D1216628

PURSUING
MELVILLE
1940–1980

MELVILLE IN 1861. Drawn by Francis Day for the *Century Illustrated Monthly Magazine*, 50 (August 1895), 563, from a photograph by Rodney Dewey of Pittsfield that Mrs. Melville provided. (Courtesy of the Memorial Library, University of Wisconsin–Madison.)

PURSUING MELVILLE 1940–1980

Chapters and Essays by
Merton M. Sealts, Jr.

> I have been building . . . some shanties
> of chapters and essays. I have been
> plowing and sowing and raising and
> painting and printing and praying,—
> and now begin to come out upon a less
> bustling time, and to enjoy the calm
> prospect of things. . . .
> Melville to Hawthorne, 29 June 1851

THE UNIVERSITY OF WISCONSIN PRESS

Published 1982

The University of Wisconsin Press
114 North Murray Street
Madison, Wisconsin 53715

The University of Wisconsin Press, Ltd.
1 Gower Street
London WC1E 6HA, England

First printing

Printed in the United States of America

For LC CIP information see the colophon

ISBN 0–299–08870–7

For Stanley T. Williams

(1888–1956), in whose graduate
seminar at Yale so much fine
scholarship began

Contents

PART IV / Pursuing Melville: A Letter to Henry A. Murray   337

Preface

A mong unpublished manuscripts in Harvard's rich Melville Collection I once found the following admonitory fragment in Herman Melville's hand, which I quote with the authorization of The Houghton Library:

> I was considering how best to anticipate possible objections, conciliate, and as by the adjustment of screens set my performance judiciously in the light; in fine I was meditating an original masterpiece of its kind, when by chance, picking up at a Nassau Street book-stall an old volume of miscellanies, I fell upon the following anonymous maxim—
> In reading a book skip not the preface: before publishing a book, if preface you have, drop it.

Mindful of the maxim that Melville cites, I have already dropped one draft preface to this volume; now, on the ground that there ought to be *some* accounting for the particular chapters and essays I have selected for inclusion here, I am venturing another in its place.

Since 1940, when I first wrote on Melville in a graduate seminar given by Stanley Williams, I find that—for good or for ill—I have published nearly fifty pieces concerning him, ranging from minor notes through reviews, essay-reviews, and journal articles to full-length books. In retrospect I see that except in reviews where the subject matter was given, I have been an explorer of five recurrent topics or themes: (1) Melville's reading, first in philosophy and then in general literature; (2) his shorter fiction, from "I and My Chimney" and other magazine writing of the early 1850's through *Billy Budd, Sailor*, the fruit of his last years; (3) his three seasons of lecturing between 1857 and 1860; (4) his relations with certain relatives, friends, and early biographers; and, along with all the rest, (5) his distinctive personality and temperament, which are as enigmatic and alluring as the books he wrote. In addressing these matters I have invariably written out of a compelling personal motivation to try first to solve a problem for myself and then to offer my findings to others who share my abiding interest in this man and his work. Whatever their ultimate value, these writings stand as one scholar's contribution to his century's knowledge and understanding of Herman Melville.

Out of this body of material I have chosen fourteen representative items for publication in Parts I and III of this volume; Parts II and IV draw on my correspondence with two men I came to know in the 1940's, Charles Olson and Henry A. Murray, through our common interest in Melville. All of this writing suggests not only the development of my own thinking but also the direction taken by Melville scholarship generally over a period of forty years. Parts I and II include writing from my time as a graduate student at Yale through my years of teaching at the University of Missouri, Wellesley College, and Lawrence College/University. The first item in Part I is a section of that all-engendering seminar paper I have already mentioned; Part I also includes a previously unpublished selection from my doctoral dissertation of 1942, three published articles, and seminal portions of two books. Parts III and IV add eight items written at the University of Wisconsin–Madison between 1965 and 1980, including a new essay composed especially for this volume: "Melville and the Platonic Tradition."

The selections within Parts I and III are arranged in the order of their composition. The date or dates in parentheses following the title of a previously published work indicate the year or years of its earlier appearance; a date in brackets following the title of a work not previously published indicates its year of composition. Brief headnotes to individual selections concern their genesis and relevance and provide bibliographical information where it is appropriate.

The editors of periodicals and the publishers of books in which some of these writings originally appeared have generously authorized their reprinting here. For their courtesy in this matter I am indebted to permissions granted by *American Literature* and Duke University Press, *ESQ; A Journal of the American Renaissance, Harvard Library Bulletin*, Harvard University Press, *New England Quarterly*, Ohio University Press and the University of Southern California, Purdue University Studies and the Purdue Research Foundation, University of Michigan Press, and the University of Wisconsin Press.

I have made relatively few alterations in the content of previously published material, which should stand or fall as it was originally printed. Where I have introduced a change of some moment, such as the addition of new information, I have called attention to its presence in a note. Other alterations mainly involve styling: for example, page references to Melville's writings that originally appeared in footnotes are now given parenthetically within the text itself, thus greatly reducing the number of notes grouped near the end of the book. The particular editions cited in each selection are unchanged in the case of reprinted material; they are specified in the notes to individual pieces.

At the University of Wisconsin-Madison the Research Committee of the Graduate School has provided released time for writing several of the later essays and for putting much of the book together. Jane Renneberg and Cynthia Townsend of the Department of English did a good deal of my typing, and Mary Maraniss and Elizabeth Steinberg of the University of Wisconsin Press have given invaluable editorial counsel. At home over the years, Ruth Mackenzie Sealts has helped me immeasurably to get everything done.

Merton M. Sealts, Jr.

PART I
1940–1965

... and behold, ... he was now both chasing and being chased. ...

Moby-Dick, Chapter 87

The World of Mind:
Melville's Theory of Knowledge
[1940]

Originally written as Chapter III of an 81-page seminar paper submitted to Professor Stanley T. Williams on 27 February 1940, this essay proved to be germinal in my thinking and writing about Melville. For its first printing here I have omitted almost all of the original documentation in favor of a few pertinent glosses.

The seminar with Stanley Williams was my first course in American literature. As an undergraduate at The College of Wooster I had concentrated in philosophy with Professors D. Luther Evans, John Bruere, and Vergilius Ferm but also studied English literature with Waldo Dunn, Howard Lowry, and Lowell Coolidge. I wrote a senior honors thesis, "Milton and Human Freedom," for both Ferm and Coolidge and went on to Yale with the intention of doing further work on Milton. But that was before I followed friends such as Norman Pearson and Alfred Ferguson into the American seminar and first read Emerson and Melville. When I came to deal with the American nineteenth century I found myself drawing on my knowledge of philosophers from Plato to William James, of Shakespeare and Milton and the seventeenth century in England, and of Romantic and Victorian literature; my study of literary theory with Frederick Pottle was also a valuable resource. I wrote seminar papers on both Emerson and Melville; by the fall of 1940, having chosen between the two, I was at work on my doctoral dissertation, "Herman Melville's Reading in Ancient Philosophy," which Professor Williams directed.

This extract introduces a number of themes associated with Melville's metaphorical voyage in search of truth that I would be addressing again, not only in the dissertation but also in various published writings—from "Herman Melville's "I and My Chimney'" (1941) to "Melville and Emerson's Rainbow" (1980).

> . . . all deep earnest thinking is but the
> intrepid effort of the soul to keep the open
> independence of her sea; while the wildest
> winds of heaven and earth conspire to cast
> her on the treacherous, slavish shore.
>
> *Moby-Dick*, Chapter 23

In Melville's experiences before the mast he had seen enough of life to distinguish romance and reality. The world, he found, lies as "in a sharpshooter's ambush, to pick off the beautiful illusions of youth, by the pitiless cracking rifles of the realities of the age." He looked on the individual as passing through various stages of enlightenment: "infancy's unconscious spell, boyhood's thoughtless faith, adolescence' doubt (the common doom), then skepticism, then disbelief, resting at last in mankind's pondering repose of If." To this last stage had Melville come in his voyage after truth. "Where lies the final harbor," he asks, "where we unmoor no more?" Not in "this world of lies," certainly, for here "Truth is forced to flee like a scared white doe in the woodlands; and only by cunning glimpses will she reveal herself."

To the world, Melville felt, even such truth as men can attain is ridiculous—and from the antics of some of its professed discoverers perhaps there is some justification for the laughter with which they are met. Between the world and those who have grasped some advanced knowledge of a legitimate nature there is a mutual antagonism: the world scorns the learned and the learned scorn their ignorant fellow-citizens. "Fight against the armed and crested lies of Mardi" as Babbalanja did and the Mardians resent the service—as Melville found from his critics. Become an adept in the world's own wisdom and run the risk of blunting spiritual insight: men such as the Hebrew prophets who spread the most light into obscure spiritual places are "mostly recluses." Of the world's knowledge Melville would forever prune his mind in the effort to train himself "down to the standard of what is unchangeably true."

Yet spiritual truth seemed to Melville as elusive as worldly truth is vain: a fearful thing "for salamander giants only to encounter; how small the chances for the provincials then? What befell the weakling youth lifting the dread goddess' veil at Sais?" Men will not speak frankly on the deepest topics; they know not their own minds and cannot know ultimate truths in this life anyway, for as the demigod Media in *Mardi* observes, "You mortals dwell in Mardi, and it is impossible to get elsewhere." To seek truth is to seek fire, which is its symbol. And not only is the search dangerous in the extreme, but there may be no ultimate truth to seek! As Melville once wrote to Hawthorne, "perhaps, after all, there is *no* secret. We incline to think that the Problem of the Universe is like the Freemason's mighty secret, so terrible to all children. It turns out, at last, to consist in a triangle, a mallet, and an apron,—nothing more!"

This skepticism as to the uselessness of speculation which Melville had reached in 1851 explains the ridicule of the philosophers which is scattered through his works. Though he loved "all men who dive" and though he plunged deeply into philosophy himself, he realized that like Tashtego and the Ohio honey-hunter a man might "sweetly perish" in "Plato's honey head," so far removed from life as to die embalmed in speculation. The sheer audacity of the would-be profound repelled him as did Emerson, "this Plato who talks through his nose." Though he recognized the merit of the sage of Concord, he saw in him "a gaping flaw . . . , the insinuation, that had he lived in those days when the world was made, he might have offered some valuable suggestions. These men are all cracked right across the brow." The lesser American transcendentalists are the butt of Melville's satire in *Pierre*, where he exposes the ridiculous impractical diets, social theories, and speculations of the "Apostles." On their philosophy itself, he comments:

> Their mental tendencies, however heterodox at times, are still very fine and spiritual upon the whole; since the vacuity of their exchequers leads them to reject the coarse materialism of Hobbes, and incline to the airy exaltations of the Berkeleyan philosophy. Often groping in vain in their pockets, they cannot but give in to the Descartian vortices; while the abundance of leisure in their attics (physical and figurative), unites with the leisure in their stomachs, to fit them in an eminent degree for that undivided attention indispensable to the proper digesting of the sublimated Categories of Kant; especially as Kant (can't) is the one great palpable fact in their pervadingly impalpable lives.

The Transcendentalists are, in short, "a preposterous rabble of Muggletonian Scots and Yankees, whose vile brogue still the more bestreaks the stripedness of their Greek or German Neoplatonical originals."

From the freedom with which Melville alludes to the classical philosophical systems in such passages as those just quoted it becomes apparent that he did not condemn philosophy categorically without a reasonable acquaintance with its literature. Similar passages might be adduced from his other works to illustrate his familiarity with the principles of individual philosophers—some of these are registered in the notes of this paper.[1] Of particular interest is his contribution in *Moby-Dick* to the conflict between empiricism and rationalism, or empiricism and transcendentalism. The head of a whale, made fast to the side of the Pequod, throws the ship badly off balance until a second head is drawn up to the opposite rail.

As before, the Pequod leaned over toward the sperm whale's head, now, by the counterpoise of both heads, she regained her even keel; though sorely strained, you may well believe. So, when on one side you hoist in Locke's head, you go over that way; but now on the other side, hoist in Kant's and you come back again; but in very poor plight. Thus, some minds for ever keep trimming boat. Oh, ye foolish! throw all these thunderheads overboard, and then you will float light and right.

If Melville thus rejected both the world's knowledge and the philosopher's knowledge, his reader may well inquire what was left for him. That he asked himself the same question, not once but many times, admits no doubt. The remainder of this paper will be an attempt to find an answer, and the point with which to begin is the problem of knowledge itself. In Melville's own voyage after truth, he threw overboard much dead weight, as we have seen. What he had left was an alert and skeptical mind, a limited reliance upon reason, and an acute intuitional insight into human nature.[2] On the basis of these instruments rest all his constructive ideas.

To begin with reason. Babbalanja in *Mardi*, quoting his beloved Bardianna, probably gives Melville's own evaluation:

"Undeniably, reason was the first revelation, and so far as it tests all others, it has precedence over them. It comes direct to us, without suppression or interpolation; and with Oro's [God's] indisputable imprimatur. But inspiration though it be, it is not so arrogant as some think. Nay, far too humble, at times it submits to the grossest indignities. Though in its best estate, not infallible; so far as it goes, for us, it is reliable. When at fault, it stands still. We speak not of visionaries. But if this our first revelation stops short of the uttermost, so with all others. If, often, it only perplexes: much more the rest. They leave much expounded; and disclosing new mysteries, add to the enigma."

Note that in this bare-wall view of reason Melville regards it as a kind of "revelation," though not of the visionary sort. This is perhaps a link with his profound plumbing[3] of the more obscure parts of the mind which may conveniently be classed under the head of intuition. In *Pierre* he observes that

so strange and complicate is the human soul; so much is confusedly evolved
from out itself, and such vast and varied accessions come to it from abroad,
and so impossible is it always to distinguish between these two, that the
wisest man were rash, positively to assign the precise and incipient origina-
tion of his final thoughts and acts. Far as we blind moles can see, man's
life seems but an acting upon mysterious hints; it is somehow hinted to us,
to do thus or thus. For surely no mere mortal who has at all gone down into
himself will ever pretend that his slightest thought or act solely originates
in his own defined identity.

This conception of the complexity of the mind is a partial explanation for Melville's contemptuous attitude toward purely rational
analysis. "In their precise tracings-out and subtile causations," he
maintains, "the strongest and fieriest emotions of life defy all analytical insight." Even the artist is helpless in trying to express this nonrational element: "Some nameless struggles of the soul cannot be
painted, and some woes will not be told"; "whatever is truly wondrous
and fearful in man, never yet was put into words or books"; "when a
man is in a really profound mood, then all merely verbal or written
profundities are unspeakably repulsive, and seem downright childish
to him." "Words," he observes, "are but algebraic signs, conveying no
meaning except what you please." This attitude is back of the chapter
in *Mardi* satirizing the gibberish of the philosophical schools as represented in the sage Doxodox. Words are rational instruments, and
knowledge is more than a rational thing. Much more significant than
the language of the system-builders are the irrational outbursts of the
bedeviled Mardian philosopher, Babbalanja. "Many things I know,"
cries Babbalanja's devil, "not good to tell; whence they call me Azzageddi." As old Bardianna says, "all men are possessed by devils," and
all are likewise endowed with hidden knowledge.

Now Mr. Mumford has observed that Azzageddi's appearance in
Mardi "was the first sign of Melville's maturity."[4] Melville himself
knew he was wiser for having written such a book, and one source of
his wisdom was the plumbing[5] of the unconscious represented by Azzageddi. For the author himself felt the tug of a new source of inspiration that mysteriously seized his own pen as the demon seized Babbalanja. In the chapter called "Dreams" he exclaims:

My cheek blanches white while I write; I start at the scratch of my pen;
my own mad brood of eagles devour me; fain would I unsay this audacity;
but an iron-mailed hand clutches mine in a vice, and prints down every
letter in my spite. Fain would I hurl off this Dionysius that rides me; my
thoughts crush me down till I groan. . . . The fever runs through me like

lava; my hot brain burns like a coal; and like many a monarch, I am less to
be envied than the veriest hind in the land.

And like Babbalanja, he feels "something going on in me that is independent of me. . . . My most virtuous thoughts are not born of my
musings, but spring up in me, like bright fancies to the poet; un-
sought, spontaneous. Whence they come, I know not. I am a blind
man pushed from behind; in vain, I turn about to see what propels
me."

Much of *Mardi*, *Moby-Dick*, and *Pierre* is inspired by Melville's demon, and it is not surprising in the later books to find other characters than Babbalanja touched with madness. Ahab and Pip in *Moby-
Dick* spring at once to mind, and one remembers also that Pierre,
haunted by the thought that both his father and his mother died insane, contemplated fearfully his own hereditary liability to a similar
fate. Pierre's father's nurse "trembled to think of that mysterious
thing in the soul, which seems to acknowledge no human jurisdiction,
but in spite of the individual's own innocent self, will still dream hor-
rid dreams, and mutter unmentionable thoughts." As for Ahab's lunacy, Melville points out distinctly that his mad object and motive
were "only subject to his perceptibility, not to his will determinate"—
he knew his own madness but could not control it. Yet "in that broad
madness not one jot of his great natural intellect had perished. That
before living agent, now became the living instrument." In Pip, obviously modeled after the Fool in *Lear*, madness is specifically linked
to revelation: Pip "saw God's foot upon the treadle of the loom, and
spoke it; and therefore his shipmates called him mad. So man's insanity is heaven's sense; and wandering from all mortal reason, man
comes at last to that celestial thought, which, to reason, is absurd and
frantic; and weal or woe, feels then uncompromised, indifferent as
his God."

There is a temptation to compare this "uncompromised, indifferent" feeling with that of Melville himself upon the completion of
Moby-Dick. To Hawthorne he declared, "I have written a wicked book,
and feel spotless as the lamb. . . . It is a strange feeling—no hopefulness is in it, no despair. Content—that is it; and irresponsibility; but
without licentious inclination." This comparison is not meant to suggest what some of Melville's critics have claimed, that the man actually
lost his mind. It simply illustrates that Melville shared in those moments of divine madness of which Plato spoke—the wild inspiration
that comes to all men in time of creative activity. "He who has never

felt, momentarily, what madness is has but a mouthful of brains." So Melville once wrote to Evert Duyckinck. "In every the wisest Soul," reads a passage in *Sartor Resartus* which Melville must have approved, "lies a whole world of internal Madness, and authentic Demon-Empire; out of which, indeed, his world of Wisdom has been creatively built together, and now rests there, as on its dark foundations does a habitable, flowery Earth-rind."

In Melville's study of the nonrational, madness is closely associated with grief. Under the burden of affliction, he notes, some creatures find relief in a wild, perverse humorousness. This is a trait observed also by Shakespeare, as the character of Hamlet attests. Melville's insight is often strikingly reminiscent of Shakespeare's, especially in *Pierre*, which shows the strong influence of the tragedy of the Prince of Denmark. On the perverse behavior of the afflicted, Melville comments in *Pierre*: "The cool censoriousness of the mere philosopher would denominate such conduct as nothing short of temporary madness; and perhaps it is, since, in the inexorable and inhuman eye of mere undiluted reason, all grief, whether on our own account, or that of others, is the sheerest unreason and insanity." To Melville the explanation of "mere undiluted reason" is insufficient. Like the romantics of an earlier generation he comes close to a near-religious worship of sorrow, but his psychology is acute enough to make his study of melancholia rise above the level of literary nostalgia.

Witness this passage on the wisdom that comes with suffering:

If it be the sacred province and—by the wisest, deemed—the inestimable compensation of the heavier woes, that they both purge the soul of gay-hearted errors and replenish it with a saddened truth; that holy office is not so much accomplished by any covertly inductive reasoning process, whose original motive is received from the particular affliction; as it is the magical effect of the admission into man's utmost spirit of a before unexperienced and wholly inexplicable element, which like electricity suddenly received into any sultry atmosphere of the dark, in all directions splits itself into nimble lances of purifying light; which at one and the same instant discharge all the air of sluggishness and inform it with an illuminating property; so that objects which before, in the uncertainty of the dark, assumed shadowy and romantic outlines, now are lighted up in their substantial realities; so that in these flashing revelations of grief's wonderful fire, we see all things as they are; and though, when the electric element is gone, the shadows once more descend, and the false outlines of objects again return; yet not with their former power to deceive; for now, even in the presence of the falsest aspects, we still retain the impressions of their immovable true ones, though, indeed, once more concealed.

Observe that again Melville specifically sets this insight over against the ways of the reasoning process. "The intensest light of reason and revelation combined," he insists, "cannot shed such blazonings upon the deeper truths in man, as will sometimes proceed from his own profoundest gloom. Utter darkness is then his light, and cat-like he distinctly sees all objects through a medium which is mere blindness to common vision. Wherefore have Gloom and Grief been celebrated of old as the selectest chamberlains to knowledge? Wherefore is it, that not to know Gloom and Grief is not to know aught that an heroic man should learn?"

In this connection Melville goes so far as to hold that the "mortal man who hath more of joy than sorrow in him, that mortal man cannot be true—not true, or undeveloped."

The truest of all men was the Man of Sorrows, and the truest of all books is Solomon's, and Ecclesiastes is the fine hammered steel of woe. 'All is vanity.' ALL. This wilful world hath not got hold of unchristian Solomon's wisdom yet. But he who dodges hospitals and jails, and walks fast crossing grave-yards, and would rather talk of operas than hell; calls Cowper, Young, Pascal, Rousseau, poor devils all of sick men; and throughout a care-free lifetime swears by Rabelais as passing wise, and therefore jolly;—not that man is fitted to sit down on tombstones, and break the green damp mould with unfathomably wondrous Solomon.

Here Melville veers very close to morbidity, as he perfectly well realized. In the succeeding paragraph he warns the reader out of his own experience:

Give not thyself up, then, to fire, lest it invert thee, deaden thee; as for the time it did me. There is a wisdom that is woe, but there is a woe that is madness. And there is a Catskill eagle in some souls that can alike dive down into the blackest gorges, and soar out of them again and become invisible in the sunny spaces. And even if he for ever flies within the gorge, that gorge is in the mountains; so that even in his lowest swoop the mountain eagle is still higher than other birds upon the plain, even though they soar.

What spiritual anguish lay behind Melville's realization that "there is a woe that is madness" cannot now be understood. It is sufficient to say here that his insight into the subtler workings of the world of mind has few parallels in literature since Shakespeare. Unappreciated in his own day, that insight has been better understood in the light of findings of contemporary psychology, of which Melville is strikingly prophetic.

Herman Melville's
"I and My Chimney"
(1941, 1967)

This essay, my first scholarly article to be published, was written at white heat late in 1940 while I was a graduate student. It was first printed in *American Literature*, 13 (May 1941), 142–154, after Jay B. Hubbell informed me that the editorial board had accepted it "with considerable enthusiasm"; it was later reprinted in *The Recognition of Herman Melville*, edited by Hershel Parker (Ann Arbor: The University of Michigan Press, 1967), pp. 238–251. For the reprinting in 1967 I made no changes in the text but added new material within brackets to a few of the footnotes; I have retained the added material in the present version, which restyles the citations and makes one correction in note 10.

In an essay on Melville's "Benito Cereno" in 1947 Stanley Williams recalled how I had come to him with a draft of this piece, remembering, as he put it, "the excitement of my student who first discovered the equivocal nature of the innocent-appearing little story." When Williams surveyed Melville scholarship for the 1956 edition of *Eight American Authors*, edited by Floyd Stovall, he observed that consideration of Melville's short fiction "really began" with two articles: E. H. Eby's "Herman Melville's 'Tartarus of Maids'" in 1940 and my essay in the following year. Not every subsequent commentator has agreed with either Eby's reading or mine; for a survey of critical comment through the mid-1960's see my "Melville's Chimney, Reexamined" (1969), reprinted on pp. 171–192 below.

The later article makes some reference to the circumstances that led me to write on "I and My Chimney"; I remember vividly how my interpretation crystallized in a sudden flash while I was rereading the story in the Reserve Book Room of Sterling Memorial Library at Yale. After drafting and redrafting the essay I took it not only to Professor Williams but also to Eleanor Melville Metcalf, a granddaughter of Melville in Cambridge, Massachusetts; she liked what I had written and sent me in turn to Dr. Henry A. Murray and Charles Olson both to make their acquaintance and to seek their judgment on the article before it went off to *American Literature*. My long friendships with Eleanor and Henry K. Metcalf and with Murray and Olson all began in this way during the winter of 1940–1941.

When I submitted my manuscript I mentioned these discussions and conveyed Mrs. Metcalf's willingness to make my findings available to scholars. "In view of recent attention focused on the symbolism of Melville's short stories," I explained, "she is anxious to forestall possible sensational treatment of her grandfather's mental condition by someone else who might rush into print without making use of the information to which I have had access." She had given particular attention to what I had said about possible hereditary insanity, to which Melville himself had alluded in *Pierre* (1852) and again in "I and My Chimney" (1856); according to earlier letters written by two of Melville's uncles (note 16 below), his own father had died "deranged" in 1832.

These references, as I found out later, had troubled another scholar, Dr. Victor Hugo Paltsits, for many years Keeper of Manuscripts in the New York Public Library, who in 1929 had edited *Family Correspondence of Herman Melville 1830–1904* in the Library's Gansevoort-Lansing Collection. Since the summer of 1940 I had been working intermittently on Melville materials in the Gansevoort-Lansing and Duyckinck Collections, and in January of 1941 I had told him of my new interpretation of "I and My Chimney." In March, after the essay had been submitted and accepted, Dr. Paltsits wrote to tell me that he had learned "on confidential authority" that according to family tradition Allan Melvill "died of pneumonia." His unnamed "authority" was in fact Charlotte Hoadley (1859–1946), a daughter of Melville's sister Catherine. After talking with me in January he had written her to ask about the circumstances of Allan Melvill's death; his letter prompted an extensive reply of 7 January 1941 in which Miss Hoadley took great exception to treatment of the Melvill family by Herman Melville's descendants and his twentieth-century biographers. From Dr. Paltsits' letter to me I inferred that he had been in touch with someone in the family, and thinking that I ought to furnish him with a quotable statement of my position, I wrote to him on 30 March in much the same vein as I had to the editors of *American Literature*. Hearing from me evidently reassured Dr. Paltsits. A month later, at the time of his retirement from the Library, he quoted extensively from my letter when he again wrote to Miss Hoadley about "the young man from Yale" and his work on Melville.

I did not know of Dr. Paltsits' correspondence with Miss Hoadley until 1975, when I first saw her letter of 7 January 1941 and his reply of 30 April / 2 May 1941; the originals are now in the Melville Collection of the Berkshire Athenaeum at Pittsfield, Massachusetts, together with copies of his letters to me and other correspondence bearing upon "Herman Melville's 'I and My Chimney.'" In 1951, it should be added, Jay Leyda in *The Melville Log* published the passage from Peter Gansevoort's letter of 10 January 1832 to Thomas Melvill, Jr., that had aroused Dr. Paltsits' particular concern (*Log*, I, 51), but its account of Allan Melvill's "alienation of mind" has drawn little attention from later scholars.

The five years between the publication of *Moby-Dick* and his advent to the Holy Land were the most crucial in Melville's long life. . . ."[1] So Raymond Weaver has written of the obscure period in Herman Melville's career between 1851 and 1856 which included the writing of *Pierre* (1852), a number of short stories and sketches for periodicals (1853–1856), and *The Confidence-Man* (1857). At this time Melville was living at Arrowhead, his farm-house near Pittsfield, Massachusetts, which provided the setting for some of his less familiar prose. Such is the case with "I and My Chimney," a short sketch in a humorous vein probably written near the end of 1855,[2] in which "Melville makes the old chimney at Arrowhead the chief character in a sketch of his domestic life at Pittsfield. . . ."[3] But the story, as will be shown, is more than a mere descriptive sketch: it is Melville's subtle comment on a major spiritual crisis of his life. The clue to certain elements in *Pierre* is also afforded by an understanding of Melville's procedure in writing "I and My Chimney."

i

A brief account of the plot of the story should be useful in further discussion. The action turns on the affection of its narrator for his beloved old chimney, which he describes in detail, and his lengthy dispute with his wife over her proposals to alter it and later to remove it entirely from the house. Over the protests of her husband, the wife employs an architect and stonemason, Scribe by name, to make a thorough examination of the chimney. Scribe startles the family by suggesting the possible existence of a secret closet within the structure, and the wife and daughters immediately conjure up visions of treasure hidden away by the late builder of the house—the narrator's mysterious kinsman, Captain Julian Dacres. But the husband, to put a stop to such foolishness and to gain a little peace for himself, eventually bribes the not unwilling Scribe to accept fifty dollars in return for a certificate attesting to the entire soundness of the chimney. Fortified with this evidence, which he hangs prominently above the fireplace, the narrator refuses to countenance the slightest alteration to the chimney, but as the story closes he is still facing minor assaults of the opposition and "standing guard over my mossy old chimney; for it is resolved between me and my chimney, that I and my chimney will never surrender" (p. 311).[4]

This rather slight plot has attracted less attention to the story than has its setting, drawn as it is from Melville's surroundings at Arrow-

head. Weaver, noting this factual background, states that the farmhouse itself was built in 1780 by a Captain David Bush, but he does
not call attention to Bush's transformation by Melville into the narrator's kinsman, Captain Dacres. This is but one example of Melville's
free handling of details in the story, which Weaver does not discuss,[5]
nor have Melville's other full-length biographers added appreciably
to Weaver's treatment of the story. John Freeman remarks only that it
is "an example of Melville writing like Hawthorne,"[6] and Lewis Mumford says merely that it is more an essay "in character" than a tale.[7]
Yet Mumford himself sees "a glimpse of Melville's own drift of mind"
in other prose of this period,[8] and more recent investigation has
found Melville's penchant for symbolism revealed even in one of his
most matter-of-fact sketches.[9] With this in mind, the extent of Melville's departures from literal truth in "I and My Chimney" should be
carefully considered.

First, as pointed out above, Melville makes the builder of the house
a kinsman of the narrator, naming him "Dacres." Secondly, he places
in the story a household of four persons: the husband and wife with
their two daughters, Anna and Julia. Melville's own daughters were
younger than these two characters: Elizabeth was born in 1853 and
Frances in 1855, both before the probable time of composition of the
story. In addition, the family at Arrowhead included two older sons,
Melville's own sisters, and his mother. The presence of Melville's
mother is significant because of a notation made by Melville's wife
concerning the spouse of the story: "All this about his wife, applied
to his mother—who was very vigorous and energetic about the farm,
etc." If Mrs. Melville is correct, this represents still another departure
from literal truth. The nagging spouse, far from an attractive figure,
is scarcely typical of Melville's own wife, whereas according to family
tradition his mother was persistently critical. More than one writer
toys with the idea that the domineering Mary Glendinning in *Pierre*
is based on the character of Maria Gansevoort Melvill, and the wife
of "I and My Chimney" may be cut from the same pattern. But Mrs.
Melville's notation goes still further: "The proposed removal of the
chimney," she continues, "is purely mythical."[10] Not only the characters, then, but also the motivation of the plot itself shows Melville's
inventive touch—and Melville never invents without purpose. In
Mardi, Moby-Dick, and *Pierre,* Melville's myth-making is intentionally
allegorical and symbolic. If the removal of the chimney is "purely
mythical," has Melville more to communicate than the mere spinning
of a yarn? And why should he write of a chimney?

In *Pierre,* published four years before, Melville had described "the gray and grand old tower" of the Church of the Apostles, "emblem to Pierre of an unshakable fortitude, which, deep-rooted in the heart of the earth, defied all the howls of the air" (p. 378). The chimney in the present story is a similar emblem of fortitude, "for it is resolved between me and my chimney, that I and my chimney will never surrender." Again in *Pierre* Melville writes: "Deep, deep, and still deep and deeper must we go, if we would find out the heart of a man; descending into which is as descending a spiral stair in a shaft, without any end, and where that endlessness is only concealed by the spiralness of the stair, and the blackness of the shaft" (p. 402). So Melville in his writing, like the poet Lombardo in *Mardi*, "got deeper and deeper into himself" (II, 326). It is with the same purpose that in the present story he traces the shaft of the chimney: "Very often I go down into my cellar, and attentively survey that vast square of masonry. I stand long, and ponder over, and wonder at it. It has a druidical look, away down in the umbrageous cellar there, whose numerous vaulted passages, and far glens of gloom, resemble the dark, damp depths of primeval woods" (p. 283). As it would be vain to search for the bottom of the endless shaft described in *Pierre*, so the narrator of "I and My Chimney" digs in vain about the foundation of the chimney. The vast area of this lower part of the structure is emphasized: " . . . large as it appears above the roof," says Scribe, the architect, "I would not have inferred the magnitude of this foundation, sir" (p. 295).

The significance of all this may be summarized briefly: the shaft is the image of "the heart of a man"; the chimney is an emblem of fortitude; what lies at its bottom is hidden in darkness. Like a pyramid in its shape, the chimney is thus discovered to have its greatest area shrouded in mystery. This consistent likening to the pyramids is important: "The architect of the chimney must have had the pyramid of Cheops before him; for after that famous structure it seems modelled" (p. 280). Had the wife's projected tunnel been thrust into the chimney "some Belzoni or other might have succeeded in future ages in penetrating through the masonry, and actually emerging into the dining-room" (p. 292). Belzoni was an Egyptologist. And again: "We seemed in the pyramids; and I, with one hand holding my lamp over head, and with the other pointing out, in the obscurity, the hoar mass of the chimney, seemed some Arab guide, showing the cobwebbed mausoleum of the great god Apis" (p. 295).[11] A commentary on this passage is afforded by an often-quoted sentence in *Pierre*: "By vast pains we mine into the pyramid; by horrible gropings we come to the central room; with joy we espy the sarcophagus; but we lift the lid—

and no body is there—appallingly vacant as vast is the soul of a man!"
(p. 397).[12] What Melville is saying in the story is that in pondering
over and wondering at his "chimney" he is introspectively surveying
his own soul—and that introspection is an endless, empty-handed
search.

Melville's identification of the chimney with himself is made certain
by the amusing connotations of other passages in the story. Built
around the structure were "the most rambling conceivable" rooms
which (like the organs of the body), "as it were, dovetailed into each
other. They were of all shapes; not one mathematically square room
among them all" (p. 306).[13] Almost every rooom "was in itself an entry, or passageway to other rooms . . .—never was there so labyrin-
thine an abode. Guests will tarry with me several weeks, and every
now and then, be anew astonished at some unforeseen apartment"
(pp. 292 ff.). This jocular anatomizing depicts perfectly the enigma
Herman Melville presented to his acquaintances, who were anew astonished every now and then by what he said and did. Carrying on
the anatomical figure, Melville's narrator exclaims at his wife's proposal "*in toto* to abolish the chimney":

"What! . . . abolish the chimney? To take out the backbone of anything,
wife, is a hazardous affair. Spines out of backs, and chimneys out of houses,
are not to be taken like frosted lead-pipes from the ground. Besides, . . .
the chimney is the one grand permanence of this abode. If undisturbed by
innovators, then in future ages, when all the house shall have crumbled
from it, this chimney will still survive—a Bunker Hill monument. No, no,
wife, I can't abolish my backbone." (p. 294)[14]

"Backbone," the colloquial term for fortitude, together with the reference to the enduring Bunker Hill monument (like the church
tower in *Pierre*), further amplifies the connotation of the chimney. No
wonder that to Scribe "this house would appear to have been built
simply for the accommodation of your chimney" (p. 295); that "I and
my chimney could not be parted" (p. 298); that "it is never out of my
house, and never out of my mind" (p. 297); that "I look upon this
chimney less as a pile of masonry than as a personage" (p. 284). All
this is entirely true, for the "chimney" is the heart and soul of Herman Melville.

ii

The identification of the chimney with Melville's own personality
would constitute nothing more than a piece of subtle ingenuity on

the part of both author and reader were it not for the larger implication of "I and My Chimney." This centers in the "purely mythical"
proposal to remove the chimney and the subsequent examination
made of it by Scribe. Scribe's report of his findings reads in part as
follows:

> It is my solemn duty to warn you, sir, that there is architectural cause to
> conjecture that somewhere concealed in your chimney is a reserved space,
> hermetically closed, in short, a secret chamber, or rather closet. How long it
> has been there, it is for me impossible to say. What it contains is hid, with
> itself, in darkness. But probably a secret closet would not have been con-
> trived except for some extraordinary object, whether for the concealment of
> treasure, or what other purpose, may be left to those better acquainted
> with the history of the house to guess. (p. 300)

The wife and daughters, on receipt of this report, immediately conclude that the mysterious kinsman who built the house must have
hidden something away—another excuse for probing the chimney:

> Although they had never before dreamed of such a revelation as Mr.
> Scribe's; yet upon the first suggestion they instinctively saw the extreme
> likelihood of it. In corroboration, they cited first my kinsman, and second,
> my chimney; alleging that the profound mystery involving the former,
> and the equally profound masonry involving the latter, though both ac-
> knowledged facts, were alike preposterous on any other supposition than
> the secret closet. (p. 302)

From this point on, the secret closet becomes the central topic of
argument: over its possible existence the family quarrel bitterly. The
wife argues that "when you think of that old kinsman of yours, you
know there must be a secret closet in this chimney" (p. 304).[15] The
husband, unable to silence his wife by out-talking her, finally resorts
to the bribing of Scribe to certify, as "a competent surveyor," that having examined the chimney he "found no reason to believe *any unsoundness; in short, any—any secret closet* in it" (p. 308; emphasis added).
This studied phrasing makes the secret closet signify unsoundness,
so that the reason for probing the chimney becomes to ferret out its
weakness. The likelihood of such "unsoundness," it will be recalled,
was corroborated by "first my kinsman, and second, my chimney."

In the story the specific kinship of the highly mysterious Captain
Dacres is never disclosed. But in *Pierre* the immediate relatives of the
hero are all marked at one time or other by mental unsoundness.
Isabel, whom Pierre takes for his half sister, had been kept in a mad-
house (pp. 168 ff.); Pierre's father had died in delirium (pp. 96 ff.);
and Pierre's mother also had died insane (p. 398). "Nor did this re-

markable double-doom of [Pierre's] parents wholly fail to impress his mind with presentiments concerning his own fate—his own hereditary liability to madness" (p. 400). And behind this fear in Pierre lay Melville's knowledge of what had befallen one of his own parents. His mother was still living when *Pierre* was written, but in 1832 his father had died under the cloud of mental derangement. His condition on his deathbed is briefly described in a letter to Lemuel Shaw, Herman Melville's future father-in-law, from Thomas Melvill (Herman Melville's uncle): "I found him *very* sick—induced by a variety of causes— under great mental excitement—at times fierce, even *maniacal.*—in short, my dear sir, Hope, is no longer permitted of his recovery, in the opinion of the attending Physicians." [16]

The pattern of "I and My Chimney" now begins to emerge, becoming more clear as the plot of the story unfolds. Following the bribing of Scribe, the narrator cites the certificate attesting to the chimney's soundness in an effort to put an end to the argument:

"Wife, . . . why speak more of that secret closet, when there before you hangs contrary testimony of a master mason, elected by yourself to decide. Besides, even if there were a secret closet, secret it should remain, and secret it shall. Yes, wife, here, for once, I must say my say. *Infinite sad mischief has resulted from the profane bursting open of secret recesses.* Though standing in the *heart* of this house, though hitherto we have all nestled about it, unsuspicious of aught hidden within, this chimney may or may not have a secret closet. *But if it have, it is my kinsman's. To break into that wall would be to break into his breast.*" (p. 309; emphasis added)

The tone of this passage contrasts with the general light tone of the earlier part of the story, as even a casual reading will show. The sudden seriousness here, in speaking of the "profane" meddling with any secrets of the kinsman, is more in keeping with the reverent mood of Pierre in approaching the image of his "sacred father" (*Pierre*, p. 89) enshrined in his mind (p. 93), or in retiring to the "locked, round-windowed closet . . . , *sacred*" to his privacies, where the ambiguous chair-portrait of his father is hung (p. 98; emphasis added). Though the beloved image is later so tragically shattered, the memory of his father "for right cause or wrong" remains "ever *sacred and inviolate*" to Pierre (p. 267; emphasis added). That such a mood was also Herman Melville's is strikingly indicated by the name given the kinsman in "I and My Chimney," "Dacres" being simply an anagram for *sacred!* This is startling confirmation that both Dacres and Pierre's father are based on memories of the unfortunate Allan Melvill.

Besides explaining the first of the two reasons given for the possible unsoundness of the chimney, this analysis is important in an understanding of Melville's intentions in *Pierre*. Many of the details of Pierre's situation, from his surroundings at Saddle Meadows to the torture of his failing eyesight, are unquestionably drawn from Melville's own life. Some critics, cautioned by Melville's distinct warning that "the thoughts we here indite as Pierre's are to be very carefully discriminated from those we indite concerning him" (p. 233), object to any interpretation of *Pierre* as its author's spiritual autobiography. But from this new evidence it is obvious that a fundamental element in Pierre's situation is taken straight from his creator's experience. When Pierre "dropped his angle into the well of his childhood, to find what fish might be there" (p. 396), he brought forth dark memories of the unhappy death of his father. And Isabel, supposedly his father's illegitimate daughter, is mysteriously connected with the father's fate just as the chimney in Melville's short story is related to the mysterious kinsman. There is general agreement among recent critics that Isabel, again like the chimney, symbolizes the depths of Melville's mind.[17] As it was impossible to reach the bottom of the endless shaft of the soul, the ultimate foundation of the chimney, so Pierre "renounced all thought of ever having Isabel's dark lantern illuminated to him. Her light was lidded, and the lid was locked." Such is the dark mystery surrounding the girl; though, Melville continues, by interrogating relatives "on his father's side" Pierre "might possibly rake forth some few small grains of *dubious and most unsatisfying things*, which, *were he that way strongly bent*, would only serve the more hopelessly *to cripple him in his practical resolves*. He determined *to pry not at all* into this *sacred* problem" (p. 199; emphasis added). So in "I and My Chimney" Melville warns against the profane disturbance of secrets relating to his sacred kinsman.

I interpret this passage as the expression of Melville's own fear that, "were he that way strongly bent," he would experience the same fate as his father's by continued delving into the depths of his mind. His dilemma was something like that of Pierre over the symbolic Isabel: to acknowledge her publicly is impossible without hurting his mother; to vindicate openly her relationship to him means tarnishing his father's honorable memory. Melville's advice to his hero is to "quit Isabel" and to "beg humble pardon of thy mother," but Pierre is unable to free himself so easily from his problem. In the confusion of his soul at these "absurdities" he "would fain have disowned the very *memory* and the *mind* which produced to him such an immense *scandal upon his common sanity*" (p. 239; emphasis added). This sounds suspiciously like the two reasons offered for the existence of the symbolic secret closet, in "I and My Chimney." At the time of *Pierre* Melville had nevertheless continued his introspection just as Pierre in the novel gave himself over to Isabel. No wonder that he later concluded in "I and My Chimney" that he had been "a little out of my mind, I now think," in trying to lay bare the very *foundation* of the structure which his kinsman had established (p. 283).

That Melville's family shared his uneasiness is suggested by Mrs. Melville's private account of this portion of her husband's career, from the writing of *Moby-Dick* "under unfavorable circumstances" in 1850 and 1851 until the period now under discussion.[18] "We all felt anxious about the strain on his health in spring of 1853," writes Mrs. Melville: she is confirmed by authentic tradition. At the time of the publication of *Pierre*, Melville, says William Braswell, "had worked himself into so frightful a nervous condition that his family had physicians examine him for insanity. The physicians pronounced him sane and assumed responsibility for his actions; but authoritative tradition survives that tells a pathetic story of his life during this period." In a note Braswell adds: "I base this statement upon personal talks with Mrs. Eleanor Melville Metcalf [Melville's granddaughter] and with Professor Raymond Weaver."[19]

Mrs. Metcalf, with whom I have also discussed the entire situation, agrees with me that "I and My Chimney" is an allegorical version of the circumstances leading to this examination. Melville's own serious mental condition was the primary cause, made doubly distressing to his family by the tragic memory of his father's death, which Melville himself had recalled in *Pierre*. Hence the relation of the chimney itself and the "kinsman" of the story to the possible unsoundness of the structure. It is conceivable that Melville's analysis of his own condition in writing *Pierre* played a part in the decision of the family to have his mind examined. According to tradition the subtler meanings of his work were a mystery even to his closest relatives,[20] but the pointed allusion to Pierre's father probably did not escape the notice of those familiar with the facts of Allan Melvill's death—particularly Maria Gansevoort Melvill and Lemuel Shaw. It is significant that Melville's mother is said to be the original of the character in "I and My Chimney" who instigates the examination, who is actively hostile to the narrator's "philosophical jabber,"[21] and who even after Scribe's report continues to tap the wall of the chimney after the manner of a physician examining a man for life insurance (p. 308).

The possible identification of one other character in the story is worth considering—that of Scribe, the examiner. Again referring to

Mrs. Melville's journal we find that Melville's physical health remained poor for several years after the writing of *Pierre*. "In Feb 1855 he had his first attack of severe rhumatism [*sic*] in his back—so that he was helpless—and in the following June an attack of sciatica. Our neighbor in Pittsfield Dr. O. W. Holmes attended & prescribed for him."[22] The relation between Holmes and Melville was more than that of doctor and patient. Holmes's "The Last Leaf" was written about Melville's own grandfather, Major Thomas Melvill, and interesting records survive of vigorous conversations between the two younger men when both were in residence at Pittsfield.[23] Reviewing these points, we find that the literary doctor was on familiar terms with Melville and had served him in a professional capacity twice during the very year in which "I and My Chimney" was probably written. It has been shown that as the architect found no unsoundness in the chimney, that is, in Melville's mind; so doctors had "pronounced him sane and assumed responsibility for his actions." Is it possible that Holmes had been one of the doctors, and that Melville meant to indicate the fact in the story by giving the examiner there the name of "Scribe," or *writer*? In view of Melville's general procedure in composing the story, this identification is at least not implausible.

The significance of "I and My Chimney" may now be summarized briefly. It is Melville's account of the examination of his mind made a few years before the story was written, at the instigation of his family. This meaning is conveyed in disguised form by the plot itself, with the aid of symbolism parallel to that of *Pierre* though the terms are dissimilar. The examination was made because of anxiety over Melville's nervous condition, represented by the speculation concerning the chimney, and with the knowledge of the tragic circumstances surrounding the death of his father, represented by the mystery concerning the late kinsman of the story. This fear of possible hereditary insanity was alluded to by Melville himself in *Pierre*. The characterization of "I and My Chimney" points to Melville's mother as the person responsible for the consultation of physicians, one of whom may have been Dr. Oliver Wendell Holmes. The examination revealed that Melville's nervous condition was not a manifestation of insanity, and the subsequent course of his life confirmed the judgment of his examiners.

Of the evidence afforded by records of Melville's career after this time, Forsythe observes that "no one who has any knowledge of Melville in his later years" needs such testimony. "For thinking people, the question . . . of Melville's sanity has long since been completely settled."[24] With these words there can be only thorough agreement.

In the present study Herman Melville himself has been allowed to explain how the question was first raised: it cannot be too strongly emphasized that any suspicions based on his own nervousness and associated with memories of his father had been entirely groundless. This is not to minimize the seriousness of his condition in 1852–1853, though in a day when a better understanding of nervous disorders prevails than in Melville's own lifetime there is no reason for describing his difficulties in sensational terms. Had modern mental therapeutic knowledge been available to Melville himself, he and his family would doubtless have been spared much of the distress they were forced to endure. More important than misguided amateur psychologizing at this late date, however, is an appreciation of the unexpected extent to which, through employment of symbols, Melville committed his deepest spiritual problems to subtle analysis in print. There is further evidence for this practice in other work of the period of "I and My Chimney," as I plan to discuss in a future publication, but for the present it is sufficient to take leave of him still "standing guard over my mossy old chimney; for it is resolved between me and my chimney, that I and my chimney will never surrender."

Melville and the Philosophers
[1942]

This essay originally constituted the "Summary and Conclusion" of my doctoral dissertation, "Herman Melville's Reading in Ancient Philosophy" (Yale University, 1942; copyright © 1964 by Merton M. Sealts, Jr.), pp. 191–203; this is its first publication. In the present version I have provided a more descriptive title and shortened a few passages (as indicated by ellipses: . . .); I have also added one footnote (note 1), restyled citations, and renumbered subsequent notes.

The dissertation was begun in the fall of 1940 under the direction of Stanley Williams and completed during my one semester of teaching at the University of Missouri in Columbia before I entered military service in February of 1942. After the close of World War II, when I returned to teaching at Wellesley College and later at Lawrence College, I adapted other parts of the dissertation for articles in scholarly journals: "Melville's 'Friend Atahalpa,'" *Notes & Queries*, 194 (22 January 1949), 37–38; "Melville's 'Neoplatonical Originals,'" *Modern Language Notes*, 67 (February 1952), 80–86; and the nucleus of certain entries in my "Melville's Reading: A Check-List of Books Owned and Borrowed," published serially in the *Harvard Library Bulletin* between 1948 and 1950, that concerned books Melville bought from his publishers, previously listed in an appendix to the dissertation.

The most significant chapters of the dissertation, those exploring Melville's response to the dialogues of Plato, I did not consider ready for publication in the 1940's or 1950's. For one reason, I needed to establish his knowledge of Emerson before I could write with authority about his debt to earlier philosophers of the idealist persuasion. My findings are reported in two long essays of the 1980's which conclude Part III of this volume: "Melville and Emerson's Rainbow" (1979) and "Melville and the Platonic Tradition" [1980].

> Finally: It was stated at the outset, that this
> system would not be here, and at once, per-
> fected. You cannot but plainly see that I have
> kept my word. . . . For small erections may
> be finished by their first architects; grand
> ones, true ones, ever leave the cope-stone to
> posterity. God keep me from ever complet-
> ing anything. This whole book is but a
> draught—nay, but the draught of a draught.
> Oh, Time, Strength, Cash, and Patience!
>
> "Cetology," *Moby-Dick*, I, 179

i

M elville's most extensive reading in the field of ancient philosophy was in the dialogues of Plato, beginning in 1847 or 1848
before the completion of *Mardi* and continuing at intervals throughout his subsequent career. At about the same time that he began reading Plato he purchased a volume of Seneca, and he may later have
read the works of other Stoic philosophers, notably Marcus Aurelius
and Epictetus. The Platonic and Stoic systems of thought were two of
the major influences on Melville's own ideas, though he accepted neither uncritically. The Neoplatonists, on the other hand, had little to
offer Melville, and no mention of Epicurean thinkers occurs in his
work at all. During the composition of *Mardi* Melville looked into the
commentary of the Neoplatonist Proclus on Plato's theology, but he
found the system of Proclus, particularly his terminology, difficult
and even ridiculous.[1] Sometime before writing *Pierre* he may also
have read a translation of Plotinus, with whose work there are parallels in the thought and imagery of Melville's book, but this evidence
alone is inconclusive. With the works of Plutarch Melville was acquainted before he himself began writing professionally. He probably
knew Plutarch's *Morals* at the time of *Mardi*, and from both the *Morals*
and the *Lives* he learned much about the civilization and thought of
the ancient world.

Plutarch's philosophical treatment of Greek, Persian, and Egyptian
myths attracted Melville, who had long been familiar with classical
mythology. Allusions to Greek, Roman, Egyptian, Persian, and Indian myths are nearly as frequent in his works as references to the
literature of the Old and New Testaments. Plato, too, taught Melville
both the theory and the practice of the philosophical myth, and Fran-

cis Bacon's *Wisdom of the Ancients* pointed out to him the symbolic implications of classical fables. His interest in Zoroastrian theology and mythology was stimulated by his purchase in 1849 of Pierre Bayle's philosophical dictionary, notable for its exposition of the Manichean and Gnostic dualistic heresies. In the works of these authors Melville found the material for much of the philosophical allegory of *Mardi*, *Moby-Dick*, and *Pierre*, in which he assumes the role of myth-maker and symbolist. Plato, Plutarch, and Bayle were largely responsible for his adherence to the philosophical position of dualism, which he had adopted as early as *Mardi* and which is the most striking feature of his thought as it developed in the works which followed.

Bayle's dictionary was the most important secondary source of Melville's knowledge of ancient thought. His familiarity with ancient philosophers and schools other than those mentioned above came either from Bayle, from an unidentified manual of philosophy, or from his extensive general reading in ancient and modern literature. Many allusions to historical thinkers in Melville's works can be traced to his fondness for the essays of Montaigne and Bacon and the writings of Sir Thomas Browne and Robert Burton, whose temperament, literary style, and encyclopedic range of mind influenced him profoundly. Melville's taste for their works was fostered early in his career by his friend Evert Duyckinck, who was himself well read in philosophy and who placed the resources of his large library at Melville's disposal. The influence of Melville's childhood training in orthodox Calvinism, which conditioned his thinking throughout his life, has been acknowledged in this study, although his reading in purely religious literature is beyond the strict scope of the present investigation. In addition to a thorough grounding in the Bible, Melville had some knowledge of the history of the early Christian church and the rabbinical tradition of the Hebrews. He probably knew the works of Augustine at first hand. and acquired additional knowledge of the Fathers of the early Church from his religious training and later from his background reading for *Clarel*, his long poem on the pilgrimage to the Holy Land published after the close of his great creative period. . . .

The investigation of Melville's reading in modern philosophy . . . should include a treatment of his use of theological works written during the period of the Renaissance and after, including those of Ethan Allen, Burnet, Calvin, Edwards, Jebb, Massilon, Paley, Servetus, Swedenborg, Jeremy Taylor, Tillotson, and Wesley—all mentioned by Melville. Of medieval and Renaissance writers . . . Melville knew little at first hand apart from the works of Machiavelli, Erasmus, and Sir Thomas More, none of which constituted a major influence on his thought. Among the modern philosophers, the British empirical thinkers, the French encyclopedists, and the German and American transcendentalists were familiar to Melville, directly or indirectly. . . . Another aspect of his reading which may yet be covered, depending on the results of further research, is Melville's knowledge of alchemy, magic, and esoteric beliefs and cults. Many of his allusions, however, are so brief and so general as to provide no adequate clues to books and authors whom he actually read and used.

ii

Both internal and external evidence show that Melville's interest in philosophy began about 1847 and 1848, its most striking manifestation being his alteration of *Mardi*, which was then in process of composition, from a story of South Sea adventure to a philosophical romance. Like its predecessors, *Typee* and *Omoo*, *Mardi* is more directly dependent upon literary sources than is Melville's later and more mature work. Plato and Sir Thomas Browne are echoed in *Mardi*, as one scholar has said, to the point of ventriloquism, and Melville's philosophical borrowings can be shown by comparison of parallel passages in their work and Melville's. *Moby-Dick* likewise contains striking reminiscenses of Plato's phrasing and imagery and of Browne's prose cadences, but Melville's indebtedness to philosophers is, on the whole, of a more general nature there than in *Mardi*. The ideas he had found in Plato and Browne—preexistence, innate ideas, poetic inspiration, metempsychosis, ethical and metaphysical dualism, and the like—were no longer new and strange, but part of his own habits of thought. His borrowings from Bayle, whom he had read more recently, can be illustrated only by broad comparisons; the technique of citing parallel passages is entirely inapplicable. In *Pierre* there is specific warning against the domination of literary sources, Plato being mentioned by name as a writer to be resisted. Melville evidently made a deliberate effort to perfect his own ideas and style independently. Records of his reading at this time show also that he was reading less Plato and Plutarch, more Shakespeare, Dante, and other writers of general literature.

The years 1847–1849 can therefore be taken as the date of Melville's most extensive reading in ancient philosophy, although neither his interest in the subject nor his reading terminated at the end of that period. What his philosophical reading had done was to force his reexamination of received truth; the new ideas which he encountered did not simply provide him with a new stock of beliefs. "For the more we learn, the more we unlearn," he declares in *Mardi*; "we accumulate not, but substitute; and take away more than we add" (II, 80). Even *Redburn* and *White-Jacket*, his next books, demonstrate his critical temper, though they are not in the philosophical vein of *Mardi*, *Moby-Dick*, and *Pierre*. In *Redburn* he remarks that "you know nothing till you know all; which is the reason we never know anything" (p. 154). In *White-Jacket* is the observation that philosophy, though "the best wisdom that has ever in any way been revealed" to man, is still "but a slough and a mire, with a few tufts of good footing here and there" (p. 231). These words are straws in the wind, for in *Moby-Dick* is an implicit denial of much orthodox philosophical doctrine and in *Pierre* an explicit rejection of all faith, all stoicism, and all philosophy as deceptive and worthless. Critics who stress Melville's preoccupation with metaphysics have too often overlooked the increasing bitterness of his attitude toward philosophy in the books which followed *Mardi*.

What was Melville's quarrel with the philosophers? First of all, he realized that the influence of philosophy upon his manner of writing in *Mardi*, *Moby-Dick*, and *Pierre* had alienated his reading public. In one of the short sketches written after *Pierre* his narrator declares that even his family, "like all the rest of the world, cares not a fig for my philosophical jabber."[2] Secondly, he had come to look upon further speculation as unprofitable. In the same story the narrator's old farmhouse is likened to "a philosophical system," in which "you seem to be forever going somewhere, and getting nowhere," for "if you arrive at all, it is just where you started, and so you begin again, and again get nowhere" (pp. 292–293).[3] This slur at systematic philosophy contrasts with his praise of "old Montaigne," the unsystematic essayist, one of those "unconventional writers who, free from cant and convention, . . . honestly, and in the spirit of common sense, philosophise upon realities."[4] By implication, the system-builders lack honesty, common sense, and realism.[5] Another fault was their want of what Melville called "heart." This criticism has been excellently stated by Stanley Geist:

The philosophers—all of them, and not simply one or another—were infuriating and absurd not because their systems were opposed to his, but because their thought was systematized, hence heartless. . . . All philosophic unity was both analytic and eclectic; while any unity which was to be valid for Melville had to be intuitive and inclusive—in other words, perceived by the great heart, not by the watchmaker's brain.[6]

The philosopher whom Melville considered to have "mere watch-maker's brains" (*Pierre*, pp. 294–295) was Francis Bacon, one of the founders of modern experimental philosophy and science. Melville was evidently familiar with Bacon's place in the history of ideas,[7] but though he respected Bacon as a commentator on ancient mythology, he had little regard for Bacon as a representative modern thinker. His "Club for the Immediate Extension of the Limits of all Knowledge, both Human and Divine" (*Pierre*, p. 351), is a satire on the spirit of Bacon's *Advancement of Learning*; modern science, Melville believed, enlarges not the scope of human knowledge but the scope of human ignorance. "Why then do you try to 'enlarge' your mind?" he asks in *Moby-Dick*. "Subtilise it" (II, 63). Science deals with external nature, not with the human heart or conscience (*Mardi*, II, 71); in fact heartlessness may even be, to Melville, "of a purely scientific origin" (*White-Jacket*, p. 314). His conviction that science deals with nature rather than with human nature helps to explain Melville's distrust of a large segment of modern thought and his humanistic bias in favor of belles-lettres, including the literature of antiquity.

Among the ancient philosophers Melville's favorites are seen to be those who wrote least like system-builders and most like authors of creative literature. He had little to say of Aristotle, the greatest systematizer of the ancient world, but much of Plato, who is as readily claimed by the poets as by the philosophers. Though Melville could not accept Plato's transcendental dogma of ideas, he responded warmly to the myths and figures in Plato which kindled his own imagination. And though Melville came to reject Plato and the Platonic system, he never uttered a harsh word concerning Plato's greatest literary creation, his portrayal of Socrates. The attraction to Melville in Zoroastrianism, similarly, was not so much the bare concept of metaphysical dualism, but the mythology of Persian fire-worship— the personification of good and evil as eternally warring deities of light and darkness. Melville's handling of the theme of darkness illustrates his manner of dealing imaginatively with intellectual concepts. Writing of the power of "blackness" in Hawthorne, he found its force to lie in its appeals "to that Calvinistic sense of Innate Depravity and Original Sin, from whose visitations, in some shape or other, no deeply thinking mind is always and wholly free."[8] To Melville, it may be surmised, the imaginative concept of blackness was as definite and real as the intellectual concept of evil and sin to the systematic theologian or philosopher.

This same blackness in Shakespeare was for Melville one of "the things that have made for Shakespeare his loftiest but most circumscribed renown, as the profoundest of thinkers," as he wrote in "Hawthorne and His Mosses." The "intuitive Truth" in Shakespeare (p. 130) meant far more to Melville than "the mere undiluted reason" of "the mere philosopher" (*Pierre*, pp. 259–260). The man of imagination—Hawthorne, Shakespeare, and presumably himself—"is immeasurably deeper than the plummet of the mere critic. For it is not the brain that can test such a man; it is only the heart. You cannot come to know greatness by inspecting it; there is no glimpse to be caught of it, except by intuition; you need not ring it, you but touch it, and you find it is gold" (p. 129). The heart rather than the brain, intuitive truth rather than reason, poetic inspiration rather than systematic thought, imaginative symbols rather than intellectual concepts—these are the preferences that place Melville not with the formal philosophers, but with the poets and makers.

iii

The conflict of heart and head in Melville is one of the primary causes of the spiritual crisis that came with *Pierre*. Since the time of *Mardi* he had sought to maintain equilibrium between the critical, skeptical, analytic tendencies of his intellect and the eclecticism of his creative, synthesizing imagination. The power of imagination had succeeded in *Moby-Dick* in welding the seemingly disparate elements of factual background, narrative, characterization, and philosophical allegory; in *Pierre*, an artistic failure except to the initiate, the attempted synthesis breaks down. There Melville's passion for analysis led him into an almost pathological anatomizing of his own soul that defied adequate literary treatment. By reference to the sources of Melville's symbolism, Plato, Burton, and possibly Thomas Taylor, it has been possible in this study to suggest a reinterpretation of *Pierre* which throws new light on the course of Melville's speculative thought.

The hero of *Pierre*, like Melville himself, had through exposure to unconventional truth become "distrustful of himself, the most wretched distrust of all. But this last distrust was not of the heart; . . . it was . . . distrust of his intellect" (p. 234). This was exactly what had befallen Melville in his adventures both in the world of experience and in the world of mind. Like Pierre, Melville too had continued to trust the heart, but if the symbolism of the novel represents his own condition, he felt himself deceived in following the heart just as Pierre is deceived by the ambiguous nature of Isabel. The source of error is actually in neither the heart nor the head, but in the dissociation of the two which is portrayed in the novel. This interpretation is suggested by the following remarkable passage of self-criticism:

That all-comprehending oneness, that calm representativeness, by which a steady philosophic mind reaches forth and draws to itself, in their collective entirety, the objects of its contemplations; that pertains not to the young enthusiast. By his eagerness, all objects are deceptively foreshortened; by his intensity each object is viewed as detached; so that essentially and relatively everything is misseen by him. (pp. 244–245)

Melville's own eager and intense passion for analysis had, in other words, destroyed the synthesizing power of imagination of which he had read in Coleridge, so that his imagination and intellect were working not in harmony but at cross-purposes. This same warfare within the self had been going on since *Mardi* and had found expression in the baroque characterization of all three of Melville's symbolic novels. *Mardi* dramatizes the conflict between the ideal and the sensual in Yillah and Hautia and the struggle of understanding with will in Babbalanja and Taji, each representing an aspect of Melville's own character. Ahab's soul in *Moby-Dick* is likewise "dissociated from the characterizing mind" (I, 252) through his monomaniac passion for vengeance. Babbalanja, Taji, and Ahab are each in pursuit of the Ultimate, but after *Moby-Dick* and its imaginative vision of spiritual terror, Melville himself had turned in retreat from "those Hyperborean regions" in which all maxims "begin to slide and fluctuate, and finally become wholly inverted." Neither by imagination nor by intellect, he had learned, must man "follow the trail of truth too far, since by so doing he entirely loses the directing compass of his mind; for arrived at the Pole, to whose barrenness only it points, there, the needle indifferently respects all points of the horizon alike" (*Pierre*, p. 231).

The ambiguity of truth and the psychological conflict within himself between the powers of creation and destruction[9] brought an end, for all practical purposes, to Melville's public career as an author. With his eventual achievement of reintegration, his anti-intellectualism gave way to a new wholeness of vision, and his interest in philosophy reawakened. By the close of his life, in *Billy Budd*, Melville had come to terms with himself and the universe in a constructive mingling of Socratic wisdom, stoic serenity, and Christian love. Philosophy, particularly ancient philosophy, thus played its part in his intellectual development from the time of *Mardi* until his death.

The Records of Melville's Reading
(1948, 1966)

In its original form this essay constituted the first installment of "Melville's Reading: A Check-List of Books Owned and Borrowed," which appeared serially in the *Harvard Library Bulletin* from the spring of 1948 until the winter of 1950 with a supplement in 1952. From 1946 to 1948 I was teaching at Wellesley College, where I compiled "Melville's Reading" at the urging of Jay Leyda and by the invitation of George William Cottrell, Jr., the first editor of the *Bulletin*; Leyda was then working on *The Melville Log* (1951) and pooling information with many of us who were engaged in research on Melville. My project had the continuing encouragement and active support of Eleanor Melville Metcalf, a granddaughter of Melville, and William A. Jackson, then Librarian of The Houghton Library at Harvard. An amplified version of the essay under its present title appeared eighteen years later as Part I of *Melville's Reading: A Check-List of Books Owned and Borrowed* (Madison: The University of Wisconsin Press; © 1966 by the Regents of the University of Wisconsin), pp. 1–26. The book was a major revision and expansion of the six installments and the supplement that had appeared in the *Bulletin*.

Further information on the origin and progress of the monograph, both as it was published in the *Bulletin* and as it was later amplified, will be found in "A Correspondence with Charles Olson," pp. 91–151 below, *passim*.

The present version of "The Records of Melville's Reading" is essentially the revised text of 1966 plus a few paragraphs incorporating new information that has since come to light. Much of it was reported in two "Supplementary Notes to *Melville's Reading* (1966)" that I contributed to the *Bulletin* in 1971 and 1979; in an appendix, pp. 347–354 below, I have consolidated additions and changes to Part II, "A Check-List of Books Owned and Borrowed," that were reported in these supplements. William H. Bond, the present Librarian of The Houghton Library, and Edwin E. Williams while editor of the *Bulletin* have continued to support this ongoing project as warmly as their predecessors, Messrs. Jackson and Cottrell. Nine footnotes to "The Records of Melville's Reading" in its present form identify new information that is not self-evident; they replace the ubiquitous notes of 1966,

109 in all, which may be consulted in *Melville's Reading* by any scholar wanting further documentation of some point.

I first conceived of this essay as a way of orienting potential users of the "Check-List of Books Owned and Borrowed" to the resources on which the listings are based, thinking of it as a convenient clothesline on which to hang all sorts of information about Melville and his reading that could not readily be stowed among the alphabetical entries. But in 1967 a generous reviewer of *Melville's Reading*, Professor Herman Spivey, delighted me by singling out these introductory pages as easy to read and going on to commend them to any student interested in "the self-education of a major writer." Professor Spivey's reassuring glimpse of the larger horizons suggested by the essay has given me further reason to include this updated version in the present collection.

The work of Melville scholarship and criticism since the late 1930's has properly emphasized the role of books in shaping the intellectual and literary development of the author of *Moby-Dick*. As Melville wrote of one of his own heroes:

A varied scope of reading, little suspected by his friends, and randomly acquired by a random but lynx-eyed mind . . . poured one considerable contributory stream into that bottomless spring of original thought which the occasion and time had caused to burst out in himself.

And as F. O. Matthiessen declared, "the books that really spoke to Melville became an immediate part of him to a degree hardly matched by any other of our great writers in their maturity." A succession of articles and books has demonstrated the effect of travel literature, philosophical writings, the Bible, Shakespeare, Milton, Bayle, Sterne, Byron, and Arnold—to name but a few—in releasing his creative energies; other studies await publication or completion. The point of departure, as in Charles Olson's illuminating studies of the relation of *King Lear* to the conception of *Moby-Dick*, has frequently been examination of the comments and notes which Melville penciled in volumes from his own library in the course of his reading.

Melville's Library

Although markings and annotation cannot of course indicate the full extent of Melville's response to a book, it is fortunate for those interested in the man and his work that many of the volumes he read and used were kept by his widow after his death in September, 1891.

Mrs. Melville's feelings about his library are indicated by a quotation she found and marked in one of them (Check-List, No. 187):

"My ideas of my husband," she said, "are so much associated with his *books*, that to part with them would be as it were breaking some of the last ties which still connect me with so beloved an object. The being in the midst of books he has been accustomed to read, and which contain his *marks* and *notes*, will still give him *a sort of existence* with *me*. . . ."

But her removal to smaller quarters in the following April made it necessary to dispose of a portion of the library. A few books were presented as mementos to relatives and friends (Check-List, Nos. 284, 539), but many more were sold early in 1892. Mrs. Melville's basis for determining which to part with and which to keep is not known; as her granddaughter Mrs. Metcalf once suggested, she may have given up some of the larger volumes simply because it was difficult to shelve them.

After Mrs. Melville herself died in 1906, nearly all of those books which she had kept were retained in the immediate family until recent years, when the majority of them were presented to the Harvard College Library by three of her granddaughters, Mrs. Henry K. Metcalf of Cambridge, Mrs. Walter B. Binnian of Cohasset, and Mrs. E. Barton Chapin of Andover, Massachusetts, and to the New York Public Library by a fourth granddaughter, Mrs. A. D. Osborne of Edgartown, Massachusetts. Still other books that once belonged to Melville but were given away or sold have been acquired by Harvard, by the New York Public Library with or for its Berg, Duyckinck, and Gansevoort-Lansing Collections, by the Berkshire Athenaeum and the Berkshire County Historical Society, both of Pittsfield, Massachusetts, by other university libraries (Brown, Columbia, Princeton, Virginia, Yale), by the Newberry Library of Chicago, and by private collectors. Some of the books placed on the market have been listed in various sale catalogues; the catalogue descriptions constitute all that is known of a few volumes now in undisclosed locations. Exclusive of copies of Melville's own works, approximately 390 titles that once belonged to him have now been tabulated, as against 350 when *Melville's Reading* was first published, 379 in 1966, 384 in 1971, and 389 in 1979. Of such books that apparently survive, numbering 257 titles, 229 have now been located. In 1948 the number located was 191; in 1966 it was 219; in 1971 it was 223; in 1979 it was 228.[1]

Just how large a part of Melville's lifetime collection of books these figures represent is difficult to say, for there is indication that his library continued to change as well as to grow. Some books he bought solely as gifts; others he gave away after reading and annotating them himself—perhaps after acquiring different editions more suited to his own purposes. Books which Melville and his family inherited and exchanged among themselves are often difficult to classify unless they bear inscriptions by their successive owners. Some of the volumes which survive contain no clues beyond their dates of publication for establishing the length of Melville's ownership and the extent of his use of them. Even less evidence of ownership and disposition is available concerning books which have apparently not survived, and which are known only by references in Melville's correspondence, journals, and accounts: of books billed to him by his publishers, for example, an unspecified number actually went to his brother Allan, who acted as his business agent, and possibly to other relatives as well. Melville once intended cataloguing his books, but after obtaining a blankbook and labeling it "Catalogue of Library H. M." he made no actual entries. Following his death the appraisers of his estate took only an approximate inventory, valuing at $600 his "Personal books numbering about 1,000 volumes." Whether the estimated "1,000 volumes" included the collected editions by general title or in terms of component works is unclear, and whether the appraisers regarded copies of his own writings as part of the library is unknown; according to acquaintances he owned few of his early works during his last years.

Not many of the books that Mrs. Melville gave away or sold have been specifically identified; fewer still have been currently located. Those she determined to sell were offered to John Anderson, Jr., whose shop at 99 Nassau Street in New York her husband had patronized. According to Oscar Wegelin, who in late 1890 and 1891, as Anderson's young assistant, had delivered orders to Melville's residence, 104 East 26th Street, the total ran to at least 500 volumes—possibly more. Anderson himself selected a number of what he considered the best books before calling in other dealers, but there is no surviving record of the price he paid or of exactly what titles he bought. Among Anderson's choices, it appears, were several volumes of Melville's own poetry including *John Marr* (1888) and *Timoleon* (1891), which Melville had printed for private circulation in editions of twenty-five copies and which have now come to be regarded as rarities of great value. Several unspecified items, says Wegelin, went from Anderson's shop into the collections of Thomas J. McKee, Henry C. Sturges, and Daniel Parish, Jr., but only two titles have been subsequently traced: a copy of *Timoleon* and a volume of Southey's *Oliver Newman* (Check-List, No. 482), each described in the extensive

McKee sale catalogue of 1900–1902 (issued by Anderson) as carrying Melville's signature. The Southey, apparently the first Melville association volume to be so catalogued by a dealer, was again offered for sale in 1931 by Newark Galleries, Inc., but its current ownership is unknown. As for titles sold by Anderson to Sturges and Parish, the Parish library is not represented among collections listed in McKay's *American Book Auction Catalogues* (1937), and no books autographed by Melville were noticed by Wegelin when he catalogued the Sturges library for auction in 1922.

For the books not taken by Anderson, Thomas E. Keane of 25 Ann Street "greatly disappointed" Mrs. Melville, in Wegelin's words, with an offer of $100; returning later to raise his bid, Keane found that she had already sold them to A. F. Farnell of Brooklyn, who took a "cartload" to his shop at 42 Court Street. The late Carol V. Wight, who bought several titles from Farnell on 14 April 1892 (Check-List, Nos. 95, 105, 112, 113, and 369), was told at the time that many "theological" works acquired from Mrs. Melville were regarded as a dead loss and had been scrapped for waste paper: it was the preponderance of such works, Farnell remarked, that led New York dealers to decline purchasing the entire lot. Although Anderson, Keane, and Farnell are the only dealers mentioned by Wegelin in connection with Mrs. Melville's sale, the late Henry A. Farnell, in talking with Charles Olson in 1934, recalled that F. H. Bangs and Andrew Merwin of the New York auction house of Bangs & Co. had also evaluated the library. And according to the late Lathrop C. Harper, Mrs. Melville sold still other books to the shop conducted by Mr. Harper and his elder brother, which they had opened in the Astor House, Barclay Street, in 1885, and which Melville himself had visited "many times." The purchase was handled by Francis Harper, and any records that may have been kept were destroyed when the two brothers later dissolved their partnership.

Even though a sizeable part of Farnell's acquisition from Mrs. Melville may indeed have been scrapped, the rapid and profitable movement of the books he placed on sale made the whole transaction "one of the best buys of his career," as Wegelin remembers his telling Anderson sometime later. There are a few more details concerning the sale, supplied by Henry Farnell, to be added here to the recollections of Wegelin and Wight. The price paid Mrs. Melville, $10 higher than the figure of $110 mentioned by Wegelin, was recorded in an entry that A. F. Farnell made in his diary as of 25 February 1892: "Mr Anderson telegraphed me to come to see a library—Went with him to Mrs Melville 104 E 26th St & bought the lot for $120"; within the next two or three days, according to a further notation, he had already resold books to the amount of $30 to Michael Hennessey of Brooklyn, a writer for the New York *Times*. Other Brooklyn buyers included James A. H. Bell, John E. Norcross, William E. Rawlins, Edward M. Smith, Daniel M. Tredwell, and one of Melville's old teachers, Professor Charles E. West, formerly of Pittsfield and Albany, who had recently retired from the Brooklyn Heights Seminary. The libraries of three of these men, West, Hennessey, and Tredwell, were later catalogued for auction, but with no indication given as to which of their books had once been Melville's. Bell's collection of 10,425 volumes was presented in 1896 to what is now the Brooklyn Public Library, but the accompanying manuscript catalogue, though it lists works *by* Melville that Bell had acquired, also fails to distinguish any association volumes bearing Melville's signature.

Since the revival of Melville's fame in the 1920's and after, books from his library have come to be regarded as collector's items of considerable value: for example, a single volume imperfect in itself but containing Melville's extensive notes brought $2100 when auctioned in 1945 by the Parke-Bernet Galleries, Inc., successor to the firm once headed by John Anderson, Jr. This was Owen Chase's *Narrative of the Most Extraordinary and Distressing Shipwreck of the Whale-Ship Essex* (Check-List, No. 134), drawn upon for Melville's account in *Moby-Dick* of the destruction of the Pequod. Prices commanded by Melville association volumes as they occasionally appear on the market have risen steadily in more recent years. One instance is an 1844 anthology of poetry that Melville presented to his sister Frances in 1868 (Check-List, No. 404b; see the Appendix below), which is priced at $2750 in a 1980 catalogue of The Current Company. There has also been talk among dealers and collectors that spurious items have been offered for sale as books that once belonged to Melville. Of the surviving books included in the alphabetical Check-List, all those examined by the compiler himself—with the possible exception of the intriguing No. 223a—are believed to be genuine. But he is unable to vouch for other books, especially those offered at some time in various sale catalogues but now unlocated, which he has had no opportunity to see.

The Early Years (1819–1839)

Among the books owned by Melville, kept by his widow, and later given in turn to a daughter and a granddaughter there is a volume of extracts from Burton's *Anatomy of Melancholy* (Check-List, No. 103) that was once part of his own father's library. In it is a note in Melville's hand:

I bought this book more than four years ago at Gowan's store in New York. Today, Allan [his brother, Allan Melville, Jr.] in looking at it, first detected the above pencil signature of my father's; who,—as it now appears—must have had this book, with many others, sold at auction, at least twenty five years ago.—Strange!

Pittsfield July 7th 1851

Except for this volume, a few other books which did not leave the family, and occasional references in letters and journals, there is little objective evidence concerning the literary tastes of the senior Allan Melvill—to use the spelling he himself employed. But in two of Herman Melville's books, *Redburn* (1849) and *Pierre* (1852), the heroes display a marked fondness for reading nurtured within their boyhood homes. Redburn tells of his fascinated interest in the large library-case which during his father's lifetime had held "long rows of old books . . . printed in Paris, and London, and Leipsic," including a six-volume London edition of the *Spectator* and "D'Alembert in French." He also recalls an "old family Plutarch" and "an old copy of the *Letters of Junius*" which had belonged to his father. And Pierre had "spent long summer afternoons in the deep recesses of his father's fastidiously picked and decorous library; where the Spenserian nymphs had early led him into many a maze of all-bewildering beauty"; he specifically remembers the appearance of his father's set of the works of Plato. It is by no means unlikely that in these passages Melville drew upon recollections of his own boyhood, either at home or in the Albany library of his mother's brother Peter Gansevoort, as Henry A. Murray has suggested. In his "Fragments from a Writing Desk" (1839), contributed to a newspaper ten years before *Redburn*, he had quoted from a volume in the Melville family library (Check-List, No. 118); and of the nine "old European and English guidebooks" listed in *Redburn* itself at least two had actually belonged to his own father. But none of the other books mentioned in *Redburn* and *Pierre* are among the volumes known to have been the property of Melville's parents.

As for Melville's formal education, his schooling began in New York City, where he studied between 1825 and 1829 at the New-York Male High School. Like his Redburn he may have "spouted" Byron's "Address to the Ocean" from its stage; in February of 1828 he won a prize as "best Speaker in the introductory Department." In that same year, according to a letter he sent to his maternal grandmother ("the third letter that I ever wrote"), his class was studying "Geography, Gramar [*sic*], Arithmetic, Writing, Speaking, Spelling" and reading in "the Scientific class book." As David K. Titus has recently observed, the letter suggests that he was pursuing the standard elementary curriculum of the day. During the previous school year, when Herman was eight years old, he had been selected as a monitor; the school was conducted on the "Lancastrian" plan "whereby faculty taught student monitors, who then instructed other pupils," though by 1831 the institution failed "because of the difficulty of adapting the monitorial method to the higher subjects."[2] Meanwhile, in 1829, both Herman and his older brother Gansevoort had been transferred to the Grammar School of Columbia College, Gansevoort enrolling in the Classical Department on 14 May and Herman in the English Department on 28 September.[3] But Allan Melvill's business reverses led the family to move from New York to Albany in October of 1830, and there both Gansevoort and Herman entered the Albany Academy.

Unlike the New-York Male High School, the Academy was a "classical school" whose students were preparing for college, and from October of 1830 until October of 1831 Herman took its standard preparatory course in the Fourth Department, studying "Reading and Spelling; Penmanship; Arithmetic; English Grammar; Geography; Natural History; Universal, Grecian, Roman and English History; Classical Biography; and Jewish Antiquities."[4] One of his schoolbooks survives, along with a book he won as a prize in 1831 for "Ciphering Books" in the standard arithmetic curriculum (Check-List, Nos. 380, 331); in 1863, when he was named a member of a committee to arrange for celebrating the Academy's semicentennial anniversary (see No. 8a), a friend gave him a copy of another textbook used there during his student days (No. 390).

For unknown reasons young Herman left the Academy in October of 1831, three months before his father's death, although both Gansevoort and a younger brother, Allan, continued in attendance for a somewhat longer period. After a brief tenure at the Albany Classical School, where he wrote English compositions for Dr. Charles E. West in 1835, Herman Melville returned to the Albany Academy for two quarters from September of 1836 until March of 1837. As Titus has shown, his study of the "Latin Language" at this time may have involved recitations in both Latin and Greek. Although Melville's knowledge of the classical languages was limited at best, his continued interest in the Latin derivations of English words is reflected in his own writing as late as *Billy Budd, Sailor*.[5]

Perhaps more important than schoolbooks was Melville's other early reading, in his father's library or elsewhere. At some time during his boyhood, according to his own later testimony, he was strongly influenced by the works of Fenimore Cooper, read "long ago, and far inland," but no work of Cooper's has been kept among his father's books or his own. The rather ostentatious literary allusions in "Fragments from a Writing Desk" imply his youthful familiarity with other standard authors—Shakespeare, Milton, Chesterfield, Sheridan, Burke, Campbell, Scott, Byron, and Coleridge—and with the *Arabian Nights*. While the Melvilles were living in Albany they had access not only to the personal library of Peter Gansevoort but also to books drawn in his name from the Albany Library, of which he was a member. Gansevoort Melville, Herman's older brother, patronized the reading room of John Cook and held membership in the Albany Athenaeum; entries in a journal which he kept for the first three months of 1834, which has been published in part by Jay Leyda, make it plain that books he borrowed during the Albany years were likely to be read and discussed by other members of the family as well. For this reason their titles are included in the alphabetical Check-List along with other borrowed books accessible to Herman Melville.

Also to be mentioned is the family library of another uncle, Major Thomas Melvill, Jr., with whom young Herman spent nearly a year at Pittsfield, Massachusetts, probably in 1834. Surviving booksellers' bills list twenty-one titles, many of them school texts, which Major Melvill bought at intervals between 1814 and 1832. These listings give some indication of the character of his library, which may also have included books acquired during his earlier residence in France. But since this information is fragmentary, and especially since Herman Melville's acquaintance with the volumes has yet to be demonstrated, the known titles have not been incorporated into the Check-List.

On 29 January 1835, when Melville was back in Albany, he joined the newly formed Young Men's Association, and for two years had access to its reading room and library of a thousand volumes. The library's records of books charged to members during this period are now lost to sight, but both a manuscript catalogue and a printed version of 1837 still exist. Included in these compilations are works known to have influenced the "Fragments" of 1839; the printed catalogue of 1837, as William H. Gilman observed, "forms the basis for Melville's first known reading list."

In December of 1837, having returned to Pittsfield for a try at school-teaching, Melville wrote to Peter Gansevoort describing his situation and acknowledging his uncle's recent gift of helpful books (see Check-List, Nos. 456a, 497). These he had found "of eminent usefulness," particularly J. O. Taylor's *The District School*; as for American education on the common-school level, the young teacher concluded, "when reduced to practise, the high and sanguine hopes excited by its imposing appearance in *theory*—are a little dashed.—" Melville did not resume teaching in 1838 but enrolled for two quarters in the academy at Lansingburgh, New York, where his mother had moved. There, apparently seeking to qualify himself for employment on the Erie Canal, he completed what Titus has called "a crash course in engineering and surveying." This was the last formal schooling he received. Though the position he sought never materialized for him, his work at the Lansingburgh academy was probably not without profit: in its library and scientific laboratories, as Gilman conjectured, he may well have "laid the foundation for his mature interest in natural science."

The Years at Sea (1839–1844)

As Ishmael remarks in *Moby-Dick*, "The transition is a keen one, I assure you, from a schoolmaster to a sailor." In 1839, unable to find other employment, young Melville began his career at sea with a voyage to Liverpool—the experience that was to provide the major factual basis for *Redburn* ten years later. After his return he read with "strange, congenial feelings" Dana's *Two Years before the Mast*, as though "tied & welded" to its author—so he was later to tell Dana himself—"by a sort of Siamese link of affectionate sympathy." The search for sympathetic and congenial companionship is a recurrent motif of Melville's writings from the beginning. *Redburn*, as we now know, is anything but a literal transcription of what befell its author in 1839; the book probably projects Melville's own situation, however, in stressing its narrator's education and literary tastes as setting him off from most of his shipmates, for this same theme is repeated in all of the books that grew out of Melville's observations of life among sailors and wanderers. Late in 1840, after a second brief experience of schoolteaching and a trip to Illinois, finding himself again with no employment in prospect ashore, he signed for another voyage, this time for the South Pacific aboard the whaleship Acushnet, on which he sailed early in January of 1841. Among his later books, *Typee*, *Omoo*, the setting of *Mardi*, and the whaling background of *Moby-Dick* are related to his life on shipboard and his sojourn in the Pacific islands; *White-Jacket* is associated with his return home in 1844 as a member of the crew of the American frigate United States.

Professor Wilson Heflin in his continuing study of Melville's whaling years has found new information concerning books and magazines available to Melville during the 1840's. Using papers discovered by Edouard Stackpole, he has published a list of the small library carried to the Pacific by the Charles and Henry, the whaleship on which Melville served for approximately six months between November of 1842 and May of 1843. Bought by the ship's owners, Charles G. and Henry Coffin, before her sailing from Nantucket, this library

consisted of thirty-seven books and two magazines (presumably bound volumes of several issues). The choice of these books—many of them juvenile, didactic, and sentimental in character,—seems to indicate in the Coffin owners, or their stationer, a shrewd assessment of the levels of literacy and taste among whalemen, plus a concerted effort to provide moral suasion. Dominant symbols in these volumes are home, fireside, country, and church. But this small library was intended to entertain, too. Much of it was popular fiction, including nautical yarns, romances, and adventure stories. There were also works of history (even one on banking) and biography. A good number of these volumes were published in the year of the ship's sailing.

From a bill submitted to the Coffins by their stationer, Andrew Macy, Professor Heflin has identified the thirty-seven books; the two magazines—"Abbott's Magazine" and "Family Magazine"—were probably *The Religious Magazine and Family Miscellany,* edited by Jacob Abbott and published in Boston, and *The Family Magazine; or Monthly Abstract of General Knowledge* . . . , vols. 1–8 (20 April 1833–1840/41), New York, Redfield & Lindsay, 1834–1840.[6]

Professor Heflin has also discovered new evidence concerning the libraries aboard the frigate United States, on which Melville served between August of 1843 and October of 1844; his findings go beyond the information previously published by Charles R. Anderson in 1939. In addition to her regular officers' library, the United States, during Melville's tour of duty on board, carried a small library for enlisted men, in accordance with a "List of Books to be allowed for the Libraries of seamen on board vessels of the Navy," proposed by the Board of Navy Commissioners on 31 May 1841. From this list the purser at the Norfolk Navy Yard, who saw to the provisioning of the frigate before her sailing, sent aboard the United States a seamen's library of more than a hundred volumes, including "Selections from [Harper's] Family Library" and nine bound volumes of the *Penny Magazine* (which Melville drew upon in his later writings, notably *Red-*

burn). Professor Heflin is preparing a detailed study of the titles probably aboard the United States during Melville's period of service.[7]

Melville apparently kept no journal during his years at sea, and no book from his library survives from this period. But in his own published works there are occasional passages that raise a special problem for the student of his reading. When the narrators of these works allude to books and authors, is Melville writing fact or fiction? Did he himself read what they report having read, and if so, did his own reading occur at the times and places described? Answers to these questions cannot be given without qualification. The Acushnet may have carried a ship's library while Melville was a member of her crew, but in *Typee*, based on his voyage to the South Pacific aboard her, it is said that the oppressive heat of the tropical latitudes made reading impossible: "take a book in your hand, and you were asleep in an instant." And though Melville's Ishmael declares in *Moby-Dick* that "a whale-ship was my Yale College and my Harvard," there is only one passage in the entire book to mention reading as part of his education at sea. This occurs in an account of Owen Chase, first mate and one of the few survivors of the whaleship Essex, which in 1820 had been rammed and sunk by an eighty-five-foot sperm whale. Ishmael states specifically that he had seen Owen Chase, had read Chase's published *Narrative* on shipboard, and had conversed with his son, "all this within a few miles of the scene of the catastrophe." At one time Ishmael's detailed assertion was regarded as pure fiction, intended by Melville to heighten and color his book; later, with the recovery of his own copy of Chase's *Narrative* (Check-List, No. 134), acquired in 1851 during the writing of *Moby-Dick*, it was made clear that here at least Ishmael was speaking for Melville himself. According to his manuscript notes bound into the book, Melville had "first become acquainted" with the story of the Essex in forecastle conversations aboard the Acushnet. Later, when the ship spoke a Nantucket whaler at sea and the two crews met for a "gam," the young man he described as a "son" of Owen Chase—presumably William Henry Chase—loaned him Chase's *Narrative*, and reading "this wondrous story upon the landless sea, & close to the very latitude of the shipwreck had a surprising effect upon me." Still later, the notes continue, another speaking brought him a glimpse of a ship's captain whom Melville took—erroneously—to be Owen Chase himself, "the most prepossessing-looking whale-hunter I think I ever saw."

On the ground that Melville's copy of Chase corroborates Ishmael's anecdote in *Moby-Dick*, it might be argued by analogy that other accounts of a similar nature in the earlier books are probably true to their author's experience. Thus in *Omoo*, sequel to *Typee*, the narrator may well be speaking for Melville himself when he recalls his hunger for literature while he roved the South Seas and when he tells of his delight in finding a companion of kindred literary interests. This was the man known as Long Ghost, who "quoted Virgil, and talked of Hobbes of Malmsbury, besides repeating poetry by the canto, especially 'Hudibras.'" Long Ghost's Australian newspapers and battered books he read through "again and again, including a learned treatise on the yellow fever," and both men greedily devoured three volumes of Smollett's novels unexpectedly provided them by a Polynesian native. Although such stories probably lost nothing in the telling, the essential situation of the narrator and his friend reflects that of Melville and the living original of Long Ghost. There are similar passages in *White-Jacket*, Melville's fifth book, where again the narrator-hero is pleased to find friends with tastes in literature akin to his own. One was the incomparable Jack Chase, also drawn from the life, who "talked of Rob Roy, Don Juan, and Pelham; Macbeth and Ulysses; but, above all things, was an ardent admirer of Camoens." Another, who had "seized the right meaning of Montaigne," was Nord: one night in his company White-Jacket "scoured all the prairies of reading; dived into the bosoms of authors, and tore out their hearts; and that night White-Jacket learned more than he has ever done in any single night since."

On the other side of the argument, however, are passages in *White-Jacket* and still others in *Redburn* that make demonstrably fictitious references to literary topics. In direct contrast to Jack Chase and Nord is the Neversink's chaplain, a "transcendental divine" more bookish than humane, who carried *Biographia Literaria* in his hand, learnedly cited the *Phædon* of Plato, and in his preaching was "particularly hard upon the Gnostics and Marcionites of the second century of the Christian era" instead of attacking the everyday vices of the man-of-war world. White-Jacket's critical description of Sunday services on the Neversink obviously does not square with a matter-of-fact sketch of religious activities written by the official Ship's Scribe of the United States, as Anderson has shown, nor is his inventory of the Neversink's library at all similar to the surviving records examined by Professors Anderson and Heflin. Like much of *White-Jacket*, which Melville presented as a generalized picture of naval life rather than a record of his own experiences, these fictional passages serve his purpose of exposing the American navy's disregard for the welfare of its common seamen. His own reading—not that of his years at sea but in works he came upon more recently—helped him to drive home his point through caricature and satire: in 1848 he himself had acquired a copy of Coleridge's *Biographia Literaria*; in 1849 he referred in a letter both to the *Phædon* and to his recent purchase of Bayle's *Dictionary*; in 1850 and 1851, in *Moby-Dick*, he was to reflect his own knowledge of the heretical "Gnostics and Marcionites" in passages deriving in part from Bayle. As for the books said to be provided for the ship's crew, so thoroughly inappropriate that they "must have been selected by our chaplain," at least two of the titles mentioned in the "Man-of-War Library" chapter are taken over from a literary source used elsewhere to fill out the content of *White-Jacket.*

Redburn, like *White-Jacket*, supplements and heightens its author's own recollections with material borrowed from other writers; both volumes followed shortly after *Mardi* (1849), Melville's third book, in which for the first time he had avowedly written not a "narrative" but a "romance," as its brief Preface asserts. And there are other similarities in their references to books and reading—particularly those passages written in the comic or humorous vein. During young Redburn's voyage he takes up a copy of Adam Smith's *Wealth of Nations*, described as a gift from his brother's friend Mr. Jones, but the volume proves as inappropriate fare as the books White-Jacket finds in the Neversink's library: instead of improving his mind it merely puts Redburn to sleep. After reaching Liverpool he attempts to make his way about the city with an outdated guidebook that had supposedly belonged to his father, *The Picture of Liverpool*; Redburn's drawn-out account of this volume and his efforts to use it helped Melville to stretch into book length a hastily written story that he dismissed as no better than a potboiler. Although neither *The Wealth of Nations* nor *The Picture of Liverpool* is numbered, like Chase's *Narrative*, among his surviving books, there is no question that he wrote *Redburn* in 1849 with copies of both under his eye. But whether he had actually taken either volume on his own voyage to Liverpool ten years before is a more dubious matter.

Equally questionable as applying to Melville's voyage of 1839 are Redburn's accounts of still other reading matter purportedly belonging to his shipmates, including Blunt's "extraordinary-looking pamphlet . . . entitled the *Bonaparte Dream Book*" and two impressive works loaned to him by the sailor Max: "One was an account of shipwrecks and disasters at sea, and the other was a large black volume, with *Delirium Tremens* in great gilt letters on the back. This proved to be a popular treatise on the subject of that disease; and I remembered seeing several copies in the sailor bookstalls about Fulton Market, and along South Street, in New York." In *White-Jacket* too the sailors are said to prefer authors "such as you may find at the book-stalls along Fulton Market; they were slightly physiological in their nature." That two books written in 1849 include similar references to "the sailor bookstalls" of the city where Melville had been living since 1847, suggests that their author was recalling works examined more recently than during his years at sea.

It is no longer necessary to labor the point that Melville's books are something other than thinly disguised autobiography, as they were taken to be by some interpreters before the objective facts of his career came under intensive scrutiny. The position to be established here is simply that internal evidence alone is not always reliable when a book is named by one of his narrators: clearly Melville himself must have known something of the works he writes about, though not necessarily under the conditions the narrator describes. As a general rule, therefore, the titles of books mentioned in Melville's published writing are excluded from the alphabetical Check-List unless objective records confirm his ownership or document his borrowing and reading them. Thus the *Narrative* of Owen Chase is listed twice, first as a book he borrowed in 1841, No. 133 in the Check-List, and again as a book surviving from his own collection, No. 134; but *The Wealth of Nations, The Picture of Liverpool,* and other books mentioned in the published works are unlisted, since no external documentary evidence has been found that records Melville's owning or borrowing them as he did the Chase. In some instances this policy has necessarily meant the omission of demonstrated source material, such as the Liverpool guidebook, but no other course has seemed practicable in a compilation of this scope.

One further instance from *White-Jacket* will illustrate application of the principle. In Chapter 24, "Introductory to Cape Horn," the narrator mentions four books by author and title: three "remarkable and most interesting narratives" record the passage round the Cape by Lord Anson's squadron in 1736, and "White-Jacket has them all"; the fourth is "my friend Dana's" *Two Years before the Mast.* As we now know, Melville himself had read Dana's book in 1840, but there is no evidence to establish whether he borrowed a copy or owned one—either then or later. *Two Years before the Mast* clearly belongs in the alphabetical Check-List (see No. 173), on the basis not of the narrator's allusion in *White-Jacket* but of Melville's letter to Dana, where he is writing in his own person. As for the other three books named by White-Jacket, one at least, John Byron's *Narrative* (No. 113), was owned by Melville himself, and his copy survives. But since White-Jacket's library is not necessarily identical with Melville's, the two other books mentioned must be omitted from the Check-List until external evidence can be found that will establish them also as belonging to Melville himself.

Author and New Yorker (1844–1850)

It is fortunate that for the years following Melville's return from the South Seas the records of his reading are far more complete and objective than for the earlier periods. In his own judgment, the most important time of his life was not that of the career of adventure which terminated in 1844. "Until I was twenty-five," he declared to Nathaniel Hawthorne in 1851, "I had no development at all. From my twenty-fifth year I date my life. Three weeks have scarcely passed, at any time between then and now, that I have not unfolded within myself."

In the years between 1844, when Melville turned twenty-five, and 1847, when he married and settled in New York, he established himself as a popular author with the double success of *Typee* and *Omoo* and began to move in prominent literary circles of the city. And as he gravitated once again to other men interested in books, so too did he find his way to the city's libraries and bookstores. In January of 1848, through the agency of his literary friends the Duyckincks, Melville became a shareholder in the New York Society Library, which he had perhaps begun to use even earlier on payment of the fee asked of non-members. As his new bride reported late in 1847, writing to her family in Boston, it was his daily habit to interrupt his work with a walk downtown and a visit to an unnamed "reading room" to look at the "papers." At that period the New York Society Library maintained two reading rooms, one reserved for newspapers and periodicals, the other a book room described as separated from the open-shelf room by two "studies for those authors who desire to pursue their investigations with their authorities around them, or who wish to make new books on old Burton's recipe, 'as apothecaries make new mixtures, by pouring out of one vessel into another.'" With both "old Burton" and his recipe Melville, we know, was thoroughly familiar. As his household was a crowded one, including his brother Allan's family, his mother, and his sisters, the library rooms may have provided him with a welcome retreat as his writing continued. Between 1848 and 1850 he withdrew only four books (Check-List, Nos. 85, 243, 450, and 451), but probably made more extensive use of the library's facilities during his visits there than its record of charges would show.

The new range of Melville's reading attracted the notice of his friends, who became aware of a decided change in his literary tastes from the travel literature he had diligently studied for the enrichment of *Typee* and *Omoo*. "By the way Melville reads Old Books," Evert Duyckinck reported early in 1848. "He has borrowed Sir Thomas Brown[e] of me and says finely of the speculations of the Religio Medici that Browne is a kind of 'crack'd Archangel'"—adding with apparent surprise, "Was ever any thing of this sort said before by a sailor?" What Melville absorbed from *Religio Medici* is evident enough in his third book: *Mardi*, as Matthiessen said, echoes Browne "to the length of ventriloquism." Though neither an artistic nor a commercial success, *Mardi* is clearly the work of a developing and aspiring talent. Into it went the immediate fruits of Melville's reading in 1848, much of it done in Duyckinck's large private library. Twenty-nine widely varied titles are charged to Melville over the years in his friend's memoranda of "Books Lent," which does not include additional books and magazines he may have dipped into at Duyckinck's residence, the gathering place for his literary friends. Melville was also a frequent visitor in the Boston home of his father-in-law, Lemuel Shaw, Chief Justice of Massachusetts, whose library was by no means limited to law books. Shaw subscribed to such journals as the *North American Review* (to which he contributed), the *Christian Register*, the *Edinburgh Review*, and the *Quarterly Review*, and was a frequent borrower—perhaps on Melville's behalf—from the shelves of the Boston Athenaeum. Titles charged to him there during the known periods of his son-in-law's visits to Boston have been included in the alphabetical Check-List.

But though Melville "swam through libraries," and admitted that they "have an imposing air, and doubtless contain invaluable volumes," he nevertheless felt that "somehow, the books that prove most agreeable, grateful, and companionable, are those we pick up by chance here and there; those which seem put into our hands by Providence; those which pretend to little, but abound in much." It was in this spirit that he began collecting books of his own, visiting the bookshops and auction sales of New York and Boston, and later of Europe. Thus he first read Emerson "in Putnam's store" and happened upon his father's copy of Burton in that of William Gowans. He and his brother Allan, his business agent, received a professional discount on books bought from his publishers, Wiley and Putnam (succeeded by John Wiley) and Harper and Brothers; their purchases are recorded by date and usually by title in the statements of Melville's accounts rendered at intervals by each of the firms. Allusions to some of these books and their authors soon appear in the works Melville was writing, but in other instances it is not certain whether individual titles were intended for him or for his brother. Since Allan Melville's purchases were readily accessible to him, as were the books belonging to his mother and sisters, such volumes are included in the Check-List. So too are surviving books that had belonged to Gansevoort Melville, who died in London in 1846; some of them are unmarked, but others are inscribed and annotated by Herman Melville.

In Melville's correspondence of this period and his journal of 1849–1850 there are further records of books which he himself bought and read, notably in a letter written to Evert Duyckinck from Boston early in 1849: "Chancing to fall in" a few days previously with an edition of Shakespeare "in glorious great type" suitable to his weak eyes (Check-List, No. 460), Melville reports with enthusiasm, he has been enabled for the first time to begin a really "close acquaintance with the divine William." In Matthiessen's words, he

had just begun to meditate on Shakespeare more creatively than any other American writer ever has. This meditation brought him to his first profound comprehension of the nature of tragedy. This was the charge that released *Moby-Dick*, and that carried him in *Pierre* to the unbearable desperation of a Hamlet.

In October of 1849 Melville sailed for Europe to negotiate for the London publication of *White-Jacket*. Hoping to travel on the Continent, he carried several European guidebooks borrowed from George Duyckinck. During November and December his itinerary included libraries, bookshops, and publishers' offices in London, Paris, Coblenz, and Cologne. His journal of the trip includes references to shipboard reading (Check-List, Nos. 182, 315), congenial discussions on shipboard of literary and philosophical topics, and acquisition by purchase or gift of over two dozen books. Other volumes were tempting but beyond his limited means: "Saw many books I should like to buy—but can not," runs his journal entry for 17 December, in London.

From the text of his journal for 1849–1850 and Melville's itemized list at its end, together with the letters, publishers' statements, and records of library loans already mentioned, come many of the entries in the alphabetical Check-List, since relatively few of the numerous books he acquired have survived. Undoubtedly Melville received copies of those publications that Duyckinck asked him to review for the New York *Literary World*, to take one obvious category of titles, but none of them is to be found among the surviving volumes. Some of the purchases he brought home from Europe in 1850 were presented as gifts—for example, a volume of *Hudibras* he inscribed to Evert Duyckinck (Check-List, No. 104); other books were disposed of in later years when Melville's interest waned, or when he secured better editions; what became of still others has not been determined. And it must be remembered that Melville read and sometimes in his own works cited more books than can be found in records of purchases and library loans. Important as they are, therefore, these listings tell less than the full story of his voluminous reading during his productive years.

The Years in Pittsfield (1850–1863)

In the summer of 1850, following his return from Europe and the commencement of another new work—"the 'whaling voyage'" as yet unnamed—Melville took his growing family to board with the widow and son of his late Uncle Thomas in Pittsfield, and in the autumn settled nearby on the newly purchased farm, Arrowhead, that was to be their home for the next thirteen years. During July he began acquiring books of regional interest, such as *A History of the County of Berkshire* and a volume on the Shakers (Check-List, Nos. 216, 459a), that were to yield material for his own writing. More important, his Aunt Mary Melvill gave him on 18 July a copy of Hawthorne's *Mosses from an Old Manse* (No. 248). Reading Hawthorne at this time affected him as powerfully as did his study of Shakespeare during the winter and spring of 1849; indeed, Melville associated the two. In a long and enthusiastic review contributed to the *Literary World*, "Hawthorne and His Mosses," he praised the Shakespearean qualities he detected in Hawthorne's writing—the very qualities he was seeking to embody in the work taking form under his own hand. In August of 1850 began his momentous friendship with Hawthorne himself, for fifteen months his neighbor in nearby Lenox and his companion in occasional talks on such now-familiar topics as "books, and publishers, and all possible and impossible matters"; though their conversations sometimes "lasted pretty deep into the night," Melville as a houseguest at Lenox was "very careful not to interrupt Mr. Hawthorne's mornings," according to his admiring hostess, and on one occasion "shut himself into the boudoir & read Mr. Emerson's Essays" while his friend was writing.

During the Pittsfield years Melville's own library continued to grow. He and Hawthorne exchanged presentation copies of their new works and also other volumes (Check-List, Nos. 157, 178a, 194), and

from Berkshire friends such as Richard Lathers and Mrs. J. R. Morewood he received additional books (Nos. 292a; 247, 333, 334, 350),
but he missed the resources of the "long Vaticans and street-stalls" of
New York. Though the local Pittsfield Library Association was open
to him, for special titles needed as his work on *Moby-Dick* progressed
he found it necessary to place orders in the city with his publishers
and with George Putnam, who imported at least one volume for him:
Beale's *Natural History of the Sperm Whale* (Check-List, No. 52). From
Evert Duyckinck he borrowed more books during 1850 than in any
previous year. In a letter to Duyckinck, acknowledging a quotation
that had reached him too late for inclusion among the "Extracts" that
preface *Moby-Dick*, he wrote in 1851:

Why didn't you send me that inestimable item of "Herman de Wardt" before? Oh had I but had that pie to cut into! But that & many other fine
things doubtless are omitted. All one can do is pick up what chips he can
buy[?] round him. They have no Vatican (as you have) in Pittsfield here.

To help make up for the deficiency of books in the Berkshires, not
only Duyckinck but also Melville's brother Allan (Check-List, No. 171)
and his father-in-law assisted in the collection of material for *Moby-
Dick*. Lemuel Shaw attempted in particular to secure certain needed
books concerning the island of Nantucket and its ships and men. The
times at which two of these volumes reached Melville are worth noting, for they constitute terminal dates for passages based in part upon
them. Early in 1851 Shaw received a copy of Lay and Hussey's *Narrative of the Mutiny, on Board the Ship Globe of Nantucket*, inscribed
"Hon^e. Lemuel Shaw presented by his friend Thos. Macy 1 ṁ [Janu-
ary] 1851" (Check-List, No. 323); this volume he in turn gave Melville, who added the inscription "Herman Melville from Chief Justice
Shaw 1851. Pittsfield." Three months later Macy wrote to Shaw from
"Nantucket 4 ṁ [April] 1851," sending "a mutilated copy" of Owen
Chase's *Narrative*, "the only copy that I have been able to procure"; in
the book itself (No. 134) is Melville's inscription: "Herman Melville
from Judge Shaw April. 1851." More than a year later, after *Moby-
Dick* had been published, Macy gave Melville a third book (Check-
List, No. 345), Obed Macy's *History of Nantucket*, which he himself
inscribed "Herman Melville from his friend Thos Macy 7 1/m [7 Janu-
ary] 1852"—perhaps in return for a copy of *Moby-Dick*, though no
record of such a gift has come to light.

Throughout the Berkshire period, reading of all kinds, including
newspapers and magazines, provided Melville with recreation as well
as source-material. At times, when his eyes troubled him after a day

given mostly to writing, he spent his evenings "in a sort of mesmeric state in my room," as he told Duyckinck, "not being able to read—only now & then skimming over some large-printed book." But J. E. A. Smith of Pittsfield, compiler of Berkshire history and friend of Berkshire authors, recalled in after years that it was Melville's usual habit, after his daily writing was finished, to

emerge from his "den," join in family or social intercourse, indulge in light reading—which was not so very light; as it included much less of what we commonly call "light literature" than it did of profound reviews, abstruse philosophy in prose or verse, and the like—visit or entertain his friends or otherwise enjoy himself: But no more formal serious work for him until the next morning, although, consciously or unconsciously, his mind was always gathering material for it.

With his increasing dependence on reading and meditation for the substance of his literary output Melville had developed a strong distaste for the fame which his earlier books of adventure such as *Typee* had brought him. "What 'reputation' H. M. has is horrible," he wrote to Hawthorne in June of 1851. "Think of it! To go down to posterity is bad enough, any way; but to go down as a 'man who lived among the cannibals'!" And in *Pierre* (1852), commenting on "inferior instances of an immediate literary success, in very young writers," he observed that almost invariably they are "chiefly indebted to some rich and peculiar experience in life, embodied in a book." (Such had been exactly the case with the author of *Typee* and *Omoo*.) But, he goes on to explain, an author who has exhausted or forsworn the material furnished by his own past life cannot hope to replace it simply by appropriating the second-hand experience found in "mere reading," for "the heavy unmalleable element of mere book-knowledge" is all too likely to domineer and dictate to the would-be writer instead of proving "an exhilarative and provocative to him."

Melville's failure to solve this dilemma to his own satisfaction after *Moby-Dick* was one contributing cause of his ultimate abandonment of professional authorship; another was his refusal to pander to popular taste for more books like *Typee* and *Omoo*. To Hawthorne, in the letter already cited, he had put the case as follows: "What I feel most moved to write, that is banned,—it will not pay. Yet, altogether, write the *other* way I cannot. So the product is a final hash, and all my books are botches." After *Pierre*, which damaged his standing with critics and the public, came a series of magazine pieces (1853–1856) plus three more books: *Israel Potter* (1855) and *Piazza Tales* (1856), collected from *Putnam's Magazine*, and *The Confidence-Man* (1857). The works were

the product of a constant application that drained Melville's energies
and alarmed his family. In 1856–1857, physically and spiritually exhausted, he traveled to the Near East in search of renewed health.
On his return, having failed either to sell his farm or to secure a
consular appointment, he took to the lecture-platform (1857–1858,
1858–1859, 1859–1860), consenting for financial reasons to draw to
some degree on personal experiences in discussing "Statues in
Rome," "The South Seas," and "Traveling." But his uneven performance compared unfavorably with that of such crowd-pleasers as the
less reticent Bayard Taylor, and his own opinion of popular taste remained low. On one occasion, stopping in New York to call on Evert
Duyckinck for some "winter reading" at Pittsfield, he observed that
"the mealy mouthed habit of writing of human nature of the present
day would not tolerate the plain speaking of Johnson, for instance, in
the Rambler—who does not hesitate to use the work *malignity!*" Four
months later he was again at sea for the sake of his health, this time
as a passenger aboard the ship Meteor, commanded by his younger
brother Thomas and bound for San Francisco. With him went "a
good lot of books . . . —plenty of old periodicals—lazy reading for
lazy latitudes"; left behind was the manuscript of a volume of poems
which Duyckinck tried without success to place with a publisher. On
Melville's return it seemed clear to him that his career as a professional author was over. Checked and underlined in a book he had
read aboard the Meteor is this line:

> The work that I was born to do is done!

Return to New York (1863–1891)

In 1863 the Melvilles sold Arrowhead to Herman's brother Allan
and moved from Pittsfield back to New York. When a consular appointment once again failed to materialize, Melville accepted in 1866
an obscure position as Inspector of Customs on the New York water-
front. His work there kept him out-of-doors and away from his desk
during the day, but freed him at last to write as he pleased—not for
money—during his leisure hours. He was composing in verse during
the 'sixties, despite failure to place the manuscript poems he had already completed; in 1866 he published his new work as *Battle-Pieces
and Aspects of the War*. Sometime in 1862 or after he had marked,
checked, and underlined a statement by Monckton Milnes that another poet's poetical vigor had advanced "just in proportion as his

physical health declined"; though he may have taken the words as applicable to his own situation, he now clearly thought himself no more than an occasional writer, no longer a professional. Reading in Arnold's *Essays in Criticism*, he was attracted by a remark Arnold quoted from Maurice de Guérin: "The literary career seems to me unreal, both in its own essence and in the rewards which one seeks from it, and therefore fatally marred by a secret absurdity." To these words he added his own: "This is the finest verbal statement of a truth which every one who thinks in these days must have felt."

Except for *Battle-Pieces* and *Clarel* (1876), the bulk of Melville's extensive writing during the years in New York was either privately printed for the eyes of his family and friends or else left in manuscript. From 1866 until his voluntary retirement in 1885 he retained his post in the customs service, carefully guarding his privacy. Had he "been willing to join freely in the literary movements of New York, his name would have remained before the public and a larger sale of his works would have been insured." So wrote his literary executor, Arthur Stedman, following Melville's death in 1891. "But more and more, as he grew older," Stedman continued, "he avoided every action on his part and on the part of his family that might look in this direction, even declining to assist in founding the Authors Club in 1882." Something of what his husbanded leisure meant to Melville after his escape from the demands of professional writing is set forth in a newspaper clipping pasted into one of his books in the year he left Pittsfield—a volume of Hazlitt that had once belonged to his brother Gansevoort (Check-List, No. 266a). "Regular education," the passage begins, "introduces the mind of the pupil to the *difficulties* of knowledge, and keeps it in *constant contact* with them, and it is able to do so because it has all the freshness and strength of the pupil's mind at its command." (Italics denote Melville's underlining.) Then come the sentences that particularly struck home:

Leisure [heavily underlined] *is the nurse of art and scholarship,* the *gradual untier of knots,* the guide that ushers into the *depths and mysteries* of knowledge, the *gradual* former of that *discrimination* and *perception* which distinguishes the man of *high education.* Irregular and anomalous education[,] which can take a hasty advantage of the odd moments and the spare attention of a busy life, cannot be expected to produce these effects, because it has[,] in truth, not *the whole man,* but only a fragment of him at its command. It takes a sharp mind under such circumstances even *to skim the surface;* the *secrets* of the *depths below* are the prize of a *gradual struggle,* which it requires time even to commence, for *we do not even see our difficulties* till we have been a considerable time looking about us.

Under the clipping, having noted its source ("Editorial in London Times") and the date, March of 1863, Melville added a sentence of his own:

> How un-American is all this, and yet—
> —how true.

This observation is but one of the many thoughts that Melville confided to his books in the absence of like-minded companions such as he had once known—even his friendship with Evert Duyckinck, which had cooled after *Pierre* and then been renewed, was never of the same intensity as his feelings for Jack Chase and for Hawthorne. Since most of the surviving books, like his surviving manuscripts, date from the later decades of his life, it is possible that he disposed of part of his existing library when he left Pittsfield in 1863. His collection as Stedman later knew it in New York consisted, "in addition to numerous works on philosophy and the fine arts, . . . of standard books of all classes, including, of course, a proportion of nautical literature." Many of these volumes were editions of the English poets that Melville had begun buying at second-hand during the late 'fifties when he turned to composing verse; they are of particular interest to students of his poetry in that they contain numerous marks and notes on versification and diction made as he schooled himself in his new medium, seeking to acquire "that *discrimination* and *perception*" he perhaps felt might have come to him sooner had he been given a more "regular" education.

The "numerous works on philosophy" mentioned by Stedman and the "theological" books reportedly scrapped by Farnell after Melville's death may have concerned research done in the 'sixties and early 'seventies for *Clarel*, his long narrative poem based partly on the journal of his travels in 1856–1857 and partly on his reading. After Melville's retirement in 1885 he evidently devoted much time to his collection of works by and about Balzac (Check-List, Nos. 27–37, 436, 543), whose writing he had known at least as early as 1870 (see No. 28). Among these volumes are a number bearing Melville's characteristic marks and notes but not his autograph—books that would not be readily identified as his had they not been kept in the family. Absence of an identifying signature might account for the seeming disappearance of other volumes he is known to have read and probably owned, such as "the 'Mermaid Series' of old plays" that occupied him during the last weeks of his life, according to Stedman, and "in which he took much pleasure." Among his persistent interests, as Stedman indicated, was his collection of prints and of books on painters and painting, some of them obviously expensive volumes (e.g., Check-List, No. 298). Although his wife, who managed the household finances, was able to allow him $25 a month for pictures and books after 1884, when she received an inheritance, it was rumored in the New York book trade that he spent more on books than the family liked. Mrs. Melville gave him other works associated with his interests and hobbies, such as growing roses (Check-List, No. 275a), but according to tradition he often bought as "presents" for his wife and children those books which he wanted at hand but felt he could not afford for himself. These gifts are properly a part of the alphabetical Check-List, like other books owned and borrowed by members of the family circle.

While Melville's mother was alive and a resident of his household it was customary for the women in the family to read aloud in the evenings (Check-List, Nos. 304, 556a, 556b, 567); in later years his wife continued the same practice (No. 396.1). Much information of this kind comes from the Melville correspondence of the New York period. Family letters frequently allude to books bought, given, and read by various branches of the Melville clan; other letters by Melville himself acknowledge books sent him by admirers and friends both at home and abroad; E. C. Stedman, Richard Henry Stoddard, the British novelist W. Clark Russell, and a group of English correspondents that included J. W. Barrs, James Billson, and H. S. Salt. In addition, Mrs. Melville made the following notes of books and articles received from this last group, who shared a mutual interest in Melville and in the poet Thomson.

Mr James Billson of Leicester England—friend of James Thomson poet— sent Herman "Vane's story" a poem by Mr Thomson Oct. 1884 Also, "The City of Dreadful Night," by the same author Jan. 1885.

In Liverpool "Daily Post" Mr Billson wrote an article on Thomson & sent it to Herman Feb. 18. 1885 [cf. Check-List, No. 435]—
Mr. Billson sent Thomson's "Essays & Phantasies" and "Satires & Profanities"—
In letter of Jan 31. 1885 Mr Billson writes of Mr. Barrs—a friend of Mr H. S. Salt who wrote notice in the Scottish Art Review
"Mr Barrs one of your readers desires to forward you 'A Voice from the Nile' &c by James Thomson. Mr Barrs had Thomson for a visitor, and Mr Barr[s] also figured in the poem 'Belvoir'—Mr Barrs['] sister was the subject of the poem 'The Sleeper' in the above named volume["]—sent Feb 15th

1886—At same date Mr Billson sent a "semi-manuscript" copy of a poem of "Omar Khayam["] translated by Fitzgerald—

Dec 4. 1888 Mr Billson sent Thomson[']s "Essay on Shelley" long out of print and very scarce—a copy at "Scribners["] was 7.00—

Mr Salt sent his "Life of James Thomson" Feb. 2ᵈ 1890

Though a number of the works specified here are among Melville's surviving books, no volumes have been found of other authors whom he obviously knew, as can be seen from allusions in his letters and late manuscripts. A conspicuous example is Whitman, whom he mentioned to Billson in a letter of 1885 and of whom he said "much" in later discussion with E. C. Stedman.

As in earlier years, Melville continued to read newspapers and magazines; according to family tradition, as reported by Mrs. Metcalf, he subscribed to the New York *Herald* because it contained the best shipping news. He not only patronized bookstores—in Philadelphia, it is said, as well as in New York[8]—but also depended on libraries for some of his reading matter. From comments in his letters it is known that he at least visited the new Lenox Library following its opening for public use in 1877, and had met its librarian "two or three times" by August of 1878. (This was the year of Evert Duyckinck's death, when the Lenox Library began accessioning his books and manuscripts—now constituting the New York Public Library's Duyckinck Collection.) From 20 November 1889 until Melville died he was again a member of the New York Society Library, having been willed a share, "free from all annual payments," by Ellen Marett Gifford, a relative of Mrs. Melville; during 1890 and 1891 he was charged with fifty-one books, some of them clearly for his own use but others probably intended for general family reading or for that of his wife and unmarried daughter. After undertaking the posthumous *Billy Budd, Sailor,* which began in verse about the time of his retirement from the Customs House late in 1885 but grew into his final novel, he sought material for it in at least one reference library which is yet to be identified.[9]

Melville's interest in philosophy, already noted, is emphasized by those who knew him in his later years, such as Arthur Stedman and J. E. A. Smith; "when able to study" during his last illness he was reading "a set of Schopenhauer's works," according to Stedman. "Health and Content," he had written in 1888, are "the most precious things I know of in this world." In his copy of Schopenhauer's *Counsels and Maxims* is a passage to set beside these words, expressing a principle to which Melville himself had inclined since ending his career as a professional writer: "That genuine, profound peace of mind, that perfect tranquillity of soul, which, next to health, is the highest blessing the earth can give, is to be attained only in solitude, and, as a permanent mood, only in complete retirement. . . ." It is true that even after his resignation from the customs service Melville's retirement had not been "complete" in Schopenhauer's sense, for his old love of congenial companionship never deserted him. But his circle of acquaintances in New York was deliberately kept small, and several of his friends such as Edmund and Arthur Stedman were men of literary interests, As with Captain Vere in his own *Billy Budd* (dedicated to his shipmate of long ago, Jack Chase), "isolated leisure" was welcome to a man who "loved books," for in his chosen "line of reading he found confirmation of his own more reserved thoughts—confirmation which he had vainly sought in social converse." Of his findings, the marks and notes which appear in books from his library are eloquent testimony.

"Toward the Whole Evidence
on Melville as a Lecturer"
(1957, 1970)

This essay is reprinted by permission of the publishers from *Melville as Lecturer*, Merton M. Sealts, Jr., editor, Cambridge, Mass.: Harvard University Press, Copyright © 1957 by the President and Fellows of Harvard College. The entire book was reprinted by photo-offset in 1970 by the Folcroft Press, Folcroft, Pennsylvania. The essay constitutes the concluding chapter of Part I of the book, pp. 114–123; the chapter title echoes the phrasing of the late Newton Arvin's query in May 1942 that had stimulated a number of Melville scholars to locate and reprint reports in contemporary newspapers of Melville's various lecture engagements between 1857 and 1860.

Part II of *Melville as Lecturer* includes my partial reconstruction, from all the newspaper reports found by the 1950's, of Melville's three lectures—"Statues in Rome," "The South Seas," and "Traveling"—with accompanying notes and commentary showing their relation in theme and idea to his other writings. The scheme of reconstructing the lectures grew out of a conversation about several of the reports with Jay Leyda during the late 1940's: how could we recover what Melville had said on the lecture platform? Leyda was then working on *The Melville Log* (1951) and I on the never-published volume of Melville's fugitive prose pieces that I had been asked to edit for the ill-fated Hendricks House Edition of Melville. He went on to quote a number of the reports in the *Log* and to reprint one long account of "The South Seas" in *The Portable Melville* (1952); my own experiments with composite texts came to the attention of Professor Perry Miller of Harvard, who urged me to complete a book on Melville's lecturing for Harvard University Press.

To round out the story, I should add that in 1975, using additional newspaper reports that had been turned up since publication of *Melville as Lecturer*, I prepared a revised version of the reconstructed texts and added new textual apparatus for the Northwestern-Newberry Edition of Melville; this material will appear, with the concurrence of Harvard University Press, in *"The Piazza Tales" and Other Prose Pieces 1839–1860*, forthcoming as volume IX of the edition. A discussion of Melville's lecturing is included in the "Historical Note" that I also contributed to this volume.

The voyage of 1860, which marks the end of the lecturing, also marks the terminal point of this search for "the whole evidence on Melville as a lecturer." From the investigation a great deal was to be learned, as Newton Arvin recognized fifteen years ago. Though after nearly a century much is now lost to view, with disappearance of the manuscripts of the lectures along with the great bulk of the correspondence between Melville and local lecture committees, much remains: the Mediterranean journal, the notebook of lecture engagements, almost every contemporary review of the lectures, a few letters, and a scattering of other documentary materials bearing upon the man and his work between his return from the Mediterranean and his second voyage to the Pacific. Out of this considerable body of evidence has emerged a far more complete story of Melville's public appearances and their reception than could be told before all these materials were brought together and sifted; at the same time the partial recovery of the content of the lectures, made possible by collating the newspaper summaries, has enlarged the knowledge of Melville's writing before and after his lecturing as well as of what he prepared for the platform. Both features of this study have served to fill in significant gaps in the record between 1856 and 1860 which previously confronted the student of Melville. To relate the picture that has been sketched here to the larger canvas of Melville's life and times is a task awaiting some future interpreter, though even within the limits of a comparatively restricted investigation there have been clear indications of several cardinal issues. Among them is the relation to one another of Melville's contemporary reputation and his venture at lecturing; a second matter is the value of the lectures and lecturing in his own eyes; a third is their significance to the student of Melville's later career. A few words on each of these points will appropriately conclude this discussion.

Had Melville consented to begin lecturing when *Typee* was still new to the public mind, as he was in fact requested to do, the story told here of the content and reception of his lectures would surely have been very different. Between 1846 and 1850 he would have attracted to the lecture hall the same men and women who were then reading and arguing about his successive books, whether charmed by the adventures related or aroused by the author's controversial opinions about missionaries in the Pacific, discipline in the United States Navy, or politicians and issues at home. In the late 1840's Melville could thus have carried with him into the lyceum movement all three of the requirements for a successful program that Emerson specified: "a great deal of light, of heat, and of people."[1] But the idea of taking time from his writing itself to explore a new medium was not one to move a successful young author busy at his chosen work and fascinated with his craft. In the 1850's, however, Melville's prospects had drastically changed as his health declined and his creative energy flagged. When a need for money and weariness of writing finally drove him to the platform in 1857, his name, as earlier research has pointed out, still carried weight with the American public. But he was no longer the center of active controversy, not because he had ceased to publish controversial books but because the public was not buying and reading *Pierre* or *The Confidence-Man* as it had read *Typee* and *Omoo*. Though Melville was "well remembered," it was not for his serious novels but primarily as an author of "light reading"—or in his own depreciative phrase of some years before, of "Peedee, Hullaballoo, and Pog Dog." In the absence of some new or significant achievement to rival the success or even the notoriety of his earlier years, such fame as he still possessed was suffering the attrition of time: details of his books had grown dim, and even his quarrel with the missionaries was no longer an active issue. Audiences of 1857 and 1858 would still turn out for a glimpse of Melville, but in none of his programs did they find sufficient reward either to rejuvenate his reputation or to keep him permanently in demand as a speaker. Lecturing may have "in no way harmed his reputation as an author," as some students have asserted;[2] certainly it did little, especially in 1859–1860, to sustain it.

By the time Melville brought himself to think of lecturing as worth a trial, the situation confronting any would-be lecturer was less auspicious than it would have seemed ten years before. The financial panic of 1857 "hampered the lecture movement somewhat" even in New England, as Carl Bode has recently written,[3] while in other sections of the country the pressure of hard times forced some lyceums and other sponsoring organizations to curtail or abandon their customary programs. And by this time the lyceum, originally dedicated primarily to adult education, had altered significantly in character and emphasis. The discussion of art and letters which had once dominated its platform was giving way, especially in states beyond the eastern seaboard, to more utilitarian programs, and in some cities like Cincinnati the market for lectures had been considerably overexploited in recent years. Despite the imminence of civil strife, however, there was little threshing-out in the lyceums of current political and social questions, and speakers considered radical, such as Wendell Phillips, found it difficult in some cities to secure any kind of a platform. The independent Henry Thoreau, viewing the situation in

1858, held it "no compliment to be invited to lecture before the rich Institutes and Lyceums. The settled lecturers are as tame as the settled ministers. The audiences do not want to hear any prophets; they do not wish to be stimulated and instructed, but entertained. . . . They want all of a man but his truth and independence and manhood."[4]

Light entertainment and perhaps some utilitarian instruction, but less culture and nothing controversial—these were the watchwords of the day when Melville followed Curtis and Holmes to the platform. The popular speaker, as he himself was warned by the press in 1857, must supply something "modern" and "personal"; for such fare, served properly and to taste, the public was willing to pay handsomely in spite of hard times. Melville himself accumulated a grand total of $1273.50 in fees during his three seasons on tour; against this had to be charged not only the expense of travel during 1856–1857 but also the physical effort and emotional stress which lecturing demanded. In one year alone, 1856, Emerson, who was still actively writing, made about $1700 from lecturing; Bayard Taylor, who was much more in tune with the public and its demands than either Emerson or Melville, could confidently expect to "clear $5000 each season."[5]

Since money had been the principal object that turned Melville to lecturing, his record of comparatively low returns makes it surprising that he continued to lecture even for two seasons, let alone three. Perhaps his modest gains were worth the trouble for the first two winters, when he had little to do in Pittsfield. But by 1859 he had grown increasingly interested in poetry, and when he left for the Pacific in 1860 a collection of his verse was being copied for submission to a publisher during his absence. Poetry, not lecturing or fiction, had become his real concern even before he gave up lecturing; for the manuscripts of the lectures he showed no such solicitude as for the proposed volume of verse, though his expectations of its success were modest. He wanted none of the "clap-trap announcements and 'sensation' puffs" customary with publishers and lecture committees— "For God's sake," he admonished his brother Allan, "don't have *By the author of 'Typee' 'Piddledee' &c* on the title-page." Other contemporary writing, as he told Evert Duyckinck early in 1860, he considered "mealy mouthed" and intolerant of "plain speaking," a remark similar to what Thoreau had said about the character of the lyceum. But concerning the "Lyceums, Young Men's Associations, and other Literary and Scientific Societies" that Melville had satirized in *Pierre* he had nothing directly to say that is now known. Some years afterward, however, when at work on the third book of *Clarel*, he introduced two references to the lyceum, the speaker in each case being the acid-tongued Mortmain. In the course of a discussion of religion turning on the question of a future life, Mortmain remarks that he and his companions have

"touched a theme
From which the club and lyceum swerve. . . ."

Later he pours scorn upon the familiar motto of the lyceum movement:

"Curse on this store
Of knowledge! Nay, 'twas cursed of yore.
Knowledge is power: tell that to knaves;
'Tis knavish knowledge: the true lore
Is impotent for earth. . . ."

Melville is of course not to be identified wholly with Mortmain any more than with any other single character of *Clarel*, but certainly his own final opinion of lecturing was not markedly higher.

What then, it may well be asked, did he think of the three essays he had written for the lecture platform? All his books, he once told Hawthorne, were "botches" in his own eyes, spoiled by the necessity of trying to compromise between what he was most moved to write and what the public would buy; "dollars damn me," he had said, and the pursuit of the dollar was what sent him finally into lecturing. In referring on earlier occasions to *White-Jacket* and particularly to *Redburn*, which he despised as hack-work turned out solely for money, he twice likened himself to a wood-sawyer sawing such "wood" for sale by the cord—a figure that recurs in his stories and sketches written for the magazines a few years later, under the continuing financial pressure that lasted throughout the fifties. In his private scale of values the lectures probably ranked even below *Redburn, White-Jacket*, and the magazine work. Though after two seasons on tour he may possibly have offered "Statues in Rome" and "The South Seas" to an editor of some unnamed magazine, the truth of the matter is more likely that he destroyed the manuscripts of all three lectures in 1860 or after—a gesture indicative of the value he set on them. But though Melville looked down on all his work written wholly, or even partly, for money, he was too good a craftsman to turn out altogether shoddy products. Some of his highest achievements, for example, are to be found among the pieces written for magazines. No such claim is being advanced here for any of the lectures, although ignorance of their content has led some commentators to undervalue them as it has obliged all students to neglect them unduly. There are times when the work of an author's left hand affords valuable clues to the intentions guiding his right; such is the importance of these minor writings to the understanding of the mind that was still to produce both *Clarel* and *Billy Budd*.

When the significance of the lectures was last argued in print it was taken for granted that Melville did not regard them "as any part of his seriously imaginative writing." Such was the contention of the editors of *American Notes and Queries*, B. Alsterlund and Walter Pilkington,[6] in commenting upon the study by Merrell Davis of "Melville's Midwestern Lecture Tour, 1859." What Davis took to be the "failure" of "The South Seas," not having access to reports of its favorable reception in Boston, New York, and Baltimore, he attributed in part to Melville's

inability to display upon the platform the narrative vividness which had so fascinated the Hawthornes some years before. But in a large part it may also be attributed to the fact that he had so completely exhausted his personal experiences that his attempts to please the public led him into commonplace generalities and verbal repetitions of himself. Consequently, these newspaper reports of his Midwestern lecture tour provide some evidence that he stopped writing because he could offer the public nothing new.[7]

But to accept this point of view, as Pilkington and Alsterlund pointed out, "one would have to assume that the lectures were Melville's idea of a kind of outlet for old stock in literary materials." Even with "The South Seas," a topic to which he returned only with considerable reluctance, such was hardly the case. First, Melville had deliberately avoided a "narrative" type of lecture, despite the promptings of his Gansevoort relatives and the conspicuous triumphs of Bayard Taylor with just that sort of offering. Second, Melville had not in fact lost altogether the "vividness" of his earlier stories—witness the comments of Henry Gansevoort and William Cramer, both of whom evaluated "The South Seas" favorably in the light of Melville's private storytelling over the years, or consider the favorable newspaper reports from Boston and New York. "Melville's criterion throughout this rostrum interlude," in the words of Alsterlund and Pilkington, "was moderation, restraint," and some listeners of course found such qualities little to their liking. Then too, as Mrs. Metcalf has rightly observed, the quality of his performance evidently depended directly upon the quality of his listeners. Third, though "The South Seas" was composed with an eye on public taste, Melville had followed another standard in writing "Statues in Rome," when as Leon Howard has pointed out he was making a serious attempt "to order his thoughts on art." Lastly, after his three seasons on the platform there still remained untouched, in his journal, page after page of detailed notes on his Mediterranean trip—grist enough for a series of Tayloresque travelogues had he felt moved to write and deliver them.

While it is true that after 1859 Melville could not—or would not—offer the public anything new about the South Seas, he had obviously not "exhausted his personal experiences" so long as this other material lay unused, if not in lectures then possibly in additional magazine articles, either of which could have been collected in the travel book envisioned by Peter Gansevoort. But where his real interest was tending involved no concern with narration in prose and no obligation to please the public. Coupled with his turning to poetry, which he was writing not for money but for his own satisfaction alone, the significant anticipations of *Clarel* in the three lectures, especially the first, suggest that he was husbanding the material for purely private purposes. In some shape or other the conception of a major work related both to his recent travels and to his views on the course of modern civilization may well have been taking form as early as 1857, when he wrote "Statues in Rome," though the poem itself was probably not begun until well after he had commenced to experiment with his new medium through the writing of shorter verse. This first lecture in particular, with its gathering together of earlier themes and images and its suggestions of the writing still to come, is a bridge between his prose written before the trip and his later poetry. The other two lectures are less significant, being work of the moment to provide material for the platform while he tried his hand at something new, though all three embody a projection of his immediate situation during this transitional period of his career.

As the first literary fruits of the latter half of Melville's life the lectures are the product of a mind grown alien to mid-century America. Among the ancients whose civilization he so much admired Melville felt more at home, removed from the contemporary scene into the timeless world of mind. Distant too, in memory, was the Pacific of his youth, to which the voyage of 1860 proved no return; the reemergence in his verse of the unforgotten story of the "Typee-truants" is a sign of how deeply the events of former days were engraved on his memory—too deeply, perhaps, for exploitation in public without pain. In the writing which lay ahead, the persistence of memories and the value of the past are major themes, not the fresh enchantment of a first glimpse of "novel objects" that had given *Typee* its popular appeal. A synonym for travel, according to the third lecture, is change, but to those interested in Melville's later thought it is his affection for things permanent and stable that strikes the dominant chord. Only after he had written *Mardi*, *Moby-Dick*, and *Pierre* did this element take on significance in his work: in the magazine pieces written between 1853 and 1856. Essentially romantic at heart, he had come by 1857 to value, in the reported words of "Statues in Rome," that "tranquil, subdued air such as men have when under the influence of no passion"—strange words, seemingly, for the creator of Ahab and the chronicler of his "fiery hunt." But to the Melville of this period, unlike his earlier self, the best that life has to offer appeared to be receding inevitably into the past. This was true of his own vigor and youth; it was true also, he now felt, of Christianized civilization in general.

To the young collegians Gulick and Coan, Melville said as much in 1859. Their reports of the interview epitomize the real message of the lectures, whose meaning, lying beneath the surface, escaped most of those who paid to be entertained by the author of *Typee*, not instructed in the personal philosophy of Herman Melville. It was with just such an attitude, never abandoned in the years ahead, that he wrote slightingly to Curtis about man's "daily progress" toward perfection, rejected in two of the lectures the "social and political prodigies" of the contemporary reformers, and praised by contrast the more spacious days of South Sea exploration, the great cultural achievements of Greece and Rome, and the virtues of tolerance and humility. In 1866, after the purgation of the national life that he hoped had been worked by the Civil War, he was once more to exhort the public in his Supplement to *Battle-Pieces*. In concluding the volume, speaking with a voice like that of the young Melville though with Aristotelian overtones, he offered a prayer "that the terrible historic tragedy of our time may not have been enacted without instructing our whole beloved country through terror and pity; and may fulfillment verify in the end those expectations which kindle the bards of Progress and Humanity." But it is the older Melville, emergent in the fifties and studied here in his brief role as lecturer, that otherwise dominates the writing after 1860. When freed at last of the need to please an audience other than himself, Melville turned almost wholly away from the present for his subject matter. In his poetry exclusive of *Battle-Pieces* and in his late prose through *Billy Budd* the time and place are the past and the distant, the characterization and themes are quieter echoes of his earlier life and writing, the prevailing mood is no longer born of change but rather of reminiscence. For the proper study of this work the journal of 1856–1857 and the lectures of 1857–1860 are the indispensable introductions.

The Ghost of Major Melvill
(1957)

This essay was written in 1956. I read a shorter version at the 1956 meeting of the Melville Society in Washington, D.C.; the complete essay appeared in *The New England Quarterly*, 30 (September 1957), 291–306. For the present reprinting I have added the epigraph, drawn from a biographical sketch of Melville by J. E. A. Smith, a Pittsfield friend, and restyled the citations.

My interest in Major Thomas Melvill, Jr., Melville's uncle, developed while I was editing Melville's fugitive prose pieces for a never-published volume of the Hendricks House Edition. One of these pieces was the nephew's sketch of Major Melvill written for and partly printed in Smith's *History of Pittsfield* (1876); a full transcript in an unidentified hand is in the Gansevoort-Lansing Collection, Manuscripts and Archives Division, The New York Public Library. Studying the sketch led me not only to appreciate the uncle's pervasive influence upon the nephew's life and writings but to explore in some detail Melville's literary use of an actual person as a basis for fictional characterizations: in "Jimmy Rose" (1855), in the Burgundy Club sketches of the 1870's, and in "John Marr" (1888). With reference to "Jimmy Rose," William B. Dillingham, *Melville's Short Fiction 1853–1856* (Athens: University of Georgia Press, 1977), pp. 303–305, believes that the title character resembles not only Major Melvill, as I had suggested, but also Melville's father and paternal grandfather as well.

Other essays of mine exploring Melville's relations with individuals include "Melville and Richard Henry Stoddard," *American Literature*, 43 (November 1971), 359–370, and a section of *The Early Lives of Melville: Nineteenth-Century Biographical Sketches and Their Authors* (1974), dealing with Smith (pp. 29–41), Titus Munson Coan (pp. 41–47), and Arthur Griffin Stedman (pp. 47–64)—Melville's biographers of the 1890's. Like "The Ghost of Major Melvill," these accounts help to fill in the brief biographical sketches of "some of the chief actors in Melville's drama" that Jay Leyda provided in *The Melville Log* (1951), I, xxiii–xxxiv.

> In Pittsfield he did not exclude himself from
> the entertainments of the local social circle
> in which his family moved, nor was he ever
> neglectful of any of the reasonable obser-
> vances required by its etiquette. He rather
> seemed to have modelled himself as a
> "gentleman of the old school" upon the pat-
> tern of his Boston-born and Parisian bred
> uncle, the democratic aristocrat Major
> Thomas Melville.
>
> J. E. A. Smith, "Herman Melville"
> (1891–1892)

In the brief prose sketch which introduces the first verses of *John Marr and Other Sailors*, a privately printed volume of poems is-sued in 1888,[1] Herman Melville described his title character as a sailor "from boyhood up to maturity" who, "disabled at last from fur-ther maritime life by a crippling wound received at close quarters with pirates of the Keys, eventually betakes himself for a livelihood to less active employment ashore" (p. 159). As Marr moved from place to place his feeling of isolation among landsmen increased, even his occasional correspondence with former shipmates having lapsed with his "last and more remote removal" (p. 162). Still he continued to think of them; and though they "could not all have departed life," in Melville's words,

yet as subjects of meditation they were like phantoms of the dead. As the
growing sense of his environment threw him more and more upon retrospective musings, these phantoms, next to those of his wife and child,
became spiritual companions, losing something of their first indistinctness
and putting on at last a dim semblance of mute life; and they were lit by that
aureola circling over any object of the affections in the past for reunion
with which an imaginative heart passionately yearns. (p. 164)

Marr's invocation of these "visionary ones" constitutes the substance of the verses which immediately follow, lines which to anyone familiar with the course of Melville's own career suggest an autobiographical interpretation. The character of John Marr seems another of Mel-ville's *personae*, one of the latest in a long line which includes Tommo and Taji, Ishmael and Ahab, Clarel and Rolfe, perhaps even Billy Budd and Captain Vere.

There is nevertheless one obstacle to the complete identification of character with author in the story of John Marr after he leaves the sea. Marr, we are told, at last settled down "about the year 1838 upon what was then a frontier-prairie, sparsely sprinkled with small oak-groves and yet fewer log-houses." There he married, but soon lost his wife and infant child, carried off by a fever, "the bane of new settlements on teeming loam" (p. 159). Though Marr's sense of alienation during his last years may well have derived from Melville's own feelings, the outward circumstances in which he found himself are of course quite dissimilar. Worth noticing, however, are certain resemblances between his later career and incidents in the life of one of Melville's relatives, his father's brother, Major Thomas Melvill, Jr. (1776–1845), of whom, as William H. Gilman remarks, Melville "was very fond despite or perhaps because of his many misfortunes." [2] Born like John Marr "toward the close of the last century," Melville's uncle had sailed for France at the age of seventeen, during his young manhood becoming a successful banker in Paris. After severe reverses abroad, however, he was obliged during the summer of 1811 to return to his father's roof in Boston, accompanied by his family. "The War of 1812 breaking out about this time, he received an appointment as Commissary with the rank of Major, and was stationed at Pittsfield." So Herman Melville wrote in a memoir contributed to the *History of Pittsfield* (1876) compiled by J. E. A. Smith. [3] The death of Major Melvill's wife at Pittsfield was followed within a few days by the further loss not only of her infant child but also of a six-year-old son. [4] Major Melvill remained in Pittsfield following the war, remarrying in 1815, but experiencing new misfortunes there, "and living in the plainest way, became a simple husbandman." His character and personality, reflecting his earlier life in the great world, set him apart from his humbler Pittsfield neighbors, who watched with curiosity the "exchange of salutations and pinches of Rappée" between the Major and the more sophisticated magnates of the village. Such a spectacle, according to a passage of his nephew's memoir judiciously omitted from the published *History,*

presented a picture upon which the indigenous farmers . . . gazed with eager interest, and a kind of homely awe. It afforded a peep into a world as unknown to them as the Vale of Cashmere to the Esquimaux Indian.

To the ensuing conversation, also, they listened with the look of steers astonished in the pasture at the camel of the menagerie passing by on the road.

In 1837 Major Melvill, "though advanced in years," removed like John Marr to the western prairies, settling at Galena, Illinois, where his nephew visited him in the summer of 1840 "and was anew struck by the contrast between the man and his environment." [5] Although this contrast is not elaborated in the memoir, the situation of John

Marr as described nearly twenty years later presents certain parallels: the fictional character is about the same age as Major Melvill, settles on the prairie at about the same time, experiences a somewhat similar loss of his wife and infant child (though at a different place and period), and in general finds his new surroundings far different from the scenes of his earlier life. As with Major Melvill and the farmers of Pittsfield, so with John Marr and his uncomprehending neighbors: lacking "a common inheritance," which in the words of the sketch "supplies to most practical natures the basis of sympathetic communion," they feel a barrier which inhibits even casual conversation. The difficulty is explained on the ground that

the past of John Marr was not the past of these pioneers. . . . They knew but their own kind and their own usages; to him had been revealed something of the checkered globe. So limited unavoidably was the mental reach, and by consequence the range of sympathy, in this particular band of domestic emigrants, hereditary tillers of the soil, that the ocean, but a hearsay to their fathers, had now through yet deeper inland removal become to themselves little more than a rumor traditional and vague.

When "naturally enough he would slide into some marine story or picture," Marr "would soon recoil upon himself and be silent, finding no encouragement to proceed." Upon one occasion of this kind an elderly blacksmith frankly pointed up the situation in a brief sentence: "Friend, we know nothing of that here" (pp. 160–161).

What Melville says of John Marr on the prairies is thus strikingly similar to what he had previously written of his uncle, the earlier life of both remaining a subject beyond the comprehension and interest of their less cosmopolitan neighbors. For Melville himself in later years, "as the growing sense of *his* environment threw him more and more upon retrospective musings," his stories of earlier adventures became literally closed books to his contemporaries. Increasingly reluctant toward the close of his life to speak even of his published works, Melville reserved the memories of his youth for expression only in private writings such as those included in the *John Marr* volume. Through these pieces move phantoms like those which haunted the imagination of the old sailor, "lit by that aureola circling over any object of the affections in the past for reunion with which an imaginative heart passionately yearns." Among these ghosts of the past, as the details of the sketch of John Marr suggest, was the figure of Major Melvill, toward which Melville was so strongly drawn. His first memories of his uncle were associated with recollections of his own childhood; allusions to Major Melvill can be traced in his writings over a period of more than thirty years. According to the memoir previously cited, his first clear image of the Major dated from 1831, when he himself was twelve;[6] three years later he spent several months upon the Melvill farm at Pittsfield,[7] and from this period came the most vivid glimpses of the Major's distinctive appearance and personality. It was Thomas Melvill at fifty-eight that he recalled long afterward in the memoir as being

gray-headed, but not wrinkled; of a pleasing complexion; but little, if any, bowed in figure; and preserving evident traces of the prepossessing good looks of his youth. His manners were mild and kindly, with a faded brocade of old French breeding, which—contrasted with his surroundings at the time—impressed me as not a little interesting, nor wholly without a touch of pathos.

He . . . would at times pause . . . , and taking out his smooth-worn box of satin-wood, gracefully help himself to a pinch of snuff, . . . quite naturally; and yet with a look, which—as I now recall it—presents him in the shadowy aspect of a courtier of Louis XVI, reduced as a refugee, to humble employment in a region far from the gilded Versailles.

Melville particularly recalled his uncle seated before the kitchen hearth "just before early bed-time, gazing into the embers," and like John Marr remembering things past, while

his face plainly expressed to a sympathetic observer that his heart—thawed to the core under the influence of the genial flame—carried him far away over the ocean to the gay Boulevards.

Suddenly, under the accumulation of reminiscences, his eye would glisten, and become humid. With a start he would check himself in his reverie, and give an ultimate sigh; as much as to say, "Ah, well!" and end with an aromatic pinch of snuff. It was the French graft upon the New England stock which produced this autumnal apple; perhaps the mellower for the frost.

Sixteen years later, in the summer of 1850, Melville boarded at the same old farmhouse in Pittsfield, to which his uncle's family had returned following Thomas Melvill's death in Galena in 1845. There Melville, having since become prominent as an author, used for a writing-desk "an old thing of my Uncle the Major's" which had been "packed away in the corn-loft";[8] "Banian Hall" itself, as he called the old residence, provided the setting for the introductory section of "Hawthorne and His Mosses" (1850), parts of *Pierre* (1852), and at least one of his short stories, the little-noticed "Jimmy Rose" (1855). Though in this sketch the "great old house" described in the opening paragraphs is given an urban rather than a rural setting, its identity with Broadhall, as the house was then known, is unmistakable. Because of alterations, according to the story, the front of the house

presented an incongruous aspect, as if the graft of modernness had not taken in its ancient stock; still, however it might fare without, within little or nothing had been altered. The cellars were full of great grim, arched bins of blackened brick, looking like the ancient tombs of Templars, while overhead were shown the first-floor timbers, huge, square, and massive, all red oak, and through long eld, of a rich and Indian color. So large were those timbers, and so thickly ranked, that to walk in those capacious cellars was much like walking along a line-of-battle ship's gun-deck. (p. 803)

Key descriptive phrases in this passage, it will be noted, recur in Melville's brief reference to the house in his later memoir of Major Melvill, where it is mentioned as

somewhat changed, and partly modernized externally.
    It is of goodly proportions, with ample hall and staircase, carved woodwork and solid oaken timbers, hewn in Stockbridge.
    These timbers as viewed from the cellar, remind one of the massive gun deck beams of a line-of-battle ship.[9]

As described in "Jimmy Rose" the rooms of the house were similarly ornamented with "heavy-moulded, wooden cornices, paneled wainscots, and carved and inaccessible mantels" of an older period. Even "the very covering of the walls still preserved the patterns of the times of Louis XVI"—just as Major Melvill is thought of in the memoir as "a courtier of Louis XVI, reduced as a refugee . . . in a region far from the gilded Versailles."
    Particularly emphasized in the story is the design adorning the largest parlor in the house, of which the narrator writes:

Instantly we knew such paper could only have come from Paris—genuine Versailles paper—the sort of paper that might have hung in Marie Antoinette's boudoir. It was of great diamond lozenges, divided by massive festoons of roses . . . ; and in those lozenges . . . sat a grand series of gorgeous illustrations of the natural history of the most imposing Parisian-looking birds; parrots, macaws, and peacocks, but mostly peacocks. Real Prince Esterhazies of birds; all rubies, diamonds, and Orders of the Golden Fleece.

As the narrator explains, this "old parlor of the peacocks or room of roses (I call it by both names)" was long associated in his mind with one of the original proprietors of the house, "the gentle Jimmy Rose," who had been "among my earliest acquaintances." Like Major Melvill, Jimmy in his prime "had an uncommonly handsome person," with bright eyes, curling hair, and red cheeks glowing with "health's genu-

ine bloom, deepened by the joy of life." Adding to his moderate com-
petence by success in "a large and princely business . . . ,"

he was enabled to entertain on a grand scale. For a long time his dinners,
suppers, and balls, were not to be surpassed by any given in the party-giving
city of New York. His uncommon cheeriness; the splendor of his dress; his
sparkling wit; radiant chandeliers; infinite fund of small-talk; French furniture; glowing welcomes to his guests; his bounteous heart and board; his
noble graces and his glorious wine; what wonder if all these drew crowds to
Jimmy's hospitable abode? (pp. 803–804)

So it was, though on a less lavish scale, with Major Melvill in Paris at
a time when "any young countryman of Washington, if possessed of
the requisite manners, found his way easy and delightful in the bright
circles of the City on the Seine." As his nephew explained the circumstances,

In certain departments the business of a European banker makes it his
interest to be hospitable. If his disposition coincide with his interest, his
entertainments may be often extremely agreeable from the piquant mixture
of the company. The polite Bostonian's dinner in Paris lacked not, as I have
been told, this quality, nor the zest of a very social nature in the host. Many
distinguished countrymen did he from time to time entertain at his table,
together with Frenchmen of note invited to meet them. Among others,
I have frequently heard him name Lafayette.[10]

But for Major Melvill and his fictional counterpart "times changed,"
both experiencing the "sudden and terrible reverses in business" that
engulfed Jimmy Rose (p. 804) and sent the American banker home
to his father's roof in Boston. Here, however, their stories diverge.
That of Major Melvill is already familiar; as for Jimmy Rose, he re-
tires to "an old house of his . . . in C— Street," where he repels the
narrator's efforts to see him (p. 805).[11] "I was a young man then," the
narrator observes, "and Jimmy was not more than forty"—approximately the age of Major Melvill when he "became a simple husbandman" at Pittsfield. "It was five-and-twenty years ere I saw him again,"
the narrator continues, going on to describe Jimmy Rose as he appeared at about the same age as Major Melvill when his nephew visited him in Galena in 1840. "He whom I expected to behold—if behold at all—dry, shrunken, meagre, cadaverously fierce with misery
and misanthropy—amazement! the old Persian roses bloomed in his
cheeks" (p. 805).[12]

Neither did Jimmy give up his courtly ways. Whenever there were ladies
at the table, sure were they of some fine word; though, indeed, toward

the close of Jimmy's life, the young ladies rather thought his compliments somewhat musty, smacking of cocked hats and small-clothes—nay, of old pawnbrokers' shoulder-lace and sword belts.[13] For there still lingered in Jimmy's address a subdued sort of martial air; he having in his palmy days been, among other things, a general of the State militia. There seems a fatality in these militia generalships. Alas! I can recall more than two or three gentlemen who from militia generals became paupers. I am afraid to think why this is so. Is it that this military learning in a man of an un-military heart—that is, a gentle, peaceable heart—is an indication of some weak love of vain display? But ten to one it is not so. (p. 806)

Though Jimmy is a bachelor, and though the pathetic details of his pauper's existence go beyond anything known of Major Melvill's later career, the broad outlines of their lives are not dissimilar: both fell from prosperity to adversity; both were pursued by creditors "as carrion for jails" (p. 805);[14] both had an old-fashioned courtliness, a taste for French furnishings, and a measure of "military learning"—contrasting strangely with the "gentle, peaceable heart" that saved both from misanthropy despite their misfortunes.

After Jimmy Rose's death, the narrator, sitting within the parlor of the peacocks,

still must meditate upon his strange example, whereof the marvel is, how after that gay, dashing, nobleman's career, he could be content to crawl through life, and peep about . . . where once like a very Warwick he had feasted the huzzaing world with Burgundy and venison.

And every time I look at the wilted resplendence of those proud peacocks on the wall, I bethink me of the withering change in Jimmy's once resplendent pride of state. But still again, every time I gaze upon those festoons of perpetual roses, mid which the faded peacocks hang, I bethink me of those undying roses which bloomed in ruined Jimmy's cheek. (p. 807)

Just so did Melville remember his uncle's "pleasing complexion," and his "mild and kindly" manners, with their "faded brocade of old French breeding"—symbolized by the "faded peacocks" amid the "undying roses" in the parlor of Broadhall. And with Major Melvill at the last, as with the house in which he had lived, "however it might fare without, within little or nothing had been altered." The persistence of imagery and detail through the fifteen years which separate "Jimmy Rose" and the later memoir are a token of the deep impression which the uncle's cosmopolitan air, reflected in the very furnishings of his home, had made upon his young nephew long before. And there is still further evidence of his influence upon Herman Melville's imagination.

In a series of little-known prose sketches upon which Melville worked intermittently during the 1870's and after, the central character is Major Jack Gentian, a Civil War veteran originally conceived as the narrator of two of Melville's longer poems, "At the Hostelry" and "Naples in the Time of Bomba." [15] Although of a different generation from that of Major Melvill, Jack Gentian too had lived in Europe and among frontiersmen, was fond of "over-sea reminiscences," held the same military title, counted high-ranking officers his friends, and dispensed "old-school hospitalities of the board"—or in the words of the earlier "Jimmy Rose," "feasted the huzzaing world with Burgundy and venison." Like Jimmy, the Major is a convivial bachelor, relishing "the rare qualities" of his friend the Marquis de Grandvin—clearly a personification of wine; he is in fact Dean of a sociable group of New Yorkers known as the *Burgundy* Club. And like Herman Melville himself he is "of double Revolutionary descent," proudly wearing his inherited badge of the Society of the Cincinnati. [16] In a passage of the fragment printed under the title "Major Gentian and Colonel Bunkum" occurs the following recollection:

I remember long ago in my youth the eldest son of a Revolutionary officer and as such the inheritor of the Cincinnati badge, saying, over the Madeira to his own son then a stripling, "My boy, if ever there is a recognized order of nobility in this land it will be formed of the sons of the officers of the Revolution."

The same scene is described in a canceled passage of another sketch, "Note: The Cincinnati," where the speaker directs the quoted remark not to "his own son" but to "the writer of this note," who is addressed there as "Nephew." The reference is obviously to Major Melvill, who had himself inherited the badge from his father; the episode is probably to be classed among Herman Melville's always vivid recollections of the time he had spent upon his uncle's farm in 1834, as certain traits of Major Gentian surely derive from the well-remembered personality of Thomas Melvill, Jr.

One further point. In his last major work, *Billy Budd*, which Melville was composing in the same year that *John Marr* was published, his mind like that of the old sailor lingered over memories of friends of the past. The story is dedicated to his former shipmate Jack Chase, "wherever that great heart may now be here on Earth or harbored in Paradise"; in its pages are recollections of the *Somers* incident of 1842 in which his cousin Guert Gansevoort was a leading figure. To its composition the persistent ghost of Major Melvill may also have contributed. The events of the narrative take place against the background of the French Revolution, from which was kindled the flame of mutiny within the British navy whose existence conditions the sentence imposed upon Billy. "The opening proposition made by the Spirit of that Age," in Melville's words, "involved the rectification of the Old World's hereditary wrongs. In France to some extent this was bloodily effected. But what then? Straightway the Revolution itself became a wrongdoer, one more oppressive than the kings" (p. 131). This unfavorable view of the French Revolution, as R. R. Palmer has recently suggested, may well have been influenced by Melville's Uncle Thomas, whom Palmer identifies with a certain "Mr Melleville de Boston" recorded as being an active supporter in France of constitutional monarchy and the conclusion of peace with England.[17] What Melville himself wrote of his uncle in the memoir has direct bearing upon this suggestion. During his stay at Pittsfield in 1834, Melville recalled, the Major

often at my request described some of those martial displays and spectacles of state which he had witnessed in Paris in the time of the first Napoleon. But I was too young and ignorant then, to derive the full benefit from his pictorial recollections.

Nor though he possessed so much information and had a good understanding was his mind of that order which qualifies one for drawing the less obvious lessons from great historic events happening in one's own time and under one's eyes.[18]

So in *Billy Budd*, having remarked that under Napoleon the Revolution "enthroned upstart kings, and initiated that prolonged agony of continual war whose final throe was Waterloo," Melville observes that "during those years not the wisest could have foreseen that the outcome of all would be what to some thinkers apparently it has since turned out to be, a political advance along nearly the whole line for Europeans" (p. 131).

If "not the wisest" at that time comprehended the ultimate significance of the Revolution, certainly not Major Melvill, whose grasp of public events is characterized in the memoir as something less than profound. Though his conservative political outlook may well have influenced Melville's own complex attitude toward "the Spirit of that Age," as Palmer suggests, even more important than his political opinions was the subtler effect of his patrician image lingering through the years in the memory of his nephew as "a cherished inmate," to quote the memoir once more. What Melville particularly recalled was his aristocratic figure projected against the incongruous backgrounds of his later environment, "in the shadowy aspect of a courtier of Louis XVI, reduced as a refugee, to humble employment, in a region far from the gilded Versailles." To the nephew Major Melvill thus seemed another "isolato," another Ishmael driven into the wilderness, sometimes presenting himself in the altered guise of a John Marr, a Jimmy Rose, or a Jack Gentian. All of these roles, moreover, are semi-autobiographical characterizations as well, through which Melville himself, in Lewis Mumford's phrase, "plays with his possible fate" as man or as author.[19] The aging veteran outliving his best days, unable to come to terms with an unsympathetic environment, yet unalterable within "however it might fare without"—such was the recurrent character-type suggested to Melville the writer by the example of his uncle's personality and career, with which he tended to identify his own.

Tracing Major Melvill's ghostlike presence through successive writings of his nephew[20] has revealed certain familiar attributes of Herman Melville and his work. In his attitude toward his uncle can be seen both his patrician pride of family and a sympathy with worldly failure which at times, as in "Jimmy Rose" though not in the more restrained "John Marr," approaches sheer sentimentality. Here too are illustrated both the persistence and the vividness of his memories over the years of whatever deeply stirred him, as shown in recurrent patterns of situation and characterization as well as of imagery and phrasing. Though Melville's creative impulse, which required external stimulus, drew heavily upon literary source-material, he was equally responsive as a writer to personalities who had strongly affected him. With those to whom he felt drawn he tended to identify himself, and in characters who show their influence he mingled autobiographical elements. The stories of Jimmy Rose, Jack Gentian, and John Marr, all examples of such composite figures, thus reflect as much of Melville himself—or an image of himself—as of the life and personality of his uncle. During the later and less eventful years of his career Melville's writing grew increasingly dependent upon the resources of memory as he too, like these same characters and the figure from whom they were partially drawn, found "phantoms of the dead" his chief spiritual companions when "the growing sense of his environment threw him more and more upon retrospective musings." Out of that vivid sense of the past, along with the ghost of Major Melvill, emerged in *Billy Budd* the major work of his final period.

Melville's Burgundy Club Sketches
(1958)

This essay originally appeared in the *Harvard Library Bulletin*, 12 (Spring 1958), 253–267. Like "The Ghost of Major Melvill," it grew out of extended work with Melville's late prose manuscripts for a never-published volume of the Hendricks House Edition. My efforts were not altogether lost, however, since my knowledge of this material helped to prepare the ground for the Hayford-Sealts edition of Melville's *Billy Budd, Sailor* (1962).

Harrison Hayford and I agreed in 1955 to collaborate on a new edition of *Billy Budd*, beginning with a fresh transcription of the manuscript and an analysis of its growth—a project that occupied both of us for the better part of eight years. At the annual meeting of the Melville Society in 1957 I presented a shorter version of this essay and Professor Hayford spoke concerning the manuscript of *Billy Budd*; our intention was to outline a method of tracing and dating the successive stages of Melville's late prose compositions. The Burgundy Club sketches of the 1870's are among the relatively few prose pieces that Melville wrote between his lectures of 1857–1860 and the headnotes to poems in the *John Marr* volume of 1888. Besides their implications for textual scholarship the sketches also throw light on Melville's cast of mind during the long period that Willard Thorp once called his "silent years." The essay considers both their textual and their thematic significance.

With the completion of his long narrative poem *Clarel* and the labor of seeing it through the press before its publication on 4 June 1876, Herman Melville turned to another composition, in a lighter vein, that was to occupy him at intervals during the last fifteen years of his life. At some earlier date he had already composed, at least in part, two sketches in verse, "A Symposium of Old Masters at Delmonico's" and "A Morning in Naples," which were first published by Raymond Weaver in 1924 under their final titles of "At the Hostelry" and "Naples in the Time of Bomba."[1] To introduce the fictional narrators of these pieces he began writing, perhaps as early as 1875,

a series of related prose sketches concerning the Marquis de Grandvin and his friend Major Jack Gentian, the former a personification
of wine and the latter Dean of an imaginary "Burgundy Club." Melville devoted a good deal of his leisure time to these prose compositions in both 1876 and 1877, but then apparently lost interest until at
least ten years later, after his retirement from the Custom House,
when he made further additions and revisions. Finally, however, the
prose sketches were dropped altogether, as Melville explained in a
prefatory note to the poems that he drafted in pencil, probably in
1890, and left among miscellaneous papers at his death in the following year.

"As the caption to the first section of '*At Delmonico's*' will be found
to intimate," Melville's note reads in part,

> one there styled The Marquis is to be considered as the teller of the
> story. . . . Moreover, toward the close of the concluding section of the same
> Piece, the aforesaid Marquis introduces one Jack Gentian his friend as the
> narrator in the Piece following, *An Afternoon in Naples* [originally "A Morn-
> ing in Naples"].
>
> Now it naturally belonged to the original design of this volume, that some
> account of each of these gentlemen should precede the Pieces respectfully
> [*sic*] ascribed to them. That design, however, if carried out would overmuch
> enlarge the volume. And it is as well to bear in mind that tho good measure
> is not without praise in a huckster, not always is it commendable in an
> author.[2]

What had evidently occurred, as the proposed volume took form in
manuscript, was that the combined length of the various prose
sketches as they were revised and, in the process, greatly enlarged,
finally threatened an eclipse of the poetry; their original function,
after all, had been merely to introduce the verse sections by giving
"some account" of their supposed narrators. Another consideration,
if the projected book was intended only for private circulation, like
the later *John Marr* (1888) and *Timoleon* (1891), may have been the
cost to the author of printing a long work. Whatever his motives for
omitting the prose pieces, Melville kept the manuscripts among his
papers, and from them Weaver printed the sketches of the Marquis
and his "disciple" Gentian in 1924.[3] Since that time the Burgundy
Club sketches have received little attention from Melville's critics and
biographers, though close study of the manuscripts reveals that they
have a considerable story to tell.

i

From a series of draft title-pages, some scattered among miscellaneous papers and others enclosed in a cover-sheet bearing Mrs. Melville's penciled notation "Contents / at the Hostelry," the growth of Melville's proposed book can be traced in broad outline. All the title-pages presuppose the existence of the two poems; not all, however, mention the prose sections, either because they had not yet been written or because of Melville's ultimate decision to discard them from the projected volume. The initial working-title of the book, "Parthenope," takes the name of one of the legendary Sirens, mentioned in the poem that became "Naples in the Time of Bomba."[4] This heading occurs in what appears to be the earliest of the title-pages, written by Melville in ink in a hand corresponding to that of other manuscripts known to date from the 1870's:

PARTHENOPE / *A Morning in Naples* / *In the time of Bomba*: / with / An Introduction / merging into / A Symposium of Old Masters / at Delmonico's. / Liberally rendered from the ideal / of / The Marquis de Grandvin.[5]

"Parthenope" is retained in only a single redrafting of the title-page, one which announces the poems alone as "versified by Herman Melville from the original suggestions of the Marquis de Grandvin." Jack Gentian, unmentioned in either of these versions, is first named in what was probably intended as a subtitle to precede the prose accounts of the narrators when these sections were added to the poetry. Another subtitle, this one for the verse sections, is noteworthy for its reference to Gentian as a member of the "Falernian Old Fellows Club"—later amended to read "Horatian," then "Falernian" again, and finally "Burgundian Old Fellows Club." Such is the ancestry of the "Burgundy Club" of the prose sketches, a name not found in the text of either poem.

Both "A Morning in Naples" and "A Symposium of Old Masters at Delmonico's," to employ the phrasing of the "Parthenope" title-page, are associated with Melville's visit to Italy in 1857; Howard Vincent has suggested that they were drafted originally as part of the volume of poems for which Melville failed to find a publisher in 1860.[6] If Jay Leyda is correct in assigning the "Parthenope" title-page to the spring of 1875 (*Log*, II, 741), Melville may have been either composing or revising the two poems at that time as a means of recreation and a welcome change from his demanding work on the manuscript of *Clarel*, which seems to have been completed during that year.[7] Though the earliest drafts of the prose sections may also date from

1875, it is clear from an accumulation of internal evidence that most of the prose was of later composition. In the spring and summer of 1876, after Melville was freed from the burdensome task of proofreading *Clarel*, he became particularly fascinated with the developing character of Jack Gentian, in whose gaiety he may have found relief from the sorrow of his sister Augusta's death the previous April. Further revision and expansion of the prose manuscripts, as will be shown, took place during the following year, 1877, when Melville evidently spent considerable time on the sketches.

In the present state of the prose manuscripts there are but two pieces primarily concerning the Marquis: "The Marquis de Grandvin," twenty-eight pages in length plus three discarded pages,[8] and "To M. de Grandvin," four pages. For the longer sketch a date of composition ca. 1876 is suggested by internal references to Lafayette and Bartholdi, the French sculptor whose statue of Lafayette was presented to New York City in that centennial year of American independence and who sent to America in the same year the first section of his Statue of Liberty, begun in 1874. The sketch also mentions Encke's comet, which made appearances in December 1871, April 1875, July 1878, and so on, and it exhibits a number of verbal parallels with poetry and letters written by Melville during the mid-seventies. The four pages of "To M. de Grandvin" seem to have been pieced together from fragments of the original introduction of the Marquis, as indicated by canceled pagination showing omissions; an earlier date of composition therefore seems posssble for the original version. Assembly of these fragments into the briefer version may have taken place in later years when Melville came to feel that "The Marquis de Grandvin" might be overlong for his projected volume.

The various prose pieces concerning Jack Gentian present a more complex but much more interesting problem. Probably the first of these to have been written is "Portrait of a Gentleman," an eleven-page manuscript that may have been composed, like the longer version of what is now "To M. de Grandvin," as early as 1875. Probably next in order came "Jack Gentian," a thirteen-page fragment of the first version of what became "To Major John Gentian, Dean of the Burgundy Club"; the fragment is therefore to be dated not later than the spring of 1876. The longest and most important manuscript is that of "To Major John Gentian, Dean of the Burgundy Club," the final form of which ran to forty-one pages. This sketch was presumably begun after Melville had discarded the "Parthenope" title-page and had also finally decided upon the name "Burgundy Club"; it contains a reference to the passing of Charles Sumner, who had died in

1874. Melville probably undertook the sketch in late April or early May of 1876 after the proof sheets of *Clarel* had been read: there is an allusion in the manuscript as first written to Memorial Day as celebrated "the last Tuesday of every May," and Memorial Day fell on Tuesday, 30 May, in 1876. Later revision is indicated by correction of "last Tuesday of every May" to "Thirtieth of every May"; by mention of Independence Day as "getting along now in its second century, this anniversary"; by allusion to the past presidency of General Grant, whose second term expired on 4 March 1877; and by reference to a trip to Saratoga, which Melville himself visited in August 1877.

Other manuscripts concerning Gentian are to be associated with this same sketch, "To Major John Gentian." Two of at least four stages in Melville's treatment of Gentian's supposed aristocratic tendencies, symbolized by his hereditary badge of the Society of the Cincinnati, are represented by a deleted passage of three pages and a longer episode of seventeen pages, the latter separately printed by Weaver as "Major Gentian and Colonel J. Bunkum." The Gentian-Bunkum episode in its complete form became a part of "To Major John Gentian" not earlier than the termination of Grant's presidency in March 1877, as shown by the reference mentioned above; Melville revised it slightly between 1886 and 1890, with an added allusion to a meeting of his characters during the Civil War "now more than five and twenty years ago," but subsequently removed the entire passage from the sketch. "Note: The Cincinnati," also separately printed by Weaver, relates in turn to the Gentian-Bunkum episode. A briefer version but a single page in length was probably first written ca. 1877; this was replaced between 1886 and 1890 by the eleven-page manuscript that Weaver printed. Like other very late Melville manuscripts this longer form of the "Note" was written in pencil on paper salvaged from earlier compositions and with page numbers added in colored crayon. The "Note" and other parts of the prose sketches were evidently put aside before composition of the new preface quoted above, which bears the notation "June 6"—probably 1890, a year in which Melville "looked over" and similarly dated a number of his manuscripts, that of "The Marquis de Grandvin" ("Feb 8th") among them.

Along with the internal evidence that thus makes it possible to date portions of the Burgundy Club manuscripts, there are other factors also bearing upon their history. During this period, as F. Barron Freeman has already shown in the case of *Billy Budd*,[9] Melville followed the general pattern of elaboration he had always pursued in composing: reworking a short and concise first draft into a much longer, more complex piece of writing not only by making changes in phrasing but by inserting additional passages throughout, many of considerable length. In the absence of surviving manuscripts of the earlier novels it may be assumed that such had been the situation with both *Mardi* and *Moby-Dick*, which were radically altered after reportedly nearing completion, and with *Pierre*, which turned into "a larger book, by 150 pages & more," as Melville told Richard Bentley, than he had thought it would be (*Log*, I, 450). So too with the Burgundy Club sketches, notably "To Major John Gentian." These pieces, like all other extant manuscripts in Melville's hand later than *The Confidence-Man* (1857), are written on small sheets of approximately 7 by 5¾ inches that could be slipped into his pocket if he so desired and perhaps carried along to the Custom House for attention during a lull in the day's business.[10] In the process of revision and expansion new pages were inserted and appropriately numbered (1^2, 1^3, 1^4, etc.); old pages were salvaged in part through cutting, pinning, and pasting; completely discarded pages were turned over and reused, according to Melville's frugal custom, for later composition. The resulting preservation of many rejected passages and the clues afforded by the continued visibility of original page numbers have made it possible, through a kind of archaeological study of stratification in the entire mass of Melville's late manuscripts, to trace the development of individual pieces through several distinct stages, which in a number of instances can be satisfactorily dated. At the present time, however, this somewhat formidable task has been accomplished only in part.

What can be done along these lines is amply illustrated by study of the comparatively brief Burgundy Club sketches. "To Major John Gentian" and its associated fragments constitute an excellent example of Melville's elaboration of a manuscript, since adequate evidence has survived to permit following its development through at least ten distinguishable stages and even to make possible the reconstruction of much of the sketch substantially as it existed in the various stages. This development can be summarized briefly with the aid of an analysis of its component sections as they stand in the final version. Code letters A through G have been assigned to these sections according to the order of their probable addition to the manuscript. The analysis follows:

A. Introduction.
B. Major Gentian does not wear a Civil War badge or speak ill of the South.
G. The Fourth of July: patriotism of youth contrasted with patriotism of age.

C. Major Gentian's Virginia campaigns and European travels; the "Afternoon in Naples" (formerly "A Morning in Naples").

E. Major Gentian reproached for his supposed exclusiveness, signified by the Cincinnati badge with its connotations of hereditary aristocracy.

F. Transition: Major Gentian's nomination to a consular post in Naples unconfirmed because of whispers about him.

D. Conclusion: Major Gentian laughs at the enthusiasm occasioned by his "Afternoon in Naples," which the editor has versified.

In addition there are: (1) a discarded section, Z, the thirteen-page fragment referred to in previous discussion as "Jack Gentian"; and (2) the other fragments once a part of section E that include the Gentian-Bunkum episode and the appended material concerning the Society of the Cincinnati.

The initial draft and immediate revision (stages I and II) of what became "To Major John Gentian" comprised the sections identified here as A and Z: substantially the present Introduction plus the "Jack Gentian" fragment. The numbering of surviving pages indicates that the revised manuscript (stage II) ran to sixteen pages. The second version of the sketch, including both a major redrafting and its immediate revision (stages III and IV), replaced section Z with new sections B, C, and D, which somewhat shortened the characterization of Gentian but led more directly to the narrative in verse, "An Afternoon in Naples," which the sketch was intended to introduce. The second version at this point (stage IV) was about fourteen pages in length. References occurring in the pages comprising these sections suggest that the first and second versions through stage IV date from the spring of 1876. Further expansion and revision (stages V and VI) probably began during the following summer, autumn, and winter with addition of the transitional section F, the long section G on patriotism, and then a linking section E on Major Gentian's supposed exclusiveness. This lengthened the manuscript to about thirty-six pages. A general revision and recopying (stages VII and VIII) seem to have followed in the spring or summer of 1877, increasing the length to about forty-six pages. The longest version of the sketch (stage IX), fifty-six pages, resulting from the further expansion of the troublesome section E into the Gentian-Bunkum episode, also appears to date from 1877. But from this time until the period of Melville's retirement from the Custom House beginning in 1886 the entire manuscript apparently lay untouched. Very minor revisions of the enlarged section E were made between 1886 and 1890, when the

supplementary note on the Society of the Cincinnati was also expanded from one page to eleven. It was presumably in 1890, when
Melville "looked over" his various manuscripts, that the Gentian-
Bunkum episode and the related note were deleted entirely, leaving
the manuscript in its final form (stage X), forty-one pages in length.

For the editor and ultimately for the critic and biographer interested in the work of Melville's so-called "silent years," the foregoing
analysis has implications more important than the intrinsic value of
"To Major John Gentian" and the other Burgundy Club sketches.
The same general method of tracing and dating the successive stages
of a manuscript is applicable to other work of this period; the thorough scholarly treatment of Melville's shorter poems that remains to
be done will employ similar procedures. Other projected works that
like "Parthenope" embody a combination of verse and prose demand
more attention than they have yet received: even *Billy Budd*, along
with these Burgundy Club sketches, "John Marr," and still other
pieces, may have begun as a brief prose introduction to an existing
composition in verse, since the ballad of "Billy in the Darbies" may
well antedate the novel[11] Until the entire body of late Melville manuscripts has been studied in this manner the interpreter of the final
phases of Melville's career will remain severely handicapped.

ii

Turning now to the content of the Burgundy Club sketches, which
to Lewis Mumford "have the air of juvenile compositions, done just
for practice,"[12] one notes that their prevailing tone is epitomized in a
single brief poem, "Hearts-of-Gold," which Melville probably wrote
during the mid-seventies. The sociable Burgundy Club, it will be recalled, was first thought of as a "Falernian" or "Horatian Old Fellows
Club"; in the poem are celebrated such "Falernian fellows" as "Hafiz
and Horace, / And Beranger," whose "memory mellows"

> Embalmed and becharmed,
> Hearts-of-gold and good fellows![13]

Hafiz the Persian poet is mentioned in "The Marquis de Grandvin"
and Horace in "To Major John Gentian." At Christmas in 1876 Melville gave to Abraham Lansing a copy of Béranger's poems he had
owned since 1860, praising its contents in a subsequent letter of 2
January 1877 (*Log*, II, 756, 758). In concluding another letter, that to

John C. Hoadley of 31 March 1877, Melville dismissed his preceding paragraphs as "a queer sort of an absurd scribble" but added that

if it evidences good-fellowship and good feeling, it serves the purpose. You are young . . . but I aint; and at my years, and with my disposition, or rather constitution, one gets to care less and less for everything except downright good feeling. Life is so short, and so ridiculous and irrational (from a certain point of view) that one knows not what to make of it, unless—well, finish the sentence for yourself. (*Log*, II, 760–761)

With Melville's old love of sociability restricted by the sense of isolation from his times that increased during his residence in New York in the last decades of his life, the imagined atmosphere of the Burgundy Club afforded a kind of compensation. To "a man wonted" to the free-and-easy ways of sailors and their haunts, if one may adapt Melville's own words in "John Marr," "something was lacking. That something was geniality, the flower of life springing from some sense of joy in it, more or less." The references to geniality in "John Marr" are a continuation of those in the Burgundy Club sketches. Though geniality was exactly that quality his literary contemporaries professed to find lacking in the reserved and retiring Melville, who declined membership in the Authors Club and abstained from all measures that he might have taken to promote the recovery of his dwindling fame during these late years, he was in fact genial himself "without sharing much in mere gregariousness, which, with some, passes for a sort of geniality."[14] His wit, occasionally revealed to a few intimates such as Evert Duyckinck, with whom he was again exchanging visits in the spring of 1876, "was meant for keen society," as Mumford has aptly remarked: "small wonder he created Jack Gentian to keep him company."[15]

Gentian, the genial bachelor Dean of the Burgundians, is of the same stamp as "R. F. C." and his companionable London friends— "the very perfection of quiet absorption of good living, good drinking, good feeling and good talk"—whom Melville had described long before in "The Paradise of Bachelors" (1855). Both that sketch and the Burgundy Club pieces are examples of what Richard Chase dismisses as "that hearty, jocose, rather clumsy wallowing in luxurious foods, drinks, and literary allusions which Melville liked to write from time to time."[16] Melville's fondness for good drinking and good talk was certainly of long standing, abundantly expressing itself in his writing as early as *Mardi* (1849). Then he had been one of Duyckinck's convivial circle of New York literati; later his conversations with Hawthorne in the Berkshires had taken place over bottles of brandy, gin, and champagne. Refusing to believe in "a Temperance heaven," he had then looked forward to sharing "a basket of champagne" with Hawthorne even in Paradise (*Log*, I, 412–413). So Jack Gentian, in his bachelor residence at the Burgundy Club, draws all his inspiration from the Marquis de Grand*vin*, whom Melville considered referring to not as the Marquis but as the "Magnum." The Marquis is "an honorary member of most of the Fifth Avenue clubs" to which Melville himself did not belong, one whose appearance in social gatherings is applauded by members of both sexes, at home and abroad. He is celebrated for his ability to inspire and kindle his friends, Melville as "Editor" of the sketches of course included. Of such a "magnanimous spirit" Jack Gentian is "ever fain to imbibe." He even "wears his colors, so to speak. And sometimes after coming from communion with him, his shining countenance, like that of Moses descending from the Mount declares the recentness of the elevated interview." [17]

The characterization of de Grandvin offered Melville few problems except that of giving life to an abstraction, but beside the more fully realized figure of Jack Gentian the Marquis seems at best pale and shadowy. And though the creation of Major Gentian may have been an afterthought with Melville, the character so intrigued him as to encourage a series of expanded treatments that defied subsequent cutting. Basically, Jack Gentian is a projection of Melville's own personality, embodying not only characteristic traits but also certain attributes that, were it not for his "disposition, or rather constitution," he would have liked to call his own. Gentian appears to be of the same age as Melville, and equally conscious of his years. His vivid memory of the past recalls a childhood in New York, his friends of the stirring days there during the Mexican War,[18] his own Civil War campaigns, his travels abroad. Like Melville, he has a high regard for Scripture and for the writings of "Charlie" Hoffman and Nathaniel Hawthorne, Shakespeare and Horace. Both had unsuccessfully sought consular appointments in Italy; both are of "double Revolutionary descent" and almost aristocratically proud of their distinguished lineage. The principal differences are that Jack Gentian is a bachelor and a Civil War veteran.

Melville's health would not permit the military exploits so gloriously performed by Major Gentian, though he had once journeyed to the battlefront as a civilian guest of another Union officer with a distinguished record of service: his cousin Henry Gansevoort. Recollections of this visit and of his late cousin, who had died in 1871, may well have contributed to Melville's characterization of Gentian. Since the war he himself had been seriously concerned by the problems of reconstruction, foreseen in his prose "Supplement" to *Battle-Pieces* (1866), treated again in *Clarel*, where the embittered Confederate veteran is portrayed in Ungar, and touched upon less directly through the moderation of Jack Gentian, both during his military service and after, toward the Southern half of his country.

For his two symbols of Major Gentian's supposedly hereditary military prowess—his empty sleeve, betokening an arm lost "in the Wilderness under Grant," and his Revolutionary badge of the Society of the Cincinnati, inherited from a grandfather—Melville drew once more on material, or rather friendships, out of his own past. First there had been the gallant Jack Chase, "a gentleman" with "an abounding air of good sense and good feeling," "a stickler for the rights of man, and the liberties of the world," as he is described in Chapters 4 and 5 of *White-Jacket* (1850).

> No one could be better company in forecastle or saloon; no man told such stories, or sang such songs, or with greater alacrity sprang to his duty. Indeed, there was only one thing wanting about him; and that was, a finger of his left hand, which finger he had lost at the great battle of Navarino.

Chase was, in short, another good companion, teller of stories with "interspersed ballads and ditties," combat veteran, and "maimed" hero—one of the many in Melville's writings. His given name "Jack" may well be echoed in the nickname of Major Gentian. Thoughts of him were certainly in Melville's mind during the seventies, since he figures in poetry written at the time and later under such names as "Jack Roy" and "Jack Genteel"—the latter strikingly similar to "Jack Gentian." The Major is of course a soldier rather than a sailor like these other figures; here Melville perhaps drew not only upon his cousin Henry Gansevoort but also his uncle, Thomas Melvill, Jr., commissioned a major during the War of 1812 and subject of Melville's sketch for the *History of Pittsfield* that had appeared in the pivotal year 1876.[19] Both majors had lived in Europe and among frontiersmen, mingled familiarly with high-ranking officers, and dispensed "old-school hospitalities of the board." A recollection of Major Melvill appears in both the episode of Major Gentian and Colonel Bunkum and in a canceled passage of "Note: The Cincinnati," where he figures as "the eldest son of a Revolutionary officer and as such an inheritor of the Cincinnati badge."[20]

The frequent allusions to this emblem in even the earlier sections of the sketches suggest that the badge and its significance had been leading elements in Melville's conception from the very beginning. The "grandfather" who is several times mentioned is obviously another relative of his own, in this case his maternal grandfather General Peter Gansevoort, the Revolutionary hero of Fort Stanwix who proudly wore the emblem of the Cincinnati while sitting for his portrait by Gilbert Stuart.[21] Though the General had died seven years before Melville was born, the relics of his life were so vital and his memory was so reverently tended by Melville's mother that "the image of Peter Gansevoort," as Raymond Weaver first pointed out, "was one of the most potent influences during Melville's most impressionable years."[22]

Confirmation of Weaver's remark is to be found not only in the Burgundy Club sketches but also in the proud though half-hidden allusions to General Gansevoort scattered through the first three chapters of Melville's earlier *Pierre* (1852). Henry A. Murray, commenting upon this "pride of heritage" transmitted to Melville by his mother and its emergence in *Pierre*, suggests its interpretation as "a backward solace-seeking movement of Melville's spirit, a reaction to the crushing presentiment that he was not capable of attaining the far better standing-ground for self-respect which he had once envisaged."[23] The same motif is operative in the Burgundy Club sketches, continuing the return to the past characteristic of all Melville's literary productions but especially manifest in the last quarter century of his life in an inhospitable Gilded Age.

In this connection the successive revisions of "To Major John Gentain" traced above are particularly revealing. Its earliest form, later discarded, constitutes the most cutting prose satire of Melville's last years, directed against the conservative, well-to-do clubmen of New York who reproach Jack Gentian for being too much of a democrat and humanitarian. In the revised form of the sketch Gentian is reproached for tendencies regarded as aristocratic, even monarchical, symbolized by his pride in the hereditary badge of the Cincinnati. It was this passage that was expanded at one stage of composition to include the rabble-rousing speech of Colonel Josiah Bunkum in opposition to Major Gentian's candidacy for public office. A caricature of campaign oratory, the speech reveals how clearly Melville comprehended the tactics of politicians in a demogogic era of which the present generation is heir; in the light of it one better understands why "the Burgundy's eccentric philosopher," author of "Note: The Cincinnati," "never votes," and why in a rejected passage of the later *Billy Budd* Melville was moved to write of "the primer that deters some superior minds from taking part in popular assemblies; under which head is to be classed most legislatures in a Democracy."[24]

None of the several Burgundy Club sketches, it is true, can be counted of much artistic worth; indeed, with the one exception of the "Supplement" to *Battle-Pieces*, all of Melville's occasional prose works from 1856 until the writing of *Billy Budd* have more biographical interest than literary merit. As poetry became his preferred medium there set in a further decline in the vigor of his prose style, partly from disuse and partly as a continuation of tendencies already visible in his magazine work of the fifties. Such surviving prose manuscripts of his later years as these sketches are of value chiefly in revealing the practices of Melville's workshop, many of them persistent throughout his career as well as during the thirty-five years when writing was no longer his principal occupation. The content of the Burgundy Club pieces, of no great significance in itself, does help to suggest the nature of Melville's detachment from the American scene during intervals of his "silent years" after the Civil War, when under the negative influence of an uncongenial environment his subject matter became increasingly retrospective, his characters developed the traits of friends of his past and turned into idealizations of values not found in his own life, and his settings remained distant in place and time from nineteenth-century New York. For fully rounded interpretation the prose sketches must be read in context with their companion poems on the one hand, and on the other with *Clarel* and with *Billy Budd* as the culminating work of this period of belated flowering. But a comprehensive and at the same time genuinely thorough examination of all these late writings considered together has yet to be undertaken. The material of these years needs further attention and understanding from the editors, the critics, and the biographers of Melville than it has yet received. To such consideration this present study looks forward.

PART II
A CORRESPONDENCE
WITH CHARLES OLSON

Why don't you use me as a resonator? Anyway, I offer myself as a
target, for any, & all letters you care
to write, to feel yr way in. (It is,
sometimes, letters, that is, a more organic way to arrive at form, than
outlines or plans)

Charles Olson, 16 June 1950

Introductory

The letters that comprise this correspondence were written between 1940 and 1964; my last telephone conversation with Charles Olson took place in the spring of 1965. The original letters on both sides are now part of the Charles Olson Archives at the University of Connecticut. Those by Olson are printed here by special permission; the entire essay, written in the summer of 1980, is copyright © 1981 by the Estate of Charles Olson. Selected passages were previously published in "Olson, Melville, and the *New Republic*," *Contemporary Literature*, 22 (Spring 1981), 167–186.

Olson's letters to me have been available to scholars since 1972, when I made copies for the Charles Olson Archives, but only a few excerpts have appeared in Olson scholarship and none in work on Melville. I have quoted them extensively here in the belief that the letters do honor to the man and will help to keep his memory green with others as they have done with me. Our perennial subject, of course, was Melville, with special emphasis on Melville's reading and on locating books that were once part of his library. The letters on both sides naturally reflect the ambience of their period, when Olson was becoming known as a poet and I as a scholar. They also give some idea of the kind of scholarly detective-work we both practiced— work that lay behind the successive versions (1948, 1966) of "The Records of Melville's Reading," pp. 31–57 above. My own letters acknowledge indebtedness not only to Olson but also to others interested in Melville with whom I shared information over the years.

Late in December of 1940, when I was a graduate student at Yale, I wrote my first letter to Charles Olson. His address in New York had been given me by Eleanor Melville Metcalf, a granddaughter of Herman Melville, who wanted Olson to see an essay I had just drafted on one of Melville's short stories, "I and My Chimney." At the time I knew of Olson not as a poet but as someone writing on Melville—someone with first claim on important source-materials then on deposit in the Widener Library at Harvard, thanks to Mrs. Metcalf's warm interest in Olson and her support of what he was doing.

I needed a second letter and a telephone call to arrange a meeting with Olson, which took place on the fourteenth of January at Olson's New York "office" and over lunch at a nearby bistro, as he called it. I remember him as he met me at the door: a tall, heavy-set, shaggy bear of a man. He was wearing a long overcoat against the chill of a poorly heated room; there was a wool scarf wrapped around his neck; later I saw holes in his shoes and the thick socks that didn't match but served to ward off the cold. Wasting no words, he motioned me to sit down, reached for my manuscript, and began reading, puffing on his pipe and occasionally nodding his head as he turned the pages. While I sat watching him and looking at his surroundings, I kept thinking of another writer at work: Melville's Pierre.

Pierre's chamber, according to Melville, was "meager even to meanness."

No carpet on the floor, no picture on the wall; nothing but a low, long, and very curious-looking single bedstead, that might possibly serve for an indigent bachelor's pallet, a large, blue, chintz-covered chest, a rickety, rheumatic, and most ancient mahogany chair, and a wide board of the toughest live-oak, about six feet long, laid upon two upright empty flour-barrels, and loaded with a large bottle of ink, an unfastened bundle of quills, a penknife, a folder, and a still unbound ream of foolscap paper, significantly stamped, "Ruled; Blue." (*Pierre*, Book XIX, Ch. ii)

Olson's room may have lacked the bedstead and the chintz-covered chest—I simply don't remember. But I can still see that wide board, this time laid between a small table and a window-sill, and loaded not with ink and quills but with typewriter and paper (some of it crumpled), pipes and tobacco, and various bottles, cartons, and cans that held or had held food and drink. More paper and containers had spilled over onto the floor.

Finally Olson came to the end of my essay, puffed two or three times on his pipe, and looked off for a moment before speaking. Then, staring straight into my face, he at last gave his verdict—on me and on what I had brought him. "Well," he said, deliberately, "I see . . . that . . . THE WHITE DEATH . . . has descended . . . upon YOU . . . too!" And with that pronouncement delivered, we went out to lunch.

All that we talked about at the bistro was Melville and particularly his reading. Both of us had been tracking down books from Melville's library, and Olson, liking what he saw and heard of my work, proposed a sharing of information that began that same afternoon and continued through intermittent correspondence over nearly twenty-five years. Though we managed only this one face-to-face meeting, we wrote each other more than eighty cards and letters, with some of the longer letters running to seven or eight typed pages. Melville's library was always our central theme. Most of what we wrote to one another about it is summed up in my *Melville's Reading*, which first ran serially between 1948 and 1950 and later appeared in book form, revised and expanded, in 1966. But as Olson became more than a writer on Melville, his letters sometimes went beyond book-hunting to comment on "the Hyde Park Prince Roosevelt,"[1] to report the shutting down of Black Mountain College, or to remark on the birth of a daughter or on the state of the world. Still, the perennial scholar in him kept revealing itself, even as it does in his poetry. Though he frequently lashed out at academics as a generally deplorable lot, he wanted all the same to keep in touch with Melville studies, repeatedly asking me to name new books and articles I thought he should know and writers whose work he should watch for. Occasionally he wrote about poetry, ranging from Homer's and Shakespeare's to Olson's own, and once he sent a copy of his "Arcana Zero." Sometimes he lashed out at me.

Since Olson's death in 1970 and establishment of the Charles Olson Archives at the University of Connecticut, scholars have had access to our correspondence, and quotations from a few of his letters to me have already appeared in print. The details of our literary detective work would be of interest mainly to specialists, but there are some letters of his that ought to be known by anyone concerned with either Olson or Melville. What I offer here from his side of our correspondence is used with the authorization of Charles Boer, Administrator of the Estate of Charles Olson, and his colleague at Connecticut, Professor George F. Butterick, Curator of the Charles Olson Archives and now Olson's literary executor. I am grateful for their kindness as I have brought the Olson-Sealts correspondence together in preparation for this running account of it.

1941–1949

After Olson and I finished talking in the early afternoon of our meeting, I went straight to Brooklyn in pursuit of a lead he had given me. Following Melville's death in 1891 certain books from his library were sold through a dealer to James A. H. Bell of Brooklyn, Olson had learned, and Bell's library in turn was presented in 1896 to what is now the Brooklyn Public Library; could any Melville association volumes possibly be located on the Library's shelves? At Brooklyn I was told in a pleasant conversation of an hour with Jesse B. Cross, then the Library's Reference Librarian, that the books and records we would need to consult would not be usable for some time because of an impending move into a new library building. In a letter to Olson of 16 January 1941 I summarized what I had learned:

(1) after the fifteenth of February the complete catalogue will be available in the new building. Any cards marked *B* indicate books in the Bell accession. (2) Most of these books are boxed, and will not be opened until more pressing jobs are done in connection with the moving program. (3) If anything relating to Melville turns up at any time, Cross will write me. (4) When the task of opening, sorting, and cataloguing the Bell books is finally undertaken, which won't be very soon, I will be informed. I think you and I will be invited to come around and go through the books at that time and, in return for helping the library locate possible treasures, will be given first rights on use of anything we find. (5) This unofficial, informal arrangement between each other and Mr. Cross will remain unknown to anyone else. I'll of course send along immediately any information I have from him from now on.

Given the situation in Brooklyn, there was little we could do pending further word from Cross. After sending Olson some other information I had found for him in New Haven I went back to work on my dissertation, writing through the summer of 1941 and then moving in the fall to my first teaching job: Instructor in English at the University of Missouri in Columbia. That December came Pearl Harbor, and by February of 1942 I was in uniform. I heard nothing from either Cross or Olson until July of 1945, while I was stationed in India; Tyrus Hillway, Secretary of the newly organized Melville Society, had evidently passed word to Olson that I was asking about him. "It is a pleasure to know how to reach you," Olson wrote me from Washington on 28 July, taking note of my position as an Air Corps major and going on to tell me that he had just completed his book on Melville: *Call Me Ishmael* (1947).

I got back to the Melville book this spring and finished it yesterday. I've been thinking about you. I liked you and your work better than your contemporaries. You knew that anyhow. I am curious to know what if anything further came out of Brooklyn. I dare say the war 10 months after your first visit knocked the plan you worked out with Jesse Cross. But would you write me a letter about Melville? If Cross ever let you know the Bell boxes were ready? If so how far you got? What your plans are ahead? Are you still interested in the Brooklyn proposition?

Unless I'm called out of the country by political developments, I thought, now that the book is off my hands, and so little of all the years of research is on its surface, that I would spend a few weeks ordering and disposing of whatever I have, or know, that might be useful to others. One thing is Brooklyn. I want you to finish it, if you're of a mind. And I am curious about you. Please write. And as WIDE a story as possible. Except for you I stay out of touch with the Melville Society, and I would prefer to have what's new screened thru your intelligence. IF YOU RETURN MY CONFIDENCE! In any case, I'll look forward.

and it's swell to say hello. and I hope you are all right.

Olson's letter reached Calcutta while I was on a series of trips into Assam, Burma, and China, and I was unable to answer until 2 October, on the eve of my transfer from India to North Carolina, when I brought him up to date about myself. "Absolutely nothing ever came of the Brooklyn proposition," I wrote, adding that of course I was still interested and would be even more interested after returning to civilian life. "One thing is certain," I told him:

I will have no opportunity to follow through on the Brooklyn matter for some months, and should be glad to see you go ahead meanwhile if you have the time and the inclination. . . .

I look forward to hearing from you and if at all possible to *seeing* you before too long. I have no idea what you may have been doing for four years, and would enjoy nothing more than a good talk about things in general. You asked whether I return your confidence—of course! I think that can be demonstrated before many months have passed; not years this time.

But we didn't meet in 1945, when I finally returned to the United States, or in 1946, when I left the service in February to resume teaching as Instructor in English at Wellesley College.

Our correspondence also resumed following publication of *Call Me Ishmael* in 1947, when I sent Olson on 7 April what I called "a rambling, disjointed letter" occasioned both by the book and by the comments of two of its reviewers, Ferris Greenslet and Lewis Mumford. "Granted your principle of suggestive brevity," I told him, the controversial form of *Call Me Ishmael*

is the inevitable one—Greenslet saw that, if Mumford didn't, or wouldn't. As for being "intuitive," Mumford himself wrote at the highest voltage when he let his intuition go, except that he made the fatal error more than once of not starting with scholarship. Now he blames you for not stopping there. It seems strange to see him now lament the absence of what he himself was attacked for, but in no spirit of charity. . . .

You are at your best on the primal things. I wish you had found room somewhere for the Galapagos turtles, not as handled in "The Encantadas" so much as in *Clarel*. I much prefer "The Encantadas" to "Benito [Cereno]," chiefly, I think, because I resent the anthologists letting "Benito" alone represent Melville. . . . Maybe I belong in your camp on *Billy Budd*; at least it bothers me for reasons I can't clearly formulate.

As I went on to explain, I had two Melville projects under way: editing the miscellaneous prose for the projected Packard—later Hendricks House—edition, undertaken "with certain misgivings" on my part, and writing for the *Harvard Library Bulletin* a long monograph "on the Melville books" intended "to assemble in one place all that is now known ʃor at least *printable*ʃ" about Melville's library "and perhaps stir up some more finds." As I well recognized,

this brings me to *your* particular territory. What do you think of the project as a project? Remembering our conversations of some years back, would you be interested in doing the article yourself, collaborating with me, lending your blessing? Or would you be either uninterested or actively opposed? Whatever is done with the article, or by whom, nothing you gave me or suggested to me as a lead will be used without your full authorization. When you wrote me in India, you mentioned two things: CONFIDENCE and the prospects in Brooklyn. The first still holds as far as I'm concerned, and I hope it does with you; the second, the Brooklyn matter, is your province to

do with as you will. Needless to say, however, I am extremely curious to
know whether you have returned to the hunt, whether you've found anything if you have, and whether that possible "anything" is of real importance.

This letter brought a rollicking response from Olson, written from
Washington on 17 May 1947.

Such a pleasure to learn yr story—and to find you intension. Words on
ISH most gratifying. Brevity? Just a nervous system. Plus language as hog-
wash. The law of discourse is ... then stop. Work 'em: if the space is there
they damn well got to take the time. (Hoooh! that I might do such deeds!
Hoooh! that I might sing the Dausi!) Note: pay me no mind. Washington
heat: just turned on. Plus a gayety over you. Plus obscure tasks disposed
of. . . .
   Now as to HLB job on books. You are the one to do it (at the same time I
think I ought to say you owe it to yourself, to sharpen edge already there, to
give your time to those materials which are themselves directly feeders:
viz., CHIMNEY [Melville's "I and My Chimney"]). Do the books, please, for it
is only in yr hands that I trust them.
   About me: you do certainly have my blessing—and any info I have which
is yet not overtaken. As to collaboration, at this moment, I don't know. I'm
thinking of Brooklyn, but I'm also aware of the old hanker to block out that
reading from start to finish in a way nobody does it because they kneel
down to the man instead of standing up with him. I drafted a chapter for
ISH as of reading for MD [*Moby-Dick*] which, naturally, had to include all
time '44 on. And it was fun, but was wrong for tone, and discarded. . . .
   Look, let's be practical. Any chance to see you and get some talk over this
business? How late are you in New England? It's likely I'll get up to Gloucester this summer. Actually, if I'm going to do anything about Brooklyn or
anything else it'll get done damn soon, or not at all, and I want to be precise
with you. My schedule works out this way: ISH comes out in France (Gallimard) fall, England maybe same time, and perhaps Italy. Wife Constance
and I want to go over come late summer or fall if we can by hook or crook
manage it. So you see how simple it all is.
   It's summer here (a two season town) but spring must be [in] New England, and I do hope with it your purgatory has eased. I wish you would
write again—for both yr letter fr India and this last have been rare pleasures.

When I replied in late June with a postcard to Gloucester, Olson
sent me a handwritten note on 30 June to say that he was on the point
of leaving there for Boston en route to Seattle for lectures at the
Northwest Writers' Conference; could we meet in late September?
Yes, I wrote in July, when I summarized my progress on the *Bulletin*

article. But meanwhile Olson had gone on to California instead of back to Washington, and in August I decided to visit Brooklyn alone, reporting to Olson on the twenty-eighth that I had found Cross on vacation but talked instead to a man in the main building of the Public Library about the Bell Collection. The books, my informant had told me, were uncrated and partly shelved, but still largely uncatalogued because of a lack of help and funds. He and I examined two sets of Thomas Warton's *History of English Poetry* looking for Melville's marking or annotation, as Olson had suggested I do, but found nothing to identify either set as having once been part of Melville's library. Olson replied from California on 6 September, proposing that we meet in New York in "early October, with a good 2–3 days to do the Brooklyn Library complete. For the Wharton [*sic*] I am sure of, have notes on it." Once more I agreed, telling Olson on 13 September that for the *Bulletin* article I had already "written or seen forty or fifty people" while pursuing leads on books Melville had owned, that I had identified the full titles of most of those he was recorded as borrowing, and that I was now ready to set an exact date for our meeting in New York and joint expedition to Brooklyn. But the Olsons were staying on in California, as I learned from Mrs. Metcalf, and it wasn't until February that I next heard from him. Answering a query I had sent in January about Melville's reading in Matthew Arnold, he wrote from Washington on 6 February 1948, enclosing his six-page transcription of Melville's many notes in his copy of Arnold's *Poems* (Boston, 1856), a volume Olson had borrowed from Dr. Henry A. Murray. "I think you can depend on me now to be a more regular correspondent," he assured me, adding that perhaps we could soon meet and "go over all the ground." Meanwhile he offered to send me his notes on other books besides the Arnold that he had examined.

Too many developments were taking place for me that year for me to reply fully to this letter, though I acknowledged it with a postcard on 25 February. The six installments of "Melville's Reading: A Check-List of Books Owned and Borrowed" were all in type and had to be proofread, with the first of them scheduled for the Spring 1948 issue of the *Harvard Library Bulletin*. Nathan Pusey, then President of Lawrence College in Appleton, Wisconsin, invited me to go there as Assistant Professor of English, and I accepted. During the spring and summer the Sealtses had a house in Wellesley to sell and a move to arrange. It was 22 March 1949 before I heard again from Olson, who had learned from a reference in Dr. Murray's new edition of Melville's *Pierre* (1949) that I had left New England for Wisconsin. "Now the shoe is on yr foot," his letter began.

This is the MT coming to Mahomet. I want to dig you as abreast of things factual. So that I don't fall on my face before you young & knowing characters, and be trampled of the puss in the public sheets, will you do me the large favor to tell me

(1) all texts now known and ⸢and/or⸥ [*sic*] available that HM can be sd to have acquainted himself with the KING JAMES VERSION by

& (2) ditto by which HM ditto HOMER by

I do not think that in either case there is anything comparable to the SHAKESPEARE, and what I am after is any like thing that can be used likewise. Yet I want you to correct me. Have you, for [e]xample, or anyone succeeded in restoring the scissored notes in the NEW TESTAMENT? (Or found M's OLD, with notes: that would be a haul!)

And do I remember right, that he had Chapman's HOMER, and no other?

I am also clearly asking you to direct me to any other sources for information or direct quotes <with HM's> concerning HM's familiarity with either of above major fountains. (You will understand this in the most complimentary sense: you are my touch with those old places where I now go blind.)

And I think there is a great discrepancy between his knowledge of (1) and of (2)? Is not his acquaintance with Homer a passing one, that cultural kissing he and Whitman indulged in? (But, of course, in this instance, it <does not> did not matter. He is Homer, and I seek to prove it.)

There in a nutshell was Olson's conception of Melville and his objective in any future writing about the man: "He is Homer, and I seek to prove it." As the letter went on to observe, "HM IS LARGER THAN EVER (and this without reference to numerous present publications. . . .)"— meaning the spate of books on Melville that began to appear once World War II was over. Olson was particularly impressed with two new editions. One was the Hendricks House *Pierre*, edited by Dr. Murray; Olson rightly praised "Harry's wondrous additions via analysis." Another was *Melville's Billy Budd*, in which F. Barron Freeman extracted from Melville's manuscript what he offered as the text of an earlier short story that he called "Baby Budd, Sailor." Freeman was in error, as the Hayford-Sealts edition of 1962 was to demonstrate, but in 1949 Olson thought the factitious "Baby Budd" to be a better piece of writing than *Billy Budd* itself as Melville left it at his death. As for me, Olson had "recriminations":

I do not know what you are up to. If you ever did do that listing for HCL [*i.e.*, "Melville's Reading" for the *Bulletin*], you never did send me same. And what else have you published (this is my fault)? Here I am ready to go to bat for you against all newcomers, and you don't put the bats in m[y] hand!

so: write. Or, on above, send me penny post card. And then write
Love,
Olson

I replied promptly on 25 March, agreeing with Olson's praise of
Dr. Murray though wishing he had given us "the biography instead"—
Murray had long been at work on a life of Melville. After accounting
for my move from Wellesley to Lawrence I explained that Olson
would soon receive a forthcoming offprint of "Melville's Reading"
that would include all six installments. As for his questions about
copies of Homer and the Bible, I transcribed from the monograph
every entry concerning editions of both that Melville had owned,
commented on Nathalia Wright's study of his biblical allusions, and
expatiated on Melville in relation to Whitman and Keats, concluding
with a brief account of my own recent writing.

My letter prompted an immediate answer: a revealing three-page
letter typed single-space that defies summary or even quotation in
part. Dated Monday, 28 March 1949, and addressed "My dear Sealts,"
it reads as follows:

Yr letter has just come, and I *am* obliged. It is the works, and I thank you.
It is pretty much as I figured, and I am disappointed—or relieved, actually,
out of that stupid American hunger to be in the clear. It is the Chapman
at Harvard, of all, that I ought to see. [*Marginal insertion in ink:* ↑P.S. And the
Osborne Bible at NYPL↓—*i.e., The New York Public Library*] Yet I no longer
move, am become utterly geotropic, and do not want to wait until such time
I am back in New England. If you should recall the density of the annotations, or their character (if there is any characterization of Homer by HM in
them) I should be obliged. (I am thinking out loud: do not impose on
yourself. I dare say I can ask EMM [Eleanor Melville Metcalf] to look it over
for me and give me a resume.)

I am actually writing to offer you something which popped into my head
again yesterday reading Traubel on Whitman. This may or may not be a
lead. (If I remember rightly it was either the Whitman bookseller Green-
berg (?) or that fool Birss who passed it on to me). I was told then (1934)
that there was either a possibility or an indication that, in the unpublished
Traubel mss., there was some observation of Whitman's on HM. (It may be,
that, in the intervening years, the Traubel barrels have been opened by
the Whitman characters. If so, I should like to know that, if you know it.
Otherwise, if you are interested, you may want to follow it up.) (The more
that century goes off behind the more the thinness of the ties between these
two men is remarkable.) (If either of them had ever edited a magazine!
amazing they didn't take up that alternative. Yet I know. I don't do it either,
fool.)

The other idea I had was to send you the piece on HM and the King James Version which I wrote in December. It was provoked by reading Freeman's Baby, and doing the article on it (did I tell you to keep a weather eye out for the next WESTERN REVIEW—if they accept it!). But I haven't looked at the draft ⌈of the "BIBLE"⌋ since (it is as it was, running water off the ribbon) and I wonder if I better get off on it today. For if I look at it, and start a copy for you, I'll start to rewrite, and then I'm in to my ears for days. I better not, but when I do, I'll send it to you. (I get the impression I'm winding up to just such an act—and to do the Homer job.) [*Marginal addition in ink:* ⌈P.S. you see what happened anyhow!⌋]

[*Marginal addition in ink:* ⌈P.S.S. It was here→I went off the rails!⌋] But I better say this, for your digestion. It is true that neither the Bible nor Homer were in the nature of discovery, as the Shakespeare. But my purpose, in adding two more essays to the original Shakespeare piece, comes from the obsession that, with those two other points established, the size of the square of Herman Melville [*Marginal addition in ink:* ⌈This is a theosophistic diagram: △ ⌋] inside that triangle will be more apparent than is now clear. What the King James piece does, is to argue how clearly and painfully Melville saw his loss in the dying off of *folk* [*marginal addition in ink:* ⌈I more & more see him in these terms. And believe it is the best way to expose the PRIMORDIAL about him.⌋] knowledge of the images and narratives of the Bible. (The crucial point here is that *it happened in his lifetime*) (<It> ⌈The point⌋ is of so much greater importance than what has heretofore been the emphasis of HM & the Biblum: Clarel, and his troubling himself with the questions of "faith". On this level he is no larger than his time and is thus smaller than himself. He shrinks to an Arnold, in fact.) What I am interested in, is the restrictions thus placed on his metaphor, which ⌈was crucial⌋ in his case, due to the nature of himself as "makyr" (I use the folk word advisedly), ⌈and⌋ <attacked> bound and choked the whole imaginative process.

The intent of the "Homer", on the other hand, is to explore his extensions, to suggest in what manner this man who was launching himself into MOBY-DICK just about exactly 100 years ago today, is <the most important creator> ⌈the only creator of his particular kind⌋ SINCE HOMER, is precisely such a "starter" as was Omeros, gave up out of the intelligence and perception of himself a measurement of man and universe so revolutionary that he will stand to the future as fountainhead as has that Greek man and woman man or woman man and/or woman for the 3000 year civilization now dead.

At which point Sealts must h[e]ave a great sigh, and say, that olson! But I don't think so, or I dare say I'd not be saying to you what I have not sd to anyone so familiar with Melville as yourself. I suppose HM ain't, for the precise reason that his language is too careless to live/ I could weep over that/ Whitman less so, tho 100 lines must be his limit too/ the American tragedy is, it was not Melville who had Whitman's diaphragm or ear. It would have helped.

But I think the valuation holds, if it is recognized that the old bases of judgment (art can be confused, is confused by, as society, by the chaos of) are not sufficient to measure our whale. It is a matter of mind, 1st of all, intelletto ((one thing I like about R[ichard]. Chase[2] (tho I abhor the snobbery he does not know he is a victim of, the elite-prinkip rot he'll reveal in the end) is his recognition of that dimension in HM). HM had a mind rare of men, and, as of the present considerations, capable of founding a new humanitas. Which I say he did (and Whitman did not. Whitman derives. M is prospective—I blocked these things out in ISHMAEL, is what lies under the "Noah" part, but I despair to think <it> †I↓ was understood.)

Th[e] most immediate proof is DOCUMENTATION, his. His methodology. (Here, for example, his language is impeccable, is only to be compared to one A. Lincoln, letter to McLellan Oct, 1862 (or 3?) in the gamut of Anglo-american tongue since Philmullholland †& King James translators↓]). <His> [*Marginal addition in ink:* †The point is a double one. He based himself on document. & that, I argue, is in turn a via of life, now most clear to us characters who face the 20th century world. (For further elucidation, if curious, see poem "La Prèface," book *Y & X* published Black Sun Press, 1948, by Olson & Cagli)↓]

2, his METAPHOR
3, his PEOPLING   ) Moses, his only antecedent(
                         a propos 2 & 3

4, his NARRATIVE. This is so far unexamined by anyone for what reason I'm damned if I can understand. Here he burst out like proteus himself. There is nothing like it since Homer. Nor is it just M-D, or, rather, the dimensions of narrative. It is the guerdon of many narratives that he gave. (Why I keep hammering BENITO, BARTLEBY—and not pre-Kafka, only, BABY BUDD—as against BILLY, THE ENCANTS, the CARPENTER, the lost turnings (such as you were after in yr job on the chimney, such as I have heard "The Piazza" talked of as "like Alain-Fournier's The Wanderer"). They talk of James! Jeezus. Melville can-opened archaic narrative, the which ain't been done since above-mentioned Greek, (tho we can talk about the satyra and fabliaux of the Middle Ages (Eng., specifically) and Theophrastus, without loss. [*Marginal addition in ink:* †Nor is this s[ad?]. I again ride herd on you <saps[?]> without allowing you to know what is au fond. It is 1, all over again: M's attack on the starting-point. He is not *fictive.* He begins from, & proceeds by the method of, observed reality.↓]

((Right here a whole school of scholiasts should go to work. Here is a mine for technical examinations. 4 slides over into 3, 2, and even 1, but the place to start is NARRATIVE. (It is another sign as symbol of you, Merton Sealts, that it is the "stories" you are concentrating on. You are right. Dig it. There is no end.)* [*Marginal addition in ink:* †*Idea: pull out "The Town-Ho" [chapter from *Moby-Dick*], & publish it as one of yr [sto]ries! That'll stir em u[p]—and make a valid point: HM is STORE HOUSE.↓]

FIVE, something else, not so easy to put in a word precisely because here we are barking at the heels of (barking our shins on) the real business back from which goes the more obvious evidences of power. 5 is why, some distance above, I sd "universe". It is also what I made so much so loosely about, SPACE. It is where the old man as of art takes his place alongside the secondary giants now thot of as the princes of science. And to get at it you have to use analogies borrowed from their more obvious advance. Let me, for now, simply put it thus:

5, his NON EUCLIDIAN SPACES

HM had a hold of *plastic secrets* I find no where else previously except in some certain archaic stone work—and Mister or Miss Omeros (notably the Phaeacian "world"). He had them because his own physiology had 'em. This, 100 years ago, was a NEW MAN (what Whitman was crying for, and wasn't), what we all are now, as particles. (If you will think of Ahab's dimension, say, or MADAME WHALE, and forget all that has been sd about how he come by it out of America and Shxper, and go down (yup, Cluny), and fergit Saturn (Keats', or HM's, or Phidias'), forget the Classical base of our behaviours (HM's), all derivations,

        and then consider the PROCESS of the creation of such dimensions (their shiftings in Babo, Benito, the Carpenter, the Chola, even Baby, or yr Chimney [*marginal addition in ink:* †More of same apologues, & hints↓]) you will agree, I think, that one has to grapple with things still unknown from yr organism and mine straight out to the geometries of SPACE. I say unknown, better, not yet understood. But HM understood them, and used 'em, (without, I suppose, consciousness: flashes into my mind Leyda's extraordinary discovery of Malcolm's birth certificate).

Oi, yoi. You're getting it, today, Sealts. I better stop, poor man. But I thank you, that you led me out. Anyhow, there's only one more point before I wrap it up, as of now.

And that's—6—where we come acropper, where HM did, LANGUAGE. This is where he did *not* add dimension. Why why why (Or were Homer's hexameters no advance, if the ante-H mss had survived?) I myself <don't> am not particularly bothered by this subtraction; read him without the pain per page other poets stay away from him for, think they are too "nice" in this, disclose they are derivatives, YET, where it is more important, the *people* do not read 'im, (will not?), Or is this important? If you do, I do, Montale has, Lorca should have, Cagli does, what does it matter. Perhaps here I go patriotic, religious, want the god to be perfect, would add that little bit of Whit<man>. Shit: let's leave him a man, and let it go at that. All the rest above adds up to HERMAN MELVILLE, EXCELLENTLY BRIGHT.

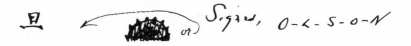

1950–1951

It was May of 1950 before the offprints of "Melville's Reading" were ready; Olson wrote me promptly on the twenty-fourth after receiving his copy. "I am most pleased," he told me, and "tho I should be at work, I have sat with it over coffe[e], poking my way in, to see what is there and if, for what is not there, I might have some answers." He was delighted that serial publication of the monograph had led to the reporting of several additional books once owned by Melville; he was sure that still others would be located: "somewhere in my notes" he wrote, "there is a lead that, in Troy, N.y., there is more evidence—this is from memory, but can, I think, be checked." He had one reservation, and in making it he had a story to tell that was entirely new to me:

I am rather suspicious of those bookseller stories you have been given. It looks like athlete's mouth from jumping on bandwagon. For I talked to Lathrop Harper in 1934, was it, when I flushed the "Sale" business, and he had no such things to say. On top of that you may, one day, want to make clear that it was lovely old John Anderson who broke the thing open. I found him in a little hotel at 23rd Street, and we <became> really pieced the thing out (it was from that day that [Oscar] Wegelin emerged: I wrote him, and he met me a few days later in a beanery on Broadway. I had the Farnell lead from Anderson. All that Wegelin did, was to confirm it. I dare say that is why I have been somewhat miffed at Wegelin crowding and crowing. It was actually out of John Anderson['s] good brain that the story came.)

Olson's objection, which he was to raise again in later years, was that by citing Harper and Wegelin I had lent credence to inaccurate accounts of the sale of Melville's books following his death. My response, which never quite registered with him, was that I could report only what I had learned, whether from written records or from oral testimony; if he had additional *facts* to correct anything I had reported, I naturally would welcome them—but meanwhile I had been working under handicaps. Of course I had been enjoined by Olson himself not to reveal his Brooklyn leads, and as for his meeting with "lovely old John Anderson," *that* feature of "the story" was utterly new to me in 1950! Then and later, Olson continually assumed that I knew more of the details of his earlier sleuthing than he had ever told me, either in our meeting nine years before or in any of his letters.

Now Olson was thinking again of a joint expedition to Brooklyn, speculating that there might be "some fund, or something, which could pay eating and sleeping bills while we pick up the track where I left it." Meanwhile, he would try to put all his information into "coherent order" so that I could "go after it" on my own, though he was "just sentimental, and curious, to do it together, particu[l]arly, to run along the Bell stuff until I hit another like the Waller [Warton], and prove, by the handwriting, that it was HM's!" As for Melville, "I love himm, more, now than ever. (This spring, for the 1st time, I lectured on him, two days, 3 hrs each, at the Institute of Contemp. Arts here [in Washington, D.C.]. It was such a pleasure.)"

On either 2 or 3 June of 1950 Olson sent me two more letters (one of them evidently misdated) prompted by a more detailed study of "Melville's Reading" in a duplicate copy that Mrs. Metcalf had sent him. The two letters were a mixture of praise and blame for what he found, together with several pages of the further detailed information he had been promising and some pointed suggestions for any new edition. Forgetting what we both knew by this time—that Jay Leyda was soon to publish *The Melville Log: A Documentary Life of Herman Melville* (1951), which would provide exactly what he had in mind—Olson called for a chronological listing of the books Melville had owned and borrowed, juxtaposed with records of his concurrent writing. To illustrate the value of a chronological table, Olson noted that he had first learned from my alphabetical check-list that Melville bought a translation of Aeschylus in March of 1849; he must therefore have been reading Greek tragedy at the very time when he was making what he himself called "close acquaintance" with the plays of Shakespeare. Purchase of the Aeschylus in 1849 Olson regarded as "one of the most imp. discoveries yet made on Melville," one he found especially significant for his own study because it might "essentially shift" his argument that "it was the Spring of '50, rather, which thru him so far forward."

If Olson was excited by the new vistas that my compilation seemed to open, he was dismayed once again to think of things he was sure I knew but hadn't said about the books and what had been done with them since Melville's death. His hot words scorched then, thirty years ago, and they scorch now as I read them over:

It is such a valuable thing you have done, and so you will the more measure my valuing of you, if i raise up, how irked i am, that you too play the scholar's game, the academic back-scratch—& leave things that you know, unsaid. When you came in to my office in New York in 1941–42 (the winter), I liked yr difference fr [Stanley] Williams' breed. I go by my nose, and, I think you will acknowledge, I went by it then, and openly gave you what I had never given any of the Harvard, or more g[ener]al scholars.

And yr letter after you left the army, or just at separation, was the kind of confirmation a man of my business, and nature, values more than honors.

And this Sealts I go on believing in, to whom I wrote—& that was too a mark—such letters as I wrote you last spring (still the 2nd is unacknowledged). And, again, two weeks ago.

so, given such conditions of regard for fellow-work, it is an irony that, to this date, (with even a Sealts' job out, specifically on the reading, and the books) it should still be only one F. Barron Freeman (and he, fr no personal cause whatsoever) who, in print, has had the accuracy to state Olson's <"sole"> relationship to the deposit of mss in The Harvard Library, let alone that which would seem, would it not, of much more importance, the same's relation to the use of the path of Melville's reading to understanding of him, and Olson's acts in the re-creation of the topography of his library.

Look, friend Sealts: it won't be so very long before my own proper work is seen in a perspective sufficient to establish clearly the use to which I have put my time. (I am not speaking of the Melville work.) And that is what a man cares for.

So I am not speaking fr any professional hungriness for coups, on which jobs, or the support of my family, might rest.

Nor does it essentially matter, simply because it is minor business: if I were querelous, I'd long ago have taken up arms against the Mumfords, the Thorpes, the Matthiessens, the Vincents.

It is just that I am proud, and that I value you, and that it does no good in life to let one's friends be careless without remarking it.

And just because it is already too late for you to make corrections, I can be free to speak to you.

What particularly hurt Olson was that I had cited the work of F. O. Matthiessen in *American Renaissance* (1941) where—in his judgment—

I should have named Olson himself and his pioneering study of Melville and Shakespeare, "Lear and Moby Dick" (1938). I understand now what I didn't realize then: that I had unintentionally rubbed new salt into an old wound, recalling to him a personal grievance I knew nothing whatsoever about in the 1940's, either from Olson or from anyone else, until I read this letter. Matthiessen I never met, though we exchanged notes about a book from Melville's library that he owned. His *American Renaissance* I valued highly; it had served to confirm the faith of my generation of scholar-teachers in the worth of our native literary heritage and the possibilities then opening to us for the study of American literature. Olson's "Lear and Moby Dick" was a shortened version of a paper he had written for a Harvard course given by Matthiessen.[3] But their formerly close relation had evidently soured, as his letter reveals. The tangled sentences which follow are a measure of the pain I had brought forth; whether the target in some of them is Sealts, Matthiessen, or both of us is difficult to tell from their tangled syntax.

I want merely to call the attention of that Sealts whom I bet on, to the kind of emphases (note yr topping of Olson, and scattering, for those who do not know the facts, the impression of his work, by Matthiessen, p. 141, and, conspicuously, on the Shake reading, p. 155) which make life intolerable— that a man's work, when it has been done hard, and has actually turned out to be leadership (to whom did Matty come that day, spring, 1934, and from whom did he take the card notes of HM's reading of Emerson, Hawthorne, etc.?) should—I say this quite quietly—be smudged, even by the one man who, most directly and well, has taken on the work?

A man's simplest wish, if he is an honest worker, is not coups, or the riding on the back of other men, but simply this—that the time I gave to such labors as you, more than a[n]yone else, has carried on, should, by you, of all people, not be slurred, or washed away in the general seas. For a man's hours *are* his fate.

I'm going to quit. For I am unhappy. Yet I do not want you to be pushed to any wall. Let me just add this, for a starter. You can <carry> fill it in, as of the 1st Harvard acquisition (the purchase of the Shake, <whom[?]> I think you know how that came abt), and as of the opening of the whole sale in NY & Brooklyn. Let me, then, leave it at, yr lst sentence:

who lst emphasized this "role of books"—cf. Olson MA thesis, Wesleyan-Yale, 1933, on deposit Wesleyan Library, Midd[le]town, Conn; also confirm date Olson arrival Cambridge, fall 1933, and work at Metcalfs; also trip Dec. 1933, to Orange, N.J., on which trip he located 97 volumes at home Mrs Osborne, and got her permission to deposit same Widener Library.

Go[o]d luck, and let me hear from you further, on what remains undone.

Olson's distressing letters caught me at a bad time. I was grading final examinations, but I replied immediately on 5 June to say that I had been in poor health for a year and though still "pretty shaky," I would shortly be answering his "four fulsome letters" as I had much to tell him. Back came a warm response with "a poem—for your health" enclosed: "Arcana Zero," from *y & x*. "Please, please, don't let that bull olson, who charged in and bellowed and pawed, and didn't know you were not well, let it add to yr boidens. . . . write me only when you can." On 12 June, after hunting out his unanswered letters that had piled up since May of 1949, I sent him six pages of single-space typing in reply to each of them in turn. Most of what I said dealt with minutiae—the luck, good or bad, I had had in running down leads he had suggested concerning individual books; there were also comments on other Melville scholarship, including the relation of "Melville's Reading" to Leyda's forthcoming *Melville Log*. Then I came at last to "the hard part," as I called it. I began by saying, "I have hurt you, and I am sorry"; I went on to mention some facts about the history of "Melville's Reading" that he might not have remembered or even known; perhaps they should be recorded here as well, as a part of the whole story. It was Jay Leyda, I acknowledged, who first

started the wheels turning in the summer of 1947 while in Cambridge and Wellesley and Boston, and after seeing what I had done with the books and the records in my dissertation. I think he talked it over with Mrs. Metcalf first; I know he sold [G. William] Cottrell at Harvard [editor of the *Harvard Library Bulletin*], and got him to ask me to do it. There were some ground-rules laid down from the beginning concerning *Bulletin* publication. It was to be a discreet way of calling attention to one segment of Harvard's Melville holdings without actually shrieking; there was to be no puffing of any scholar, group of scholars, books, projects, societies, etc., nor any of the reverse unless errors of fact were corrected . . . ; since the list would obviously be long and might be longer as it went along, everything must be factual, abbreviated, concise, but clear. . . .

After mentioning Mrs. Metcalf as being " 'in' on every stage of the whole business" I went on to recall how she had told me of Olson's "coming to her door years ago," and I expressed my gratitude to them both for their much-needed help. But I also felt obligated to set forth to him, in addition,

the completely unselfish sharing of literally hundreds of items on the part of Jay Leyda; I remember that Walt Bezanson in a way started this whole business when he first sent me to the publishers' accounts at Harvard to look again and see what I had previously missed; I remember that even Jack Birss, secretive as he is known to be, likewise turned his files inside out for me, and gave the hint for what I consider my best bit of pure detective-work in the whole Check-List (#270 [George Herbert, *The Temple*], which the Library of Congress said I would never identify from the quotation and in the absence of relevant Philadelphia copyright records). In short, my list of obligations is so long and so complicated and so personal that I despair of ever giving credit, publicly or privately, where it is rightly due, my own effort being chiefly that of questioner, recorder, and writer of several hundred follow-up letters.

Lastly, the Check-List was not intended as a history of modern Melville scholarship, but as a compilation of "all that has been learned to date concerning the disposition of Melville's library," "as a guide to the location of known books, and [a work that] may lead to the recovery of others." (Pp. 144–145) The quotations I used were chosen because of what they said, not because of who said them or how he happened to be in a position to say them (Matthiessen). As for you, I thought you would notice that in listing Matthiessen, Anderson, Olson, *et al.*, on my very first page, it was only Olson's studie*s* (documented) which were at all characterized. . . . On p. 144, the order "Murray, Olson, Birss, and Leyda" is strictly chronological; on p. 383 the footnote listing obligations is simply to save others the trouble of following the blind alleys, along with the noncommittal recording of my own obligations to others than the libraries and collectors themselves.

Olson's answer was a four-page handwritten "note of acknowledgment," dated 16 June 1950, on the eve of his leaving Washington "for a few days in N.Y." He wrote immediately, he explained,

because I want you to know how the dignity of yr answer to my truculence is itself reward.

(The hell is, in this business of the making use of our lives, how much it is, go blind, like animal, fight for, in this corner. And how, when another person speaks, how animal one is shown to be!)

Then he went on to discuss an idea I had broached to him: a book that would bring together the best criticism of Melville that had so far been written. "It is most exciting," he wrote;

as a matter of fact it is the *other* publishing idea to the one [James] Laughlin offered me, a year ago, (to do an "iconographic" Melville—the obvious mate to ISH, a sort of Olson LOG—†via‖ document) which causes me to spring up. (The Laughlin thing is on the shelf, at the moment, because he hasn't the funds, sez he!)

For a starter, do, in yr thinking of yr book, and its plan, think of yourself as *critic*, <rather> beyond selector; think of the introduction as only one act of judgment, in other words, that the marshalling of the material itself be, a critique. I say this, because, it is the only way any of us can create *values*, (which is, actually, the fragrance of form, and the form a book takes, if it has value, is found out *only* by the man under whose hand it is.) Yr own pride in "[Herman Melville's] I & My Chimney" is the very stem I, for one, would trust.

        (Why, Merton, it occurs to me: *in this book you have the very device of health*, the *act* to bring to bear the ten years you have finely put to the record of this man, whom we are honored (as I sd this week to Leyda) that we have done work on.

    Do, very much, do it. (A caution, fr a burned hand—it is too good an idea for you to rush the plan of, for one publisher. Give yourself the joy of blocking it out *in yr own image* FIRST, without regard to the *commerce* of books.

        (Why don't you use me as a resonator? Anyway, I offer myself as a target for any, & all letters you care to write, to feel yr way in. (It is, sometimes, letters, that is, a more organic way to arrive at form, than outlines or plans)

        (And, as to a publisher, have no doubts. Here, too, eds use Olson—Viking, ↑New Directions,↓ or wherever: I'll back you to the limit.)

    I must run: but this, for you to turn once, in yr mind:

      FORM IS NEVER MORE THAN   [which I
      AN EXTENSION OF   make this
      CONTENT.   corollary of:
                          Right form. . . .
                          the precise, & only
                          possible.]
                          Affections,

                                          Olson

    In retrospect I find this letter even more remarkable than I did at the time, considering Olson's resentment at Matthiessen for appropriating ideas he believed to be his: once again I too had conjured up a project Olson himself had already thought of, but instead of warning me off, as he might properly have done, he generously offered to help with it at every stage. To Olson I sent a postcard on 27 June calling his attention to articles on Melville in the May issue of *American Literature*; meanwhile I had already sounded out one publisher about the proposed collection of critical essays. But I went no further. My health remained uncertain over the next year, my teaching schedule was heavy, and outbreak of the Korean War raised the real possibility of my being called back to active military duty as a Reserve officer. It was 27 March 1951 before I ventured another letter to Olson, writing during spring recess in a rather discouraged mood about the proposed book and other matters we had been exploring. "I keep thinking about the critique," I assured him, "but look at the remaindering of such ventures as the James volume"—I may have been thinking of *The Question of Henry James*, the collection of critical essays edited by F. W. Dupee—"and the continued delaying of Jay [Leyda]'s [Melville] Log. I think a quiet scuttling of the [Hendricks House] Melville edition may be in progress; I'm not sure." With the uncertain fate of my volume in the edition "and possible active duty both hanging over my head," I explained, I had done little on Melville except to prepare a supplementary note to "Melville's Reading" for the *Harvard Library Bulletin*. Olson's essay on *Billy Budd* in the *Western Review*[4] I liked, the letter affirmed, "but of CJO I really know nothing."

My next news of Olson came not from a letter to me or through Mrs. Metcalf, who had often sent me word of him, but through the broadside in verse headed "Letter for Melville" that he wrote "in a moment of flame" during the summer of 1951. In September of that year the Melville Society was holding a meeting at Williams College to commemorate the centennial year of *Moby-Dick*; Olson thought the celebration "damned stupid," and in a prose preface to his poem charged that a heroic man—Melville—was being "used" by "a bunch of commercial travelers from the several colleges." In the poem itself he first berated his good friends the Metcalfs and Henry Murray for mixing themselves in "such salads / as these caterers will serve" at Williamstown; then he launched into invective against clearly recognizable individuals for trading on Melville in academic market-places, attacking Howard Vincent as editor of Melville's poems for Hendricks House (1947) and author of *The Trying-Out of Moby-Dick* (1949), probably F. O. Matthiessen, and certainly Perry Miller, who spoke at Williamstown.[5] I attended the conference but was not on the program; I heard there that Olson had distressed Mrs. Metcalf by what he had sent, but I did not see the "Letter" at the time. Had Olson known of my own presence among "these caterers" he might well have ended our correspondence forthwith.

1952:

Olson and the New Republic

M y letter from Olson dated 5 March 1952 was the first of a series of four that came during that same month from Black Mountain College in North Carolina. Written in longhand, it ran to seven full pages, most of them concerned with Melville and Melville scholars. Olson had not answered my last letter of the previous March, he acknowledged; he "was then in the Yucatan, & by some inconceivable error" he did not see it until "last September, when a bundle of things was brought to me here from Washington." In October a daughter named Kate had been born: "a *pleasure!* & somewhat handsome, & shrewish as she shld be, having her mother & her name! Conceived in Vera Cruz!" He had recently talked with Jay Leyda, he continued, and had singled out Leyda himself, Murray, Nathalia Wright, and Sealts as the Melville scholars he took special note of: for their clear-headedness and for "exhibiting a clear & present sense of the limits." With that point established, he next reported that the *New Republic* had asked him to review the Hendricks House *Moby-Dick* (1952), edited by Luther Mansfield and Howard Vincent, and though he liked "Mansfield's long study of M's †literary↓ sources for his characterization of Ahab †[pp.] 637–652↓, especially the *Goethe* portion †648–49, & *678–679↓*," he had serious reservations about "the several scholarly problems the *disproportion* of this Centennial MD raises."

Although "I do not usually do reviews," he went on to say (presumably because they pay little or nothing), "I shall do the NR job." But he also proposed a longer and more scholarly treatment of the volume in a professional journal (1) if I could suggest one immediately, or (2) if I should hear later on of a journal that might be interested, or (3) if "we might together *lead* some mag to let us do a joint job" that would cover the *sources* and *composition* of *Moby-Dick*—two topics, or rather "levels, . . . which you and I come loaded for bear on."

OK. Three ideas—& the last one you might well wish to disengage yrself frm (especially now that I learn ((fr [Richard] Chase's review of Leyda [*The Melville Log*] in the Nation, *Dec.* [1951, p. 478], that Olson's ISH is looked upon, in correct circles, as "indefensibly wild, 'Freudian', & intellectual"!)

In any case, give me yr best thoughts on this. I am so out of touch with such matters, even what, if any, new scholarly mags. have been added to "American Literature"—if so, what are they, & which of them engage themselves in the important task of weighing the worth of such 250 pages of notes, in estimating the pretensions of Mansfield & Vincent therein?

I shall be obliged, & shall be as discrete as you might rightly find it necessary to ask me to be about yr information.

Thus under way, Olson "hate[d] to stop, now that I am with you at last. Want to talk again about Brooklyn, & when we get there, the two of us. And much else." He had checked the latest catalogue from Lawrence College to see what I was teaching; he hoped I wouldn't give up "the *critique* job," and he wanted to hear about the other volumes in the Hendricks House edition. Could we "flush the whole Brooklyn *covey*" together? I was to write "any time: you stay my one sure man in this more & more complicated business we all seem to stay deeper and deeper in years & years later".

As of Olson: he lectures here on verse, & sundry other aspects of writing & reading

& so far as his own work goes, in the last couple of years, it's mostly in #'s 1, 2, 3, & 4 of the Boston mag ORIGIN (51 Jones Ave Dorchester 24, MASS)

Earlier in his letter Olson had said of his projected review that he would be "working this forward slowly for the next couple of months," but by Sunday, 7 March he had written me another installment on the same subject that ran to eight single-spaced pages typed with a red ribbon—clearly one of his great letters. What prompted it was more reading in the new volume, this time

in MD itself! (1st time in a long time, and very heartening: read THE TAIL & then THE FOUNTAIN, and got wholly involved again in this man's knowingnesses, his incredible natural knowingnesses. For surely (as I once horrified Mat[t]hiessen over a beer in Clancy's, was it, that bar on Mt Holyoke St, next to the Hayes Bickford, was it, when I sd, Matty, I think I'll do a rewrite—clean up—MD) surely any professional could clean up that prose at all points YET, so what, for what counts—what he gets in there—is something the like of which (I still say, repeating that long spume to you three years

ago just about this time) aint happened since Homer: that absolute familiarity with *sensation* as it really is, that impeccable swiftness of register of the
faster-than-light intricacies of *the motion* of experience. I still find it crucial to
speak of it as a space-power. For it is objective reality, and its workings,
which he is as delicate to as his whale's tale ⎰(*tail*!)⎱ that lovely statement, its
power even in its play (in fact, any rewriting is always where the "play"
gets playsome, is coy or cute or so avoiding of sexual hardnesses (their
"zones", e.g., as against Montaigne's straightness about the same elephant:
"and now and then over her band put his truncke into her bosome, and
feele her breasts") that he gets to writing fit for the family parlor!

But ΄la! how reality springs up from his hands *as it damn well is!* The accor-
dioning of it, in & out, the speed, there, the telescoping of time & of space
as any of us are presented to its bearing, the way the human system buzzes
its way through it to its death!

It is an extraordinary *man*, this phe-
nomenon, HM, an extraordinary system—and none of us can rest, in our
explanations, short of a continuing examination of the nature of this *kinetic*.
For the closest one can get to an extrapolation of this literal magic is to
recognize the import of motion. And I would venture to think that a way of
understanding why Melville did suddenly appear, did have this thing unsaid
since the Odyssey, is that man had gone away from that "truth" of the
nature of Nature which the Ionian physicists had not lost and which the
non-Euclidean geometers contemporary to Melville made it possible for
modern physics to discover anew: that the minute particles of substances
(including any one of us) is in vigorous & continual motion.

And how pre-
cise an instrument for the recording of this motion on all of the <interio>
planes on which it asserts itself he was, how spontaneously & completely
he was able to express those interlockings of those planes which make up
th<e>⎰at⎱ sphere which we then call reality!

One further observation pro-
voked by <th>a footnote beyond those two chapters I reread: the footnote
[by Melville] on *gallow* [in Chapter 87: p. 382 in the Hendricks House *Moby-
Dick*]: <T>that time, in his hands, historical time, in this instance, gets the
same *fluency* (or, better, to make clear the difference from time-bound men,
the same *manuable* character that substance has: this is a determinable difference from others handling of time, and is of some importance, simply, that
Melville apprehended history proper in this strong image-ish way (metaphor as not separable from object, but <a>is *another* character of object—
and with no needed reference to spirit, simply, that substance also exists
because of its space-time loci, that this location of its motion is a factor of its
motion, a qualitative determinant as well as a positional & mass determinant.

Then, objecting strongly to the "flat words" in which Mansfield and
Vincent had summed up Melville's relation to Horatio Nelson, by

baldly identifying Nelson as "one of Melville's greatest heroes" (p. 616), Olson charged ahead:

How such phrasing destroys the very relevance of Melville, the still insufficiently explored singularity & usefulness of him to any of us—one needs only to turn immediately to Billy B[udd] and see how M was trying to cope with Nelson as fix for the situation he wanted so much to give the proper dimensional & kinetic life to—and how he felt bitterly the *loss* in his audience (or the absence, still, 1890, of a comprehension of man in time & space. . . .

> you see, Merton, there *is* this important likeness of HM to Rimbaud, that both of them, in wholly different ways, got exasperated because a reality equivalent to their own penetration of reality *had not come into being in their time*

(You will recall how I argued this point—as of the King James Version—in that Western Review piece, David Young, David Old. But I now see it as much more crucial than I then understood: these two men were deeply balked just because <their manu> they had in themselves manumitted the *inaccurate* estimate of reality man had gone by since the Ionians—due to a loss of a recognition of the absolute tenacity of the space-time context in which all things, including man, <rest. it> are set—and yet, because of the lag of events (it was not until, say, August 1945 that man as a whole was shocked into the recognition), these two men (because any of us, even a Rimbaud? certainly a Melville, are not possibly ever that sure that they are right, however firm they feel their "intuitions", Melville called his sense of his own exactitudes) were *hindered*

Melville & Rimbaud were made (made themselves) capable of engaging reality *as it is*. And if Melville grabbed on to Nelson as a figure of his "system", then any of us had better gauge that <gr> "prehensile" (is his word for what he wishes the whale's tail might have more of, so that, like an elephant it could woo, & pick out the darts thrown into itself—as Nelson couldn't the splinter which took off his eye) †the prehensile↓ necessity *seriously*, SIMPLY
          modestly. . . .

Here, after a digression on the Henricks House editors, Olson proceeded to "take it another way" by "pick[ing] up on that word *hero*," declaring that

one of the central preoccupations of man today—one of his central necessities—is exactly this problem of *hero:* which is, any time, man's measure of *his own possibilities*—how large is he?

now one of the greatnesses of HM's
work is the very way he cleared man in his attack now upon the heroic as a
dimension   (the Specksynder is the first created
          measure of the Dictator
                    (((curiously enough, the one *major*
contribution these men have made (so far as I have yet found) is their
evidence of what Goethe contributed to Melville's thinking on exactly
this point

Melville "stays, is now valuable," Olson then asserts, "because he had
found out the secret of apprehending reality lost since Miletus—what
is now again a common property of all of us, even if not yet taken up
and acted by, seen by, experienced by" us—and because he "cleared
the HERO problem of history in the one-planed and romantic sense in
which even Goethe was defeated."

Olson's reflections here on "that word *hero*" require further elucidation. He was thinking particularly of a passage in Chapter 33 of
Moby-Dick, "The Specksynder," where Ishmael in characterizing Ahab
speaks of the "sultanism of his brain" (p. 144.22 in the Hendricks
House edition). What Olson calls the "*major* contribution" of Mansfield and Vincent, in their explanatory note on this passage (pp. 678–
679) and in an earlier note on Ahab, is their suggestion that this "de-
fining ingredient of Ahab's character" was "shaped largely" by Melville's reading of Goethe's *Truth and Poetry: From My Own Life*. What
Goethe wrote there of the characters of Mahomet, Prometheus, and
his own Egmont "must have greatly interested Melville," according to
Mansfield and Vincent (p. 648), "especially since Goethe had ultimately to abandon the drama he projected about the first and the
poem meant to deal with the second, confessing that these personalities afforded no suitable material for his poetic art. Perhaps Goethe's
failure merely spurred Melville to attempt Ahab," they continue,
since many of his traits "would seem to have been suggested by
[Goethe's] analyses of the Arab prophet and the Greek god." What
Goethe could not deal with in these figures, Olson believed, was the
"demonic element" that reappears in Ahab's "sultanism." In Olson's
words, "Goethe had to give up just because he lacked what Melville
had: proof evident—he settled for Egmont, when M took on both
Prometheus *and* the Prophet."

The remainder of Olson's long letter defies summary, since his
original train of thought was continually being sidetracked by his anger at contemporary scholars and their work like that of his earlier
"Letter for Melville"—the outburst in verse provoked by the centennial conference on *Moby-Dick* at Williamstown in 1951. His initial in-

tention, he explained, had been to outline for my "fine correction" what he was thinking of writing for the *New Republic*. At first he planned an essay to be called "SOME FIRST PRINCIPLES TOWARD THE PROBLEMS OF THE EDITING OF THE WORK OF HERMAN MELVILLE," one in which he would try "to lay down some canons such as Greg, & Pollard have brought to Shakespeare emendation." But then he had begun to reflect on "the immorality of the politics & economics of our time" as seen even in academic scholarship, and he had fallen back "in despair."

Who is ready to see how *crucial* it is that Melville's work be left in its own "life"? who of any of us is yet ready to guage [*sic*] the *import* of this man's heave? If I, after 20 years of preoccupation with him, still find each day a little entrance into the depth of his act—a new thing more blinding to me than the day I read Benito Cereno (it happened to be the first, by some accident of it being to hand one afternoon I was not well and had a chance to read something)
   I don't know. Two weeks ago I finished a long go called CULTURE, in which this point—of how seriously do any of us take the work of a book (by comparison, say, to those obvious acts of history—like the Bomb o<f>r Adolf Hitler—we are all convinced are important)—was put out there.
                                                                                But
when I am confronted with the *uncleanness* of thinking, feeling, self-taking— of even the scholarship—in such work as this edition, I am bewildered as to how to expose it, how to carry out what I am sure is the moral imperative of any worker in any field: to be responsible to the public for the conduct of the other workers in that field:::
                                that is why I beg you to follow me. For who but us who are inside *know* what is being done here?
                                And Question #2: how can we together arrive at any determination of action to keep our house clean by exposing those who dirty Melville?

To these questions Olson added a series of others, of which the third is most relevant here:

Let me ask you the same help I asked Leyda: because you are much more current to the work than I, can you tell me of any one I should add to yrself, Leyda, Miss [Nathalia] Wright, [Harrison] Hayford, [Henry A.] Murray (as psychologist) as they who have done clean work because they have stayed inside the recognizable limits of *research* & of its announcement, its presentation

You see, the *hinge*, it turns out, on which the whole thing does hinge, is this thing you & I in particular are experts in: *sources*

And if I do do those PRINCIPLES of EDITING, I shall have to make clear in
what way <sources> the <handling> presentation of the sources has to be
governed

(it is not a personal matter: the problem is as definable & delimita-
ble as emendations, say. . . .

As examples of what he meant, Olson went on to cite not only my
"Melville's Reading" and Leyda's *Melville Log* but articles by Wilson
Heflin, William H. Gilman, Hayford, and Leon Howard[6] that do not
claim to be other than they are. Each, in Olson's phrasing, "is exactly
an act of mind precisely because it (1) presents the known facts; (2)
recognizes that these are only the known facts, that others obviously
also existed which have disappeared or have not yet been recovered;
and (3) leaves those facts as facts, and does not claim to analyze Melville's use of them." By contrast, Olson had harsh words for two books
in particular: *The Trying-Out of Moby-Dick* (1949) by Howard Vincent,
who in Olson's eyes could do nothing right, and *Melville in the South
Seas* (1939) by Charles R. Anderson, both of which he measured
against "Kittredge's superb book on Chaucer" and, "as fullest measure of *all* Melville work, the scholarship of Victor Berard on THE
ODYSSEY." Winding up his letter with what he called the "$64 Ques-
tion," Olson then concluded as follows:

have we any moral right to leave it to any one else—any reviewer—any
editor—†[*in ink*] to anyone but ourselves↓—to MAKE THESE THINGS CLEAR[?]

I'm going to shut up. If you have got this far, do see it all as working my
way through talking to you this day. I should be most aided if you give me
answers to the questions spotted thr[ough]out. But please: don't let any
of this (except the reading) be a burden. Only what it provokes you to say.
Don't feel it calls for an answer in its own terms: these are my headaches,
and the only reason I toss them around with you is my respect for you.

OK.   Much left unsaid!   Loce, Loson

I answered briefly on 15 March 1952, promising a longer letter
after searching out the new edition of *Moby-Dick*; meanwhile, I said
with reference to his detailed comments on Vincent et al., "I have not
read such elegant, eloquent, and thoroughly grounded vituperation
in years!" On the same day Olson wrote again from Black Mountain
with "an idea" and "two hunches." The idea was to push the projected
anthology of Melville criticism as a collaborative effort; the "hunches"
were that Olson could place such a book in this country and also in
Europe, where *Call Me Ishmael* was due shortly in French translation
from Gallimard. Reporting that he had just received another book
for review in the *New Republic*, Lawrance Thompson's *Melville's Quar-*

rel with God (1952), he asked, "what in hell *is* it?" But before I could comment on any of these matters he wrote again on 17 March to say that he had "done a most unusual thing for me, which hearteneth me: had, in one page, and after the shortest sort of reading, knocked off a 'review' of Thompson's book! (Crazy, that I shld ever be that fast abt a matter of HM's!)" Meanwhile, he was "in full sail" on Mansfield and Vincent. In the margin of this letter, in answer to a postscript inquiry of mine about Black Mountain College, he wrote this:

Black M is where I work—& that I do find it possible *to work* is enough of reason for me to enjoy it, even if, ultimately, I would prefer to be where I am "alone" (what a "college," even this, the best one I could ever dream up, can never be for a pedagogue like myself!) —▸ I love the young too much —▸ and because I am, alas, still a younger myself. . . .—

(The arrows and punctuation throughout are Olson's own.)

The remainder of the letter of 17 March was occasioned by Olson's further meditations on Melville and Melville scholars, all with his *New Republic* review obviously in his mind. He began and ended with comments on a published note of mine that I had recently sent him: "Melville's 'Neoplatonical Originals.'"[7] First came the praise: he liked my emphasis on Melville's linking of Emerson with Proclus as Transcendentalists ancient and modern; he liked my own references to "other problems of HM than the one under yr hand at the moment," and he seized upon an image I had cited from Chapter 176 of Melville's *Mardi* in suggesting that for Melville, Emerson "seldom makes us open our eyes under water"—the image itself, like many of the ideas Olson had been exploring in this whole sequence of March letters, turns up in the essay he finally published in the *New Republic*. As for blame, he rightly pointed to "a flaw" in my presentation: the suggestion that reading Emerson might have led Melville to look into Proclus:

not only do I not think you have any evidence for such a speculation, but what is more important you have plenty of evidence for M's own natural movement to such a name, to such an exciting thing to him as "Proclus on Plato", such an exegesis, such a sort of Confucian disciple act

—and this sort
of impulsion of HM's to other writers, particularly to the grand past, is as important an element of his greatness as is, say, what I was writing to you about last, his depth-drive to heroes

you see, by cutting this sort of a drive
back to some notional idea of Emerson as provoking it, you *limit* HM—and actually contradict the openness of your own tone [*added in ink:* ↑—you

even—this once—<are> fall for the very thing HM *did not* and all historians *have* since, Emerson's *importance*↓]

 for you <know> *are* free of that ugly trap these other ignorant writers about writers are caught in—that terrible thing th<at>ey pass off to people: that writers live by <writers> †books↓!

 what a lie, and what a sign of the debasement of culture, that books are somehow presented as though they were library things, dead paper & cardboard & vellum, instead of what they forever are to any writer, the live things some other man made as you yrself are trying to make live things—a book—too, are trying to get yrself as human being so totally inside the written word that it stands in your stead as—YOURSELF, yr life, yr vision, yr commitment, your ACT OF LANGUAGE, like theirs was, is, if it is of any use to you, even when it is negative use, as Emerson or Proclus finally were to HM. . . .

What I mean by yr own evidence to the contrary of that sentence is in yr own text:

 that M, in *Mardi*, (the very text in which you show his direct & negative use of P[roclus]—as, finally, a gi[b]berish like he was *later* to find Em[erson])

joins Proclus to divine Plato and to Bacon as his counsel![8]

 This is so typical of him—of his excitement in *names* as magical, and invocatory—that he shld use him this positively, this enthusiastically as name, despite the fact he <will> does dish him, even as he will dish Plato in the honey-head of MD, and Bacon as the watch-maker brain in Pierre![9] [*added in ink:* †A Melville wld never *need* an Emerson to go to—for— a Proclus!↓]

 These are the lovely ambigu[i]ties (quite *right*, by the way: I know it on my own self, how, a thing will live two ways, or a thousand, inside one) which you so successfully disclose, in your work. . . . And if I pull you up on one miss, it is only that we are all full of holes! . . . Love, again, and please don't be snowed under by these long go's—it is a joy to sit and talk to you

I quote these full extracts from the letter of 17 March because they show Olson at his best as both an astute scholar and a remarkably prescient critic. As a scholar he was absolutely correct in saying that Melville read Plato and Proclus *before* reading Emerson—though it took me many years to confirm laboriously what Olson had seen immediately. Behind his perception lay his intuitive realization of Melville's response to the power of names, the power of language itself—something that Olson as poet understood because the very same powers operated so tellingly within himself. Moreover, the quoted words explain his objection elsewhere in the letter that Lawrance Thomp-

son "shows no 'ear' at all" for what Olson calls Melville's "geometric
intervals"; instead, he and other current critics "are either posing
their own readings as the common-sense ones [*added in ink:* †(by back-
ing away from the real engagements called for, and then passing their
simplicimusses off on the public as HM's!)|] or are—as [Newton] Ar-
vin,[10] say, or [Richard] Chase—exploiting †crudely| contemporary
disciplines like those proceeding from Freud and from Marx."

What interested Olson himself, as he affirmed in this same letter,
was

> to lay home for all to see that the under-water sights of Melville are what
> makes him essentially worth all the pother about him
>> that if I can join him to Rimbaud, that several can talk of his
>> "anticipations"—of Kafka, say, or (more far-reaching) of depth-
>> psychology—or his close preceding of Dostoevsky—or now the
>> attention his verse is receiving from several contemporary
>> practicers
>> that such values in him are from his blindness:

like "the dragging of him back to Carlyle, even Goethe, Emerson etc."
This is to see him in historical, or as Olson put it, in "temporal" terms
at the expense of his vision of "the eternal (what stays interesting as
the human common anytime)." Melville, Olson argued, gave "continuing attention to *both*" the temporal and the eternal, and in books
like *The Confidence-Man* and *Clarel* "left behind him *a critique* of the
temporal." To illustrate his point, Olson proceeded "to misuse a distinction of Keats about Shakespeare"—his *negative capability*[11]—in
characterizing Melville's "incisive *measuring* (measurement) of his
day." Melville's power as a critic of his times was *negative*, Olson explained, in the sense that it corresponds to

> the marginal notes any of us keep registering about the multiplicity of ex-
> perience as it asserts itself daily on us. For a man's time *is* the package in
> which life comes to him, willy-nilly, and it was one of Melville's limits that his
> despair over his time was always subtly discouraging him and pulling him
> away from the confident assertion of his own *positive penetrations:*
>> in fact (again) i keep going back to the notion that exactly the absence
>> of a tradition of such critique—a clear understanding on his part
>> that what he did so much of was a sine q[ua] non of any writer any-
>> time anywhere
>>> (one gets the inverted happy side of this in his excite-
>>> ment over Hawthorne & America as Elizabethan in THE
>>> MOSSES essay ["Hawthorne and His Mosses" (1850)];
>>>> one
>>> gets the severity of the cost to him—not the niggling of it

⸸referred to just above⸸, but the huge actuall PRICE of the
turning of time which the 19th Century was—the dying
of the Greek and Judeo-Xtian West—in BILLY BUDD, in his
stated despair that the Testaments and the Heroic had
died off in his people, leaving him with an audience he
mistakenly felt he could not bounce his full-blown image
and seizure of the imaginative side of life against—he, a
narcissus in the pure sense of any man (that ultimately we
have to love ourselves, simply, that we are our own only
instrument, and aloneness is absolute—that the egocentric
predicament is inextricable) had lost Echo

The point of all this with respect to Melville criticism, as Olson explained next, is that one has to join Melville's use of a given source
"to its pertinence in his own wrestle with the coming-at-him of his
own contemporary time—and that time is a matter of *himself* as well
as, subtly, of his contemporaries (Emerson, in your instance)." But the
academic critics, ignorant of "what the life of a writer always amounts
to—includes, . . . don't seem to have any inkling that a man, even if
he didn't know a single one, lives elbow to elbow with *the men of his
time*, that these are also a conspicuous part of his 'reality.'" The "twist
of it, the gimmick," Olson continues, is "that the man himself is to a
very definable if subtle degree a 'contemporary' of himself! that he is
always measuring himself exactly in terms of the success of his penetration of his reality, of the 'progress' of his own incisiveness." As a
fine example in Melville, Olson cites his prose "Supplement" to *Battle-
Pieces* (1866), the book of Civil War poems, where "he takes on *this
responsibility*" of so "measuring himself" in terms of his times. "M's
concern there," in the "Supplement," "needs emphasizing," according to Olson, especially "by comparison to such a contemporary as
WHITMAN."

To counteract what he called "the mis-dance of all these others now
piling out books on HM," Olson then prescribed the comprehensive
study he wanted done of the man, his reading, and his writing—all
three. The book he had in mind must deal with "the *sources* of M's
materials and perceptions," which "*cannot* be treated in isolation from
each other *unless* there is either an unconscious apprehension of these
sphericities i have been dwelling on or ⸸a⸸ governing & stated recognition of them." As defined by Olson these three *sources* are:

(a) Melville's BIOGRAPHY—(I am trying to cover the experiential as it exists
for any human being in all that he goes through: birth, family, society, loves,
aging, death) and (b) and (c), those two aspects of M's life which he shares

with writers in particular: (b) M's READING, and (c) HIS WRITING, the *total* act
of it—and here I would stress, as above, *the critique & the creation:*
> (I think this is as spherical as one need be, that these THREE are
> the distinguishable MAJOR sources of HIMSELF
>
> his LIFE, his READING, his WORK

Addressing me directly, Olson proposed the writing of such a book as
an appropriate goal for me. "My desire is, to suggest to you, that you
look to the day when you will want to bind up all yr work into something called MELVILLE'S ORIGINALS":

> you could apparently be exploring the act of his WORK, and with a certain
> tendence of it to be primarily a full clarification of his READING, yet . . . end
> up with a "LIFE" of him which would stand free because of the propriety
> of the interaction & juxtaposition of all three of the triad which does seem
> to [be] the sphere so ignored or unknown [*added in ink:* †or badly balanced↓]
> by *all* present workers . . . as to essentially *invalidate* their work.

Taken literally, Olson's proposal was more than flattering to a new
young associate professor with a head full of Melville and a book still
to write. At the time I supposed that he meant just what he told me:
that some day *I* ought to produce the triple-stranded work described
in the last of his four March letters. Now, as I read over the whole
series, it's not Olson writing to Sealts that I see; it's Melville himself in
1850, with "Hawthorne and His Mosses" in print and *Moby-Dick* under his hand, writing to Hawthorne. For it was not so much Nathaniel
Hawthorne that Melville was addressing, but rather an idealized projection of himself, and it was far less for Sealts than for Olson that
these letters of 1951 were written. "Sealts" was simply the "reasona-
tor" for Olson that he had once volunteered to be for me, offering
himself as "a target" for my own letters when I cared to write—"to
feel yr way in," as he put it, adding that sometimes letters are "a more
organic way to arrive at form, than outlines or plans." Comparison of
what had gushed forth in these four letters with what he was to say
in his published essay of the following September shows how Olson
was organically feeling his own way toward form—and "FORM" (as he
had assured me in 1950) "IS NEVER MORE THAN AN EXTENSION OF CON-
TENT." What still greater work he may have been groping his way
toward, beyond *Call Me Ishmael* and the immediate requirements of a
commissioned review, one can only conjecture.

After Olson's March letters, both our remaining correspondence of
1952 and even the *New Republic* review itself seem almost anticlimac-
tic. On 5 April I attempted an answer to all four of his letters in seven

and a half pages of single-spaced typing that I forbear to sample at any great length here, though there are a few paragraphs that will serve to round out the story of our mutual concerns. For example, I wrote that his second letter

opens with one of those wonderful comments on M's *style*, which nobody has really done and which you could and should and I hope will do. Here again you illustrate what you're discussing not only by quoting but by your own touch—and it's that matter of touch that the Mansfields and Vincents and I fear the Sealtses of this world just damned well do not have. It is what you mean, I think, in saying that *composition* as such needs to be handled by someone with creative writing of his own in his background who can get at Melville's accomplishment from the inside and not from a set of rules. In some ways the worst possible critic of *M-D* I can think of, worse even than the pedants, would be the formula boys in the lit. comp. racket!

. . . the passages on Rimbaud, Nelson, Einstein . . . capture your meaning exactly and communicate it by marrying the idea to the expression. That I can't do; that is my limitation; that is why I ought to stick to check-lists unless some day the spirit moves me again as it did in the chimney piece— which even though my best has still the Ph.D. stigmata all over it. This is to discount your very kind and charitable remarks on the Proclus thing as well as to drive home by personal illustration what I meant in the paragraph above.

In the third letter Olson had proposed a collaboration between us in editing an anthology of Melville criticism; to this idea I was obliged to reply that I had already made a tentative commitment in another quarter. Harrison Hayford, I told him, had thought of such a book "at the same time I did."

We both took preliminary steps with different publishers; we happened to compare notes; we tentatively agreed last summer to join forces and collaborate; I have done nothing on it since and have not heard from him, but suppose with this other book and the *Omoo* job [an edition for Hendricks House] in the mill that he hasn't either. I have rather run out of steam on this, though might get it up again in the summer. Suppose I let you know whether Harry wants to proceed, defer, or withdraw, and then we take up the matter ourselves if he withdraws? I have no idea how serious he may still be on it, but I feel obligated unless and until released by him. As for doing it with you, it would be fine for me—but would you really want to drag Sealts along on it?

Nothing came of any of this; the first full-scale collection of Melville criticism was not to appear until 1967: *The Recognition of Herman Melville*, edited by Hershel Parker.

As for his fourth letter, with its praise of my note on Melville, Proclus, and Emerson and its suggestion that I think of a major book on Melville's reading, his writing, and his life, I had this to say on these particular topics:

> I accept your gig on the Emerson-to-Melville-to-Proclus; I cannot accept your praise of the Proclus article as commensurate with the article itself (jerked out of my dissertation . . .). And for reasons stated above, I cannot accept your invitation and urging for me to do a book I am not prepared to do. By *prepared* you mean that I see and feel certain things, sense certain things, and know certain things which validate and support the intuitions. Yes, with limitations. But to do what you propose a man needs a desire, a compulsion, and a readiness which I do not now have, and without it I would not attempt such a task. If I ever have that compulsion I'll probably set about *a* book, perhaps not that one; meanwhile, aren't you, of all of us, not excluding anyone, the man to do it? I am not being modest or coy or nice here, this is what I think; this is what I ask.
>
> I had better stop here. I am late in answering; I'm sorry—I wrote when in more than one way I was ready to, and I hope you will answer when you are ready to. Thank you for all the letters, and for making me write this one.

From Olson I heard nothing directly until after his review appeared: in the *New Republic* for 8 September (pp. 20–21) and 15 September (pp. 17–18, 21) 1952. I must have written him after reading the review, but my letter or postcard has apparently not survived; his own postcard of 12 October, mailed from Washington, implies that he had heard from me:

> Ya. Only—you shld have had the mss, they so garbled Part I: not only the errors you cld see (like making poor [Walter] Bezanson equivalent to *Moby-Dick*!), but the way the scare-de-cats cut out swipes at THE ENEMY! (Fact is, I was more proud of Part I, it did have, in mss., such proportion!)
>
> OK. Say more. (Back home, & files on Brooklyn in hand!)

One "error" Olson didn't mention appears in the very title of both installments: "Materials and Weights of Herman*n* Melville." I infer from his complaint about "the scare-de-cats" that Part I as he drafted and submitted it must have epitomized many of his fulminations against "THE ENEMY" in his letters to me of six months before. What survived the *New Republic*'s cautious copy editing is obviously far less specific than those letters had been, both in their blasts against bad scholarship and in their bitter personal animadversions, though the published text does retain Olson's blanket objection to "the soddenness of the scholarship of the new edition of *Moby-Dick* and the perverseness of thinking in *Melville's Quarrel with God.*" Over against these American books Olson sets an English study of Melville given him by a friend, *The Spirit above the Dust* by Ronald Mason (1951), praising not only "its intelligence and limpidity" but also "its decency, its seriousness and the deftness of its proportion."

Whatever Olson may have written originally about Thompson's book, his verdict on *Melville's Quarrel with God* is clear enough from the fourth paragraph of the published review: "this Mr. Thompson has written a 450-page book on the subject of Melville and God—and has given only four pages to *Clarel!*" As for the Hendricks House *Moby-Dick* and its editors, Olson had "toyed with the notion of using this space to try to establish Some Principles Toward a Correct Editing of Moby-Dick, as severe a list of such simple demands as, say, George Lyman Kittredge might have expected from anybody doing a book on Chaucer" (p. 20). This sentence will be recognized as a simpler version of what he had written me on 7 March about laying down "SOME FIRST PRINCIPLES TOWARD . . . EDITING" Melville's works— even to his use of Kittredge on Chaucer as a standard of scholarly excellence. In that same letter, it will be recalled, he mentions several scholars who had "done clean work" on Melville; in the article he names most of them again, adding F. Barron Freeman and Walter Bezanson to his earlier list and scolding the Hendricks House editors for overlooking in their commentary the two chapters on Melville in D. H. Lawrence's *Studies in Classic American Literature.* In one of his closing paragraphs in Part I Olson cites Lawrence as "the one man of this century to be put with Melville, Dostoevsky and Rimbaud (men who engaged themselves with modern reality in such fierceness and pity as to be of real use to any of us who want to take on the postmodern)" (p. 21).

When he conceived his review, according to a paragraph in Part I, Olson's larger objective was "to bring the total Melville picture into some sort of focus, and to offer whatever insights five additional years of work of my own might bring to correct or add to the measurement of Melville I offered in *Call Me Ishmael.*" Having discussed Melville scholarship in his first installment, Olson turned in the second (that of 15 September: Part II) to an assessment of "Melville's importance, greater than ever," to a twentieth-century reader. It lies in three factors, he goes on to say. The first is Melville's "approach to physicality," illustrated by praise of a chapter of *Moby-Dick* Olson had reread early in March while examining the new edition. That chapter is "The Tail," of which he had written so glowingly to me on 7 March, citing both Homer and Rimbaud as he does here (p. 17). The second factor is Melville's "address to character as necessary human force"; in discussing it, Olson draws on his letters of 7 and 17 March—including his reservations about Melville scholars who exploit "contemporary disciplines like those proceeding from Freud and from Marx." (In March he had specified Arvin and Chase; neither is named here.) In one passage worth quoting he expands on what he had written to me about "The Specksynder" chapter of *Moby-Dick* and its reflection of Melville's reading in Goethe. Now, acknowledging Luther Mansfield's demonstration, in the Hendricks House edition, of the influence of *Dichtung und Wahrheit*, Olson observes that

the sultanism that Goethe enabled Melville to expose by way of Ahab leaves such achievements of Melville only prophetic, like his discoveries in *Pierre* which the Freudians find pioneer or those meta-physic ones in *Moby-Dick* which Jung has acknowledged. In "The Specksynder" passage [Chapter 33] Melville even uses just such signal words of recent political and economic fact as "dictatorship" and "centralization" ("the plebian herds crouch abased before the tremendous centralization"). (p. 18)

Olson is at his strongest when he comes to discuss Melville's "application of intelligence to all phenomena as *the* ordering agent—what [Robert] Creeley and I have elsewhere called the Single Intelligence." This is the third factor in Melville's present-day importance as Olson assesses it; what Olson has to say, distilled directly from his March letters, deserves generous quotation here as the end product of his thinking in mid-1952 about Melville and also about modern man. "Melville can stand examination and more serve us," Olson writes, in what he calls "more thorough depths of his engagement with what men are—less substantive, and more to do with the morality implicit in form."

In creating the anti-hero Ahab and in trying to go beyond him, Melville put himself squarely up against the hero, and thus at the heart of narrative and verse now. I throw down the proposition that Billy Budd is a Christian Hero (it is an oxymoron: a Christian can only be a saint). And it is as perverse of the Neo-Christian critics to read Melville's Christianity their way (to fail to see what *Billy Budd* cost him) as it is for Marxians and Freudians to put Melville's pains their way. For Melville grasped the archeological man and by doing it entered the mythological present. *Moby-Dick* is the evidence. The rest of his work is the defeat which is still our own. (p. 18)

In developing his idea of Ahab as anti-hero Olson draws at length on what he had written to me about Melville's negative capability, about his attitude toward Nelson, and about Melville and the example of Rimbaud. First comes Melville's "negative" confrontation of "any good or evil" as Olson sees it in *Moby-Dick:*

> Melville already knew what none of the moderns today yet know by having, in the anti-hero Ahab, confronted any good or evil negatively, and the rest of his work was a huge effort to do it the other way—to achieve personage instead of characterization. He did not see man as measure of man (Ahab got him over that Renaissance stile) but as limit. Thus he had the totalness to lend any of his creations such insides that only in his work among the moderns (not in Joyce's, say) can any of us involved in the postmodern struggle find lessons proper to the dimensional rather than the essential problem of the Hero (all that I read is either the essence or the documentation, never the act). (p. 18)

Then Olson repeats his complaint to me that Mansfield and Vincent had put Melville's use of Nelson "in such flatness as: Nelson was 'one of Melville's greatest heroes,'" adding now that the text of *Billy Budd* "shows how bitterly Melville felt his failure to give Nelson (or Billy, for that matter) the proportions, sufferings and relevances he knew man as hero to be."

This observation prepares Olson for his concluding paragraph. The "failure" he detects in Melville's characterization of both Nelson and Billy Budd serves to mark

> that limit of Melville which might also be seen to have been Rimbaud's, that both of them, in wholly differing ways, were prevented from work beyond what they did do (what cannot be said of Dostoevsky or Lawrence except in a dull absolute way) by an exasperation that a reality equivalent to their own penetration of reality had not come into being in their time. They both had, in themselves, manumitted man from the inaccurate estimate of reality men have had to go by since the Ionians. Both had seen ideality for the discrepancy it is. There are signs that Rimbaud had been so fierce as to come to totality, the condition of the Hero. Melville couldn't; the appeal of Christ was so strong on him. But he knew. For he had got as far as Ahab in the attack against organization or false form in men, society, or nature. Christ did stay so much the image of perfection to Melville, who had gone so far back into the nature of things that he had also given men their first image, since the biblums, of Chaos or Pre-Form, the Dragon as White Whale. In any case, the debate in his nature rove Melville, and left the job he was so much the most capable to do still to be done. He was too American to have the logic Rimbaud had—to quit, and to make money. (pp. 18, 21)

1953–1965

Another year passed before Olson and I were again in touch. On 7 October 1953, he wrote to me from Black Mountain:

my dear m. s. :
catch me up on what's doin' in the melville buiseness, won't you, please?
i think i last heard from you as of the N[ew] R[epublic] article (nice thing abt that was, that, last spring, [Ronald] mason finally caught up with my remarks abt him—thru [Howard] vincent—and since, i have been in a lot of correspondence with him:
he's a very patriotic melville lover, and i have told him to keep his eye out for any of your work

What he wanted from me this time was "a newsletter—all yr own acheivements [sic], plus any gossip of how the professors etc. continue to whack the Old Man"; he particularly wanted to know about "Murray's book" on Melville and "any further thots in yr own mind abt that book i suggested you were the precise one to do??????"

Olson's letter was forwarded to me in Massachusetts, where I had gone after a summer in England for a year's reading at Harvard as a Ford Fellow, concentrating on American social and cultural history; it was Nathan Pusey's first year as President of Harvard. Answering Olson on 23 November, I said that Dr. Murray seemed for the time to be out of sight, but I had seen the Metcalfs and read a paper Olson had sent them on Melville's "Bartleby," written by one of his students. I had "done nothing on HM except a little more tinkering with my work on the lectures." The Hendricks House edition of Melville was

131

"stirring again," I had been told, but I was dubious about the actual publication of any more volumes—"including my long-waiting one"— beyond the two said to be in production: *The Confidence Man*, edited by Elizabeth Foster, which indeed was published in 1954, and *Clarel*, edited by Walter Bezanson, which was held back until 1960; my own work on *Stories and Sketches*, like several of the other volumes, was simply never issued by Hendricks. Apart from the edition, I could report that "[Merrell] Davis and [William] Gilman are editing the letters; [Harrison] Hayford is at work on a handbook of some kind; [Howard Horsford] has done what I hear is fine work on the 1857 journal." As for myself, the summer away from my desk and my fellowship year were giving me "a sense of perspective that I've long needed," I said, but the uncertain status of the Hendricks House volume was inhibiting any new projects: "Until I get the Incubus off my back, meaning *Stories and Sketches*, I dread to take on more writing."

I had hoped to see Olson while I was still on the Atlantic seaboard, as I saw Dr. Murray, whose lectures at Harvard I audited during the spring term. But Olson did not answer, and I did not write again before returning to Wisconsin. I suppose now that poetry rather than Melville had taken first place with him, and for poetry I was never the kind of resonator that he needed. More than three years went by until either of us was moved to resume the correspondence. On Sunday, 19 May 1957, he found himself unexpectedly typing a letter to me, and before I could answer he was writing another in longhand on the following Wednesday. Black Mountain College had closed, he was about to leave North Carolina, and "that Brooklyn thing" of years before was again on his mind.

Suddenly yesterday again talking to a 17 year old neighbor with whom I exchange arrowheads! (I have Cherokee points one can pick up here after any heavy rain, and he has Cata[w]ba points from over Statesville way) who wants to go to Harvard—

there it was: our secret—the books, Brooklyn. And I told him, where I had stopped (not mentioning the city nor your name) you had been stopped by the war

But, I sd, this man's list of what books Melville's library   is   than which

SO: *what is new??????????*

I don't imagine my movement will turn back BUT Black Mt College has closed, I am the only one here to sell it off against debts and soon that will be over so I am planning the next step (s)

Actually I shall try to go to England to one small old West England port to pick up one line of one of the *Maximus* poems!

But I shall also be north for the first
time in so many years (almost, indeed, since you came to see me on 4th
ave, just before the Washington move!)

and I was wondering: maybe I'd stick my finger in to that Brooklyn thing,
maybe

In other words, what is it there? and (2) wld i in any way upset any apple-
cart if i did?

Wld you bring me up to date?

The letter of 22 May is more specific, and more important to me for
its frank acknowledgment of something I had long suspected: Olson
had never told me all he had learned about the sale of Melville's library—and now at last he had come across documents that drove the
point home for him. "Brushing up (in anticipation of yr reply)," it
begins, "I am aghast to find one piece of info. (on the *back* of a card)
whc I have no memory of having passed on to you"; an enclosure
transcribes it:

#1   H A Farnell's diary
        Feb 25, 1892 "Mr [John] Anderson telegraphed me to come †to↓ see
                a library—Went with him to Mrs. Melville 104 E 26ᵗʰ st &
                bought the lot for $120"

&
#2   James A.H. Bell [died Feb 2, 1901]
        "Presented 10,425 volumes to 'The Brooklyn Library'
        June 30, 1898"
                        !

                        IT SHOULD BE A PIPE
                        —for two of us!

The letter then continues: "†also have (in package marked 'To be held
for Sealts')↓ Wegelin's original letter to me May, 1934, on the details
of the sale: which is much more interesting & truthful than his Colophon article!" Olson's reference was to Oscar Wegelin's essay "Herman Melville as I Recall Him," which had appeared in *The Colophon*
in the summer of 1935. To compound matters, he had further information about the provenance of one volume, Melville's copy of Robert Southey's *Oliver Newman*, which he "didn't send in 1950?" (The
question is his; the answer was no, he had not.) Finally, Olson concludes,

I also find curious mention of book titles in my notes which will only bear
fruit by checking against the Bell Collection——WHEN DO WE START??!!

It
would be the craziest if you were East this summer, & I was up there, & arm
in arm we picked that crazy thing up, after 23 years for me & 16 pour
vous! Fondly & awaiting yr word, Olson

Olson's two letters "after long silence" caught me during "a siege of
the MUMPS," as I told him on 10 June 1957, which had struck just in
time for final examinations; I was expecting galley proof shortly on
my first book, *Melville as Lecturer* (1957), and had agreed to collaborate with Harrison Hayford "on a new edition of *Billy Budd* intended
to go way beyond [F. Barron] Freeman on both text and analysis."
Olson had mentioned a projected paperback edition of *Call Me Ishmael;* I was pleased, and replied that students would then "stop wearing out my copy and library's (which gets periodically stolen—real
tribute!)." As for Brooklyn, I was "delighted to hear that . . . you're"
proposing to tackle the job once again." When I had visited the new
building of the Public Library, I went on to say,

I was put off with the story that lots of things were still crated after the move
. . . , but that I would be notified by letter when I could come back and do
the kind of digging I had spoken of. After hearing nothing for months I
wrote, as I remember, to the man I had talked with, but received not even
an acknowledgment of the letter if memory serves me right. But too much
time has intervened for me to remember just what happened and when.

Th[i]s whole Brooklyn thing is and has been really your baby, and if you
turn up crown jewels you should certainly make any and every use of them
you care to. In view of your kind invitation to join the invading party I
would, if I were closer to NYC and less hedged in by previous commitments,
say flatly right now, "Name the date," but it isn't quite that simple for me
nor is it altogether right that you should open prospective finds in advance
by ringing me in on the show.

Let's therefore put it something like this. Go dig when your schedule
permits, and Godspeed. If you find things, use 'em. If you find so much of
such moment that the physical task of filling the ore sacks is too much for
even your broad shoulders, send me an SOS and if I can possibly manage it
I'll catch the first submarine for Brooklyn with my shovel in hand. Whatever
you do, wherever you go, moreover, good luck, and keep in touch.

Olson did not answer my letter, and to the best of my knowledge
he did not go to the Brooklyn Public Library. The longest lapse in
our correspondence now set in, and during the late 1950's I lost track
of him altogether. These were years of intensive work on the Hayford-Sealts *Billy Budd* (1962), which we edited directly from Melville's
manuscript, providing extensive analysis and commentary. During
our last stint at the Houghton Library, Davis and Gilman, who had

since published the Melville letters (1960) and turned next to Emerson, asked the two of us to join them and other friends we had known at Yale in editing the new Belknap Press edition of Emerson's *Journals and Miscellaneous Notebooks*. In the fall of 1962 I was back in Cambridge as a Guggenheim Fellow to work on Emerson, and on 2 October, hearing from Henry K. Metcalf that Olson was in Gloucester, I wrote "to inquire whether in the course of the winter you would still like to go digging in Brooklyn for HM treasures." With the "earnest support" of William A. Jackson, the Houghton's Librarian, I was planning a revision of "Melville's Reading" in book form, I explained, and was already seeking additions and corrections. Then I raised an old question once again.

For years now we have written back and forth about really going after the possibilities in Brooklyn. In my case at least, this is the ideal year to do it. Are you for it? What sort of campaign would you envision—write first, go down in person, or what? And when?

If you say the word, I can easily come out to Gloucester at your convenience, or we'd be delighted to see you here. I'm at the Houghton most of the day; my wife helps me there in the morning. But the schedule is of our own making, and all we need is the word.

I look forward to seeing you.

Olson promptly replied with a brief note, mailed from Gloucester on 4 November 1962. He was "delighted to hear" from me, but would "need still a little more time" before going to Brooklyn: "I'm sure the way to do it is to walk in there, not inquire ahead of time." Although he promised to write, I heard nothing until the following March in reply to a long letter of mine, which I had written from Cranford, New Jersey, on 10 February 1963 to report discouraging news about Brooklyn. As I explained, my wife and I had been called away from Cambridge by the illness of a relative, and our visit to the New York area had prompted me to investigate the Bell Collection once more.

For the better part of two full days I have worked in the main building of the Brooklyn Public Library—the building about to be completed years ago when I first approached the late Jesse Cross about Melville items. The first job, of course, was to find the right librarian; I think I did so in the person of Miss Louise Turpin of the History Division, who has jurisdiction over matters associated with the Bell Collection, and who put various underlings to work chasing down books and records. There is a manuscript catalogue of the Bell Collection in 65 bound volumes, each bearing the date of 1889 on the spine; the collection, as we knew, was presented to the library in 1898. In vol. 32 is a section on HM that includes newspaper clippings (obit, picture of "the late . . . ") and a list of 17 items in the collection: most of the novels, *Battle-Pieces* & *Timoleon*, and reviews as spotted in periodicals also in the collection. But there is no reference to anything from HM's library, and a sampling of listings in other volumes of the catalogue was of no help: whoever did the catalogue for Bell added no tidbits to any entries concerning provenance or association.

The other obvious gambit was to examine actual books. After all these years there are still a few boxes waiting to be unpacked—more accurately, to be culled and catalogued on the basis of hand-lists done years ago. I was given the lists, and in turn selected what seemed like possibilities—i.e., titles that might have interested HM. One of the male librarians began looking at these books themselves, and is in fact going to continue the search for me, but to date he has turned up none with an autograph or any of the marks I told them to watch for. I myself put in some time examining other titles off the shelves that came with the Bell Collection, but I too had no luck— and I *still* have failed to find there the copy of Warton's *History of English Poetry* that you once examined in Brooklyn. There may be some explanation in the attitude of one of the librarians I talked with. A volume with writing in it is a "mutilated" volume, he explained to me in magisterial tones, even if the writing is Shakespeare's—let alone Melville's. And it is the policy of the BPL to *discard* all mutilated volumes as rapidly as they can afford to. It is his opinion that if books that had been HM's ever did find their way to the shelves, either before or since the move to the new building, they have probably gone with the wind by now.

One other possibility also led to a dead end. For a long time, cards for books in the Bell Collection were marked with a "B"—thus simplifying the job of checking on a likely title: no "B" meant it had come to the library from some other source. But since the 1940's—I'm not sure just when—this practice has been discontinued. The Bell Collection has long since ceased to be regarded as a separate entity; I gather that there is a Bell endowment which interests the present-day librarians far more, as a source of funds for purchasing new books, than the old books left by Bell, which are admittedly being retired [read "destroyed"] to make shelf-room for items of interest to the modern customers. (High-schoolers seem to be in the majority.)

Having exhausted every gambit I can think of, I've now come to the reluctant conclusion that Brooklyn is probably a dead end—the only possibility . . . is that since the staff, or part of it, is now alerted, they may just by chance stumble upon something and write me about it. There seems to be no explanation for the fate of the Warton; if you remember, it eluded me in the 1940's also. Incidentally, there was one question I couldn't really answer when it was put to me by the librarian: "What makes you think that any of Melville's books went into this collection in the first place?" Beyond explaining that Mrs. Melville sold to a Brooklyn dealer, Farnell, I couldn't say— have *you* ever established a connection between Farnell and Bell?

This leads me to another point. Five years ago you startled me by a letter

(22 May 1957) with which you enclosed a quotation from *H. A.* Farnell's diary about his going with Anderson to buy from her; Wegelin's references are all to *A. F. Farnell.* (According to the 1892 Brooklyn directory, there was a third Farnell, F. W., with a shop in New York—4th Avenue.) Two questions: (1) May I quote the entry you sent, and if so, with what kind of citation? (2) Is there anything else relevant from the same source, wherever it may be? (In the same letter, as I recall, you said you had had a long letter from Wegelin giving a more accurate version of the transaction than what he printed in *The Colophon.*)

After adding a page of specific questions for Olson, I concluded by offering to show him the entire manuscript: "I'd be delighted to bring or send a copy to Gloucester or to see you in Cambridge, whatever your pleasure. Meanwhile, I'd like very much to know of any further ammunition that might occur to you with respect to the Brooklyn matter." In a postscript I added that I had bought Olson's *Maximus* (1960) "in the Square before Christmas."

This letter was not mailed until 14 February, after we had returned to Cambridge, when I enclosed a three-page trial draft of a passage intended for the projected book that dealt with the sale of Melville's library after his death. Olson's response, to put it mildly, was explosive. On the eighteenth he returned my letter and the draft, writing in pencil on the backs of both after scrawling his enraged comments in the margins and between the lines of my original typing. Much of his language was sulphurous. Some of the particular explosions were touched off by what I had said in either the letter or the draft, but there must have been still other provocations I cannot identify even when the writing itself is at least semidecipherable; perhaps Olson himself was simply erupting.[12] Here and there are points for a projected letter, but he managed to send only an unfinished note addressed to "My dear Merton" that begins: "(*No more paper: Terrible* news on B'lyn (same experience *here* Gloucester: . . . buying *new* books." Also enclosed, on both sides of two small envelopes (one originally addressed by Olson to Leroi Jones in New York but never sent), are additional words about what Olson called my "*misleading* report— & note—on the Brooklyn *sale* If you *haven't* got the persons (as well as the B plic Library) which I at first knew 1934—for X's sake get THE Notes on [Jeremy Taylor's] HOLY LIVING & HOLY DYING. . . ." These notes were in the second envelope, which along with other scrawled writing carries the notation "Everything sd here is *exact*" and asks me, "*Why* didn't you send me a copy of your *Billy Budd* WHY NOT? WHY NOT?"

On 2 March 1963, Olson followed all this with a handwritten note of seven pages in a very different key. His copy of the Hayford-Sealts edition of *Billy Budd, Sailor,* had just reached him from the University of Chicago Press, and he was writing to thank me for "the present of Billy . . . before I read any more than the introduction."

I do this also first to excuse, as I have wanted to, for 10 days is it, that scratch of any imaginable sort which you must have <throw> thought was not quite right when you probably did what one does when mail comes in, opened it.

It *was*, by the way, A—— Farnell, Court Street (it was the son H, whom I dealt with, and led me to forget †that↓ the father's name—the original buyer—was different. [I called there, a year ago, and H himself is now not any longer living]

I also wanted to remind you (I do think I must have told you) that the one Melville I examined in the Brooklyn library (in 1934, if I have the year right) was Thomas Wharton's Hist. of the English Literature, and though it lacked his autograph it was profusely (I'd recollect) marked with even I'd say notes in the margins.

Also, that (Thomas?) Fuller's (the Bishop's) Holy Living & Holy Dying was at that time in the hands of the Hennessey (I'm pretty sure) family [who were living around something like Cathedral Parkway or some such pretentious part of Brooklyn or any new part of new any city address. That, I recall, was autographed (with I think date of purchase [[70's?]] and sparse if any more than one or two, if that, any thing inside.

Also did that fellow Wegelin in his published article <say any> give any number of <the> books the Farnell cart took away from was it 17th St? In his †prior↓ letter to me he said "500".

I wish you very well and hope you will favor me again with all the news on our matter; and that there is recovery in the situation despite what you learned at the place recently. For example, could it be possible that, as I remember, there was a 'red' mark of some sort (like a star or asterisk possibly) on Bell books in <in a card for> the cards of the general catalogue †at that time I first went there↓??

and do you need to take that person's word (which sounds most modern and kitchen clean) about any books with markings being removed? That is, it is my experience that books such as Herman Melville would have read would not too likely have been taken out by *any* reader in these recent 30 years, and thus that they had annotations be called to any †desk↓ librarian's attention (thus discarded)

Not at all to raise up the old labor in front of you! But at least to lay †out↓ before you some of the beliefs of my own mind that those Bell books etc

Well, to get word to you
Fondly,
Charles Olson

Three days later, on 5 March 1963, Olson had gone far enough into the new *Billy Budd* to send a few criticisms in another handwritten note. He didn't like our commentary on Melville's subtitle, "An Inside Narrative," which he thought misleading; he felt free to say so to me "(and I hope Hayford)" in view of the good things we had done, beginning with my essay on "I and My Chimney" so long before. "Well, don't mind if I play fly on Io's back, or something, because as you well know I do believe you work genuinely, and probably will for your lifetime and there is reason to give Melville the best of his own intention. . . . LOVE, & best wishes [& nice turn on me in the quote on Baby Budd!]" This last reference was to a passage that Hayford had contributed to the Editors' Introduction; Olson's compliment illustrates not only his graciousness but his recognition that our editorial scholarship had led to a significant critical generalization: as Melville developed the manuscript of *Billy Budd* he consistently rendered dramatically what at earlier stages he had simply reported. "The point may be served," the Introduction reads, "by a quotation from Charles Olson." In his "David Young, David Old" (1949), Olson had hailed F. Barron Freeman's publication of what he took to be an earlier short story by Melville that Freeman called "Baby Budd"; Olson considered it more dramatic than *Billy Budd* as Melville left it at his death.

In expanding the story, Olson declared, Melville "worked over and over as though the hand that wrote was Hawthorne's, with his essayism, his hints, the veil of his syntax, until the celerity of the short story was run out, the force of the juxtapositions interrupted, and the secret of Melville as artist, the presentation of ambiguity by the event direct, was lost in the Salem manner." Actually, as we have shown, *Billy Budd* developed in almost the opposite way, from exposition into dramatization. Yet the terms of Olson's criticism, if not the conclusions, are highly relevant. (pp. 35–36)

I replied to Olson's two letters on 17 March, explaining that "a copy of *Billy*" had been on hand for him "since September, in the expectation that I would be seeing you shortly; since we didn't get together, and you weren't sent a review copy, I would have mailed one from here if I hadn't just run out. Hence the copy from Chicago." I assured him that in a second printing we would be correcting the sentence he thought misleading, together with several minor slips that had escaped us in proofreading; I was "pleased *you* were pleased about the 'turn,' as you call it." Then I took up various matters related to the projected book on Melville's reading, including questions raised in my letter of 10 February that had provoked what I have called Olson's "eruption." Enumerating various bits of information about the several Brooklyn booksellers named Farnell, I wrote:

Do you see why *I'm* a little confused?

It looks to me as though the key to the whole puzzle may lie in your "package marked 'To be held for Sealts'"; I hope you still have same and can put your hands on it! Was it "the son H" who showed you "H A Farnell's diary"? If so, *when?* And what do you suppose has become of the diary itself? And what about "Wegelin's original letter . . . May, 1934, . . . which is much more interesting and truthful than his Colophon article"? Anything that would sharpen and clarify what I set down about the sale would be *most* welcome, since the draft as it stands is admit[t]edly weasel-worded and I don't like it any better than you did when you fired it back to me last month with outraged comments!

Yes, I too believe there are Melville books in the Brooklyn Library—and so, I dare say, does my friend Miss Turpin there; it's one of the male librarians who gave me the business. But what to *do* about the situation as it stands has me absolutely stopped.

In concluding the letter I proposed a face-to-face meeting "to catch up. . . . Do you come into Boston? Would you want a Gloucester visitor? I'm mobile." I also thanked him for both "the kind words on *Billy,* which now seems like something done years ago; thanks too for the jabbing, past or to come, wherever needed."

To my four-page letter came an undated handwritten reply, written in pencil on the backs of what I had sent and the envelope originally enclosing it.

My dear M: Why not tell *the* FORD [FOU]ND[A]T[ION] there are the '*bulk*' of 500 of HM's own personal books—with his *notes*—in the B.P.L.: and that you are the man to lead a *search team* to find them as truffles are found by pigs with rings in their noses, such rings & pigs' time to go through the 5 million books ⎸(the no.⎸ reduced by yr sagacity) TO BE PAID FOR BY THEM?

Or—(2)—using the fact that you are about to 'tell the whole story', *which will leave the Library open to losses of Grreat value,* why not ask the *Board* of the BPL to put a staff at yr disposal to do as told??

Or (C) how many days have you got to take range on sd *bulk?*

From my own experience once you get into the 'swing' of it—had yr wind up—you'd be *surprised*

OK. I shld think—if you tell me that a H. A. [Farnell] shows 1892—that the H A I dealt with (spring, 1934(?)) did mean *his* father, & that A F may have been the older brother & firm name ⎸*in margin* [sticker on #343 *proves* business name was A F- F]⎸ (—or at least 'boss' so Wegelin had it that way, but I'd *trust* my quote of the telegram, remembering that H A 19[3]4 either looked that diary up at home (I don't 'feel' he showed it to me. [If you

wanted to, go by the store—it's still there—mostly stationery & office supplies—& an *old* geezer fr at least H A 1934's period, is there—& *might* have
memorie[s]

Enclose my two earliest—& last (except for coffee with him in between)—
communications fr that bug *Wegelin*

PS/ You *ought* by the way—though this is my 'feeling'—mention or give
great credit to the memory of John Anderson for making this whole 'get-
ting-there' possible. He was a most distinguished man (did a *beautiful* book
on Turner's drawings, built I think, on his own collection) & was what today
is Parke-Bernet & was Anderson Galleries; he was (as against all others I
looked & looked on, to find out) *most* courteous gracious & generous—and
little fart Wegelin wld never have come back from mosquito-land (meaning
↑the↓ Jerseys) if it hadn't been for Anderson's *valuable* memory. . . .

By the way—*don't* you have in mind [who's Emerson ? ? ? ? to do the *real*
book: a study of HM's reading ? ? ? based on known books owned, & his
notes ? ? ? in them? My God his job in [Emerson's] Conduct of Life alone is
enough to *reform America*

PLEASE ANSWER ME ON THIS. With what you have done—plus the interest of
what [you] did on *Chimney* . . . etc——you are AN IDIOT not to bring—or
come to rassle with——*this* is one of the most important book[s] BY MELVILLE
which is sitting around waiting to be RELEASED

And I'd be *happy* (even tho they have been in the rain, but I *think* are still
legible—actually only musty) to give you my 5 × 8 cards of *all* his notes
(and located page & line-wise to the edition used by him) in the books of his
which were known to me (to date whatever. But it wld enable you to work
anywhere eventually[?] (that is, if they are still READABLE! (meaning, not my
hand-writing, which I then did decently I *think*

etc

BUT THE THING IS:
    are you or are you not contemplating such a book??
I can assure you (1) no such thing etc

&

      (2) no man more interesting than it be done on—<a>
   & (3) <and> an evidence of anti-taxonomic knowledge
which <is> wld show something very few readers—or anyone else—*guess*
goes (went (was done by—

     & *so far* I have seen no USE made of his notes
which comes within distance of what *lieth* therein (due to (1) timidity (2)
academicism & (3) the horrible *fallacy* of comprehensiveness (which, in 20th
[century], replaced comprehension[?].

Please rush reply
I am *shocked*—(EMERSON!

now suddenly dawns on me: if Farnell put stickers in books, *is another way*
to check BPL—(tho I *believe* he wldn't have done that until *after* the open

table sale which was the way the '500' were dumped (acc. to H A F 1934)—&
that Daniel Bell, one & biggest of 5 <cust> choice customers (inc. Hennessey) wldn't have liked such stickers in their books. *But* it *is* a thing to use with
Ford Fndt BPL yrslf

Once again Olson had surprised me with new information—especially about "the open table sale" at the Farnell shop. While still absorbing his letter and the notes he had sent me, I mailed him two
items, the Melville number of *Modern Fiction Studies* (Autumn 1962)
and a "Directory of Melville Dissertations" compiled for the Melville
Society by Tyrus Hillway and Hershel Parker (1962). Then on 2 April
1963 I replied to this latest letter. "Among several enclosures," I
wrote,

you'll find all the notes you sent plus a carbon copy of my typed transcription of most of them. On the transcript are a few comments and queries—
every time I went through, I spotted something else.

Also enclosed are two copies of the latest of many drafts for the revised
Check-List [of Melville's Reading]; again, every time I went at it in the light
of your notes, another juxtaposition lit up something new. Even though I've
been working through three or four removes, I've a feeling I'm *beginning*
to get some sense of what really happened. Did Merwin and Bangs perhaps
go *first* to 26th St when the value of the estate was being determined? If so,
they set a higher value on the books—or somebody did—than E[liza-
beth] S[haw] M[elville] seems to have realized: $600. It's significant that the
books weren't *auctioned.* The fact that they were not seems to me to light
up the comments of both Wight (a fine man, whose word I'd bank on) and
Harper, whose description of the library (my note 13) rings true even if one
wonders about how much he really remembered about HM. I'm inclined
to think now that ESM really *peddled* books.

(This raises unpleasant thought that what she kept may have been partly
what the buyers declined! But why *did* she keep what she did—as against
revealing books like Wight's copy of HM's Byron, which I recall as a set she
shouldn't have let go.)

On the draft—the copy for you—are some further notes, including a
point I want to restate here. The Farnell business is *yours. I will print only
what you are willing to see printed, in a form that meets your approval,* or I won't
go into it at all. If you spot *anything* that you want cut or altered, or if you
think of anything to add, in either text or notes, please indicate it on the
second copy and fire it back; I will proceed accordingly before things go any
further.

If this or a further revision does seem printable, I have two further gam-
bits in mind. Since I was recently told that Wegelin is still alive, I'm attempting to find out whether he's still in New Jersey; if so, how would he react—
assuming he isn't now merely senile—to his story in the context of the other

information? (Incidentally, the biggest discrepancy between what he wrote you and his *Colophon* article is in the matter of whether or not there were signatures in the books that went to Farnell.) My other idea is to have one more go at Brooklyn, armed with the written-up story so as to drive home the point once more that BPL ought to be really digging for its treasures.

What about a go at the present Farnell establishment? Do you suppose the diary ⎰etc.⎱ is still around? (Your note to me says you think Henry F. didn't actually show it to you.) Also, as I read your note-card, it sez "A". . . .

I turned next to the materials I had mailed Olson, which would give him "some notion of the tone of recent work" on Melville, singling out for special comment a Harvard dissertation then in progress: "Melville's Marginalia" by Walker Cowen, with whom I had been exchanging information as I worked to revise "Melville's Reading." Cowen's project, as I knew, had already begun to assume massive proportions: though he hadn't yet "tackled all of the books at Harvard" or visited more than one or two of the other libraries with Melville holdings, he had told me that he "already has amassed 1000 pages of typescript!" (I had been urging him to make photographs or photocopies of Melville's markings and marginalia rather than typed transcripts.) How Cowen's ambitious compilation might bear on "any other project involving M's reading" I didn't know, though the question of course concerned me. "As for that book you keep saying I shld someday write," I told Olson, "I don't honestly think Cowen's transcription service is going to cut others out—me, you, or anybody else—but instead may actually *help* by doing much of the drudgery and bringing raw material together for convenient reference." In conclusion, I called Olson's attention to three new paperbacks issued by Corinth Books, one of them Bruce McElderry's 1963 edition of Owen Chase's *Narrative of the . . . Shipwreck of the Whaleship Essex* with plates reproducing Melville's notes in his surviving copy and what I called "pats on head" for Olson.

Then on 15 April I wrote Olson again, reporting that I had recently "talked to Mrs. Wight of Chatham," Massachusetts, "whose late husband bought the Byron items from Farnell." She had told me two things he should know:

1. Wight himself lived right around the corner from the Farnell store in Court St., was a good friend of the son, Henry, whom she also remembers, and—as she put it—"educated himself" by reading for hours on end in the Farnell store and off the Farnell shelves. I am sorry that I didn't lead the conversation more in that direction when I talked with Wight 15 years ago.

2. Mrs. Wight, nee Stallknecht, was a neighbor of the Henry Thomases

in the Oranges before she married, but the families were not well acquainted. She says it was "common knowledge" that Melville was mistreated by his family, and used to shut himself up in his room to get away from them. (An interesting variation on the usual theme, which puts the shoe on the other foot.) I tried to get more details, but could not keep her on the subject without putting ideas into her mouth—since I expect to talk with her again, I thought no information preferable to managed misinformation.

In one of Byron books is notation '103 E 10th St.' Does that address jibe with anything concerning HM? It doesn't for me. I've checked Davis-Gilman ed. of *Letters*, which I brought with me, but not Leyda's *Log*, which is in Wisconsin—will look in <Houghton> Widener [Library].

My sister-in-law [in New Jersey] reports no Wegelins now in Roselle, N.J. I am going to Pittsfield again. . . .

Shall I go back to Brooklyn—B[rooklyn] P[ublic] L[ibrary] and Farnell shop?

Olson replied in a penciled letter postmarked 10 May 1963; the envelope is endorsed: "Sorry to have delayed this so long. Hope all goes well. (Received all)." The letter itself, which crossed one of mine dated the twelfth, was another blow, as my own had evidently been to Olson himself. His animus against Wegelin—whose published article I could not simply disregard—led him to reject the latest draft I had sent for his comments, but not to suggest a better way for me to handle the discrepancies in Wegelin's various accounts and the contradictions between Wegelin and what Olson had learned from Anderson and Farnell. "It breaks my heart," he began,

that *again* you follow the tribe and give Wegelin such a place in the story—a secondary figure with a secondary story, in the face of real events——and if you let this stand this then will become the record. It is intolerable, to my *mind*. I don't know what to do to see if I can get you back to the story as *original research*

Any more (2) than I think *right now* you are *yourself* (under a Foundation grant) doing the most *obvious* possible *original research* yrself— like planting yourself in Brooklyn & hitting that Library where (what I mean by having the thing *to be hit* in front of yourself:

are you or are you not interested in bringing *more* of Herman Melville's *own* actual thing into re-existence? ? ?—like, under the Olin Fellowship—in *Economics* mind you— dug out for me from Wesleyan by *Wilbert Snow* the moment December 1933 [my MA thesis Wesleyan [Yale] 1933 was on the growth of <Mel> etc, & had in it the direction to go & find out more direct materials of Mr Melville's habits] it became clear (at Mrs. Metcalf's that there was books ... thus financed Dec–Jan 1933–4 Erward Matthews, Wesleyan, drove me to Mrs Osborne's & we 'found' the Shakespeare as well as 59 other volumes— *all of which Mrs Osborne allowed me to take away to Cambridge!* R[ecover?]ing

that stuff led me also to (mind you *financed by Wesleyan's* grant) go to New York, and stay in YMCAs going from bookseller to bookseller (inc. Lathrop Harper, who had no such lead) *until* I arrive at *John Anderson* (in Flatiron Bldg or thereabouts—23d st?] WHO REALLY REMEMBERED—& only thus, and after did that puppy[?] (whom only a phagocyte editor of *Colophon* [too much *bookishness* Mr Sealts] picked up on *later*) was *I* becoz of JOHN ANDERSON to dig out that little clerk & opportunist (whose memory you trust? & whom you quote *ahead* of such primary evidence as THE FARNELL VISIT??!
                                                                        Lord
place that little reporter in proportion, won't you *please*?
                                                                The leading per-
sons are: *Mrs Melville* / *John Anderson* / *the Farnell purchase*: the *known* sales fr Farnell's (inc. yr friend [Wight]) *but* still *right there Brooklyn* the BOOKS IN THE BPL
        OK. *Live animals* Mr Sealts—please: LIVE living things not these deleteri-
ous second things
                All right. In one word——
                                        Charles / Olson

My letter of the twelfth was mailed before I saw this letter from Olson and felt once again the hot blast of his displeasure. I had been to Chatham to see Mrs. Wight and bring back the volumes of Byron she had agreed to sell to the Houghton Library; I had also been to Pittsfield, where I found one book previously unlisted and also located "some but not all of the missing items mentioned in the original Check-List but now out of sight." Also, in the vault of the Berkshire Athenaeum I read a letter from Elizabeth Shaw Melville that put "another crimp in Wegelin's published story."

He said that Anderson took the remaining stock of *J[ohn]. Marr & Timoleon*—but Anderson didn't get *all* of 'em, because after ESM moved into The Florence [apartments] she wrote the librarian of the Athenaeum about copies of same she gave to round out the collection of HM's works there. She indicated that she had other volumes on hand had they too been lacking—and that remark cuts against the assertion by Wegelin (and before him by Oliver Hillard) that HM had no copies of his own works toward the end of his life. Surely one wouldn't say *he* lacked books that were in *her* hands.

I think I told you that Wegelin is no longer in Roselle, N.J., where he lived when he wrote you. Perhaps I can find him if I go to New York again this spring, as I may do. It would seem wise for me to go to the present Farnell store, and perhaps to have one more try at the Brooklyn library. But as I made it clear to you, I will not make *any* use of the information you gave me *without your express permission*.

Until I had Olson's concurrence, I went on to say, I was stymied in trying to place my manuscript with a publisher. "If you don't approve of the draft write-up I sent you in April, please say so," I wrote; "if you think it will do, with or without tinkering, please let me know." What I really hoped for from Olson, of course, was a quotable narrative of his talks with Anderson and Farnell that I could simply incorporate in the book, thereby setting the record straight and giving credit all around, wherever credit was due. When I read his letter of the tenth, however, I realized that though I had a narrative of sorts, it was scarcely the kind to be quoted, and mere paraphrase would never fill the gap. After much pondering, I finally wrote a letter on 15 May that needs to be given here in its entirety, since it recapitulates the whole story of our relationship as it had developed, faltered, and now seemed about to close.

Your letter, which crossed mine, has been here a couple of days. I have torn up the beginning of several replies. We are not communicating, and haven't been since last fall, with a few exceptions. If it's my fault, I'm sorry. Obviously you and I are—and you will say Thank God!—not the same breed of cat. You don't play in my league, or I in yours; we've known that. But neither of us is likely to change at this point. I have at least tried to play absolutely straight with you, whether you like my game or not; it would be insulting on my part to be anything other than straight, and I think too much of you (and of myself) to stoop.

Some of your letters this year have been hard to take; probably you have been infuriated with mine—there's evidence that you have been. But the hardest thing of all, for me, was your statement in this last one, *made for the first time* since we met 23 years ago, that you yourself talked *with John Anderson*.

Here I was flatly *wrong*, as I now see; I had forgotten Olson's reference to "lovely old John Anderson" in his letter of 24 May 1950, which I had supposedly reread before I began to write (as I told him below).

Then you give me hell for basing information on Wegelin's article (*all* I had in the 1948 version) and your own dealings with Wegelin (first given me this past winter)!

Of course I would prefer to play up Anderson. Ideally, I would prefer to quote him directly—but he was dead by the time I started on the original Check-List. Next best would be what he told you—but *what did* he tell you when he "really remembered," as you put it? You have given me *nothing* on this—though I would gladly quote every word of your conversation with him if I had it.

Instead of writing you, I have been sitting here reading over the whole batch of our correspondence since 1940. Do you remember how you enjoined me to secrecy about your finds? Do you remember how cagy I was when I first talked to Cross at Brooklyn—because this was *your* find, on which you had dealt me in, but which nobody else was to share? Do you remember in 1947, when I wrote you about *Ish*, that I told you the *Harvard Library Bulletin* had asked me to do the Check-List? I said then that I would be grateful for anything you cared to throw in, but would say nothing about the Brooklyn business unless we could go together and try to crack it[.]

You gave me material then, and told me to have a go at Brooklyn to prepare the gound. I did, but didn't get very far—and you were everywhere but here. Then I went to Wisconsin from Wellesley while the Check-List was still coming out, and we never did get to Brooklyn. Last fall, when I reached here, I wrote you in Gloucester bringing up once more the matter of a joint expedition, to which you answered "Will need still a little more time." Finally, with my year getting away, I went alone, with less than complete information, and got nowhere. Now that I've had your notes, I've been trying to get the story straight—but how can I be straight about information I don't have?

What *did* Anderson say? Did his version check with Henry Farnell's? What about Merwin and Bangs? How many books were there? How many did he take? What did he pay? Where they marked? Where did they go? What about the man from Ann Street? Did he contradict Wegelin on any of these points? *Was* Lathrop Harper involved somehow, or do you know definitely that he wasn't? (He told Leyda he was—and Leyda got me to write him, with the results you know of.)

As for Mrs. Melville's role, it isn't covered in the draft I sent you for the simple reason that I didn't send you everything in the new write-up. As in the 1948 version, she comes on stage first. The treatment of what she did is essentially the same this time, but works in facts I've since learned—e.g., what she gave Caroline Stewart, the Berkshire Athenaeum, etc.

As for "original research"—which you seem to think I've not done—, I thought the most important thing was first *to get the facts*, as fully and as accurately as possible, from whatever source. If the source was primary, so much the better; if it was secondary, credit and acknowledgment are imperative. I have been scrupulous about clearing with you not only the use but the *form* of everything that has come from you, and have urged you to add, subtract, or change anything that in any sense is not right. I urge it again now.

But Wegelin can't come out unless something goes in in its place.

And there the matter rests. If you prefer to pitch this into the fire and have done, that is your privilege. In that case, I have, it seems to me, only two alternatives. One is to forget the whole thing—as Harvard Press advises. The other is to let this section stand without anything of yours. Neither prospect pleases. Nor does the situation as your last letter presents it. Again, I'm sorry.

With this letter I felt that our strained relationship must either be eased or ended—I wasn't sure which; if it was to be ended, there was little I could do to fill the gaps still remaining in my tentative account of the sale of Melville's books. What I first saw of Olson's reply, postmarked 22 May 1963, was this postscript, written on the back of the envelope:

Please look my previous letter over for the *proportion* of acts, the *emphases* as of the sale, & its rediscovery—and particularly the point of all of it, the character of Melville's library/reading—and what notes or titles are *at this date* retrievable. That seems to me the nub of the problem

Inside were nine handwritten pages, again in pencil but in a tone very different from that of Olson's distressing letter of 10 May that I had found so difficult to answer.

Dear Mert, I guess I hear you on what you call the facts   And what I am hitting you on are (and you do again show the scrupulousness I have always valued from the moment you came into my office there then on 4th Avenue; as well as in such writing of yrs as the Chimney [and *did* you do that Tartarus of Maids analysis??[13] Please tell me, & if so do you have a copy? I had occasion to talk of that to some persons recently (also, if Bezanson has an extra copy of his *Clarel* thing—or was it ever published? is there a chance you cld dig me up a copy for further use?? Much obliged, if so: [one of the most valuable things yet, or possibly I am way off the pace (tho did you ever run into my review <of> in The Chicago Review, of Chicago book on Fine Hammered Steel of Woe [Milton Stern, *The Fine Hammered Steel of Herman Melville* (University of Illinois Press, 1957)]?[14]
    By the way also, has any one resolved the difference of Mat[t]hiessen's <&> or my reading of the sentence in the Shakespeare volumes on It †(madness)↓ & right reason extremes of woe (one ?[15]
                                        <Please>
You mustn't mind my hitting out at you; or abandon *any thing* on your project . . . : all you have done (and have there as is) breaks open anyway the 'Brooklyn' sale
                    [I can't add anything on Anderson except the leading fact that 1) he was the one sent for; 2) I found <th> my way to his door; †&↓ 3) he told me he thought Wegelin, who <was> †had been↓ then his runner, might add facts to the story—BUT, unless I am mighty mistaken [and you cld have checked that with the postmarks on those letters & cards I sent you (?] <I> Anderson told me Farnell, and I had already gone there, found what books I did, including the Wharton in the BPL—and still believe there are *many more* HM items right there   BPL   now to be discovered by one such as *you*
                    But look Mert: no reason for any strain between you and me. Maybe what you have up to now done is what <you> is the next step—

and satisfy yourself: do what you feel tells the story and by all means *go ahead*: don't let any of this . . . fault your progress /

every piece of work you have done is, to my mind, the decentest stuff on Mr Melville I see; and that's what counts

[I do feel you are carrying a lot more than a man can, and live in time with one man; but then I am ⌈a⌋ long-liver any way, and Melville seems to me a mountain men can gain by putting & putting their pick-axe into

Please anyway have my word on any thing you do—and very happy to have you come back and back on me as well as please keep me in touch with any & all results *which interest you* including especially your own *which interest me*

Charles

To what I called Olson's "handsome letter of last week" I responded with a postcard on 1 June, thanking him for "the word" and promising to "have another go at the write-up with your suggestions in mind." On 6 June I sent a second card to report receiving

a letter from the president of H. A. Farnell & Co., who was executor of H.A.F.'s estate. The diary of A.F.F. was not among the son's papers, nor has he seen it among the records of the firm, which he joined in 1906. Disappointing, but not surprising.

I thought you'd like to know I had made the appropriate inquiry.

By this time the fellowship period was drawing to a close, and there was much demanding work to be done on the Emerson project before I left Cambridge and the Houghton Library in early August of 1963. On first arriving from Wisconsin the year before I had of course written Olson to propose a meeting at his convenience, either in Cambridge or in Gloucester, and since then we had written back and forth about going to Brooklyn. But we had not met. Instead, there had been another long exchange of letters, as though I were still in Wisconsin, and a growing strain in our relationship that had threatened to end it completely. I should somehow have found the time to write once more before loading our belongings for the drive back to Wisconsin, but under many pressures I failed to do so. Then on 28 October Olson wrote me from Wyoming, New York, asking "What in the world did happen at the end of spring this year? was I the one who might have seemed to have let the garden gate slam, or something?" If so, he was sorry; he felt "as though things had suddenly cut off." In July, he said, he had been in Vancouver; now he was at the University of Buffalo "as Visiting Lecturer." His assignment there

suddenly included a criticism of <your> paper measuring Benito [Melville's "Benito Cereno"] by Aristotelian canons. Had a ball & it has started a few hairs

As I do (with your acceptance) regard you as the one I turn to, I should be extremely happy if you wld fill me in on what *you* take as work of recent time which makes sense or has value

Plus putting me on to where yr own work of last year is *etc*

As well that yr health & spirit be

My answer was delayed until 20 December 1963, at the close of a trying term at Lawrence. Just before the assassination of President Kennedy I had lost my voice, I told him, "and was home fighting bugs when all that happened." He "*must* have wondered what became of me—not only last spring but since [his] letter of more than a month ago." In Cambridge, I explained, we had discovered in June that "unilateral changes in the styling of vol. III of the Emerson *Journals*" undercut work already done on later volumes and required extensive revisions to volume V in July that disrupted the work schedule I had been keeping until then. We had come home in August to face major repairs on our house and to adjust to a new president and a new curriculum on campus; only in the last two days had I found time even to sort the Emerson and Melville materials I had been working on in Cambridge.

"What's going on in Melville? Lots of publishing," I told him, "but nothing to overturn all your convictions." I briefly characterized three recent books I had reviewed for *American Literature*, mentioned Hennig Cohen's two new editions of Melville's verse, and also cited "the only short piece I've seen lately that made me think": "The Shadow in *Moby-Dick*" by John Halverson in *American Quarterly* for Fall 1963 ("if you're feeling Jung enough"). The Modern Language Association, I said,

is trying to raise either government or foundation money to publish a "clear-text edition" of Melville comparable to the current Ohio State–Virginia Hawthorne: definitive text and textual apparatus, brief factual introduction, but no commentary. If it works out, the volumes previously done for Hendricks will be ignored, but stuff like the existing published letters, journals, lectures, and B[*illy*] B[*udd*] will be incorporated (cum permissions, of course), my unpublished work on the prose mss. will be updated, and all else will be redone from scratch. We'll see.

In conclusion, I apologized again for not sending "at least a card" and asked him "what goes on in Wyoming, N.Y."—a place which must really exist "if this reaches you there." It did; Olson replied with a card of his own on 6 February 1964—the last written communication between us. "Don't mind please," he wrote,

that I seem to be engaged here in so many different pursuits that I have been delayed in thanking you for your letter.—(I do find still that one of the hardest, & most valuable, forms of bibliography for scholars to offer—I dare say it does stem from keeping close to the letter, & probably exists mostly in bibliographies for courses actually given by the man, or in his own mind—but it is *the constantly fresh selecting bibliography* which men need from each other. So many thanks, & whenever you have any thing please shoot it across to me. Yrs, Charles (Olson)

I next heard from him by telephone late in the evening of 15 June 1965, when my wife and I were in the midst of packing for our impending move from Appleton to Madison and my new appointment as Professor of English at the University of Wisconsin. My typed note on our conversation reads:

Charles Olson phoned from the University of Buffalo to talk about our research into Melville's library; said visit of a man named Hatfield from California (Berkeley?) had set him going, and he called on impulse to see what I'm doing.

I told him about the Northwestern plans [for the Northwestern-Newberry Edition of Melville], my move to UW, etc.; we talked about the Metcalfs and Harry Murray. He is going to Italy; will be giving readings next winter, possibly in Madison, and may or may not be back at Buffalo.

Gloucester address is permanent; mail sent there will always reach him sooner or later.

The move to Madison took place that summer, with all the challenges of settling into a new location and a new position, and my correspondence soon fell sadly behind. Olson did not appear in Madison, that next winter or later, but I saw him once on television and thought him greatly changed—his eyes especially. I should have written him to report at least one piece of news: the University of Wisconsin Press accepted my *Melville's Reading* for publication in 1966. When the book was issued in the fall of that year I asked the Press to send a copy to Olson at 28 Fort Square in Gloucester with my compliments, but I received neither congratulations nor criticism from him in return—not even an acknowledgment. By that time more than twenty-five years had gone by since our single meeting in New York. Now at last "our secret—the books, Brooklyn" was out with publication of my book, and our long correspondence had finally concluded.

PART III
1965–1980

"Aye, he's chasing *me* now; not I, *him*. . . ."

Moby-Dick, Chapter 135

Melville's "Geniality"
(1967)

This essay, something of a sequel to my earlier study of Melville's Burgundy Club sketches, was contributed by invitation to *Essays in American and English Literature Presented to Bruce Robert McElderry, Jr.*, edited by Max F. Schulz with William D. Templeman and Charles R. Metzger (Athens, Ohio: Ohio University Press; copyright © 1967 by the University of Southern California), pp. 3–26. It was written in 1966, after I had begun teaching at the University of Wisconsin. During the late 1950's, while I was compiling material for the Notes and Commentary of the Hayford-Sealts edition of Melville's *Billy Budd, Sailor* (1962), I had collected passages from his earlier works that might throw light on his conception of Billy as "genial in temper"; the invitation to join in honoring Bruce McElderry with a *Festschrift* prompted me to explore Melville's notion of "geniality" in more breadth and depth. In 1971 Hershel Parker reprinted the fourteenth paragraph of the essay in his Norton Critical Edition of Melville's *The Confidence-Man: His Masquerade* (New York: W. W. Norton & Company, 1971), p. 331, under the supplied title "The Dialogue in Chapter 30." The present text reprints the version of 1967 except for minor revisions in the third paragraph, restyling of citations, and renumbering of notes.

"Melville's 'Geniality'" has had a mixed response from its readers. Alexander Kern spoke kindly of it in reviewing the McElderry *Festschrift* in 1969, but Marjorie Dew's reaction was strongly negative when she heard the abbreviated version that I read before the Melville Society at New York City in December of 1966. She later published a vigorous counter-statement, "Black-Hearted Melville: Geniality Reconsidered," in *Artful Thunder: Versions of the Romantic Tradition in American Literature in Honor of Howard P. Vincent*, edited by Robert J. De Mott and Sanford E. Marovitz (Kent, Ohio: Kent State University Press, 1975), pp. 177–194. Like the subject of Chapter 14 of *The Confidence-Man*, the point at issue between us is "Worth the consideration of those to whom it may prove worth considering." As I wrote to her in 1974, " . . . you think I overstate HM's inclination toward the genial; I hope I've also pointed to his equally strong feelings that geniality can be whaleishly alluring, deceptive, even destructive in a world full of man-traps under the daisies and populated by Goodmans and Claggarts. Conversely, I'll confess to thinking that you somewhat overstate the darkness and suffering, playing down 'mine infirmity of jocularity' which admittedly can betoken 'a gay, desperado philosophy.' One of my students (undergraduate) delighted me the other day by telling me she's planning a paper on Queequeg's pipe, which can be either a weapon or an instrument of genial fellowship as occasion may warrant; *there's* our man, I think, with his usual doubleness—not to say duplicity!" My conception of Melville's "doubleness" has since been extended by John Bryant, who at the 1977 meeting of the Melville Society in Chicago read a paper appropriately entitled "Genialist and Con-Man: The Comic Debate in 'Benito Cereno.'" And William H. Shurr discussed "Melville's Geniality Once Again" in October of 1981, when the University of Tennessee sponsored a conference on Melville to honor Professor Nathalia Wright on her retirement.

When completion of the Northwestern-Newberry edition of the writings of Herman Melville makes possible a full concordance of his "talismanic language,"[1] it will be found that the word "genial" and its cognates—"ungenial," "genially," "genialness," "genialization," and especially "geniality"—appear in some one hundred instances. Like other words he made peculiarly his own, such as the complementary pair studied in 1945 by R. E. Watters, "sociality" and "isolatoes,"[2] Melville's term "geniality" deserves careful attention, for it reveals one persistent strain of sensibility linking his years at sea, his career as an author, and the retrospective musings of his late private writing. "Despite the mythic identification of Melville with the tragic 'isolatoes' he created," as Edward Rosenberry has said, "he had a lifelong passion for the comforts of friendship and conviviality, founded about equally on a love of talk and a love of sharing his animal enthusiasms for food and drink."[3] Among his books it is *Mardi* (1849) that most fully expresses Melville's fondness for genial conviviality; it is *The Confidence-Man* (1857) that most caustically exposes its weaknesses and dangers. Even in his last years, when nostalgia for the idealized companions of earlier days marked much of his writing, he had praise for geniality as "the flower of life springing from some sense of joy in it, more or less," as he put it in his sketch of John Marr (1888).[4]

Because *The Confidence-Man*, of all Melville's works, has the most frequent references to "genial" characters, "genial" wine, and "genial" talk, including a long conversation on the subject of geniality itself,[5] it is the one book to receive closest examination here. First, however, a glance at Melville's use of "genial" in his earlier writings will be helpful in bringing out the principal associations and connotations that geniality evidently held for him. "The Paradise of Bachelors" (1855), written not long before *The Confidence-Man*, is an appropriate place to begin. This composition recalls the "genial hospitalities" Melville enjoyed at the Temple in London during 1849 (*Complete Stories*, p. 189)—in particular a "good, genial dinner" (p. 191). The modern Templar he salutes as "best of comrades, most affable of hosts, capital diner. . . . His wit and wine are both of sparkling brands" (p. 187). During the dinner,

as the wine ran apace, the spirits of the company grew more and more to perfect genialness and unconstraint. . . . It was the very perfection of quiet absorption of good living, good drinking, good feeling, and good talk. We were a band of brothers. Comfort—fraternal, household comfort, was the grand trait of the affair. (pp. 192–193)

To be genial for Melville was thus to be affable, comradely, even fraternal, enjoying the good drinking and good living that foster good feeling and good talk. Letters to his friends, especially Duyckinck and Hawthorne, express the same sentiments; in his books, eating, drinking, and smoking, as Rosenberry has effectively shown, repeatedly constitute "the thematic handmaidens of social intercourse."[6] *Mardi* in particular is filled with Rabelaisian feastings, its interpolated songs celebrating the "genial glow" of wine and the comfort brought by tobacco.

Except for *White-Jacket* (1850), with its admiring portrait of Jack Chase as a companionable man of "good sense and good feeling" (p. 16) and its enthusiastic praise of fraternal smoking (pp. 361–366),[7] the nature of Melville's writing after the exuberance of *Mardi* required relatively few passages in the convivial vein until "The Paradise of Bachelors." In *Moby-Dick* (1851), though Ishmael and Queequeg enjoy a "pleasant, genial smoke" (p. 51), Ahab is made to abandon his symbolic pipe, "this thing that is meant for sereneness," in the realization that on such a revengeful quest as his, "smoking no longer soothes" (p. 126); he lacks "the low, enjoying power" (p. 165). Save for Pip, who radiates "that pleasant, genial, jolly brightness peculiar to his tribe" (p. 410),[8] There is little geniality in the book, though occasionally Ishmael voices his "free and easy sort of genial, desperado philosophy," born of "that odd sort of wayward mood" in which a man "takes this whole universe for a vast practical joke," when "nothing dispirits, and nothing seems worth while disputing" (pp. 225–226).[9] The despairing young hero of *Pierre*, another of Melville's dark books (1852) which particularly anticipates *The Confidence-*

Man, comes to know this same mood—in sharp contrast with the optimism, cheerful good will, companionableness, and sterling charity that we are told marked him in the days of his boyhood (p. 324).[10]

There are scattered references to geniality in several of the magazine pieces that Melville wrote between *Pierre* and *The Confidence-Man*, but most of the stories are of a predominantly somber cast. Occasional touches of human kindliness and warmth are present, but the prevailing themes are poverty and sickness, failure and rejection, withdrawal and isolation—even naïveté and deception, as in *The Confidence-Man* itself. The poverty-stricken narrator of "The Two Temples," finished in 1854, longs to become part of some "genial humane assembly of my kind; such as, at its best and highest, is to be found in the unified multitude of a devout congregation" (*Complete Stories*, p. 160), but is rebuffed by the sexton of a fashionable New York church; Melville's satire seemed so pointed in its application that *Putnam's Magazine* declined to risk publishing the sketch. Following "The Paradise of Bachelors," with its celebration of wit, wine, and genial hospitality, "Jimmy Rose" (1855) describes a bachelor's unhappy downfall. Jimmy is "a great ladies' man" who never marries; his cheeks bloom with health and "the joy of life." But after his misfortunes, few of his friends except the narrator remember his cheeriness and sparkling wit in the old days of his great dinners, suppers, and balls, when his noble graces and glorious wine marked his "bounteous heart and board" (p. 244).[11] "Old wine" and a "comfortable pipe" (pp. 385–386) provide part of the warmth in "I and My Chimney" (1856), while in "The Apple-Tree Table" (1856) Melville deals with the eventful reemergence of a "sad little hermit of a table, . . . long banished from genial neighborhood, with all the kindly influences of warm urns, warm fires, and warm hearts" (p. 412). If bounteous hospitality, conviviality, and fraternal unity are outward signs of true geniality, humane warmth and kindliness are clearly its motivating spirit.

But there is another aspect of geniality, a negative one—and Melville never lets his readers overlook it. In "The Paradise of Bachelors," immediately following the "band of brothers" passage quoted above, comes the following observation:

Also, you could plainly see that these easy-hearted men had no wives or children to give an anxious thought. Almost all of them were travelers, too; for bachelors alone can travel freely, and without any twinges of their consciences touching desertion of the fireside.

The thing called pain, the bugbear styled trouble—those two legends seemed preposterous to their bachelor imaginations. How could men of liberal sense, ripe scholarship in the world, and capacious philosophical and convivial understandings—how could they suffer themselves to be imposed upon by such monkish fables? (p. 193)

From at least the time of *Mardi*, undertaken not long after his own marriage, Melville had repeatedly used bachelors—bachelors and sophomores—as his favorite examples of pleasure-loving immaturity and naïveté, as yet untouched by misfortune. It is so in Chapter 115 of *Moby-Dick*, for example, where the "moody" Pequod, outward bound, meets the Bachelor, a "glad ship of good luck" returning from a prosperous voyage.

"Come aboard, come aboard!" cried the gay Bachelor's commander, lifting a glass and a bottle in the air.
"Hast seen the White Whale?" gritted Ahab in reply.
"No; only heard of him; but don't believe in him at all," said the other good-humoredly. "Come aboard!" (p. 489)

As for "The Paradise of Bachelors," the earlier part of the sketch expresses honestly Melville's genuine love of "good living, good drinking, good feeling, and good talk." But its later paragraphs show his equally clear recognition that the genial way of living he describes, for all its fraternal comfort and warm attractiveness, implies a denial of the responsibilities and grimmer realities of mature life. This double evaluation carries over into *The Confidence-Man*, where spurious geniality is a peculiarly enticing bait for trapping the young or unwary among passengers of the Fidèle, the Mississippi steamboat evidently to be taken as a microcosm of contemporary society.

Geniality in *The Confidence-Man* is a principal element in those episodes involving two particular manifestations of the masquerading title character—"this apostle of geniality," as a reviewer at the time aptly described him, who beneath his affable manner is indeed what the same critic suspected: "an arch-imposter of the deepest dye."[12] These are the bogus stock salesman of Chapters 9–15, named as "Mr. Truman" by the herb-doctor in Chapter 20, and the "cosmopolitan" calling himself Frank Goodman who dominates the entire second half of the book, from Chapter 23 to Chapter 45. The seemingly open, warm, convivial manner of these two figures has an irresistible attraction for their fellow-passengers of a like disposition, though not for other characters less genially warm than suspicious, cold, and even misanthropic.

A quick résumé of the operations of the stock salesman will develop this point and set a pattern for studying the more important figure of the cosmopolitan. Entering the story with "genial jauntiness" (p.

51) as "president and transfer-agent" of "the Black Rapids Coal Company," the salesman successfully peddles his stock to three of his potential victims, though with a fourth he apparently meets defeat. In Chapter 9 a gullible young college student—appropriately, a sophomore, one fond of champagne dinners, cigars, and "fellows that talk comfortably and prosperously," falls easy prey to the salesman and his flattering remarks about the young man's caution and "genial humor" (pp. 51–56). In Chapters 10–13 a warm-hearted, genuinely charitable merchant is just as unwary—and unintentionally alerts the salesman to the presence aboard of his third victim, the miser of Chapter 15. But early in Chapter 10 the confidence-game does not work. In the ship's cabin the "ruddy-cheeked" salesman first encounters "a little, dried-up man, who looked as if he never dined," engaged in reading verses on a handbill thrown about the cabin:

> Alas for man, he hath small sense
> Of genial trust and confidence.

Though feeling momentarily "trustful and genial" after reading these lines ("not unlike a sermon," he says of them), the little man rebuffs each advance as the salesman invites him to enjoy a game of "genial cards" ("Somehow I distrust cards"), a bottle of wine, cigars, or story-telling, for all of these appurtenances of geniality are really foreign to his habits and disposition (pp. 57–59).[13] Thus Melville establishes his reader's association of geniality with mutual "trust and confidence," its absence with mistrust and suspicion.

In the later episodes involving the cosmopolitan, where Melville treats geniality at greater length and on a more philosophical level, this same general pattern also applies. The cosmopolitan makes his first appearance at the end of Chapter 23, which opens with the rifle-carrying Missourian called "Pitch"—a mature man of skeptical outlook but still one of Melville's extensive gallery of bachelors—meditating ruefully upon a bargain he has just concluded: a certain "man with a brass plate," agent of a "Philosophical Intelligence Office," has somehow managed to persuade him, against his previous experience and firm resolution, to hire a fifteen-year-old boy, sight unseen, and to advance money for his passage to Missouri. As the reader knows, the employment agent was really the masquerading confidence-man in another disguise. The Missourian, though now too late, correctly "begins to suspect him" and "half divines, too, that he, the philosopher, had unwittingly been betrayed into being an unphilosophical dupe" (p. 147). This man is obviously shrewder than the collegian and more suspicious than the merchant. How, exactly, had he been tricked?

Philosophy, knowledge, experience—were those trusty knights of the castle recreant? No, but unbeknown to them, the enemy stole on the castle's south side, its genial one, where Suspicion, the warder, parleyed. In fine, his too indulgent, too artless and companionable nature betrayed him. Admonished by which, he thinks he must be a little splenetic in his intercourse henceforth. (p. 148)

As the Missourian "revolves the crafty process of sociable chat" by which he fancies he had been duped (p. 148), he is roused by a "genial hand" laid on his "ungenial shoulder." It is the rosy-cheeked cosmopolitan, "king of traveled good-fellows, evidently," with his Nuremburgh pipe in hand, symbolically wreathed in tobacco smoke. Identifying himself not by name but as "a true citizen of the world," the "warm and confiding" cosmopolitan, in Chapter 24,[14] takes direct issue with the "unrosy" Missourian's "unprofitable philosophy of disesteem for man," charging that it springs from "a certain lowness, if not sourness, of spirits inseparable from sequestration." His remedy is conviviality. One should "mix in," he says, have a good time, and cure "sober sottishness" with a little judicious tippling, as a sick old woman was once cured by her doctor's prescription of "a jug of Santa Cruz" (pp. 149–152). The Missourian, surprised into interest by the anecdote, nevertheless prefers his customary jug of cold water to a jug of wine, thinking even "the too-sober view of life" to be "nearer true than the too-drunken" and finding "Rabelais's pro-wine Koran no more trustworthy than Mahomet's anti-wine one." The cosmopolitan, shifting his tactics, then proposes a walk among the other passengers, arguing that by natural law "men are social as sheep gregarious. . . . I say, mix with man, now, immediately, and be your end a more genial philosophy" (pp. 153–156).

At this point the irritated Missourian flings off the other's "fraternal arm," gestures with his own symbolic rifle, and cries out roundly against "any sly, smooth, philandering rat" (i.e., insincere man-lover) which may be plundering the Fidèle's "human grain-bin." But when the cosmopolitan counters by ambiguously praising the "humor" of Diogenes the Cynic above that of the openly man-hating Timon, the Missourian suddenly seizes his hand, squeezes it vigorously, and hails his companion as a brother misanthrope! "You are Diogenes," he exclaims, "Diogenes in disguise. I say—Diogenes masquerading as a cosmopolitan." The confidence-man professes amazement. Quickly retaliating, he labels the Missourian "an Ishmael" whom he had earnestly hoped to reclaim for the human race, and promptly moves away "less lightsome than he had come, leaving the discomfited misanthrope to the solitude he held so sapient" (pp. 156–157). In the prickly Missourian, once burned and now twice shy, he has met his match, and their encounter thus ends in a virtual draw.

The next episode, which also ends with the shrewd penetration—this time by the cosmopolitan—of another's disguise, introduces one more seemingly genial passenger: Charles Arnold Noble,[15] himself a Mississippi sharper in search of a victim, whose revealing countenance betokens "a kind of bilious habit" (p. 158). Here too occurs a discussion in which convivial geniality is proposed as a counterweight to misanthropy. Passing over Chapters 26 and 27, where Noble expounds "the metaphysics of Indian-hating" and relates in some detail the borrowed story of Colonel John Moredock, we find him concluding the latter account with the suggestion that the Missourian is an Indian-hater like Moredock. In such men Noble detects "something apparently self-contradicting," however, for "nearly all Indian-haters have at bottom loving hearts; at any rate, hearts, if anything, more generous than the average." Thus Moredock himself was "not without humane feelings. . . . He could be very convivial; told a good story . . . , and sung a capital song" (p. 175)—in short, he had the very attributes Melville associates with geniality.[16] But the cosmopolitan is dubious. Though ready to grant that the Missourian is not what he seems ("His outside is but put on"), and to assert that Pitch really loves men even while "snapping at them all the time," such a man is still no Indian-hater. As for the story of Moredock himself, its seeming contradictions strike the cosmopolitan as incredible.

"To me some parts don't hang together. If the man of hate, how could John Moredock be also the man of love? Either his lone campaigns are fabulous as Hercules'; or else, those being true, what was thrown in about his geniality is but garnish. In short, if ever there was a such a man as Moredock, he, in my way of thinking, was either misanthrope or nothing; and his misanthropy the more intense from being focused on one race of men." (p. 177)

As the cosmopolitan goes on to develop this line of thought, he brings sharply into focus the central issues of the book. For him, it is all or nothing: one must either love man or hate him, as in religion one must either believe or disbelieve. Misanthropy and infidelity are in fact coordinates; they spring "from the same root, I say; for, set aside materialism, and what is an atheist, but one who does not, or will not, see in the universe a ruling principle of love; and what a misanthrope, but one who does not, or will not, see in man a ruling principle of kindness? Don't you see? In either case the vice consists in a want of confidence." (p. 178)

In the conduct of social life it is the same alternative of either/or: a man must be altogether genial or else turn not merely suspicious but a thoroughgoing misanthrope:

"Can a misanthrope feel warm, I ask myself; take ease? be companionable with himself? Can a misanthrope smoke a cigar and muse? . . . Has the misanthrope such a thing as an appetite? Shall a peach refresh him? The effervescence of champagne, with what eye does he behold it?" (pp. 178–179)

With these sharply phrased views Charlie Noble readily agrees; indeed, as the cosmopolitan observes pointedly, were their sentiments "written in a book, whose was whose, few but the nicest critics might determine." Still, when Noble proposes celebrating their new friendship over a bottle of wine the cosmopolitan at first demurs, on the ground that he has already drunk so much with "so many old friends, all free-hearted, convivial gentlemen," that he finds "his head of less capacity than his heart" (pp. 179–180). Grateful for this lead, Noble endeavors to make his intended victim tipsy by plying him convivially with wine while abstaining himself, but the wily cosmopolitan shows himself thoroughly equal to this old game. Noble's fulsome praise of wine (he is not drinking) and tobacco (he is not smoking) sets the tone of their wide-ranging conversation: as given in Chapters 29–35 it is filled with "genial" thoughts and punctuated with "genial" gestures. Noble ultimately steers the talking back to the subject of conviviality, which for him "signifies the highest pitch of geniality" and "implies, as indispensable auxiliary, the cheery benediction of the bottle" (he is still not drinking). His conclusion is that the man who "loves not wine" should be hanged for an "ungenial soul" (pp. 198–199). The wine-drinking cosmopolitan, hearing from Noble much the same one-sided argument he himself had offered the water-loving Missourian, now raises an objection: "Conviviality," he asserts, "is one good thing, and sobriety is another good thing." Noble concedes the point, blaming the wine for his one-sidedness: "Indeed, indeed, I have indulged too genially" (p. 199).

Now the scene is properly set, and Noble's remark becomes the cue touching off an extravaganza of comedy. The dialogue which follows toward the close of Chapter 30 (pp. 199–201) brings to a head the whole complex of interrelated themes we have been examining: warm geniality, trust and confidence, philanthropy *versus* ungenial coldness, doubt and suspicion, misanthropy. The exchange is both comic and dramatic; the speeches will be given here as though Melville had written them for a play, with each speaker duly labeled for the reader's convenience. Noble is still holding forth. "By the way," he continues, "talking of geniality, it is much on the increase in these days, ain't it?"

GOODMAN: "It is, and I hail the fact. Nothing better attests the advance of the humanitarian spirit. In former and less humanitarian ages . . . geniality was mostly confined to the fireside and table. But in our age . . . it is with this precious quality as with precious gold in old Peru, which Pizarro found making up the scullion's sauce-pot as the Inca's crown. Yes, we golden boys, the moderns, have geniality everywhere—a bounty broadcast like noonlight."

NOBLE: "True, true; my sentiments again. Geniality has invaded each department and profession. We have genial senators, genial authors, genial lecturers, genial doctors, genial clergymen, genial surgeons, and the next thing we shall have genial hangmen."

GOODMAN: "As to the last-named sort of person, I trust that the advancing spirit of geniality will at last enable us to dispense with him. No murderers—no hangmen. And surely, when the whole world shall have been genialized, it will be as out of place to talk of murderers, as in a Christianized world to talk of sinners."

NOBLE: "To pursue the thought, every blessing is attended with some evil, and—"

GOODMAN: "Stay, that may be better let pass for a loose saying, than for hopeful doctrine."

NOBLE: "Well, assuming the saying's truth, it would apply to the future supremacy of the genial spirit, since then it will fare with the hangman as it did with the weaver when the spinning-jenny whizzed into the ascendant. Thrown out of employment, what could Jack Ketch turn his hand to? Butchering?"

To the cosmopolitan's sly suggestion that the hangman may "turn valet," in view of his "familiar dexterity about the person," Noble asks, "Are you . . . really in earnest?" Goodman's "mildly earnest" reply brings the whole discussion to its designed climax:

"I trust I am never otherwise; but talking of the advance of geniality, I am not without hopes that it will eventually exert its influence even upon so difficult a subject as the misanthrope."

NOBLE: "A genial misanthrope! I thought I had stretched the rope pretty
hard in talking of genial hangmen. A genial misanthrope is no more
conceivable than a surly philanthropist."

The cosmopolitan insists that there *is* such a being as "a surly philanthropist"; indeed, the Missourian is a perfect example:

"Does he not . . . hide under a surly air a philanthropic heart? Now, the
genial misanthrope, when, in the process of eras, he shall turn up, will be
the converse of this; under an affable air, he will hide a misanthropical
heart. In short, the genial misanthrope will be a new kind of monster, but
still no small improvement upon the original one, since, instead of making
faces and throwing stones at people, like that poor old crazy man, Timon,
he will take steps, fiddle in hand, and set the tickled world a' dancing. In
a word, as the progress of Christianization mellows those in manner whom
it cannot mend in mind, much the same will it prove with the progress of
genialization. And so, thanks to geniality, the misanthrope, reclaimed from
his boorish address, will take on refinement and softness—to so genial a
degree, indeed, that it may possibly fall out that the misanthrope of the
coming century will be almost as popular as, I am sincerely sorry to say,
some philanthropists of the present time would seem not to be, as witness
my eccentric friend named before." (pp. 200–201)

A look at the movement of Melville's skillful rhetoric through these
tightly structured speeches discloses the intensely serious thrust behind the humorous extravagance. When the comic Noble makes his
increasingly fatuous remarks about the forward march of geniality,
the witty Goodman, pretending to agree, not only caps each successive point on Noble's own level but at the same time transforms their
verbal exchange into a series of increasingly serious jabs at prevalent
contemporary assumptions about "the advance of the humanitarian
spirit" and "the progress of Christianization." His inference, obvious
to the clear-eyed reader, is that "the whole world" is just about as
likely to turn genuinely Christian as it is to become truly "genialized":
"In a word, as the progress of Christianization *mellows those in manner
whom it cannot mend in mind*, much the same will it prove with the
progress of genialization" (emphasis added). "Geniality" in this immediate context is actually Melville's rhetorical stalking-horse for an
exposure of the pretensions of humanitarianism and religion, conceived in terms of the prevailing nineteenth-century faith in inevitable "progress" that so frequently drew his fire.[17] This point once
established, the function of "geniality" in *The Confidence-Man* as a
whole is further illuminated. When the dealer in "confidence" assumes geniality as his mask, it becomes the exact equivalent of such

other humbugs as the superficial piety and charity he displays elsewhere in the book. And when passengers aboard the Fidèle cannot
resist playing the confidence-game, both its operators and their gullible victims get out of it about what they both deserve.

Beside the consummate performance of the cosmopolitan throughout every episode in which he appears, the forced geniality of the
bilious Charlie Noble during their long conversation seems ridiculous
and crude: Noble is but an ordinary journeyman sharper while
Goodman is the confidence-man *par excellence*. But in Chapter 24, we
recall, the Missourian Pitch, a shrewder observer than Noble, had
seen in Goodman a misanthrope "masquerading as a cosmopolitan"—
and conversely, in Chapter 28, the cosmopolitan had spoken of Pitch
himself as really a philanthropist in disguise. Goodman's intriguing
distinction in Chapter 30 between the "surly philanthropist" and "genial misanthrope" is of a piece with these earlier identifications: indeed his double picture here "so resembles the Missourian and himself respectively," in Miss Foster's words, "as to amount to confession"
(p. lxxii). But again what the careful reader detects is lost on Charlie
Noble, who, "a little weary, perhaps, of a speculation so abstract,"
breaks off the discussion of the genial misanthrope by repeating that
one "must be genial or he is nothing. So fill up, fill up, and be genial!"
(p. 201). The wily cosmopolitan, observing accurately that "I do about
all the drinking, and you do about all—the genial" (p. 202), is now
ready to put his "boon companion" to the test: "I am in want, urgent
want, of money," he declares, and Charlie is going to loan him fifty
dollars. But the "noble kindliness" of Charlie has undergone a pre-
dictable metamorphosis, and Noble promptly invites Goodman to "go
to the devil, sir! Beggar, impostor!—never so deceived in a man in
my life" (pp. 202–203).

There are two sequels to this exposure of the falsely genial. One of
them follows immediately, when in Chapter 32, by producing "ten
half-eagles" from his pocket, the cosmopolitan as if by magic "re-
stores" his former friend (p. 204). The other comes in the play-acting
of Chapter 39, when with a man called Egbert taking the part of
"Charlie" the cosmopolitan again requests a loan of his "bosom-
friend" and once more is met with a flat refusal. In practical terms
the results are the same, though the original Charlie is transparently
a sharper while Egbert is a professed exponent of the mystical philosophy of one Mark Winsome—a distinctly Emersonian figure who
makes a brief appearance in Chapter 36, ungenially declines to finish
what remains of Noble's bottle of wine, and enjoys instead a goblet of
ice-water (pp. 212–218). Beneath their unlike masks the ungenial

mystics and falsely genial operators are thus presented as equally cold and equally nonbenevolent.

Faced with the task of evaluating this book of variations on the theme of confidence, more than one critic has responded by writing it off as the despairing outcry of a confirmed misanthrope—thus ascribing to Melville himself the all-or-none philosophy put forth in turn by such dubious speakers as Frank Goodman and Charlie Noble. But it is clear from Melville's writing after *The Confidence-Man* that he neither renounced mankind nor forswore geniality, despite the obvious reservations he had expressed there about both. Before going on to the later writings, it will be well to examine one more passage in *The Confidence-Man* itself, again linking wine with confidence and trust, which affords a clue to his own mature view of the issues. It occurs in Chapter 29, as the talkative cosmopolitan is commenting on Noble's observation that good wine is "the peculiar bond of good feeling," even though some "gloomy skeptics . . . maintain that now-a-days pure wine is unpurchasable" (p. 182). Though ostensibly horrified at so painful an example of "want of confidence," and lamenting the consequences to "convivial geniality" if "wine be false, while men are true," the cosmopolitan is nevertheless reminded of certain reports he has heard (pp. 182–183). There exists, it is claimed,

"a kind of man who, while convinced that on this continent most wines are shams, yet still drinks away at them; accounting wine so fine a thing, that even the sham article is better than none at all. And if the temperance people urge that, by this course, he will sooner or later be undermined in health, he answers, 'And do you think I don't know that? But health without cheer I hold a bore; and cheer, even of the spurious sort, has its price, which I am willing to pay.'" (p. 183)

"Such a man, Frank," responds Noble to these words, "must have a disposition ungovernably bacchanalian." "Yes," replies Goodman, "if such a man there be, which I don't credit." After offering still further disclaimers of his "fable," he then goes on to say that from this very story "I once heard a person of less genius than grotesqueness draw a moral even more extravagant than the fable itself." According to him,

"it illustrated, as in a parable, how that a man of a disposition ungovernably good-natured might still familiarly associate with men, though, at the same time, he believed the greater part of men false-hearted—accounting society so sweet a thing that even the spurious sort was better than none at all. And if the Rochefoucaultites urge that, by this course, he will sooner or later be undermined in security, he answers, 'And do you think I don't know that? But security without society I hold a bore; and society, even of the spurious sort, has its price, which I am willing to pay.'" (p. 184)

What is said in these carefully balanced passages does not represent the attitude of the cosmopolitan himself—that genial man-hater who by the end of the book is revealed as probable surrogate for Satan. Indeed, he repeatedly disclaims the "fable" and impugns the freak who draws from it his "extravagant" moral. That anonymous "person of less genius than grotesqueness" bears a distinct family resemblance to other Melvilleian characters, however: minor figures often described as eccentric who turn up in works from *Mardi* to *Billy Budd* as spokesmen for points of view Melville preferred not to espouse directly through flat authorial comment.[18] Indeed he is very much like that "rare bird" introduced as "Hilary" in the "Inscription Epistolary" to *John Marr and Other Sailors* (1888): a "companionable" man "at once genial and acute. Genial, I mean, without sharing much in mere gregariousness, which, with some, passes for a sort of geniality" (*Collected Poems*, p. 468). This thumbnail sketch exactly hits the outline of Melville's own figure as it emerges from the shadows of his later years through the medium of his occasional writing.

Following completion of *The Confidence-Man* in 1856, Melville set out for Europe and the Near East in search of rest and restored health. He looked up Hawthorne in Liverpool, but with the old spirit of adventure gone out of him, he confessed during their conversation, he anticipated little real pleasure from the trip. ("Bachelors alone can travel freely," he had written in recalling his previous voyage of 1849.) "To be a good traveler, and derive from travel real enjoyment," he said in the lecture of 1859 called "Traveling," one "must be young, care-free, and gifted with geniality and imagination, for if without these last he may as well stay at home."[19] Geniality is a quality repeatedly celebrated, even in correspondence, throughout Melville's so-called "silent years." A verse-letter to one of his New York friends, Daniel Shepherd, extending an invitation for a Berkshire visit in 1859, promises that though Shepherd might miss his accustomed otard and claret while at Arrowhead, the "guest *unwined*" there could still count on plenty of bourbon, cold water, and "genial Friendship" (*Letters*, pp. 196–197). Melville himself praised the "genial hospitality" of his favorite "Cousin Kate" and her husband, Abraham Lansing, in Albany during his visits there from New York, where he resumed residence in 1863 (*Letters*, p. 263). And to a sympathetic brother-in-law, John Hoadley, he voiced in 1877 the hope that his letter expressed "good-fellowship," for "at my years, and with my disposition, or rather, constitution, one gets to care less and less for everything except downright good feeling" (*Letters*, p. 260).

Nor is the genial spirit banished from Melville's poetry, serious though much of it is in subject and tone. Even in *Clarel* (1876), where the mood is prevailingly subdued, there is considerable talk of wine. The word "genial" itself occurs nearly a dozen times in the poem, always with familiar connotations[20]—notably in the characterization of Rolfe, a partial self-portrait of the author, who possesses both a "genial heart" and "a brain austere" (I.xxxi.14) much as Hilary in the later *John Marr* volume combines his geniality with acuteness. The old association of conviviality with a genial temper is also renewed in the *John Marr* poems such as "Bridegroom Dick," with its celebration of the pipe and "the wine's genial cup" (*Collected Poems*, pp. 167, 173) and its recollections of Melville's cousin Guert Gansevoort, a wine-bibbing naval officer:

> O Tom, but he knew a blue-jacket's ways,
> And how a lieutenant may genially haze;
> Only a sailor sailors heartily praise.

Among other sailors so praised is Jack Chase, this time as "Jack Roy" (p. 185):

> Never relishing the knave, though allowing for the menial,
> Nor overmuch the king, Jack, nor prodigally genial.

In prose, the Burgundy Club sketches, begun about 1875 as Melville was finishing *Clarel*, feature a "genial foreigner," the Marquis de Grandvin, a personification of wine, and that "genial spirit" Jack Gentian; in his adoption of the Marquis' "genial philosophy" Gentian "may not improperly be regarded as his disciple." Thinking of the symbolic character of the Marquis, Melville specifically observed in "The Marquis de Grandvin" that "a person of genial temper is not only very likely to be a popular man's man, but also, and beyond that, a favorite with the ladies."[21] Writers as different as Shakespeare and the poet James Thomson attracted Melville as "genial";[22] so too did a figure of his own imagination, Billy Budd, whom he conceived from the first as "genial in temper, and sparklingly so" (p. 275). In *Billy Budd* itself, the culminating work of the late years, rosy-cheeked Billy is "happily endowed with the gaiety of high health, youth, and a free heart" that Melville still treasured so much, and likeable for his "genial happy-go-lucky air" (p. 49)[23]—but with Melville's earlier innocents, he proves all too trusting of mankind in a world that produces both Billy Budds and John Claggarts.

These later works, major and minor, are not the writings of an embittered misanthrope—not even of a "genial" one. Their author, one infers, was a man neither "confident" nor even gregarious, but one who never ceased to value good fellowship and good feeling, in the company of a few convivial intimates or else in memories of the past. Like Melville's "Hilary," such a man could be termed both genial and acute—perhaps more genial in later years than in the 1850's when *The Confidence-Man* was being written. In 1851 he had frankly confessed to Hawthorne, while asserting his "ruthless" and "unconditional" democracy, his "dislike to all mankind—in the mass" (*Letters*, p. 127); in 1855 he concluded "I and My Chimney"—so brightly magazinish on the surface and so dark beneath—with the narrator's wry acknowledgment that his "city friends" think he is "getting sour and unsocial. Some say that I have become a sort of mossy old misanthrope" (*Complete Stories*, pp. 407–408). But Melville himself was at bottom no more a misanthrope than a philanthropist, or no less; he was plainly something of both. In mankind, to adapt Hawthorne's much-quoted words about him in 1856, he could apparently neither quite "believe" nor be comfortable in his unbelief. Hawthorne thought him "too honest and courageous not to try to do one or the other" (*Log*, II, 529), but "one or the other" was exactly the rub—witness the all-or-none reasoning of "Goodman" and "Noble"! There is nothing in *The Confidence-Man* to align Melville himself with these spurious figures or with their dubious propositions on either side of the argument.

On the contrary, human nature impressed Melville, like the tortoise of "The Encantadas," as both black and bright: "Enjoy the bright, keep it turned up perpetually if you can," he admonishes in Sketch Second, "but be honest, and don't deny the black" (*Complete Stories*, p. 56). His work of the fifties and after illustrates his honest and courageous acknowledgment of both—even when the darker side seems more in the ascendant. "That which we seek and shun is there."[24] But skepticism is not cynicism, and a nonbeliever in "confidence" and "progress" who disliked mankind in the mass could nevertheless remain a realist, a democrat, and a confirmed lover of "good living, good drinking, good feeling, and good talk." Like the essentially good-natured, wine-drinking, but still clear-eyed man in the fable, though all too aware that wines may be sham and humanity false-hearted, Melville would settle for neither "health without cheer" nor "security without society." Geniality, even of the spurious sort, has its price—and he was never unwilling to pay.

Melville's Chimney, Reexamined
(1969)

From *Themes and Directions in American Literature*, edited by Ray B. Browne and Donald Pizer. Copyright © Purdue Research Foundation, 1969. Reprinted by special permission. The book is a *Festschrift*, subtitled *Essays in Honor of Leon Howard* (Lafayette, Indiana: Purdue University Studies, 1969); my contribution appears on pp. 80–102. As the opening paragraph explains, Melville's "I and My Chimney" has long been a subject of "friendly disagreement" between Professor Howard and myself, and it therefore seemed appropriate to honor him by reviewing critical pronouncements about the story between 1856 and the 1960's. The later sections of the essay in particular reflect changing fashions in American literary scholarship since I drafted "Herman Melville's 'I and My Chimney'" in 1940 and advanced "what must be the 'orthodox' interpretation." The quoted phrasing is not an endorsement, coming as it does from a vigorous dissenter: Marvin Fisher, in his *Going Under: Melville's Short Fiction and the American 1850s* (Baton Rouge and London: Louisiana State University Press, 1977), p. 200, note. Lively discussion of Melville's story and its interpreters seems likely to continue indefinitely.

In the notes, pp. 370–371 below, I have provided a bibliographical listing of books and articles touching on "I and My Chimney" that appeared between 1941 and 1969 and are cited in this essay. Since 1969 there have been new biographical discoveries bearing upon the background of the story and its possible implications as a reflection of its author's state of mind during the years after he published *Moby-Dick*. The Northwestern-Newberry edition of *Pierre* (Evanston and Chicago, 1971), pp. 380–381, reports that rumors about Melville's mental condition were actually circulating in New York following the appearance of *Pierre* in 1852. The New York *Day Book* for 7 September 1852 took account of them in a brief paragraph headed "HERMAN MELVILLE CRAZY," saying that he "was really supposed to be deranged, and that his friends were taking measures to place him under treatment." The long-standing concern of Melville's wife and her relatives in Boston over Melville's mental health finally came to a head in 1867. At that time her half-brother Samuel Shaw counseled a separation on the ground that "her

171

husband is insane. . . . I think she would have done this long ago," he wrote, "if not for imaginary and groundless apprehensions of the censure of the world upon her conduct"; the family physician, Dr. Augustus Kinsley Gardner, had already advised a separation, according to Shaw. But Elizabeth Melville did not leave her husband, even though a further crisis ensued later in 1867 with the death of their oldest child, Malcolm, of a self-inflicted shot from a pistol. After Melville himself died in 1891 she remained fiercely loyal to his memory: see "The Belated Funeral Flower," reprinted below as a section of "Alien to His Contemporaries: Melville's Last Years."

The possible separation of the Melvilles in 1867 was unknown to scholars until 1975, when Walter D. Kring and Jonathan S. Carey published "Two Discoveries Concerning Herman Melville," *Proceedings of the Massachusetts Historical Society*, 87 (1975), 137–141; their article has been reproduced in a pamphlet, "The Endless, Winding Way in Melville: New Charts by Kring and Carey," edited by Donald Yannella and Hershel Parker (Glassboro, New Jersey: The Melville Society, 1981), pp. 11–15, along with related documents. The pamphlet also includes commentaries on the significance of this "new evidence" by a dozen well-known writers on Melville.

B oth in private conversation and in print, the interpretation of Herman Melville's short story "I and My Chimney" (1856) has long been a subject for discussion and friendly disagreement between Leon Howard and myself. The reading of this story that I published in 1941 has recently been exhumed and reprinted, immediately following Howard's challenging early study of Melville's "struggle" in *Moby-Dick* with the art of the novel, in Hershel Parker's anthology of Melville criticism, *The Recognition of Herman Melville* (1967), where for students of the 1960's the two articles must appear as something like historical curiosities. On the present occasion it seems appropriate for me to look again at "I and My Chimney" and the considerable body of commentary which has accumulated over the years around it, distinguishing the main lines of analysis that have emerged and reexamining the story itself in the light of all that has now been said of it, wisely or otherwise.

i: 1856–1940

About the contemporary reception of "I and My Chimney" there is little to record in the absence of printed commentary. The story was first published, anonymously, in *Putnam's Monthly Magazine* for March, 1856, more than six months after its submission in manuscript, and was not reprinted until thirty-one years after Melville's death, in *The Apple-Tree Table and Other Sketches by Herman Melville* (1922), collected by Henry Chapin. Had *Putnam's* carried the story before the end of 1855 Melville himself would presumably have collected it, along with other stories from that magazine, in *The Piazza Tales*, which he assembled early in 1856 and published the following May. There it would surely have drawn favorable critical notice; in the private judgment of George William Curtis, who as *Putnam's* editorial advisor had reported on the manuscript, it was "a capital, genial, humorous sketch . . . , thoroughly magazinish," and other disinterested readers of the time probably responded to it in much the same way. For members of the Melville clan, however, the story evidently carried subtler implications to which outsiders were of course not attuned. It obviously puzzled Melville's brother Allan, in whose copy of the magazine containing the story there are penciled question marks in the margins next to six scattered passages. Melville's wife, who identified the narrator and his family in the story with the Melville household at Pittsfield, was moved to write a defensive marginal notation: "All this about his [the narrator's] wife, applied to his [Melville's own] mother—who was very vigorous and energetic about the farm, etc. The proposed removal of the chimney is purely mythical." As for Melville's mother herself, what her reaction to the story may have been can only be conjectured.

Elizabeth Shaw Melville's association of the story with Arrowhead, the Melville farmhouse at Pittsfield, and her unequivocal identification of its narrator with her husband have been echoed in much subsequent commentary, though with significant variations and, in recent criticism, a few vigorous dissents. Raymond Weaver followed her lead in his pioneering *Herman Melville: Mariner and Mystic* (1921), where he offered the first discussion of "I and My Chimney" to appear in print: in the story, he declared, Melville "makes the old chimney at Arrowhead the chief character in a sketch of his domestic life at Pittsfield: himself and his wife, both freely idealised, are the other actors." Weaver's treatment continued with details concerning the history of the house and the appearance of its largest fireplace; in 1924, when he reprinted "I and My Chimney" in volume XIII of the Standard (Constable) edition of Melville, he quoted in a footnote, without comment, Mrs. Melville's assertions about the identity of the "wife" and the "purely mythical" removal of the chimney. During the later 1920's and the 1930's, as the Melville revival gathered strength under the impetus of Weaver's biography and publication of the Constable and other reprintings of Melville's works, there were passing references to the story in books by John Freeman, Lewis Mumford, and

Willard Thorp, but full-scale evaluation of the shorter prose generally did not begin until E. H. Eby published on "The Tartarus of Maids" in 1940 and my own article on "I and My Chimney" appeared in the following year. Both essays, it might be noted, were written at a time when the relations between Melville's various writings and events of his own life were in the process of clarification as biographical research continued to provide new information; also, explication of images and symbols was then a favorite gambit with literary critics, whether the author being examined was Melville, Shakespeare, or T. S. Eliot.

ii: 1940–1955

What both Weaver and Mrs. Melville had written about the story and about Melville's family situation in the 1850's provided starting points for my analysis of "I and My Chimney," although it took a dinner-table discussion in 1940 to arouse my immediate interest and set me pondering about its possible meaning. An intelligent and sensitive individual knowing little of Melville had been powerfully affected, I was told, by something in the story—what was that something? Next day as I sat rereading "I and My Chimney" trying to account for its extraordinary emotional impact, I soon became aware of the great chimney "less as a pile of masonry than as a personage," in the narrator's words: here I began to sense a little lower layer of significance. Then I came to the arresting outcry against "profane" meddling with matters both "secret" and "sacred," where the bantering tone all at once becomes earnest and solemn: surely all this was not without meaning. Suddenly I was reminded of a Melville family tradition, known to Weaver and cited in William Braswell's doctoral dissertation (later to be published as *Melville's Religious Thought*), which I had recently read. Melville himself, it was said in the family, had been subjected to a mental examination after publishing *Pierre*—very likely in 1853, when there was anxiety about "the strain on his health" (Mrs. Melville's words) and his mother began unsuccessful maneuvering to get him away from his desk by securing a consular appointment. Here, I thought, was the key to it all!

Starting with this clue, the pattern my essay was to follow at once began taking shape, turning upon the significance of the chimney and the various comments about it by characters in the story. (1) Pointing to comparable images in Melville's earlier writing—the ascending tower, the descending shaft, the pyramid—which establish dimensions of the human personality as he conceived it, I suggested in the article that the chimney stands for "the heart and soul" of Melville himself. Then, considering its place in the action and overall design of the story, I advanced a series of further hypotheses. (2) Through the narrator's musings on his chimney Melville is commenting obliquely on his own penchant for introspection. (3) The wife's open hostility to the chimney and the "survey" of it made at her behest by one Scribe, the local architect and master-mason, reflect the reactions of Melville's own family following his publication of *Pierre* and the examination of his mind that was reputedly made some time thereafter, at their instigation. In the story, the "secret closet" that Scribe conjectures to be hidden in the chimney is associated with the "kinsman," Dacres, who built the house ("To break into that wall, would be to break into his breast"), and it is specifically equated with possible "unsoundness." In actuality, Melville's own father had been mentally deranged while on his deathbed in 1832, and in *Pierre* Melville had overtly introduced the theme of possible hereditary insanity. (4) The architect's unusual name, "Scribe," suggests that one of Melville's examiners might have been (not "was") his summer neighbor at Pittsfield, Oliver Wendell Holmes, the literary doctor who is known to have treated him for rheumatism and sciatica in 1855, shortly before "I and My Chimney" was written.

The basic point of my article, "Melville's identification of the chimney with himself," received eloquent support when William Ellery Sedgwick's *Herman Melville: The Tragedy of Mind* was published posthumously in 1945. Before his death in 1942 its author had independently linked the chimney of the story with "Melville's crotchety ego" and taken it as a symbol of his "importunate integrity and of the innate dignity which was his . . . in common with all humanity." I think now that Sedgwick must have felt much as I did when first writing about "I and My Chimney," and indeed still feel. "One dislikes to probe into the interior of this almost wholly charming piece," he acknowledged. "One feels Melville's reserve in it, which one feels called upon to respect." His discussion was less concerned with what happens in the story than with its tone. Seeing Melville himself, at the time of its writing, as "beginning to comprehend the needs of life as it composes itself to old age," he found "I and My Chimney" as a whole to be informed by an attitude of recognition and acceptance. His sensitive discussion of its central symbol is illuminated by the revealing parallels he drew with passages in the earlier *White-Jacket* and *Moby-Dick:* the chimney's "cupboards and closets" are reminiscent of the jacket which gives the narrator of *White-Jacket* his very identity;

the broad-based structure symbolizes what Melville "otherwise represented" when in *Moby-Dick* he described "those vast Roman halls . . . where far beneath . . . man's upper earth, his root of grandeur, his whole awful essence sits in bearded state." By thus relating the story to Melville's long-standing concern with personal identity, individual integrity, and human dignity, Sedgwick properly emphasized its broadest and deepest thematic implications, which in effect transcend its more immediate biographical referents though without necessarily negating them.

Meanwhile, in his *Melville's Religious Thought* (1943), Braswell had unreservedly concurred in my own reading of "I and My Chimney": Melville's family did arrange a mental examination after *Pierre*, he declared, and "Sealts has shown how Melville symbolically told the story" of it. When Willard Thorp reviewed Braswell's book in 1944 he took occasion to characterize Melville as "one of the great figures in the now century-old symbolist movement." Citing the work of Watson, Homans, Matthiessen, and myself, he observed that "in Melville scholarship the most fruitful returns can at present be got from the study of his symbols"; other commentators of the 1940's evidently shared his belief, as indicated by the general tenor of the voluminous publication on Melville which immediately followed the close of World War II. For the shorter prose in particular, Jay Leyda's collection of Melville's *Complete Stories* (1949) provided a convenient text and probably drew the attention of a new generation of critics to Melville as a story-writer. Leyda's editorial discussion of "I and My Chimney" cited my 1941 reading with full approval as removing "the last trace of innocence—but not good humor" from what Melville had written. The late Richard Chase also found it "very persuasive," remarking in his *Herman Melville: A Critical Study* (1949) that "it is surely amusing to watch Melville dealing in his bantering way with the suspicions of his family."

Other points in Chase's influential discussion of "I and My Chimney" deserve further notice here, since they were to affect the direction and tone taken by later commentary. In keeping with his regard for Melville as a significant critic of the liberal tradition in American culture, Chase had more to say than either Sedgwick or myself about ideological implications of the contest between the likeable old narrator and his "foolish, mindlessly optimistic" wife. He made further associations between the chimney and "Melville's recurring symbol of the Tower," and he also linked its supposed secret closet with earlier images of encryptment, such as the glass ship in *Redburn* and the sarcophagus within the pyramid in *Pierre*. "Always before" in Melville, Chase noted,

the impulse has been to break into the crypt and discover the inner mystery. But here we find the old man no longer wanting to break in, and indeed protecting the crypt from those who do. As usual the hidden mystery is to be connected with the father and man's search into the past for the decisive moral basis of his being. Captain Julian Dacres represents Melville's father. As Mr. Merton Sealts has pointed out, "Dacres" is an anagram of "Sacred." . . . The impenetrable secret of the chimney is the God whom it is vanity to try to understand.

A year later, in his introduction to *Selected Tales and Poems by Herman Melville* (1950), Chase recapitulated his views; with those students— and their teachers—not familiar with either Chase's earlier book or the accumulating body of Melville scholarship and criticism, it was this discussion of 1950 which earned for him the credit (or blame) attached to certain ideas about "I and My Chimney" and the circumstances of its writing. Melville's family, Chase declared flatly in 1950, without documentation, "feared that he was going insane and arranged a consultation with Dr. Oliver Wendell Holmes." Concerning "the richly suggestive and mellow" story itself, he again emphasized the meditative old narrator and his regard for the chimney, which represents,

in the old man's mind, venerableness, wisdom in the face of death, resignation before the fact of the world's vanity, the vision of things set forth in the book of Ecclesiastes. The chimney has something sacred about it (the name of its previous owner, Captain Dacres, is an anagram of "sacred"). In this story the man's wife is possessed of the spirit of confidence, as we see from her schemes for getting rid of the chimney, her foolishly conceived plans for self-improvement and renovation, her "infatuate juvenility," and her inability to admit the fact of death. If one of the characters displays an inner morbidity and an unrecognized desire for self-destruction, it is not the man but his wife, whose idea of "improvement" is only "a softer name for destruction." She it is who in her mindless optimism plants flowers every spring on the north side of the house, exactly where the north wind will be certain to destroy them.

Among other commentators of the 1940's, the late Newton Arvin, with his interest in depth psychology, was also attracted by the symbolism of "I and My Chimney." In his study of "Melville and the Gothic Novel" (1949) he glanced briefly at its "imagery of the subterranean," through which "the Unconscious is powerfully symbolized" (an accompanying footnote cites my 1941 article as "an interesting discussion of the symbolism in this sketch"), and a year later, in his *Herman Melville* (1950), he remarked that "I and My Chimney," in spite of its prolixity, would always be worth preserving because "the great spinal chimney, with its dark subterranean base, is so expressive a symbol of a man's essential self." He found "natural and touching" Mrs. Melville's comments about the "wife" of the story as representing Melville's mother, but added an interpretation of his own: "the truth is that wife and mother had been fused in Melville's mind into a single image of intrusive and oppressive hostility." No other critic had gone quite so far in relating the story to a psychological analysis of its author. Arvin cited *Pierre* along with "I and My Chimney" in support of his views, and also as evidence of the "morbid state of mind" that Hawthorne saw reflected in Melville's writings of the 1850's, but few interpreters have shared his specific conclusions about the nature of Melville's reactions to the family situation at Arrowhead. Geoffrey Stone, for example, had followed Mrs. Melville in identifying her mother-in-law with the "wife," but Stone's own biographical reading of "I and My Chimney" in *Melville* (1949) went no further than to suppose that differences existed between Melville and his mother over "management of the house." As for my particular suggestions about the story, which in Stone's version translated the "supposed secret chamber" into the "insanity" of Melville or his father, "Mr. Sealts's theory" had for him "the neat articulation of similar ones relating the measurements of the Great Pyramid to the ruins of Tiahuanaca and the sages of Thibet, and, its premises granted, is no easier to refute."

The next major pronouncements on "I and My Chimney" appeared in 1951, when a unique "cooperative venture" in scholarship culminated in the publication of two complementary works: *The Melville Log: A Documentary Life of Herman Melville* by Jay Leyda and *Herman Melville: A Biography* by Leon Howard. Though the two authors fully shared the same data, they did not always read their evidence in the same way nor arrive at the same conclusions. Leyda, as in his edition of *Complete Stories* two years before, associated Dr. Holmes's attendance on Melville in 1855 with "Scribe's" survey of the narrator's chimney, juxtaposing passages from the story itself with biographical information drawn from Mrs. Melville and the Pittsfield journalist J. E. A. Smith—plus the following suggestive meditation from Melville's own *Billy Budd:*

> Who in the rainbow can draw the line where the violet tint ends and the orange tint begins? . . . So with sanity and insanity . . . in some supposed cases, in various degrees supposedly less pronounced, to draw the exact line

of demarkation few will undertake, though for a fee some professional experts will. There is nothing nameable but that some men will undertake to do it for pay. In other words, there are instances where it is next to impossible to determine whether a man is in his mind or beginning to be otherwise.

Howard, however, was less willing than Leyda to trace the symbolism of the story beyond the more literal implications of its imagery of spines and backbones. Though finding "I and My Chimney" "the most intimately personal" of all Melville's magazine writings, he saw nothing in it reminiscent of an earlier mental examination. What Melville had done, according to Howard, was to

put into the story many observations of his real situation at the moment— his sciatica and his feeling of age and kinship to his twisted old grapevine, and Elizabeth's efforts to take over the practical management of the farm and build a new barn. Despite the wholly imaginary "plot" . . . and his exaggerated representation of his age and his henpecked condition, there was a certain amount of reality in his picture of himself. . . .

Beneath this surface was also something comparable to the biological allegory slipped into the "Tartarus of Maids." His dealings with "the master-mason" . . . included an examination such as might have been endured by a man who was suffering from a stiff back and sciatica, both of which were attributed to his sedentary habits while writing.

In later work on Melville—a University of Minnesota pamphlet, *Herman Melville* (1961), an introduction to selections from Melville in *Eight American Writers: An Anthology*, edited by Norman Foerster and Robert P. Falk (1963), and his recent essay "The Mystery of Melville's Short Stories" (1966)—Howard has set forth essentially the same view of "I and My Chimney" as recalling a physical but not a mental examination of its author; when annotating the story itself for *Eight American Writers* he observed also that "Scribe's" name "may be a personal allusion" to Dr. Holmes. As for "what was implied" in either the proposed removal of the chimney or its possible "secret compartment," the word used in the 1951 biography was "uncertain." What seemed "not improbable" to Howard, however, was "that Herman's womenfolk wanted him to have more medical attention than he was willing to receive, and that he was irritated without being too worried to hold on to as much of his sense of humor as his literary purpose demanded."

Howard's emphasis on the good humor of "I and My Chimney," which had already attracted Leyda and Chase, was echoed in Edward H. Rosenberry's *Melville and the Comic Spirit* (1955), where the story is succinctly described as "a domestic farce." Rosenberry, however, went farther with respect to its possible psychological overtones than Howard had ventured, though not to the extent of adopting Arvin's radical views. Citing my 1941 article in a footnote, he affirmed that the plot was "unquestionably"

> suggested to Melville by the well-meaning attempts of his family to alter the untidy architecture of his personality by consulting Dr. Holmes about his physical and particularly his mental health. If the incident irritated him at the time, it no doubt amused him as well: he was continually having to remind people in his admittedly eccentric letters that he wasn't "crazy."

Rosenberry's discussion adds a further suggestion in line with conclusions already advanced by Sedgwick: "If the story has serious biographical meaning," he declared, "it lies not in the domestic relations of the protagonist," which Chase and Arvin had emphasized, "but in the symbolism of his chimney." Read in this way, it became for him a chapter in Melville's spiritual autobiography, the "profoundest theme of which," in Rosenberry's view, "is the struggle for self-knowledge." The narrator's descent into his "cellar" translates into "the comic idiom" both the "common madness of Taji, Ahab, and Pierre" in Melville's earlier writings, whose reckless diving "within themselves in search of the mythical bedrock of Truth . . . had killed them all," and also the "more literal diving" that in *Moby-Dick* brought insanity to little Pip. What "I and My Chimney" particularly revealed to Rosenberry was that by the time it was written "Melville had evidently come to terms with himself and learned from all these deaths and madnesses to live with his enormous and tantalizing ego in a truce of mutual respect."

Rosenberry's conclusion that "I and My Chimney" reveals Melville as having "come to terms with himself" is in line with much previous comment ever since Sedgwick had used the terms "recognition" and "acceptance" in writing about it. By the time of Rosenberry's book it was generally agreed that the story is somehow autobiographical in nature, though there was a considerable range of opinion, as we have seen, about the direction of Melville's possible references—whether to his physical condition at the time he was writing, emphasized by Howard, or to his state of mind, most radically interpreted by Arvin. Virtually every discussion of the story touched on the chimney as symbol; several critics made comparisons with various related images in Melville's writings and speculated about possible implications of its supposed secret closet. Another facet of the story had also interested Chase, who called attention to the narrator and his wife as conducting a dialogue of ideas with cultural and political overtones. My own hypotheses concerning the name and activities of "Scribe" had a mixed reception: the argument for the idea that Melville might have been thinking of Dr. Holmes and that Holmes might have been asked at some time to examine more than his neighbor's ailing back convinced Howard only in part and Stone not at all, though Braswell, Leyda, Chase, and Rosenberry were all more receptive. Unlike several later commentators, I had been careful not to write as though a "consultation" with Holmes over Melville's mental condition were a documented fact, or, in the words of a more recent critic, to assign "Holmes's mental examinations of Melville" specifically to 1855, when his professional services were required by Melville's attacks of rheumatism and sciatica. According to the family tradition cited in my 1941 article, there had been a mental examination, but no written records are known that would confirm the report or indicate when and where such an examination may have taken place and who may have done the examining. My discussion suggested that several elements of the story throw additional light on the possible circumstances, and I still think they do. But there remains a difference between hard evidence and sheer inference or conjecture. The "exact line of demarkation" is in some cases difficult to draw—like that between sanity and insanity, Melville himself might say. But professional scholars and critics ought to be aware of the distinction, and what they pass along to their readers should certainly be labeled accordingly.

iii: 1955–1965

During the late 1950's and early 1960's "I and My Chimney" shared in the increased attention given Melville's writings after *Moby-Dick* and *Pierre*, the short stories in particular. Interest in its symbolism continued to remain high, though there have been conspicuous shifts and wide divergences in interpretation among more recent commentators. Merlin Bowen, Harry Levin, and Leslie Fiedler, in brief glances at the story, have all linked the chimney with objects or episodes in Melville's previous works not remarked by earlier criticism. Bowen, in *The Long Encounter: Self and Experience in the Writings of Herman Melville* (1960), compared it with the hearth in "The Lightning-Rod Man" (1854), seeing them as representing "the center and heart" of their fictional owners' "independent existence." Levin, whose appended bibliography cites my 1941 article as bringing out "the autobiographical reverberations" of "I and My Chimney," wrote in *The Power of Blackness* (1958) of the "defensive insight into the hidden recesses of personality" that the story embodies and termed the chimney itself "a symbol of the narrator's innermost integrity." Both Levin and Fiedler recalled an earlier chimney in Melville, that of *Moby-Dick*, Chapter 4, where Ishmael half-remembers a childish caper—"I think it was trying to crawl up the chimney." Interpretation of this "fantasy," Fiedler remarked in *Love and Death in the American Novel* (1960), "suggests itself immediately"—presumably in sexual terms—and thereby "casts light on the meaning of chimneys for Melville in such a later story as 'I and My Chimney.'" Fiedler did not elaborate, but William G. Crowley had already asserted in "Melville's Chimney" (1959) that in the story the chimney as a symbol is "ambiguous but definitely phallic," and E. Hale Chatfield, in "Levels of Meaning in Melville's 'I and my Chimney'" (1962), and Darwin T. Turner, in "Smoke from Melville's Chimney" (1963), were shortly to set forth this consideration more fully. I would agree that the chimney has certain physiological and sexual connotations, some of which I pointed out long ago, in a footnote. But they scarcely appear crucial to the overall symbolic pattern; the chimney surely represents more than a masculine counterpart of the biological imagery in "The Tartarus of Maids."

The most detailed investigation to date of the chimney in relation to comparable symbolic figures in Melville's earlier works will be found in a section of Dorothee Metlitsky Finkelstein's *Melville's Orienda* (1961), a book dealing with Melville and the Near East. In treating his preoccupation with Egypt and its ancient monuments, especially the pyramids and their explorers, Mrs. Finkelstein makes the following noteworthy observation:

> The supreme symbolical importance that Melville's vision attached to towering shapes which enclose a hidden vacancy found its objective correlative in the monuments of ancient Egypt. The image of the obelisk and the pyramid expands in symbolic significance until the identification of man with a pyramidal shape, the "I" in "I and My Chimney," is complete: "The architect of the chimney must have had the pyramid of Cheops before him; for after that famous structure it seems modeled."

(A footnote at this point in her discussion cites my 1941 article on "identification of the chimney with Melville's own personality.") Mrs. Finkelstein traces Melville's frequent allusions to various Egyptian monuments from *Typee* through the late poetry, concentrating on *Pierre* and "I and My Chimney"; she shows how earlier images, such as the entombed sarcophagus and particularly the Memnon Stone in *Pierre*, strikingly prefigure the chimney in the story. As for the action of "I and My Chimney," she demonstrates that Melville consistently maintains an analogy between the narrator's exploration of his chimney and the explorer Belzoni's operations in Egypt; even "Scribe's" measurements with reference to a secret closet "may have been inspired," she thinks, "by Belzoni's measurements and computations to determine the entrance into the Khefren pyramid." It may be claiming too much to say that Belzoni and the pyramid, in her words, "finally control the story," and certainly there are other components of "I and My Chimney" that obviously do not fall within the scope of a work concentrated on Melville's interest in the Near East. Nevertheless, Mrs. Finkelstein's study contributes substantially to understanding of the story in several respects. By throwing new light on its indebtedness to a special area of Melville's reading, she reminds us that it has roots in something besides first-hand experience. She goes farther than any of her predecessors in relating the pyramidal shape of the chimney to numerous structures appearing in earlier works, uncovering Melville's progressive development of the pyramid from incidental image to meaningful symbol. Her understanding of the symbolic values of the pyramid in Melville correlates with previous comments on the chimney by Sealts, Sedgwick, Chase, Rosenberry, and Arvin (in "Melville and the Gothic Novel"); she finds that a characteristic pattern of movement, "descent into 'the heart' of the pyramid," becomes Melville's recurrent symbolic representation of "the archetypal search for one's own soul." Not all interpreters will agree with this last point, but future critics of the story cannot safely overlook her investigation of its antecedents in Melville's reading and earlier writing.

Three other critics of the 1960's—Stuart C. Woodruff, William J. Sowder, and William Bysshe Stein—differ sharply from Mrs. Finkelstein in their reactions to the chimney as a symbol and from most earlier commentators in their general approach to the story itself. For Woodruff, whose "Melville and His Chimney" (1960) may be called the first "revisionist" criticism of the story, its chimney is neither a phallic nor even a personal symbol; it stands rather as "an emblem of the empirical reality of time and its manifestation as history." Sowder, in "Melville's 'I and My Chimney': A Southern Exposure" (1963), agrees with Woodruff that the chimney is independent of Melville; indeed, the setting of the story is not even Arrowhead but the American South, the narrator is a Southerner reflecting allegorically upon the history of his region, and the chimney represents its "peculiar

institution," slavery—specifically, "the presence of the Negro." For
Stein, in "Melville's Chimney Chivy" (1964), the chimney takes on religious connotations, appearing to him as "a symbol of warm, vitaliz-
ing faith equivalent to the ethic of love preached by Christ." A reader
of such widely diverging treatments of a common subject might be
forgiven for associating Melville's chimney with Ahab's "round gold"
doubloon and "rounder globe, which, like a magician's glass, to each
and every man in turn but mirrors back his own mysterious self." The
theories of Sowder and Stein strike me as saying less about Melville
and his story than about the preoccupations of two of its readers—
though I am well aware that all of us who write about ambiguous
doubloons are probably open to much the same charge. Woodruff is
convinced that the differences among earlier critics of the story are
negligible; the same comment hardly applies to most commentators
of the past decade.

Among the more recent essays on "I and My Chimney" I have
singled out three for closer examination in terms of their diverse
critical methodology, first comparing the articles of Woodruff and
Crowley, then moving to Richard Harter Fogle's discussion of the
story in his *Melville's Shorter Tales* (1960). In contrast to Woodruff's
deliberate break with his predecessors, Crowley may be said to round
out earlier discussion along biographical lines. His article of 1959, a
sequel to his master's thesis at Trinity College, Connecticut, begins
with a survey of what had already been said of "I and My Chimney"
by Sealts, Chase, Arvin, Leyda, and Howard; he accepts the most
radical implications of the view prevailing among them that the story
constitutes "sublimated biography, actual and psychological." Besides
giving an account of Melville's "mental-physical illness which resulted
in an examination by Dr. O. W. Holmes," "I and My Chimney," as
Crowley reads it, embodies "an attack on femininity" by Melville
(here Crowley is following Arvin closely) and "a classic picture of the
unhappy marriage—in some respects his own." Beyond all this, it also
makes "a conscious statement" of Melville's "literary position in the
fifties." Elaborating on this point, in his most original passages, Crowley argues that the chimney primarily represents "Melville's talent,
which he associates with his masculinity and, in this particular summer [1855], his poor health"; neither was what it had once been—
before "the personal catastrophe of *Pierre*." The remodeling of the
chimney recalls Melville's subsequent writing for the magazines,
something he regarded as "artistic self-mutilation." Only "the pervasive good humor" of the story leads Crowley to see in it the resolu-

tion, rather than the concealment, of "a personal tragedy or crisis in Melville's life."

Woodruff, unlike Crowley, acknowledges few ties with the commentators so far under review with the exception of Chase; his allegiance, if partly to New Criticism, is mainly to Milton R. Stern, though in *The Fine Hammered Steel of Herman Melville* (1957) Stern had passed over "I and My Chimney" altogether. Woodruff's discussion of the story begins with a flat rejection, as simply "misleading," of the bulk of previous writing about it up to 1960, when his article appeared. He particularly deplores the virtual "unanimity of opinion" he finds among his predecessors concerning its central symbol: they look upon the chimney as "some sort of projection of the narrator's soul and mind, and by extension, of Melville himself," when they ought to have taken it as standing instead for something impersonal, objective, and wholly external to both. Here Woodruff most resembles the New Critic reacting against what has been called the biographical fallacy. Charging that other commentators have read the story "solely" in personal terms, he cites as "typical" the views of Sedgwick and Arvin (which I see as barely compatible), and laments the errors of "even Richard Chase," the critic who otherwise "gets closest to Melville's intention" as Woodruff interprets it. Of all attempts to "explain" the story, however, the first article written about it is, in his words, "perhaps the most off-center." Though the article's author, says Woodruff,

is to be commended for his resourcefulness and ingenuity, he seems to be the victim of that common fallacy of *post hoc, ergo propter hoc*. If Dr. Holmes' visit to "Arrowhead" is embodied in the story, I fail to find it. . . . And if the affair is there as an unconscious exorcism, Sealts's reading becomes even more irrelevant.

. . . Despite his remarks on Melville's use of symbols, Sealts freezes the story into an allegorical mode of limited thematic value. My quarrel is not so much with what Sealts says as with what his interpretation prevents him from saying. If we are to treat "I and My Chimney" as an allegory of Melville's concern over insanity, we do a disservice to a story of richly patterned and highly significant symbolic statement.

Although the alternative treatment, on strictly New Critical principles, would be to examine the work not as personal allegory but purely as a literary artifact, Woodruff's ensuing discussion, with its concentration upon what he calls "symbolic statement," reveals that he has extraliterary concerns of his own. "In reading 'I and My Chimney,'" he remarks, "it is impossible to miss Melville's strong anti-transcendental bias." Such an attitude he finds clearly visible in "one of the main themes," defined as "the inevitable necessity and wisdom of living within a temporal, historical dimension, without . . . trying to destroy or ignore the only existence we may have—the 'sober, substantial fact' of the chimney itself." The "old" narrator must be seen as quite distinct from his older chimney, which through its association in the story with the widest ranges of time and history is made "symbolic of so much more than self": what Melville is evoking in "the 'cellar' imagery" when the narrator explores his chimney's foundation is simply the "dim period" of primeval antiquity rather than the self or the unconscious. (Mrs. Finkelstein would see here not a contradiction but a revealing correlation.) For Woodruff's purposes the significant measurement of the chimney is not its towering height but its imposing breadth: in their "shared obesity" the narrator and his chimney represent an "all-important historical, naturalistic perspective" in contrast to "a vertical dimension of cosmic idealism"; the narrator's wife, conversely, is idealistic and presumably transcendental. Borrowing a term from Stern's book, Woodruff calls the wife "a kind of quester" and describes her as "a domesticated Ahab bent on her own 'mad project' of hunting down and killing the chimney," which in the narrator's words appears "like an anvil-headed whale."

What Woodruff had found particularly attractive in Chase's handling of the story is apparent from his further interpretation of the strained relations between the husband and wife. For him "it is not hard to recognize an implicit criticism of America itself" in the narrator's "slightly sardonic portrait of a woman who refuses to act her age, who lacks all reverence for the impact of the past or a chastening sense of 'place.'" Though granting that "it is possible to understand" the story without referring to any such "cultural dimension," Woodruff is nevertheless persuaded that "the obvious parallels between the wife's shortcomings and those of Melville's America extend appreciably the significance of the narrator's courageous resistance." The contest between the pair as Woodruff describes them—the immature, credulous wife and her skeptical, cautiously pragmatic husband—comes to a head when "Scribe" (who, "of course, is a Confidence Man") captures her interest with his talk of a "secret closet" in the chimney. At this point Woodruff parts company with Chase, finding him "essentially wrong" in relating "the hidden mystery" of the chimney to concepts such as "the father" and "God." Since the chimney stands only as the empirical reality of "time and process itself," as Woodruff's own argument runs, then the ensuing search for its supposed closet must represent "the folly and futility of searching out life's secrets." Here Melville's own "belief"

in what Milton Stern has called "an epistemology and an ontology based upon pragmatism and empiricism" emerges . . . as the narrator's skepticism about the closet's very existence—about *any* benevolent, humanly oriented purpose in the universe. . . . [For him,] the "closet" is simply a phony come-on.

Now "the real theme" of the story is disclosed: "the fundamental dichotomy between a vertical and a horizontal dimension, or between the man-world and the God-world." In Woodruff's judgment, man's search for questions of ultimate meaning is "inevitably destined to fail," and the story suggests why this is so: "The trouble with idealists, Melville appears to argue, is that they embark on *spiritual* treasure hunts with *empirical* equipment," like "Scribe" taking his measurements of the chimney. What marks the superiority of the "narrator-artist," as Woodruff now calls him, is his use of "the one legitimate instrument for the contemplation of mystery—the mind itself," and particularly its "symbol-making faculty." He is both naturalist and symbolist, and his "intense devotion to his chimney is also Melville's intense devotion to the materials of his art."

Woodruff's article has historical value both as a corrective to earlier criticism and as opening new approaches to "I and My Chimney." His explication of the story as "a thoroughgoing symbolic expression of Melville's basic epistemology" is likely to seem persuasive to those who, like some of my own students, already share Stern's ideas, seeing Melville's writings as growing out of a consistently "naturalistic" perception of the external world; others, however, will regard such a reading as too conceptualized or even as too narrow. Woodruff's own protest against taking the story "solely" as disguised autobiography is no doubt timely, though his wholesale dismissal of previous criticism seems an over-reaction and his strictures against all "allegorical" readings allow for no differences of kind or degree among them, whether the critic involved is Sedgwick or Arvin. The ensuing analysis is provocative within its self-imposed conceptual framework; it ends, curiously enough, by putting Melville as thinker into the story where others had been chastized for placing Melville the man. Having opened his discussion by insisting on a "crucial distinction" between chimney and narrator, Woodruff concludes by minimizing differences between narrator and author, though to some readers "the psychological and political 'distance'" will appear as great in the one instance as in the other. The case for Melville's "naturalism," moreover, still remains moot. A writer able "to reveal at once his skeptical intellect and his strong emotional will to believe," as Leon Howard described the author of *Moby-Dick* in his edition of that work in 1950, is not to be readily or narrowly categorized, and the "bias" against a "vertical" perspective in favor of the "horizontal" that Woodruff's article develops may reside not so much in the story or in Melville as in the eye of its convinced beholder. Although a naturalistic Melville seems especially congenial to some present-day readers, only three commentators publishing between 1960 and 1965, so far as I know, have cited Woodruff's essay in advancing their own views of the story. One of them, Judith Slater, in "The Domestic Adventurer in Melville's Tales" (1965), explicitly follows Woodruff's lead with respect to "I and My Chimney," though her general comments on Melville's work of the 1850's are also reminiscent of Richard Chase; the two others, Sowder and Turner, reach conclusions far removed from the ideas of either Woodruff or Stern.

The consideration of "I and My Chimney" in Fogle's book of 1960 I regard as the most comprehensive of recent discussions. Fogle himself is among the least doctrinaire of all Melville's critics. In his reading of this one story he draws freely upon the insights of earlier commentators, as does Crowley, though with more reservations; his views of it are much closer to those of Sedgwick and Chase than to Arvin's. His distinctive approach grows out of his conviction that Melville's writing embraces several levels or layers of significance—among them the biographical—which for him are not mutually exclusive as they appear to Woodruff. "On one plane," he acknowledges, "I and My Chimney" may well be "an allegory of Melville's own condition and circumstances"; more particularly, in "the search for the treasure" there is possibly "an ironic reference to Dr. Oliver Wendell Holmes's mental examinations of Melville in 1855." Such a reading of the story, Fogle adds, besides helping "to explain the architect's invidious name, . . . would also point to a complex self-irony in Melville, surprisingly jocular and unembittered. If it is true, however, it is also limited in interest" (though not "irrelevant," as Woodruff would have it), and certainly "the 'secret' of the story" does not lie here. Perhaps "the secret is that there is no secret," as Melville once wrote Hawthorne in another connection, "none, at any rate, which would warrant the finder in destroying . . . the structure in which it lies embedded." Here Fogle's central emphasis becomes manifest: for him the chimney is a living, organic image, presenting an "archetypal form of reality and growth" (compare Mrs. Finkelstein on Melville's archetypes); it is "perhaps most obviously the life principle of the house as a structure," that vital force which the narrator is seeking to preserve against threatened extinction. The chimney can also be taken, appropriately enough, to represent Melville's writing, and a little more broadly as his genius (Crowley had said his "talent"), but beyond that it is "any genius, a possession which may burden even its owner." On this level, the narrator's "genial, conventional conservatism" is for Fogle "a veil which part reveals and part conceals a more urgent and fundamental struggle by Melville, who is fighting to preserve what is best in himself and his life's work at a time when it seems to be threatened seriously." But this still is not all, for "In its largest aspect the chimney is a symbol for universal reality, the scheme of things entire"—an identification akin to but less restrictive than Woodruff's purely "empirical reality of time and its manifestation as history."

Fogle makes one further point about the chimney comparable to what has been observed of Melville's other major symbols, notably the White Whale: throughout the story it is presented as "an indivisible, inexhaustible object in itself."

That is, many meanings are attached to it, but it is larger than any of them singly and larger than the sum of them. It preserves its own unique identity; when all has been said, it is simply (or complexly) a chimney still. It has a kind of magic about it, but its enchantment can be finally neither elucidated nor broken.

What is said in these last three sentences could scarcely be improved upon; in my judgment it is the best single comment on the chimney since Melville himself published his story in 1856. As for Fogle's general conception of "I and My Chimney" as a work embodying multiple levels of meaning, this approach has all the virtues and possible dangers of an all-inclusive eclecticism, though Fogle is less open to objection on this score, I should say, than is Crowley. While willing, as Woodruff is not, to entertain the possibility, or even probability, of subordinate biographical implications on one or more planes of interpretation, Fogle differs from most of his predecessors and contemporaries alike in a highly important way: because of his governing concern with the aesthetic values of Melville's writing, he repeatedly and rightly insists that to dwell solely on any component part is to risk doing less than justice to the comprehensive artistic whole. On this count, unfortunately, most writers on "I and My Chimney" up to the present, whether their preoccupation has been with the life of the author, his metaphysical outlook, or other hidden treasure of their own devising, must plead guilty in some degree.

iv: After 1965

Discussion of "I and My Chimney" between 1940 and 1965 reflects the general movement of Melville studies from an earlier concentration on Melville the man to a growing appreciation of his achievements as a literary artist. The continuing search for meanings has been relatively constant, especially wherever symbols are involved— white jackets or white whales or chimneys with possible secret closets. If I were asked what direction future commentary on "I and My Chimney" is likely to take, I would predict more study of *how* it means, in John Ciardi's phrase, and less concern with precisely *what*. Going back for a moment to 1962, consider *The Example of Melville*, in which Warner Berthoff, tracing Melville's artistic development, values certain advances in the short stories as going beyond the technical proficiency achieved in *Moby-Dick* itself. Along with "Bartleby," he finds "I and My Chimney" "charmingly executed yet teasingly profound and moving in implication, and full of sharp turns and recoveries of wit." For Berthoff it is among Melville's very best work, "as original in conception as *Moby-Dick*, though on a reduced scale, and as expert in performance as *Pierre* is confused and maladroit." Although he offers neither explication nor technical anlysis of the story, he suggests a profitable approach to its artistic design by classifying it among the varieties of Melville's first-person narratives—"the personal adventure-chronicle, the recital, the confession"—in which "the interposing of a narrator's voice tends to become the chief formal precipitant of interest and significance." Happily, some future critic more concerned with Melville's skillful employment of "a narrator's voice" than with the burden of its presumed message will soon turn his attention to the entire body of shorter prose, "I and My Chimney" included. What can be done in such a study is illustrated by A. W. Plumstead's rewarding treatment of "Bartleby: Melville's Venture into a New Genre" (1966), published in the recent symposium on that story. "Let us suspend for a moment the question of meaning," Plumstead begins, and consider the matter of literary genre. His methodology for treatment of "Bartleby" would apply equally well to "I and My Chimney":

To approach the story keeping in mind [Melville's] problems and past experience, the models he may have had in mind, and his awareness of the
demands of his new genre, is to go a long way toward understanding why
the story is what it is.

Such an approach does not provide a complete, satisfying interpretation
or "key to it all" (if any can), but it does enlarge "Bartleby's" stature as a
good short story in its own right, by showing its importance both to
Melville's development as an artist, and to any final assessment of his craft of
fiction. It challenges interpretations which see the story as a subtle allegory
of some despair, resignation, or even madness in Melville himself.

By quoting Plumstead with approval I do not mean to suggest that
I have turned "against interpretation," in the current fashion, or re-
pudiated my earlier reading of "I and My Chimney." Were I to write
again on the story, in 1967, in the light of all that has now been reviewed here, I should begin and end with the chimney itself, for it
dominates the tale, but pay more attention than before to point of
view and tone as provided by Melville's creation of the old narrator.
And I should keep in mind its author's "problems and past experience," personal as well as professional, not for their biographical significance so much as for their contributions to the *donnée* of the story.
First there is the matter of setting. The story certainly includes "a
geniune description of the great chimney at Arrowhead," in the
words of Leon Howard, plus "some details from the one at Broadhall." Broadhall is the nearby house at Pittsfield that had once belonged to Melville's uncle Thomas, where a chimney was actually
taken down in 1851 during remodeling by its new owners the Morewoods. "The proposed removal of the chimney," I suspect, was not so
"purely mythical" as it seemed to Mrs. Melville in after-years. From
her husband's earlier works, in tracing the further genesis of the
story, I would cite representative passages showing his long fascination with chimneys and associated structures (which Woodruff over-
looks), and I would draw gratefully on Mrs. Finkelstein's book to
bring in his reading about the Egyptian pyramids and to develop
what they had come to stand for symbolically in his imagination. With
respect to the plot, I would weigh her suggestion of a link between
Belzoni's measurement of a pyramid and "Scribe's" survey of the
chimney in the story, but I would add, in full agreement with Howard, that Melville was also thinking of Dr. Holmes's examination of
his own back, recalling those wry references to sciatia put into the
mouth of his narrator. Remembering too what drew me to the story
originally, the intensity with which its more serious passages are
charged, I should once again go farther than Howard has been will-

ing to go, and deeper into "the 'cellar' imagery" than Woodruff's horizontal commitments allow, in dealing with both genesis and content: I believe that besides writing a genial, humorous, and "thoroughly magazinish" sketch for the public, Melville was also, on another level of meaning, privately "representing the disturbance that was created in his household by what his mother took to be evidences of insanity in her son." The original "intuition" about the story set forth in these last words I still affirm; the particular phrasing I have quoted is Henry A. Murray's; the ostensible speaker—appropriately enough— is "the biographer," one of the anonymous personae appearing in "Bartleby and I" (1966), Murray's coruscating dialogue among seven differing characters in search of agreement about Melville's intentions in writing the earlier story.

But we are not to treat "Bartleby" as merely a biographical document, as both Murray and Plumstead remind us, nor "I and My Chimney" as "solely" an allegory, whether "of Melville's concern over insanity" or only with twinges in his aching back. Surely, beneath the humorous surface, it also embodies his equal concern with personal identity, individual integrity, and human dignity, as Sedgwick's study affirmed, and with the hidden mysteries of life, whether connected with the father and man's search into the past, as Chase held, or simply with time and process itself, as Woodruff insists. All these concerns, as part of the given with which Melville worked, became part of its meaning as well—but they are not what "I and My Chimney" is necessarily *about*. It is about the narrator and his chimney. The chimney is indeed an object in itself with many meanings attached, both within the story and beyond, which a quarter-century of diverse criticism has brought to light in profusion. As Fogle has said, it looms larger than any one meaning and larger than all, though in the immediate context of the story it remains, simply or complexly, a veritable chimney. Going through the surrounding commentary, to borrow the narrator's words by way of conclusion, "is like losing one's self in the woods; round and round the chimney you go, and if you arrive at all, it is just where you started"—with the chimney, now reexamined but still unexhausted.

Alien to His Contemporaries:

Melville's Last Years

(1974)

Reprinted here under this supplied title are two self-contained components of *The Early Lives of Melville: Nineteenth-Century Biographical Sketches and Their Authors* (Madison and London: The University of Wisconsin Press; © 1974 by the Regents of the University of Wisconsin System), pp. 20–28 and 64–82: "A Hermit's Reputation" and "The Belated Funeral Flower," both of which deal with "aspects of Melville's life and temperament" during his last years. (I borrow the phrasing of Professor G. R. Thompson's review of *The Early Lives*.) Arthur Stedman, Dr. Titus Munson Coan, and J. E. A. Smith, whose names appear in the following pages, all wrote biographical sketches of Melville following his death in 1891 when Mrs. Melville chose Stedman as her husband's literary executor. Kathleen E. Kier, "Elizabeth Shaw Melville and the Stedmans, 1891–1894," *Melville Society Extracts*, No. 45 (February 1981), pp. 3–8, quotes more extensively than I had space for in *The Early Lives* from Mrs. Melville's letters to Stedman and his father, Edmund Clarence Stedman. I must confess to some surprise at Ms. Kier's statement that my "principal emphasis" in studying "the attempted Melville revival in the nineties is on the role of the Stedmans . . . as the driving force," since I agree wholeheartedly with her own thesis: that Mrs. Melville herself "provided the principal impetus behind the crusade, though she was well aware that a professional man of letters would have to handle the particulars" (p. 3).

In the present text I have omitted all illustrations, parenthetical page references, and appended notes that appeared in the 1974 printing; ellipses (. . .) on p. 206 indicate the point at which extended parallel passages were quoted on pp. 68 and 70 to demonstrate Arthur Stedman's indebtedness to Mrs. Melville's memoranda of her husband's career. I have made one correction, on p. 196: we now know that the Melvilles were married at the Shaw home in Boston rather than at the New South Church. On pp. 200, 201 and 215–216 I have added new information that has turned up since 1974—notably extracts from Mrs. Melville's recently published letters to Mary Lan-

man Douw Ferris, a distant relative of Melville who wrote a biographical
sketch of him in 1901.

"A Hermit's Reputation"

If you know that fine writer, Melville, why not write his life?" This
was the question posed in 1883 by W. Clark Russell, the English
novelist of the sea, to an American correspondent, Augustus Hayes,
who wrote short stories for the magazines. Russell did not know Melville himself or even whether he was still living, but he did know his
books—"the best sea stories ever written," he called them in his letter
to Hayes, by "the greatest genius your country has produced." The
world ought to be told "as much as can be gathered of his seafaring
experiences and personal story." Hayes showed Russell's letter to a
writer for the New York *Herald*, who published an excerpt in his column. If quoting Russell was intended to test the attractiveness of his
suggestion to prospective American readers and publishers of a Life
of Melville, as it may well have been, the results were evidently not
encouraging. Although Melville's reputation in England seems to
have been continuous, his name and his books were no longer familiar in America during the Gilded Age, where even in New York there
were said to be professional authors who supposed him to be long
since dead.

Russell himself was in no position to undertake the research necessary for a biography, but he did what he could during the 1880's to
celebrate Melville's writings. In the *Contemporary Review* for September of 1884 he praised not only *Typee*, *Omoo*, and *Redburn* but also
Moby-Dick, which he regarded as Melville's "finest work." After Russell's essay was reprinted in expanded form in *In the Middle Watch*
(1885), published in New York by the Harpers, Melville acknowledged his praise in a letter delivered by their mutual friend Peter
Toft, an artist who had "accidentally discovered" Melville in New
York. Russell's reply, dated 21 July 1886, expresses his pleasure in
learning "from Mr. Toft" that Melville was "still hale and hearty."
"Your reputation here," he assured Melville, "is very great. It is hard
to meet a man whose opinion as a reader is worth having who does
not speak of your works in such terms as he might hesitate to employ
with all his patriotism, towards many renowned English writers. . . ."
Since Melville had been receiving similarly flattering letters from
other English admirers, James Billson and J. W. Barrs, he had some
confirmation of Russell's gratifying remarks about his fame overseas.

In 1888, with Russell's permission, Melville dedicated to him his *John Marr and Other Sailors*, printed for private distribution to a few chosen friends; Russell responded in 1889 by dedicating *An Ocean Tragedy* to Melville and again praising him unreservedly in a Chicago weekly, *America*. "I know not if the works of the author of 'Omoo,' and 'Typee,' and 'Redburn' are much read and esteemed in the United States," Russell wrote in his article, "but I am sure there is no name in American letters that deserves to stand higher for beauty of imagination, for accuracy of reproduction, for originality of conception, and for a quality of imagination that in 'Moby Dick,' for instance, lifts some of his utterances to such a height of bold and swelling fancy as one must search the pages of the Elizabethan dramatists to parallel."

Among Melville's own countrymen there was no contemporary voice to speak as glowingly of his achievement as Russell had done in England. As for a possible biography, apparently the first suggestion from his own side of the Atlantic that the Life of such an author was deserving of book-length treatment came later in 1889 from Alexander Young, contributor of the "Here in Boston" column of the Boston *Post* under the pen-name of "Taverner." After proposing that "some of our enterprising publishers would find it in their interest to reprint 'Omoo,' and 'Typee,'" Young added that "I do not see why the author's life should not find a place in the American Men of Letters series." Young himself, an antiquarian who at the time of his death was writing a book on "Old Boston," devoted a later column primarily to Melville's grandparents, Major and Mrs. Thomas Melvill, and their home on Green Street in Boston as an old friend recalled it, concluding with a reference to Melville. In the parlor of the house, this unnamed friend remembered, were "many curiosities," among them

a glass ship, fully rigged, modelled after the fashion of some celebrated French vessel, which was the delight of his young eyes; and, under a glass cover, some very precious tea—a part of that veritable tea which was thrown overboard when the American people resisted "taxation without representation." Major Melville [*sic*] was one of the sturdy band who, dressed as Mohawk Indians, assisted in throwing the tea into the water; and when he returned home the specimen referred to was shaken out of his high boots and preserved as a valuable relic. For his display of patriotism he was given a lucrative office in the custom house which he retained for some years. One of his six daughters became engaged to a young lawyer, who was long devoted and sincerely attached to her; but her early death prevented her union with one who was afterwards revered and honored as Chief Justice Shaw, whose daughter subsequently became united to Herman Melville.

As we now know, Herman Melville spent the summers of 1827 and 1829 with his grandparents in Boston. He long remembered the glass ship, which figures prominently in *Redburn;* the Melvill and Shaw families carefully preserved the Major's vial of tea following his death in 1832. When Melville married Elizabeth Shaw on 4 August 1847 it was Young's father, Rev. Alexander Young (1800–1854), Unitarian minister of Boston's New South Church, who performed the ceremony. Nothing has been discovered to indicate a subsequent personal relationship between the minister's son (1836–1891) and the Melvilles, but it is evident from this and other references in "Taverner's" column that he maintained a Bostonian's interest in members of the Melville and Shaw families.

Although no Life of Melville was to appear "in the American Men of Letters series" until 1950, when Newton Arvin's biography was published as part of a twentieth-century revival of that project, another Bostonian, Horace E. Scudder, may have recalled "Taverner's" suggestion on assuming the editorship of the *Atlantic Monthly* in 1890. On 14 October 1890 Scudder wrote to George Parsons Lathrop, Hawthorne's son-in-law and author of *A Study of Hawthorne* (1876), who had been an associate editor of the magazine, suggesting two possible subjects for a "miniature American men of Letters" series that Lathrop might handle: "Fitz-Greene Halleck & Hermann Melville, especially the latter." Lathrop, who had corresponded with Melville when preparing his book on Hawthorne, replied from New York that he believed Melville to be still alive and at work in the New York Custom House (Melville had in fact resigned at the end of 1885), but

very much averse to publicity. He is an excellent subject, however. I don't know of any unpublished material that I can get, relating to him. If I could find time I might go down to the Custom House & unearth him, & perhaps get at something. . . . A capital article could be made about him, even without any new material. There is enough in the *Study* & references of Hawthorne's, to suggest a picture of their friendship in Berkshire; a picture nowhere I think very clearly outlined. But I mean that Melville himself, any way, would furnish forth a good & interesting article. . . .

Scudder's response was discouraging.

I can't help thinking that there must be some good material in the subject, though probably it would be better still if Melville would only let go of life. So much more frankness of speech can be used when a fellow is apparently out of hearing. What you say of his aversion to publicity makes me pause. I hate the whole business of making papers on living men, when the appeal is not to the interest of the men as writers, or artists, or publicists or what not, but to a petty interest in personal details.

On second thought therefore, I believe we had better wait for our shot at Melville, when his personality can be more freely handled.

While Melville, with his aversion to publicity, was still alive but aloof in New York there would be no full-length Life written of him in America, as Russell and Young had proposed, or even a biographical article of the sort that Scudder had in mind for the *Atlantic*. Russell's pronouncements from England and those of Henry S. Salt, who wrote on Melville in the *Scottish Art Review* in 1889, drew less of a reaction in this country than other remarks from abroad by the Scottish poet and novelist Robert Buchanan, who after a visit to the United States in 1884 accused the New York literary community of neglecting Melville, "the one great imaginative writer fit to stand shoulder to shoulder with Whitman," in Buchanan's words, on the American continent. So Buchanan wrote in a footnote to his poem "Socrates in Camden," contributed to the London *Academy* of 15 August 1885, which praised Melville fulsomely along with Whitman. This "sea-compelling man" who raised Leviathan from the deep and

> whose magic drew Typee,
> Radiant as Venus, from the sea,
> Sits all forgotten or ignored,
> While haberdashers are adored!

So Buchanan charged in the poem; his accompanying note explained that while he was in America he had "sought everywhere for this Triton, who is still living somewhere in New York," but "No one seemed to know anything" of him. Returning to the attack four years later, Buchanan was more specific in his account of the circumstances. His "very first inquiry" in America had been for Melville, he asserted in a note to his "Imperial Cockneydom," written for the *Universal Review* of 15 May 1889.

There was some slight indication that he was "alive," and I heard from Mr. E. C. Stedman, who seemed much astonished at my interest in the subject, that Melville was dwelling "somewhere in New York," having resolved, on account of the public neglect of his works, never to write another line. Conceive this Titan silenced, and the bookstalls flooded with the illustrated magazines!

To literary New Yorkers the jab at Stedman would have been unmistakable—especially if they realized that in 1884 he and Melville had been near neighbors on East Twenty-Sixth Street: Stedman at No. 44, Melville at No. 104. Whatever Stedman's exact knowledge of Melville may have been in 1884, he had certainly been aware of his existence two years earlier, when the founding members of the Authors Club, Stedman among them, had offered Melville membership. In 1888, Ernest Rhys, another Briton then visiting Stedman, was told that Melville, "living only a few doors away," had "a hermit's reputation, and it was difficult to get more than a passing glimpse of his 'tall, stalwart figure' and grave, preoccupied face." In these words Rhys was not only recalling the occasion but also quoting one of Arthur Stedman's later articles in which the phrase "tall, stalwart figure" is applied to Melville. Buchanan's story and its repetition in America obviously struck a sensitive nerve with the younger Stedman, who did not become a visitor in Melville's residence until some time in 1888. When the old tale turned up once again in the New York *Times* following Melville's death in 1891, Stedman was moved to comment tartly in print that the complaining Buchanan was merely a literary adventurer who "apparently 'sought everywhere' except in the one place where all of Mr. Melville's contemporaries made their search when they had occasion to visit him—the City Directory."

But Buchanan was not the only contemporary figure to charge neglect of Melville by the American public and especially by his fellow writers in New York. That Melville's name "would not be recognized by the rising generation" was granted by the New York *Commercial Advertiser* in an article of 14 January 1886. "Although his early works are still popular," the paper continued, probably meaning "still popular" among older readers, "the author is generally supposed to be dead." Nevertheless, "he is not very old—sixty-five—and his rather heavy, thick-set figure and warm complexion betoken health and vigor." In recent years

he has done nothing in literature. For a long while he has been in the custom house as inspector, and is dependent on his salary. . . . He has, indeed, been buried in a government office. . . . He is a genial, pleasant fellow, who, after all his wanderings, loves to stay at home—his house is in Twenty-sixth street—and indulge in reverie and reminiscence.

Edward Bok, the young editor of the *Ladies Home Journal*, was even more pointed: "There are more people to-day," he wrote in 1890, "who believe Herman Melville dead than there are those who know he is living."

And yet if one choose to walk along East Eighteenth Street [*sic*], New York City, any morning about 9 o'clock, he would see the famous writer of sea stories—stories which have never been equalled perhaps in their special line. . . . Busy New York has no idea he is even alive, and one of the best informed literary men in the country laughed recently at my statement that Herman Melville was his neighbor by only two city blocks. "Nonsense," said he. "Why, Melville is dead these many years!" Talk about literary fame? There's a sample of it!

Bok's paragraph, syndicated in his newspaper column and re-printed both in *Publishers' Weekly* and in the Boston *Literary World*, provoked a variety of comments. Alexander Young was led to reflect in the Boston *Post* on "the difference between Boston and New York in regard to appreciation of literary men": in Boston, he insisted, "an author of Melville's genius and reputation would not be allowed to lapse into obscurity simply because he had ceased to write." In New York, according to the *Critic*, "the friends of Mr. Herman Melville have been annoyed" by the publication of Bok's paragraph. "Mr. Mel-ville, it is true, has gone out very little since the death of his son, some two years ago," the *Critic* conceded; "but in literary circles in New York it is by no means unknown that he is a resident of this city, and an employee of the Customs Revenue Service." As this inaccurate re-port suggests, the *Critic*'s information on Melville in 1890 was scarcely up-to-date. It was then fully four years since Melville had left the Custom House; if the loss of a son had affected his social life it was more likely the death of Malcolm in 1867 than that of Stanwix in 1886. Actually there had been many deaths of relatives and friends during the New York years. Melville's wife, as one of her grand-daughters recalled, "had been in mourning so often for members of her family" that whenever her grandchildren appeared in black hair ribbons "she changed them to bright colors." When the family first returned to New York in 1863 Melville had resumed his visits to Evert Duyckinck, continuing until Duyckinck's death in 1878, and was seen occasionally with such writers as Alice and Phoebe Cary, but he seems never to have sought companionship among the younger generation of authors and editors.

According to Arthur Stedman, who knew both Melville and Whit-man as well as other writers of his father's generation and his own, Melville, in spite of his "hermit's reputation," was always "an interest-ing figure to New York literary circles." Making this point in his obitu-ary notice, Stedman went on, with Buchanan's slur at his father ob-viously in mind, to cite the invitation extended to Melville—"among the very first"—to join the Authors Club. Stedman was correct; in fact, according to Charles De Kay, secretary of the Club, Melville had at first accepted but later declined the invitation because, in De Kay's words, "he had become too much of a hermit" and "his nerves could no longer stand large gatherings." Another member, Brander Mathews, recalled, however, that "the shy and elusive Herman Melville" actually "dropped in for an hour or two" at one of the Club's early meetings when "all the men of letters residing in or near New York" were invited. But in 1890 the elder Stedman, still one of the Club's moving spirits, acknowledged to a friend his disappointed surprise that he had not persuaded its members "to take an interest in Melville, one of the strongest geniuses, & most impressive *personalities* that New York has ever harbored. *He* ought to be an honorary member. He is a sort of recluse now, but we might perhaps tempt him out." Frank Jewett Mather, Jr., writing in 1919, asserted that shortly before Melville's death Stedman "managed a complimentary dinner for him and with difficulty got him to attend it"—though such an event is unrecorded by other writers on either Stedman or Melville, Mather presumably had the story from Stedman himself. Both Stedman and his son were genuinely drawn to Melville during the final months of his life; both evidently remained sensitive to the old charge that he had been ignored by New York writers, Stedman included. The implications of Arthur Stedman's rebuttal to this charge in his obituary notices were not lost "in literary circles," as a paragraph in the Springfield, Massachusetts, *Daily Republican* of 12 October 1891 (p. 4) clearly attests.

> Herman Melville's separation from his fellow-authors was voluntary, and not due to their neglect, as has been said. He was one of the first to be invited to join the Authors club at its founding in 1882, but he declined. Few literary men and women in New York knew him; one of the few, naturally, was Edmund C. Stedman, whose friendly acquaintance no recluse even would willingly forego.

Along with the Stedmans, Melville's other New York friends and visitors during his last years included Dr. Titus Munson Coan, an old acquaintance who "visited him repeatedly," and Oliver G. Hillard, who found that though Melville was "eloquent in discussing general literature" he would not talk about his own writings; Peter Toft had the further impression that he seemed to hold them "in small esteem." Melville in fact told Hillard that he owned none of his early works, and Oscar Wegelin reported delivering copies of them to Twenty-Sixth Street that Melville had ordered from the bookshop of John Anderson, Jr. Besides visiting Anderson's shop Melville, still an omnivorous reader and a wide-ranging walker, browsed also in those of Albert L. Luyster and Francis P. and Lathrop C. Harper and in at least two libraries, the Lenox and the New York Society. As for literary talk, he reminisced uneasily about Hawthorne with Hawthorne's son Julian in 1883 and more openly with Theodore F. Wolfe, probably somewhat later; there are records of both interviews in print, but nothing to suggest further discussion of Hawthorne with George Lathrop for the *Atlantic*. Other acquaintances who were not professional writers included George Brewster, whom he knew through his Albany connections the Gansevoorts and Lansings, and George W. Dillaway, a lawyer, both New Yorkers who were present at Melville's funeral along with Coan, Arthur Stedman, and members of the family. In 1885 he made a last visit to Pittsfield where according to his old friend J. E. A. Smith, poet, journalist, and historian, he "did not evince the slightest aversion to society, but appeared to enjoy the hearty welcome which it gave him" there. In later years the Melvilles were reportedly entertained at dinner by Mr. and Mrs. Gustav Schirmer in their New York apartment at the Dakota; according to Stephen Birmingham, the Schirmers "apparently found Melville charming but a little sad. He was working again on a final novel, to be called *Billy Budd*. But, he said, he was sure his book would never be published unless he had it privately printed, because his popularity of more than thirty years earlier had all but vanished."[1]

From such evidence as this it seems evident that Melville's seclusion, though deliberately cultivated as Arthur Stedman insisted, was by no means impenetrable. "He never denied himself to his friends," Dr. Coan asserted; "but he sought no one." Coan traced the cause of his withdrawal not to any particular event so much as to "his extremely proud and sensitive nature and his studious habits," both of which had been evident when the two first met as early as 1859 in Pittsfield. Though Peter Toft found "much in common" with Melville and termed him "a delightful talker when in the mood," he thought him "abnormal, as most geniuses are," and felt that he "had to be handled with care." Hillard had no such reservations, however: "With the few who were permitted to know him, he was the man of culture, the congenial companion, and the honestest and manliest of all earthly friends." Melville, it appears, selected his own intimates and correspondents as time and occasion suited him. On at least two occasions he wrote letters of thanks to men who had spoken favorably in public about his work: W. Clark Russell and J. W. Henry Canoll. When he declined an invitation it was invariably with the utmost courtesy. An illustration is afforded by his letter of 5 December 1889 to Professor Archibald MacMechan, who had written him from Halifax, Nova Scotia, proposing a correspondence and seeking "some particulars of your life and *literary methods* . . . other than given in such books as Duyckinck's dictionary." In a regretful refusal, after citing his advanced age and long service "as an outdoor Custom House Officer," Melville explained that "I have latterly come into possession of unobstructed leisure, but only just as, in the course of nature, my vigor sensibly declines. What little is left I husband for certain matters as yet incomplete, and which indeed may never be completed." His unspecified reference was of course to at least one more volume of verse to follow *John Marr* (1888) and to the prose work then in progress that he would call *Billy Budd, Sailor*. But both *John Marr* and *Timoleon* (1891) were privately printed, *Billy Budd* was still undergoing revision at the time of his last illness, and neither the public nor even his friends had reason to know that to the end the "hermit" was actively writing.

Following Melville's death on 28 September 1891 there was a flurry of renewed interest in both the man and his works that continued into the next year and beyond, both at home and abroad, though Weaver's full-length biography was still thirty years in the future. The New York *Sun, Times, Tribune,* and *World* and the Boston *Journal* and *Evening Transcript* carried obituary notices within a day or two of his passing, editorials and extended critical appraisals soon followed, and by the end of December 1891 some thirty notices or longer articles had been printed or reprinted in at least eighteen American newspapers and four magazines. With respect to purely biographical materials the most informative of these articles were written by three men: Arthur Stedman, Titus Munson Coan, and J. E. A. Smith. All three not only knew Melville but spoke with authority about particular phases of his career, such as his life in the South Seas and in Pittsfield and his dealings with various publishers. Their essays provided more new information than any other publications since the *Cyclopædia* of 1855, when the Duyckincks had said far less of what they knew about the man behind the writings than they had done in private correspondence. None of the three was moved to bring out the book that Russell and Young had called for, but the younger Stedman, who had charge of Melville's literary affairs after his death, arranged for new editions not only of *Typee* and *Omoo*, as "Taverner" had suggested, but also of *White-Jacket* and *Moby-Dick*. As an Introduction to the first of these volumes, *Typee* (1892), Stedman printed the brief Life of Melville that had been evolving, with Mrs. Melville's suggestions, in his earlier articles. Meanwhile, Coan, also with Mrs. Melville's help, had published at least one shorter piece of his own, and Smith, working indepedently in Pittsfield, had turned out a serialized bio-

graphical sketch and accompanying editorial on Melville for the Pittsfield *Evening Journal*; in 1897, after Smith's death, Mrs. Melville arranged for a partial reprinting in a thirty-one page pamphlet, of
Smith's account. . . .

"The Belated Funeral Flower"

In the first of Stedman's articles after Melville's death, the account
of his funeral published in the New York *Tribune*, occurs one of the
few glimpses of Melville himself to appear anywhere in the younger
man's essays. "He was always a great reader," Stedman wrote,

> and was much interested in collecting engravings of the old masters, having
> a large library and a fine assortment of prints, those of Claude's paintings
> being his favorite.
>
> His tall, stalwart figure, until recently, could be seen almost daily tramp-
> ing through the Fort George district or Central Park, his roving inclination
> leading him to obtain as much out-door life as possible. His evenings were
> spent at home with his books, his pictures and his family, and usually with
> them alone.

In his second article, " 'Marquesan' Melville," Stedman added these
words:

> A few friends felt at liberty to visit the recluse and were kindly welcomed
> but he himself sought no one. His favorite companions were his grandchil-
> dren, with whom he delighted to pass his time, and his devoted wife, who
> was a constant assistant and adviser in his work. . . .

What Stedman says at the outset in these passages has been independently confirmed through studies of Melville's reading and his collection of books, engravings, and prints, many of which survive. From
the manuscripts of his last years with their clear indication that Mrs.
Melville had been acting as her husband's amanuensis and perhaps at
times as his friendly critic, we know too that Stedman had reason to
call her Melville's "assistant and adviser." Finally we have the words of
two of the four grandchildren about Melville himself, with his "brave
and striking figure as he walked erect, head thrown back, cane in
hand, inconspicuously dressed in a dark blue suit and a soft black felt
hat," bound for Madison Square with Frances or to Central Park, "the
Mecca" of most of his pilgrimages with Eleanor. "I am sure he took
great comfort and pleasure in his grandchildren," Frances Thomas
Osborne has affirmed, "and he showed a side of his nature to us that
no one else knew he possessed."

Both the granddaughters have written vividly of their recollections of the house on Twenty-Sixth Street and those who lived in it; both mention a number of the same household objects and family customs. Frances, the younger, was fearful of the statues and paintings, though she liked to play among the books. She "never felt the least bit afraid" of Melville himself, however, despite his reputation among the family for "moods and occasional uncertain tempers." Her elder sister recalled that at long intervals "his interest in his grandchildren led him to cross the river and take the suburban train to East Orange, where we lived. . . . When he had had enough . . . he would suddenly rise and take the next train back to Hoboken." As she remembered, or perhaps was told, "he felt his grandchildren would turn against him as they grew older. He used to forebode as much." Eleanor was between nine and ten when "this quite special grandfather" died. During the next year, 1892, her grandmother sold the Twenty-Sixth Street house, and with her unmarried daughter Elizabeth—"Aunt Bessie" to the girls—moved into the Florence at 105 East Eighteenth Street. The Florence, as Eleanor Melville Thomas Metcalf recalled it sixty years later, was

an old-fashioned, high-studded apartment house with a spacious, darkly wooded, black-marble-pillared, crimson-carpeted dining room, where excellent meals were served to them at their own table by a faithful "Joe." Elizabeth and her crippled daughter were relieved of all further household worries and cares.

Elizabeth's main care now was for her husband's fame, but her intimate interest in all family concerns continued undiminished. Her grandchildren's memory of her is warm. She was humbly proud of their imagined gifts and attributes. And her son-in-law gave her the devotion of his own warm, sympathetic nature. When her trials were over, no one could hint that her life would be easier (and therefore happier). Indeed, one of her in-laws tried to; but an almost fierce pride that she had been Herman's wife silenced the imprudent tongue. A pride in his work and fame, which she had always cherished, grew further from this personal loyalty, and was the beginning of her inducting me into the service of him she had served so faithfully.

Mrs. Metcalf's book of 1953, *Herman Melville: Cycle and Epicycle*, gathers many family letters, including those of her grandmother, which present Melville as revealed "by his contemporaries in his personal relations" (p. x)—an aspect virtually undisclosed in the carefully circumscribed writings of Stedman and Smith. Mrs. Melville's letters in particular, like those of Evert Duyckinck in the 1850's, show more of Melville than what either she or Duyckinck set down for the record—in her case, not in print but in private memoranda written for her own use and that of her family. Her jottings, entered in a well-worn "Pocket Diary," contain much miscellaneous information having nothing to do with Melville himself though serving to bring out much of her own sense of family and of family continuity. Thus she records in the first of the surviving entries—106 pages have been torn out and other entries erased—the numbers assigned by the photographer to two portraits of her daughter and the serial numbers of two of her bank books. Next in sequence, if not in time, comes this paragraph on the volumes Stedman had edited:

A new edition of Typee, Omoo, Moby Dick, & White Jacket having been published in 1892—by Mr. Arthur Stedman—I received in royalties from the U[nited].S[states]. Book Co. and afterwards from the Am[erican]. Pub[lishers]. Corporation both of whom failed $243.40—owing me $158.13 which was never paid. Then a new edition was published in 1900 from the rented plates—by Dana Estes & Co Boston—from which on a 5 p[e]r c[en]t royalty I have received $63.47—

(Following this entry, dated 1 February 1902, is the added notation "see later accounts".) What Mrs. Melville recorded in subsequent pages includes, as Raymond Weaver said, "a brief history of Arrowhead, . . . an inventory of legacies, and notes of furniture, plate, pictures, a blue quilted petticoat and an Empire gown. There is also, in two versions, the briefest biography of her dead husband."

The first of what Weaver distinguishes, somewhat inaccurately, as the "two versions" of a biography tells about Melville's career only as Mrs. Melville herself had observed it after he had come back from the South Seas; her running comments make it the more interesting narrative of the pair. The little "Pocket Diary" was published in, or for, the year 1866; this first biographical account seems to have been copied into it from preexistent notes originally dated "May 1861". It opens with Melville's return from the Pacific in 1844; it must originally have run through the Meteor voyage of 1860, though as the account now stands it also includes references to his two attacks of erysipelas in later life. Mrs. Melville's remarks on the various events she chronicles emphasize two elements: the hard work her husband had put into his books and the deterioration of his health during the 1850's and after. In the thirteen years between 1844 and 1857, as she correctly notes, "he had written 10 books besides much miscellaneous writing." Her association of the poor health with the hard work of writing is obvious in her incidental observations, brief though they are, as she runs over the titles—especially *Mardi, Moby-Dick,* and *Pierre:*

Winters of '47 & '48 he worked very hard at his books—sat in a room without fire—wrapped up—wrote Mardi. . . .
Wrote White Whale or Moby Dick under unfavorable circumstances—would sit at his desk all day not eating any thing till four or five o'clock. . . .
Wrote "Pierre" published 1852—
We all felt anxious about the strain on his health in Spring of 1853. . . .
In Fall of 1856 he went to Europe . . . [;] came home . . . in 1857 . . . with much improved health. . . .
In Feb 1855 he had his first attack of severe rheumatism in his back—so that he was helpless—and in the following June an attack of Sciatica. . . .
A severe attack of what he called crick in the back laid him up . . . in March 1858—and he never regained his former vigor & strength—

Mrs. Melville's second version of her husband's career, which lacks the cryptic but suggestive observations included in the first, follows after an intervening sequence of eleven blank pages. This version is a factual recital of dates and events running from Melville's birth in 1819 to his death in 1891. Internal evidence suggests that she probably compiled it with the aid of one or more of the various nineteenth-century biographical sketches available to her. The occurrence here of much-used phrasing going back as far as the article on Melville in the 1852 edition of *The Men of the Time* indicates that she may even have consulted her husband's copy of that work for its record of his earlier years. For his later career, in case her own memory needed refreshing, she possibly went to *Chambers's Encyclopædia*, which she had mentioned in the earlier account because of its misstatements about Melville's Meteor voyage of 1860. That some reference work or works lay before her is not the only inference to be drawn from analysis of this second account, however, since a further point to be noted is that the very same phrases, the same erroneous dates, and still other elements in common also turn up in the second of Arthur Stedman's newspaper articles on her husband, "'Marquesan' Melville." . . .

Common to these parallel accounts, in addition to the phrases and dates that both Mrs. Melville and Stedman could have picked up from earlier biographical sketches, is just what the briefer Lives do *not* mention: they do not report Melville's attendance at the Albany Classical School or name Dr. West; they refer to a New Bedford whaler but not the Acushnet; they make no allusion to Melville's period of schoolteaching (which had been pointed to, however, in Smith's 1879 *Taghconic*). Although Stedman's successors, beginning with Raymond Weaver, have been aware of his general indebtedness to Mrs. Melville, they have missed the specific information she thus provided for him. One reason is that their attention, like Weaver's, has been focused on Stedman's later Introduction to *Typee* rather than its various antecedents: Smith's biographical sketches, Stedman's own journalistic articles that Smith too had drawn on, and the partial source for "'Marquesan' Melville" in Mrs. Melville's store of facts that were not widely known outside the family. It should now be clear that at the time when Stedman was writing that article he either had access directly to Mrs. Melville's memoranda or else had learned of their phrasing in some more precise way than through ordinary conversation; perhaps she read aloud to him parts of the Pocket Diary or, more probably, furnished him with a written extract from it. That Dr. Coan benefited in a similar way while writing about Melville for the Boston *Literary World* is an additional possibility.

How one assesses the influence of Elizabeth Shaw Melville on the essays of Stedman and Coan, and how one interprets her role in her husband's career, will depend both on personal impressions of Mrs. Melville's character and personality and on intuitions about the nature of the Melvilles' marriage relationship. That she earned the warm regard of her granddaughters is evident. Among the biographers, Stedman, like Smith, does not probe at all into the inner life of the family; both are content with conventional remarks about Melville's wife and granddaughters, though with never a word about the generation of sons and daughters between them. In a later day, Raymond Weaver, uninhibited by the restraints of the nineties, flatly blamed Elizabeth Melville for the "crisis" in her husband's life between 1851 and 1856. His Introduction to an edition of Melville's journal of 1856–1857, where he quotes the whole of Mrs. Melville's first account of her husband, describes the Pocket Diary as

a peculiarly intimate affair—the jottings of an old lady who has outlived her husband and her generation, and whose years have been crowded with tragic memories she was unable to understand and which she wished to efface. . . .

Her story of her husband, a "gaunt digest . . . crowded with 'facts,'"

reveals more about Mrs. Melville than of the subject it purports to treat. It is of Melville's achievements, and the handicap of his bodily ills. He had been a busy man, and he came to be a sick one. Such is Mrs. Melville's *apologia* for her husband. And the limitations of her piety and imagination that narrowed her vision to this, were, I believe, among the prime instigating causes to provoke in Melville the emotional crisis which she was pitiably unable to understand.

Though Eleanor Metcalf, "inducted" as she was by her grandmother "into the service of him she had served so faithfully," obviously saw her as Melville's wife in a perspective different from Weaver's, his less charitable view of Elizabeth Melville's role in their marriage still has its active proponents. In terms of the present study, however, the point to be emphasized is not the validity or invalidity of either Mrs. Metcalf's or Weaver's contentions about Mrs. Melville; what is relevant here is the changing climates of opinion within which Melville's own life and works have been interpreted over the years. Weaver, writing in the 1920's and 1930's, offered a psycho-sexual explanation of Melville's personal problems; Mrs. Melville, like her contemporary J. E. A. Smith, stressed her husband's physical ailments while Arthur Stedman, with Dr. Coan and many another nineteenth-century reader, bewailed the shade of Aristotle that seemed to rise coldly between themselves and Fayaway. "Each age," as Emerson shrewdly said, "must write its own books; or rather, each generation for the next succeeding. The books of an older period will not fit this." The statement aptly applies to the successive Lives of Melville from 1852 to 1892; it is just as pertinent to the newer conceptions of literary biography that came into fashion during the present century. As Frank Jewett Mather remarked when reviewing the third full-length Life to appear in the 1920's, Lewis Mumford's *Herman Melville,*

no man of my generation could have written so ardent and subtle a biography of Herman Melville as Mr. Mumford has produced. Whatever our conviction of Melville's greatness, such devotees as Arthur Stedman, Professor Archibald Mac Me[c]han, and myself could not but be muffled by the fact that all our weighty literary acquaintance assumed our task was to praise "Typee" and, beyond that, merely to apologize for its author. These things ought not to inhibit, but they do.

There is no indication that Mrs. Melville in her time looked forward to a full-scale Life of her husband other than Smith's projected expansion of his serialized biographical sketch. The surviving memoranda certainly do not suggest that she was assembling material for anything more ambitious than the articles written in New York by Stedman and Coan. What did engage her immediate interest and active support was the new edition of Melville's principal works; "the desire of my heart," she told Stedman in 1893, was "to see my husband's books resurrected." Since Melville himself, by Stedman's testimony in his article for *Appleton's Annual Cyclopædia,* had "avoided every action on his own part and on the part of his family that might tend to keep his name and writings before the public," the question arises of whether the new edition was in violation of his express wishes or whether the restrictions placed on "his family" applied only during his own lifetime. Of the four titles selected for republication in 1892, three—*Omoo, White-Jacket,* and *Moby-Dick*—had gone out of print by 1887. As for *Typee,* the undated directive in Mrs. Melville's hand that she turned over to Stedman—it is headed "Memoranda for re-issue of 'Typee' (made by Mr Melville)"—is tangible evidence that as her husband's "assistant and adviser" she had discussed with him a new and revised edition of at least that particular work. The matter had arisen late in 1889, when H. S. Salt wrote Melville from England about a "proposition to reprint 'Typee'" in the Camelot Series published by Walter Scott of London. Melville was ill at the time, but on 12 January 1890, when he felt well enough to reply, he addressed both Salt and John Murray expressing his interest but acknowledging Murray's rights in the book under provisions of the original agreement of 1846 for its publication in England. Murray withheld his approval, thus preventing Salt and Scott from going ahead with their new edition during Melville's lifetime—the term of the agreement. Meanwhile, however, the possibility of "re-issuing" *Typee* was evidently taken seriously enough for Melville either to draft or ask his wife to draft the revisions covered in the "Memoranda." Whether he also discussed with her the desirability of a new American edition, either of *Typee* alone or *Typee* in association with other works already out of print in this country, can only be conjectured.

Certainly Mrs. Melville did not wait long after her husband's death to authorize the new selected edition. Under terms of Melville's will (dated 11 June 1888) she had been named sole executrix of his property; since the will makes no specific reference to copyrighted books or other literary materials, any instructions concerning their disposition must have been separately communicated to her, probably not in writing. It is therefore impossible to say what wishes Melville may have expressed about his out-of-print works or unpublished manuscripts, or to know whether he and his wife had discussed the qualifications of young Arthur Stedman as a professional literary man and prospective editor, if not as potential biographer. That Mrs. Melville had lost no time in turning to Stedman for assistance during or after Melville's last illness is clear from Stedman's letter to Salt written on 17 November 1891, which explains not only that he had been in charge of Melville's "literary affairs"—originally written "publishing affairs"—since his death, but that he had also begun the campaign to bring Melville's name again before the public by writing and publishing five articles about him and above all by arranging for the new American edition of his selected works. In each of these activities Stedman was clearly proceeding with Mrs. Melville's approval and tangible support. We know that she had provided information and illustrations for Stedman's first articles on Melville and had also turned over the publishing agreements, which he had examined "very thoroughly," as he told the United States Book Company, thus becoming more familiar with their provisions than was Mrs. Melville herself. The decisions about what to include in the new edition were probably worked out jointly by Mrs. Melville and Stedman but laid before the publisher by Stedman as her agent.

As Stedman explained to Salt, the edition would comprise Melville's four "best books"; in "Melville of Marquesas"—the article which has most to say about Melville's own publishing arrangements—he had already set forth the rationale for their selection:

> Melville's most artistic work is to be found in "Typee," the first blossom of his youthful genius. This idyl, which set all the world to talking, undoubtedly will hold a permanent position in American literature, and most people will wish to read its sequel, "Omoo." . . . As for "Moby Dick" and "White Jacket," they should be read wherever men go down to the sea in ships, and until the spirit of adventure, so strong in the English-speaking race, abandons its sway over the hearts of human beings.

A year later, when the publisher—or was it Mrs. Melville?—raised the possibility of adding a fifth title to the edition if sales of the original volumes should be encouraging enough, Stedman agreed to "investigate" *Israel Potter*, though his printed comments on the book indicate that it had never been one of his favorites. A more likely candidate in his eyes might well have been *The Piazza Tales*, which he felt had been undervalued because of its publication "in an unattractive form." Like Smith in *Taghconic* (1879), Stedman mentions "The Piazza" in relation to Melville's surroundings at Arrowhead, but his favorite tales from the volume were obviously "The Bell-Tower," the one piece of Melville's prose to be selected for *A Library of American Literature*, and "Benito Cereno," both of which he described as "powerful." Stedman's articles also name two other stories: "I and My Chimney," to which Smith had called attention in *Taghconic* as "a humorous and spicy essay," and "Cock-A-Doodle-Doo!," which the editor of *Harper's Magazine*, Henry M. Alden, had praised to Stedman as "about the best short story he ever read." These references to five of the stories may suggest that a collection of Melville's shorter prose was under consideration as well. Mrs. Melville had ready a file of all her husband's magazine fiction; in addition, she listed—possibly for Stedman's editorial use—their titles and place of first publication. Beyond these pieces, as she knew though perhaps Stedman did not, was also the unpublished manuscript of *Billy Budd, Sailor*. But if a fifth volume—*Israel Potter*, the shorter fiction, or whatever—was actually under consideration by Stedman and Mrs. Melville, the publisher's bankruptcy shortly after the third and fourth titles of the new edition were released put an end to any idea of thus enlarging its scope.

In the light of Stedman's special relations with Mrs. Melville, what he had to say in print about the Melville canon and the changing course of Melville's reputation over the years deserves closer attention than it has so far been given. Mather spoke of him as "muffled" by the expectations of his professional contemporaries; to what degree was he also inhibited—or conversely, was he prompted—by Mrs. Melville, given his position as her literary advisor and spokesman? To ask the question is of course to raise the finally insoluble issue of whether his published essays reflect his own opinions, Mrs. Melville's, or a consensus of both. Whatever their ultimate views of Melville himself may have been, Stedman's approach to Melville's writings clearly had a good deal in common with hers. His Introduction to *Typee* and to the new edition offers a further explanation of the place of these "four most important books" in the Melville canon as a whole. Three of them, he asserts, "are directly autobiographical, and 'Moby Dick' is partially so; while the less important 'Redburn' is between the two classes in this respect." Here Stedman is following the division of Melville's work into "classes"—autobiographical writings and creative romances—that had been standard among commentators from the Duyckincks to H. S. Salt; he is also echoing the refrain running through the earlier paragraphs of Mrs. Melville's second résumé of her husband's career: "See 'Redburn'"; "See 'Typee'"; "See 'Omoo'"; "See 'White Jacket'". In classifying most of Melville's other long prose works as "unsuccessful efforts at creative romance," Stedman was evidently thinking in particular of *Mardi* and the disastrous *Pierre*. In his article on Melville for *Appleton's Annual Cyclopædia*, which Mrs. Melville was given in proof and which in effect she approved before its publication, Stedman singles out *Typee* and *White-Jacket* as Melville's "most consistent" books; *Moby-Dick* "is perhaps the most graphic and truthful description of whaling life ever written, although it contains some of the objectionable characteristics of 'Mardi.'" If *Mardi* was "objectionable," whether by reason of its matter or of its manner, *Pierre* was even more so, and both *Israel Potter* and *The Confidence-Man* further "detracted" from Melville's reputation.

Melville's attainment of fame with his earlier books and his loss of it with *Pierre* and its successors is a particular concern in Stedman's

"Melville of Marquesas." "Melville's success as a writer," Stedman declares here,

> was undoubtedly continuous and constantly increasing up to the publication
> of "Moby Dick" in 1851. . . . With "Moby Dick" he was to reach the topmost
> notch of his fame. "Pierre, or the Ambiguities" (1852) was the signal for
> an outburst of protest against "metaphysical and morbid meditations" which
> already had made themselves apparent in "Mardi" and "Moby Dick."

Meanwhile, Melville's publishers, the Harpers, had the "sagacity" to give him a less favorable contract for *Pierre*, as Stedman explains in another section of this same essay headed "A Disastrous Year." In this section he also introduces a matter that Mrs. Melville stresses in her memoranda: her husband's hard work at his books as the cause of injury to his health; not even Smith, in his reminiscences of Melville's Pittsfield years, had assumed such a cause-and-effect relationship. "The year 1853," Stedman declares,

> was one of ill omen to Melville. He had removed to Pittsfield in 1850 in the
> flush of his youthful fame, and while "shaping out the gigantic conception
> of his 'White Whale,'" as Hawthorne expressed it. The book came out
> and he enjoyed to the full the enhanced reputation it brought him, al-
> though six years of the most engrossing literary work had somewhat injured
> his constitution. He did not, however, take warning from "Mardi," but
> allowed himself to plunge more deeply into the sea of philosophy and
> fantasy. "Pierre" appeared, and after it a long series of hostile criticisms
> ending with a severe, though impartial, article by Fitz-James O'Brien in
> *Putnam's Monthly.*

Criticisms such as O'Brien's may well have touched Melville himself, along with responses within the family to *Pierre* and its reception, during the "disastrous year." Though Stedman of course does not say so here, we know now that at this same time the Melvilles, Shaws, and Gansevoorts were trying in every way they knew to get Melville away from his desk, out of Pittsfield, and into some occupation other than writing. Family correspondence of the fifties says little about any of his particular works, but there was a tendency to agree with the professional critics of the day that in his more recent books he had left his "proper sphere"—straightforward narrative—for "crude theory & speculation" and "metaphysical disquisitions." Along with the narrator of "I and My Chimney" (1856), Melville might well have exclaimed that his family, "like all the rest of the world, cares not a fig for my philosophical jabber." It is his absorption in "philosophy and fantasy" that Stedman too came to specify as the primary cause of Melville's declining reputation after 1851. He began assembling the evidence in "'Marquesan' Melville" and "Melville of Marquesas," both written when he was working closely with Mrs. Melville in planning the new edition. In these articles he touches on Melville's philosophical discussions with Hawthorne that began in 1850, the monologue on Greek philosophy delivered to Coan in 1859, and the contemporary protests against the "metaphysical and morbid meditations" of *Pierre*—the phrase is Fitz-James O'Brien's. In the same vein, the later biographical essay in *Appleton's Annual Cyclopædia* states flatly that Melville had been "led by his inclination for philosophical speculation to commit grave literary errors, which destroyed his popularity with the reading public." (This is the article that Mrs. Melville read in proof and found both "comprehensive and well done.") Elsewhere in the *Cyclopædia* essay Stedman again cites Hawthorne on Melville's fondness for philosophical discussion, but he does not take up Smith's earlier suggestion that this supposedly harmful trait was something Melville had been led into by Hawthorne's bad influence; instead, he affirms that Melville had habitually "indulged" in philosophical studies since the time of his "early manhood"—a point Stedman may have inferred from *Mardi* or perhaps learned from talking with Mrs. Melville. This habit grew as Melville "advanced in years," Stedman continues, "until his conversation with friends became chiefly a philosophical monologue." Here, though no names are mentioned, Stedman may have been thinking specifically of Coan's experience at Pittsfield; in the Introduction to *Typee* he modified this sentence to read: "This habit increased as he advanced in years, if possible." Indeed, philosophy as Melville's supposed "ruling passion" is virtually the theme of the Introduction, in which Stedman declares that "Mr. Melville's absorption in philosophical studies was quite as responsible as the failure of his later books for his cessation from literary productiveness."

How much Stedman knew at first hand about Melville's philosophizing, apart from his reading of Schopenhauer during his last illness, and how much he derived from Hawthorne and Coan, from critics like Fitz-James O'Brien, and from Mrs. Melville herself is difficult to estimate. Though there is of course no reason to deny Melville's long-standing interest in philosophy, one suspects that "philosophy and fantasy" had tended to become code words, among nineteenth-century critics and the Melville family alike, for all the otherwise undefined tendencies in *Mardi* and its successors that made them different from *Typee* and *Omoo*. What Stedman came to say, or was possibly prompted to say, on this much-belabored subject has been picked up and repeated by later biographers even though it goes beyond the testimony of others who knew Melville in his late years, such as Toft, Hillard, Stedman's own father, or even Coan, though Weaver chose to read Coan's recollections of Melville in 1859 as typifying his way of talking to the end. Stedman may well have done likewise, if his own experience in listening to Melville tended to confirm Coan's early impression. But not all of Melville's acquaintances would have called his conversation a "monologue" or regarded it as particularly "philosophical." Another writer—anonymous—who knew Melville in his old age remembered not only "his gray figure, gray hair and coloring, and piercing gray eyes" but even more strongly his manner of speaking: "Though a man of moods, he had a peculiarly winning and interesting personality, suggesting Laurence Oliphant in his gentle deference to an opponent's conventional opinion while he expressed the wildest and most emancipated ideas of his own." To his friends as in his books Melville continued to display that persistent quality of mind that Hawthorne had long since characterized as his "freedom of view." It had sometimes shocked the more conventional Evert Duyckinck: "To one of your habits of thought," Melville had written, "I confess that in my last [letter], I seemed, but only *seemed* irreverent." It had later disturbed John Morewood and other "good citizens of Pittsfield" who knew Melville himself; it certainly troubled a proportion of his readers—the evangelical partisans who disliked his comments on the missionary enterprise or those readers of *Mardi* and *Pierre* who wanted adventure instead of allegory and narrative instead of metaphysics. The freedom, the "seeming" irreverence, were his to the last, whatever the terminology of those who recognized and reported it—readers, friends, or members of the family.

That Elizabeth Melville herself would have said publicly what Stedman wrote and printed about her husband's "grave literary errors" may be doubted; that Stedman published such things repeatedly without her challenge or amendment is a matter of record. The *Cyclopædia* article she not only accepted but praised, and even on re-reading the Introduction to *Typee* she could find nothing to change but a few minor errors in names and titles—certainly no deletions such as the passages she omitted from Smith's biographical sketch when preparing the 1897 pamphlet. What she did object to in publications other than Smith's and Stedman's is worth noting here: she tried unsuccessfully to have certain words removed from her husband's letters to Hawthorne as they were printed in Rose Hawthorne Lathrop's *Memories of Hawthorne* (1897); she was "so incensed" by the "atrocious portrait" of Melville in Julian Hawthorne's *Hawthorne and His Circle* (1904) that she wrote "asking him to withdraw it from future editions, or let me furnish him with a good one to replace it." Would she have remembered how Melville and his Pierre had refused to be "oblivionated" by a daguerreotype? Probably not, since Melville himself had relaxed his old rule in permitting his portrait to appear in the *Library of American Literature* and even earlier in *Appleton's Cyclopædia of American Biography*. Whatever her private thoughts may have been about his life and work, she was a jealous conservator of her husband's fame, quick to respond when she sensed an injury or saw an opportunity to enhance the positive appreciation of his achievement. The 1892 edition, published with Stedman's indispensable help, was her primary effort; it was unfortunate for them and for their goals that the edition seemed headed for oblivion, along with its publisher, within the first six months after its first volume had appeared.

In addition to her reprinting of Smith's biographical sketch in 1897, "for the family and a few near friends," there are two or three further examples of Mrs. Melville's realization of every new opportunity to keep her husband's name and fame before a larger audience. In 1895 she provided a previously unpublished portrait of Melville for use in the *Century Magazine*. In the Springfield, Massachusetts, *Sunday Republican* of 1 July 1900 is an article on Hawthorne and Melville by one of her Pittsfield friends, Harriette M. Plunkett, illustrated with portraits of the two authors and consisting in part of long extracts from Melville's "Hawthorne and His Mosses," which Mrs. Plunkett credited not only with creating "a profound sensation among discriminating readers" of the Duyckincks' *Literary World* but also with leading to a phenomenal increase in sales of *Mosses from an Old Manse*. At Mrs. Plunkett's request Mrs. Melville had previously agreed to furnish that "precious document," her own copy of the essay, should a file of the *Literary World* be unobtainable in Pittsfield. A year later, when a distant relative of Melville, Mary Lanman Douw Ferris, requested her comments on a biographical sketch Mrs. Ferris had prepared for the *Bulletin* of the Society of American Authors, Mrs. Melville replied at some length in a letter of 20 September 1901 that requests a number of alterations. The projected article, she wrote,

is very interesting and mainly correct—but I should like to amend one statement where it is said that the reception of "Pierre" had any part in causing my husband to lead "a recluse life"—in fact it was a subject of joke with him, declaring that it was but just, and I know that however it might have affected his literary reputation, it concerned him personally but very little—his seclusion from the bustling outer world was but the outcome of a naturally retiring disposition, and desire of repose after what would now-a-days be called the "strenuous life" of his boyhood and youth and had long been his habit from the beginning of his home life long years before "Pierre" was thought of.

I have ventured to make a few suggestions on the margin of your proof which may be too late to act upon, and I wish I could have had communication with you personally or otherwise before your writing. I do not think my husband's manner ever could be called "gruff," though being approached at times when his mind was absorbed in some phase of his literary work it might have seemed so. And I think he would not have [been] willing to call his old Typee entertainers "man-devouring" as he has stated that whatever might have been his suspicions he never had evidence that it was the custom of that tribe.

I am very much gratified at each additional tribute to my husband's genius, and thank you for so contributing to the "Authors Bulletin"[.] I shall be very glad to see it when it appears.

The article as published in the *Bulletin* for September 1901 (VI, 289–293) deletes the reference to *Pierre* that had troubled Mrs. Melville, saying only, in its tenth paragraph, that "Melville was a recluse, chiefly owing to his natural disposition"—words that reflect some of Arthur Stedman's phrasing in his "Herman Melville's Funeral" (1891) and also Mrs. Melville's own, though without repeating her striking assertion that her husband had *joked* about the book's failure as "but just." Although Mrs. Melville's letter did not specifically request further deletions, whatever Mrs. Ferris had written concerning Melville's "gruff" manner and his opinions of the Typees as "man-devouring" must also have been cut before her essay was published, since these topics are wholly absent from the final version.[2]

Later in 1901, after an anonymous "admirer of Herman Melville" had written to the New York *Times* requesting information on Melville's various books, Mrs. Melville responded, making annotations on a list of titles that the paper subsequently published. *Battle-Pieces* was then still in print, as noted in the list; *Clarel*, she explained, had been "withdrawn from circulation by Mr. Melville on finding that it commanded but a very limited sale, being in strong contrast to his previous popular works," and *John Marr* and *Timoleon* had been printed for private circulation only. Otherwise, she remarked,

I suppose that all of the later books are now out of print, but the principal sea stories—"Typee," "Omoo," "Moby Dick," and "White Jacket"—which have always been in demand, were reissued with new plates and with a memorial introduction by Mr. Arthur Stedman, under his able auspices, in 1892, and are now in the hands of Dana Estes & Co., Boston.

Except for one later reference among her memoranda to the Boston printing, this is Mrs. Melville's last allusion to Stedman's editorial work. In 1906 she was dead, leaving her husband's papers in the hands of her invalid daughter Elizabeth; as we know, the daughter was willing enough to let Mather make use of everything for his projected biography except Melville's letters to her mother. Two years later Miss Melville too was dead; the papers passed in turn to her sister Frances (Mrs. Henry B. Thomas), to Eleanor Melville Thomas Metcalf, and to the collections at Harvard and the Berkshire Athenaeum. It was Mrs. Metcalf who encouraged Raymond Weaver, Henry A. Murray, and other pioneering twentieth-century scholars interested in a Life of Melville; Mrs. Thomas entertained written inquiries submitted through her, but would go no further. After finding a reference to herself in John Freeman's *Herman Melville* (1926), she wrote to her daughter: "I absolutely refuse to be interviewed by *any one* on the subject of H.M. I don't know him in the new light."

As Mrs. Thomas's letter suggests, it was to yet another generation that Melville was obliged to look for "the eventual reinstatement of his reputation" mentioned in Stedman's Introduction to *Typee*: "Mr. Melville would have been more than mortal," in Stedman's words, "if he had been indifferent to his loss of popularity. Yet he seemed contented to preserve an entirely independent attitude, and to trust to the verdict of the future." Until that verdict should be returned, he would figuratively keep the open independence of his sea, like Bulkington in Chapter 23 of *Moby-Dick*, in preference to the false safety of the leeward land: "in the port is safety, comfort, hearthstone, supper, warm blankets, friends, all that's kind to our mortalities," yet for the storm-tossed ship, "the port, the land, is that ship's direst jeopardy; she must fly all hospitality," for "her only friend" is really "her bitterest foe." Such land-based friends as the Stedmans were confident that "had Melville been willing to join freely in the literary movements of New York," as Arthur Stedman put it in " 'Marquesan' Melville," "his name would have remained before the public and a larger sale of his works would have been insured." This is almost to imply that the virtue of "Hawthorne and His Mosses" was that it increased the sales figures of *Mosses from an Old Manse*. The Authors Club and the Century were not for him, however kindly the suggestions were made or the invitations tendered. What Melville thought of the kind of "fame" that could be promoted by meeting and cultivating literary journalists is the burden of one of his letters to James Billson in England, that of 20 December 1885. It "must have occurred" to Billson, as it had to

Melville himself, "that the further our civilization advances upon its present lines so much the cheaper sort of thing does 'fame' become, especially of the literary sort."

The sentiment is familiar: "All Fame is patronage," Melville had written to Hawthorne over thirty years earlier. "Let me be infamous." Over the years he had thrown away the Biographico-Solicito Circulars from the compilers of dictionaries and encyclopedias, evidently little concerned with the accuracy or even the inclusion or omission of a biographical sketch of "H.M. author of 'Peedee' 'Hullabaloo' & 'Pog-Dog.'" But beneath the carefully maintained reserve of the last years one detects a difference. It is visible in the letters to his various English correspondents, in the newly made photograph that accompanied the very letter to Billson that expressed his sentiments on fame, and in the portraits that began turning up in encyclopedias and anthologies; his willingness to consider a new edition of *Typee*—when the initiative came from beyond himself and his family—is still another indication. But the clearest evidence of Melville's private thinking is in the writing of his last years, most of it known only to himself and to his wife—the "Winnefred" to whom he dedicated the never-to-be-finished volume of "Weeds and Wildings." In the language of the late poetry, true fame must grow organically; it cannot be mechanically induced, though its natural flowering may "for decades" be delayed "owing to something retarding in the environment or soil." So Melville declared, with a glance at his own age and fame, in his prose headnote to "The American Aloe on Exhibition." Any reputation is evanescent at best, during a man's lifetime or after, he wrote in "Thy Aim, Thy Aim?"

> if, living, you kindle a flame,
> Your guerdon will be but a flower,
> Only a flower,
> The flower of repute,
> A flower cut down in an hour.
>
> But repute, if this be too tame,
> And, dying, you truly ennoble a name—
>
> Again but a flower!
> Only a flower,
> A funeral flower,
> A blossom of Dis from Proserpine's bower—
> The belated funeral flower of fame.

In reading Schopenhauer during 1891 Melville came across and checked a remark by Tacitus that he may well have applied to himself:

"The lust of fame is the last that a wise man shakes off." And the familiar lines from *Lycidas* must have run through his mind—

> Fame is the spur that the clear spirit doth raise
> (That last infirmity of noble mind)

—as he wrote the Nelson chapters of *Billy Budd* and essayed his portrait of Captain Vere: "The spirit that 'spite its philosophic austerity may yet have indulged in the most secret of all passions, ambition, never attained to the fulness of fame." Thus even "the belated funeral flower" was denied to Vere, as it seemed beyond the reach of another austere philosopher who in years gone by had awakened to find himself a celebrity as "the author of *Typee*." To Melville and probably to his wife as well, the most secret of all passions was never entirely hidden; Arthur Stedman seems to have suspected it, though without ever entirely understanding its operations during Melville's last years. "With lessening fame his desire for retirement increased, until a generation of writers for the press grew up to whom the announcement of his death was the revelation of his previous existence." So runs the conclusion of Stedman's article in *Appleton's Annual Cyclopædia*.

And so Melville maintained his distance, and with it his independence. Away from the city, back in Pittsfield in 1885 or in upstate New York a year or so later, he felt more freedom and less constraint: in Glens Falls during the summer of 1886 or 1887 the young Ferris Greenslet overheard him in a barbershop spinning a tall and ribald story about his exploits in *Typee*[3]—the very subject he refused to discuss with his callers in Twenty-Sixth Street. With the grandchildren too, who also heard "wild tales of cannibals and tropic isles," he was equally relaxed; "Little did I then know," wrote Eleanor Metcalf in later years, "that he was reliving his own past." Here Melville showed "a side of his nature" that others little suspected—or if they did, considered it out of place in a formal biographical essay. As for the biographers of the nineties, what Weaver said of Mrs. Melville's memoranda is true of their Lives of Melville: these writings too reveal more of their authors than of the subject they purport to treat. Something Julian Hawthorne once wrote about his father's friends—Melville included—is relevant to Melville's own acquaintances and even his family: "Seeing his congenial aspect towards their little round of habits and beliefs, they would leap to the conclusion that he was no more and no less than one of themselves; whereas they formed but a tiny arc in the great circle of his comprehension." This is not an exaggerated observation; it applies to any man or woman of genius or even talent in dealing with other citizens of the world. "Ever the instinct of affection revives the hope of union with our mates," wrote Emerson in "Friendship," "and ever the returning sense of insulation recalls us from the chase."

While reading Schopenhauer during his last months of life Melville paused over and marked another passage in *The Wisdom of Life* that must have struck him as a comment on his own relations with his time:

the more a man belongs to posterity, in other words, to humanity in general, the more of an alien he is to his contemporaries; since his work is not meant for them as such, but only for them in so far as they form part of mankind at large; there is none of that familiar local colour about his productions which would appeal to them; and so what he does, fails of recognition because it is strange. People are more likely to appreciate the man who serves the circumstances of his own brief hour, or the temper of the moment,— belonging to it, and living and dying with it.

How to present as a man of their time this once-famous writer who had become a hermit, a recluse, in short an alien to his contemporaries—this was the problem confronting the biographers of the nineties that is unsolved in any of the early Lives of Melville. Their choices were either to apologize for the man who refused to remain "the author of *Typee*," to fly in the face of prevailing taste, or somehow to transcend both alternatives, as only biographers of a later generation and sensibility were finally able to do. That Melville belonged ultimately to posterity rather than among his fin de siècle contemporaries is a commonplace of twentieth-century criticism, but this is a conviction not generally accepted until the labors of Arthur Stedman and Elizabeth Melville were long since over and done. An essential preliminary was the "resurrection" of Melville's forgotten books: first the four titles of the much-reprinted American edition of 1892 and the corresponding edition in England, and later the Constable volumes of the 1920's that included even *Mardi* and *Pierre* as well as *The Confidence-Man*, the poetry, and the unknown *Billy Budd*. When successive generations of twentieth-century critics and scholars looked with new eyes at these books and their author they saw what was denied the vision of the first biographers. Their findings have justified Melville's own quiet confidence in the verdict of the future and his wife's unwavering faith in his work and fame.

The Chronology of Melville's
Short Fiction, 1853–1856
(1980)

This study, copyright © 1980 by Merton M. Sealts, Jr., was prepared in 1977 during a research leave underwritten by the Graduate School, University of Wisconsin–Madison, and first published in the *Harvard Library Bulletin*, 28 (October 1980), 391–403. Its substance will appear in another form in the "Historical Note" to *"The Piazza Tales" and Other Prose Pieces, 1839–1860*, forthcoming as volume IX of The Writings of Herman Melville, edited by Harrison Hayford, Hershel Parker, and G. Thomas Tanselle (Evanston and Chicago: Northwestern University Press and The Newberry Library, 1968–).

My special interest in Melville's short fiction began in the early 1940's when I wrote and published my first essay on "I and My Chimney" and a subsequent note of 1944 on "The Publication of Melville's *Piazza Tales*." I worked out a tentative chronology of his magazine pieces of 1853–1856 after World War II while I was editing what was intended to be volume XII of the projected Hendricks House edition of Melville's works, comprising his uncollected *Stories and Sketches*. The edition as a whole was never completed, and XII was one of the volumes that for one reason or another remained unpublished. I refined my chronology during the period beginning in 1964 when I served as one of several "Contributing Scholars" advising the Northwestern-Newberry editors and as volume editor for their volume IX. My service to the edition, I must add, terminated in October of 1978 when the "Historical Note" and the component texts of volume IX as I had prepared them were in galley proof and the remaining editorial apparatus was in semifinal typescript.

In public life, an official who serves at the pleasure of a governor or president is expected to resign his appointment if and when he can no longer support the policies of the administration in which he has been serving; in my judgment the same custom should apply in academic life as well. The editorial policies governing a scholarly edition are determined by its principal editors, who have the right and responsibility not only to apply those policies to individual volumes but to modify them if they recognize the need. A volume editor has the obligation to follow those policies and their modifications—provided that in his best judgment they do not conflict with the actual practice of the author whose work he is editing as he has come to understand it. Here differences of opinion may well arise. In the late summer of 1978 the Northwestern-Newberry editors unexpectedly called for major textual alterations in volume IX, changes that I could not conscientiously accept. In order to give the editors a completely free hand in revising my work as they saw fit, work I had supposed at an earlier stage to be approved, I felt obliged to withdraw from the edition. My responsibility for the published volume therefore extends only to the "Historical Note."

B etween the publication of *Pierre* in 1852 and that of *The Confidence-Man* in 1857, Herman Melville was a frequent contributor to two American periodicals: *Harper's New Monthly Magazine* and *Putnam's Monthly Magazine*. Determining the sequence of composition for his fifteen individual contributions to these magazines—the intention of this study—is largely a matter of inference, since most of the pieces are unmentioned in surviving correspondence or records and those named were not necessarily published in the order of their writing and submission. Even so, there is enough objective evidence now at hand on which to base a probable chronology of Melville's short fiction during these years.

The first magazine piece to be named in Melville's known letters of 1853–1856 to Harper & Brothers, the New York publishers of *Harper's New Monthly Magazine*, is "The Paradise of Bachelors and the Tartarus of Maids" (1855): on 25 May 1854, he acknowledged payment of "$100 on acct: of the 'Paradise of Batchelors &c" (*Letters*, p. 168). Since their magazine had already published "Cock-A-Doodle-Doo!" in the issue of December 1853, and had presumably paid for it long since, the sum of $100 "on acct:" must have represented an advance payment for the entire group of Melville's later contributions that began to appear in the spring and summer of 1854: "Poor Man's Pudding and Rich Man's Crumbs" (June 1854), "The Happy Failure" (July 1854), "The Fiddler" (September 1854), and—seven months later—the one item actually mentioned by name in his letter of acknowledgment, "The Paradise of Bachelors and the Tartarus of Maids" (April 1855). The payment was evidently calculated on the basis of total wordage rather than by the printed page unless these pieces had actually been set in type by this time; in their printed form the four items ran to 19½ pages in all, worth roughly $100 at the rate of $5.00 per printed page that Melville evidently commanded.

When had Melville written and submitted these four compositions? Certainly well before 25 May 1854, since "Poor Man's Pudding and Rich Man's Crumbs" was scheduled for the June issue; from its inception *Harper's* had appeared "in all parts of the United States on the first day of every month" and was sent to press about the tenth day of the month preceding.[1] The four pieces must have been dispatched from Pittsfield to New York no later than the early spring of 1854; two of them, it would seem, were probably sent along with "Cock-A-Doodle-Doo!" on 13 August 1853, when Melville wrote to Harper & Brothers enclosing "three articles which perhaps may be found suitable for your Magazine." That these were his first submissions is suggested by his request that they be given "early attention" and that he be apprised "of the result" (*Letters*, p. 171).[2] The Harpers evidently returned a favorable answer concerning "Cock-A-Doodle-Doo!," which was used in the December number; if the other two pieces were "The Happy Failure" and "The Fiddler," which are shorter and less well developed than any of the other compositions named and may well have been Melville's first attempts in the new medium, they were held for later use—in July and September of the following year.

Melville had also been in touch with G. P. Putnam & Co. about a possible contribution to *Putnam's Monthly*. By September of 1853 he had a first manuscript ready for *Putnam's* and either a fourth contribution for *Harper's* or a revision of one of the three manuscripts submitted in August, but apparently he erred in addressing his communications to the magazines. On 20 September Charles F. Briggs, the editor of *Putnam's*, wrote to Harper & Brothers forwarding a "Ms. and note" intended for *Harper's* but "directed to *Putnam's Monthly*"; Briggs also inquired whether, "as something was expected from Mr Melville perhaps he may have misdirected it to you."[3] The manuscript Briggs was expecting must have been that of "Bartleby, the Scrivener," which subsequently reached *Putnam's* in time for publication in the November and December issues. During the summer of 1853 Melville had thus written at least three magazine pieces for *Harper's*, "Cock-A-Doodle-Doo!" and probably "The Happy Failure" and "The Fiddler," and another for *Putnam's*, "Bartleby." Between September and the following May he submitted four additional contributions: presumably "Poor Man's Pudding and Rich Man's Crumbs" and "The Paradise of Bachelors and the Tartarus of Maids" to *Harper's* and "The Encantadas" and "The Two Temples" to *Putnam's*.

Meanwhile, Melville had also projected another book, which he proposed to Harper & Brothers in a pivotal letter of 24 November 1853 (*Letters*, pp. 164–165) that deserves quotation in full, since it bears not only upon the chronology of his writing in 1853 and 1854 but also upon his relations in these years with the Harpers.

> Gentlemen:—In addition to the work which I took to New York last Spring, but which I was prevented from printing at that time; I have now in hand, and pretty well on towards completion, another book—300 pages, say— partly of nautical adventure, and partly—or, rather, chiefly, of Tortoise Hunting Adventure. It will be ready for press some time in the coming January. Meanwhile, it would be convenient, to have advanced to me upon it $300.—My acct: with you, at present, can not be very far from square. For the above-named advance—if remitted me now—you will have security in my former works, as well as security prospective, in the one to come, (The Tortoise-Hunters) because if you accede to the aforesaid request, this letter shall be your voucher, that I am willing your house should publish it, on the old basis—half-profits.
>
> Reply immediately, if you please,
And Beleive Me, Yours
Herman Melville

The opening sentence of this letter would seem to indicate that Melville had still "in hand" the unpublished work of the previous spring; if so, he had not at this point destroyed the manuscript. That he expected to finish by "some time in the coming January" another book of "300 pages, say" means that he had already been working on it during the fall of 1853—presumably after dispatching his first magazine pieces to *Harper's* and *Putnam's*. That he proposed his new book for publication by the firm "on the old basis—half profits" attests to his assumption that by this point the Harpers might be less hesitant about bringing out another of Melville's works in the wake of *Pierre*. Their reply to his letter of 24 November has not survived, but an in-house report on the sales of Melville's books (filed with his letter to the firm) apparently justified their decision to send the requested advance on 7 December. Three days later, on 10 December 1853, the firm suffered a disastrous fire at their New York establishment in Cliff Street which destroyed nearly 2,300 bound and unbound copies of Melville's books though not the plates; as Melville explained later to his father-in-law, this meant a loss to him of "about $1000" that would otherwise have come from his share of profits and royalties.[4]

Melville's more immediate response to news of the loss may have been to open negotiations with G. P. Putnam & Co. for use of some or all of his account of "Tortoise Hunting Adventure" in *Putnam's Monthly*, perhaps in the belief that the Harper firm would be unable to publish the projected book because of the fire. All that is known is this: on 6 February 1854, he wrote a now-unlocated letter to Putnam on an unknown subject;[5] on 14 February the New York *Post* announced that "The Encantadas" would begin in the March number of *Putnam's Monthly* (*Log*, I, 484–485);[6] the March installment included an account of tortoise-hunting in Sketch Second. Meanwhile, Melville wrote to Harper & Brothers in late February about the book he had proposed two months before. When he "procured the advance of $300," his letter began, he

> intimated that the work would be ready for press some time in January. I have now to express my concern, that, owing to a variety of causes, the work, unavoidably, was not ready in that month, & still requires additional work to it, ere completion. But in no sense can you loose by the delay.
>
> I shall be in New York in the course of a few weeks; when I shall call upon you, & inform you when those proverbially slow "Tortoises" will be ready to crawl into market. (*Letters*, pp. 167–168)

Melville may have been in New York for his brother Allan's birthday on 7 April, when a work used in Chapter 23 of his *Israel Potter* was charged to his account with the Harpers (*Log*, I, 486); if so, there is no record of what he may have said about the delayed book or its relation to "The Encantadas," which continued to appear in *Putnam's* for April and May. In any event, he repeatedly sought word about "the 'Tortoises' extract," as he termed it in his letter of 25 May 1854, that he must have sent to the firm at some time after his February letter (*Letters*, p. 169). He had received no reply by 22 June, when he wrote again to inquire "whether it be worth while to prepare further Extracts":

> Though it would be difficult, if not impossible, for me to get the entire Tortoise Book ready for publication before Spring [*i.e.*, of 1855], yet I can pick out & finish parts, here & there, for prior use. But even this is not unattended with labor; which labor, of course, I do not care to undergo while remaining in doubt as to its recompence. (*Letters*, pp. 170–171)

Presumably the Harpers asked for additional extracts and Melville responded by writing on 25 July to say that he was sending by express "a parcel . . . containing M. S. S. for you" (*Letters*, p. 171). The "M. S. S." must have been "parts, here & there," of the projected book rather than additional magazine pieces, since his last two contributions to *Harper's*, "Jimmy Rose" (November 1855) and "The 'Gees" (March 1856), were not ready for submission until September of 1854. Whatever the nature of these extracts, it seems evident that Melville wrote more about "Tortoise Hunting Adventure" for the Harpers than he had published in Sketch Second of "The Encantadas" in the March number of *Putnam's*. But there is no further information concerning the fate of the "Tortoise Book," which—like that of "the story of Agatha"—can only be conjectured.

When Melville wrote to the Harpers on 25 May 1854, acknowledging their payment for magazine articles and inquiring about their response to the extract he had sent, he also broached another subject: "When you write me concerning the 'Tortoises' extract, you may, if you choose, inform me at about what time you would be prepared to commence the publication of another Serial in your Magazine—supposing you had one, in prospect, that suited you" (*Letters*, p. 169). By this time he was obviously well along in composing *Israel Potter*, "the Revolutionary narrative of the beggar" he had thought of "serving up" more than four years before when he bought an old map of London for possible use in writing it.[7] Evidently failing to interest Harper & Brothers in "another Serial," he addressed George Putnam on 7 June 1854, advising him of the shipment "by Express, to-day," of "some sixty and odd pages of MSS," part of "a story called 'Israel Potter.'" His proposal was for serial publication in *Putnam's Monthly* "at the rate of five dollars per printed page" (*Letters*, pp. 169–170). Putnam agreed to all of Melville's several stipulations except one, that of a requested advance of $100 on acceptance of his proposal. A place was found for the first installment of this "Fourth of July Story" in the issue then in press, that of July 1854; *Israel Potter* continued to appear through March of 1855, when Putnam issued the story in book form as Melville's eighth book. The nine installments ran to 82¼ pages, for which Melville received a total of $421.50 in the form of monthly payments. For his earlier contribution of "The Encantadas" he was paid $150, also in monthly payments, but still another story, "The Two Temples," was rejected in May of 1854 on the ground that "some of our church readers might be disturbed" by its "*point*" (*Log*, I, 487–488).

Both Putnam and his editor, Charles F. Briggs, wrote Melville to apologize for their decision not to print "The Two Temples"; Putnam, in addition to asking Melville for "some more of your good things," also requested "some drawing or daguerreotype" to be used "as one of our series of portraits" (*Log*, I, 485). Melville was unable to supply a likeness, he replied to Putnam on 16 May, saying also that he had already written Briggs concerning "The Two Temples" and would soon "send down some other things, to which, I think, no objections will be made on the score of tender consciences of the public."[8] The opening portions of *Israel Potter* were to follow on 7 June; "The Lightning-Rod Man," published in the August number, probably accompanied this or a later segment of the longer work. Putnam's prompt acceptance of *Israel Potter* and his apologetic letter about refusing "The Two Temples" both indicate his interest in having Melville as a contributor to his magazine. During the first six months of its existence *Putnam's Monthly* received 389 manuscripts, and 980 in all by the end of its first year;[9] clearly Putnam and Briggs singled out Melville's contributions for special handling as well as special payment.

From the evidence just reviewed of Melville's dealings with both Putnam and the Harpers it is possible to draw up a probable chronology of his magazine writing between the publication of *Pierre* in 1852 and the serialization of his eighth book, *Israel Potter*, in 1854 and 1855, though with one major reservation: there is no basis other than purely internal evidence for determining the sequence of individual compositions within certain groupings. From manuscripts by Melville on hand an editor may have selected a particular story because of its length, given the amount of space available in the next monthly issue of his magazine, rather than the period of time since its submission: was a long piece or a short one needed to fill out a number? "Cock-A-Doodle-Doo!" was the first story by Melville to appear in *Harper's*; it was not necessarily the first submitted or even the first written, since Melville may previously have tried his hand at other pieces which are shorter and less complex, such as "The Happy Failure" and "The Fiddler." "The Two Temples," first mentioned in letters to Melville from Putnam and Briggs in May of 1854, has affiliations with Melville's other two-part pieces—"Poor Man's Pudding and Rich Man's Crumbs" and "The Paradise of Bachelors and the Tartarus of Maids," which were apparently paid for by *Harper's* in that same month. Does it follow, then, that all these pieces were written and submitted at about the same time? Or was one or more than one held for an extended period before they were acted upon? Answers to such questions must necessarily be conjectural at best.

Here is the probable chronology through the summer of 1854:

Winter of 1852–1853: Work on "the story of Agatha," in all likelihood the manuscript that Melville submitted to Harper & Brothers in the spring of 1853 but was "prevented from printing."

Spring and summer of 1853: (1) Composition, copying, and submission to *Harper's New Monthly Magazine* (on 13 August?) of "Cock-A-Doodle-Doo!" (published December 1853) and two other pieces, probably "The Happy Failure" (published July 1854) and "The Fiddler" (published September 1854). (2) Either revision and resubmission of one of these pieces or submission to *Harper's* of a fourth contribution (before 20 September), misdirected to *Putnam's*

Monthly Magazine. (3) Composition, copying, and submission to *Putnam's* (after 20 September?) of "Bartleby, the Scrivener" (published November, December 1853).

Autumn of 1853 and winter of 1853–1854: (1) Work on the "Tortoise Book" proposed to Harper & Brothers on 24 November but apparently never finished. (2) Work on "The Encantadas" for *Putnam's* (possibly submitted, at least in part, on 6 February; announced as forthcoming on 14 February; published in March, April, May 1854). (3) Work on "Poor Man's Pudding and Rich Man's Crumbs" (if not already submitted), "The Two Temples," and "The Paradise of Bachelors and the Tartarus of Maids."

Spring and early summer of 1854: (1) Acceptance by *Harper's* of "Poor Man's Pudding and Rich Man's Crumbs" (probably paid for in May 1854; published in June 1854) and "The Paradise of Bachelors and the Tartarus of Maids" (paid for in May 1854; published in April 1855). (2) Submission to *Putnam's* of "The Two Temples" (rejected on 12 May 1854). (3) Work on *Israel Potter* (proposed 7 June? 1854; serialized in *Putnam's*, July of 1854 through March of 1855; issued in book form in March 1855). (4) Preparation of extracts from the proposed "Tortoise Book" (submitted to Harper & Brothers on 26 July?). (5) Composition, copying, and submission to *Putnam's* of "The Lightning-Rod Man" (published August 1854).

Between November of 1853 and March of 1855, when Putnam sold his magazine to Joshua Dix and Arthur Edwards, Melville earned $674.50 from *Putnam's Monthly* alone, as shown by ledger entries recording its payments to authors. During this same period he probably received an additional $145 from *Harper's*, allowing for an estimated payment of $45 for "Cock-A-Doodle-Doo!" (nine printed pages @ $5.00 per page) in addition to the $100 for other contributions that he acknowledged in May of 1854. There is no reason to suppose that he was paid for occasional reprintings in newspapers and magazines; for example, the *Western Literary Messenger* of Buffalo, which reprinted "Poor Man's Pudding and Rich Man's Crumbs" in August of 1854 and also copied two chapters of the serialized *Israel Potter*, was eclectic in a large degree and did not pay its authors.[10] For Melville's remaining contributions to *Harper's* and *Putnam's* in 1855 and 1856 there is only one known record of an individual payment, but if the magazines continued to pay at the same rate during these years the probable total was over $400: approximately $32.50 for two pieces in *Harper's*, "Jimmy Rose" and "The 'Gees" (total 6½ pages), and $377.50 for five pieces in *Putnam's*, "The Lightning-Rod Man," "The

Bell-Tower," "Benito Cereno," "I and My Chimney," and "The Apple-Tree Table" (total 75½ pages). The grand total of these several estimates is $1,329.50 for all of Melville's magazine writing of 1853–1856, a larger sum than that formerly reckoned before it was known that his contributions commanded $5 per printed page.[11] In addition, he received at least one payment of royalties for *Israel Potter* in book form: $48.31 on 8 October 1855 (*Log*, II, 509).

As this survey indicates, Melville sent more of his contributions to *Putnam's* than he did to *Harper's;* on the whole, his longer narratives went either to Putnam or Putnam's successors, Dix & Edwards, while his shorter pieces were awaiting action by Harper & Brothers. The fact that the Harpers held his manuscripts for such long periods, coupled with his difficulty in obtaining a decision concerning the projected "Tortoise Book," may have something to do with his apparent preference for dealing with *Putnam's Monthly*. If "Jimmy Rose" and "The 'Gees" constitute the "brace of fowl—wild fowl" mentioned in the letter headed "Sept: 18th" that Melville apparently wrote on that date in 1854 (*Letters*, p. 172),[12] then it must be observed that "Jimmy Rose" remained unpublished for the next fourteen months and "The 'Gees" for eighteen—just at the time when Melville's contributions to *Putnam's* were appearing regularly. "Jimmy Rose" has affiliations with two other pieces sent to *Putnam's* rather than *Harper's:* "I and My Chimney" (published in March 1856) and "The Apple-Tree Table" (May 1856); since "I and My Chimney" is known to have been in the hands of Dix & Edwards by July of 1855 (*Log*, II, 504, 507), it appears that the three stories were written in sequence at some time between late summer in 1854 and the summer or fall of 1855. "The 'Gees" is like both "The Encantadas" (1854) and "Benito Cereno" (1855) in its association with Melville's knowledge of the sea, but it also looks forward to *The Confidence-Man* (1857), which Melville completed in 1856. That "The 'Gees" was written as late as 1856, when Melville was occupied with both *The Piazza Tales* and *The Confidence-Man*, seems unlikely, however, and indeed there is some internal evidence for placing its composition as early as July or August of 1854 on the ground that it is in part a response to an article that appeared in the July issue of *Putnam's*.[13] In short, both "Jimmy Rose" and "The 'Gees" might well have been ready for submission by mid-September of that year.

Melville's correspondence with Dix & Edwards on 7 and 10 August 1855 concerning payment of $37.50 for "The Bell-Tower" (7½ printed pages) indicates that the new owners of *Putnam's Monthly* continued to pay him at the rate of $5 per page (*Letters*, pp. 173–174). He had evidently submitted the manuscript of "The Bell-Tower" by late May or early June of 1855, since it was included with other contributions that Joshua Dix forwarded to his editorial advisor, George William Curtis, in time for Curtis to comment on the story in his letters of 18 and 19 June (*Log*, II, 502); the story was included in the August issue and paid for immediately upon publication. "Benito Cereno" was not handled so promptly. The longer work, probably composed during the winter of 1854–1855, may have been submitted to *Putnam's* early in 1855 before George Putnam sold his magazine to the new firm, since it had evidently been set in type by March of that year. On 1 April Melville wrote Dix & Edwards returning "the proof last sent" and requesting "the whole as made up in page form" (*Letters*, p. 173); obviously he had been correcting proof of an unnamed article of some length probably intended for serial publication, and "Benito Cereno" is his only contribution published in *Putnam's* after this date that appeared in installments. Dix forwarded the story to Curtis in mid-April and received a favorable report on it, although Curtis disliked "the dreary documents at the end" and observed that Melville "does everything too hurriedly now" (*Log*, II, 500–501). For some reason Dix did not begin serializing "Benito Cereno" until the October number; on 31 July 1855, Curtis had urged him to use it in September, adding that "You have paid for it" (*Log*, II, 504). Thus "Benito Cereno" may be exceptional on at least two counts: it is the one story that Melville is known to have read in proof before its publication (there may well have been others) and the one for which he was paid in advance by *Putnam's*.

The first of Melville's two remaining stories for *Putnam's*, "I and My Chimney," was included in a batch of manuscript contributions that Dix forwarded to Curtis in July of 1855. Curtis held the manuscripts until 7 September, when he singled out "I and My Chimney" for praise as "thoroughly magazinish" (*Log*, II, 507), but Dix did not use the story until March of 1856—after the serialization of "Benito Cereno" in the October, November, and December numbers and subsequent planning of the collection that became *The Piazza Tales*. "The Apple-Tree Table," unmentioned in Melville's surviving correspondence or that between Curtis and Dix, did not appear until May of 1856. As noted above, both of these stories have affiliations with "Jimmy Rose," published in *Harper's* for November 1855, but apparently written as early as the summer of 1854. The narrator of "I and My Chimney" suffers from sciatica; Melville himself had an attack of "severe rheumatism" in February of 1855 and was treated for sciatica in the following June, when he may have been finishing work on his story.[14] "The Apple-Tree Table" was probably written later in the year, either just before or just after the "severe illness" from which he was reported as recovering in mid-September. It was in December of 1855, after the final installment of "Benito Cereno" had appeared in *Putnam's*, that Melville proposed collecting those of his stories which had been published in the magazine up to that time, and in January or February of 1856 he composed "The Piazza" as a title piece for the volume. "About having the author's name on the title-page, you may do as you deem best," he told Dix & Edwards on 19 January; "but any appending of titles of former works is hardly worth while" (*Letters*, p. 177).

The probable chronology of Melville's writing for the magazines can now be extended to summarize the remainder of this period.

Summer of 1854: Composition, copying, and submission to *Harper's* (on 18 September?) of "Jimmy Rose" (published November 1855) and "The 'Gees" (published March 1856).

Winter of 1854–1855: Composition, copying, submission to *Putnam's*, and proofreading of "Benito Cereno" (apparently in proof before 1 April 1855; publication delayed until October, November, and December 1855).

Spring of 1855: Composition, copying, and submission to *Putnam's* (by late May or early June) of "The Bell-Tower" (published August 1855) and (by July) of "I and My Chimney" (published March 1856).

Summer or fall of 1855: Composition, copying, and submission to *Putnam's* of "The Apple-Tree Table" (published May 1856).

January–March, 1856: (1) Revision (by 19 January) of the magazine pieces collected in *The Piazza Tales.* (2) Composition, copying, and submission to Dix & Edwards (on 16 February) of "The Piazza." (3) Proofreading (by 24 March) of *The Piazza Tales*, published in May.

Before writing "The Piazza" Melville was already well along with *The Confidence-Man*, his tenth book, which he had apparently begun during the previous summer;[15] there are several correspondences between its early chapters and "The Apple-Tree Table." When he finished the book later in 1856 he arranged for its publication by Dix & Edwards rather than the Harpers.[16] As a number of commentators have pointed out, there are episodes in it that might well have been published separately as magazine pieces, but no evidence exists to suggest that Melville offered *The Confidence-Man* or any of its chapters for magazine publication.

The Reception of Melville's

Short Fiction

(1979)

This essay, originally written in the autumn of 1978 as a critical review for *ESQ: A Journal of the American Renaissance*, 25 (1st Quarter 1979), 43–57, is another expression of my long-standing interest in Melville's magazine writing of 1853–1856. The introductory and concluding sections reflect more specifically my contribution to volume IX of the Northwestern-Newberry Edition of Melville. In the present version of the essay I have somewhat shortened the sections numbered i, ii, and iii, which survey and appraise studies of Melville's short fiction published in the 1960's and 1970's by Richard Harter Fogle, Warner Berthoff, Klaus Ensslen, R. Bruce Bickley, Jr., Marvin Fisher, Ann Douglas, and William B. Dillingham.

Together with "Melville's Chimney, Reexamined," pp. 171–192 above, this essay will serve to illustrate my principles as a reviewer and my personal biases. For various scholarly journals I have written both appraisals of individual books concerning Melville and longer essay-reviews touching on groups of books and articles; during a five-year period, 1967 through 1971, I covered current work on Melville in chapters of the annual volumes of *American Literary Scholarship* (Durham, North Carolina: Duke University Press, 1969–1973). My notion of the reviewer's aim is that of Matthew Arnold's critic: to see the object as in itself it really is. In practice the reviewer should point out the basic position from which a work he is treating was written, identify the thesis advanced by its author (preferably as stated in the author's own words), and estimate the degree to which the author's effort succeeds in throwing light upon his chosen subject. The review, and particularly the essay-review, should be written not only to appraise but to record, and the reviewer should therefore be something of a literary historian as well as a critical magistrate, citing antecedents and tracing affiliations of the books and articles under his examination.

My preference for a genetic and historical approach to Melville and to Melville scholarship has been called a bias; my practice of quoting an author's own words has been mistaken as evidence of a positive endorsement;

my own judgments have been dismissed as bland by those who prefer reviews written in vitriol by some Lord High Executioner. But fashions in reviewing come and go along with fashions in scholarship, and determining what is permanently valuable in the work on Melville of the past forty years will require the "longer critical perspective" of that future cultural historian evoked in this essay.

When some cultural historian of the next century, blessed with a longer critical perspective than that we now possess, charts the shifting course of Herman Melville's literary reputation, one of his or her most interesting chapters is bound to be the account of responses over the years to Melville's magazine pieces of 1853–1856. Although Melville had written on occasion for the Duyckincks' *Literary World* and Cornelius Mathews' *Yankee Doodle* during the 1840's, he continued to resist overtures from other periodicals until the utter failure of *Pierre* (1852) kept him from placing a new book-length manuscript with Harper & Brothers in the spring of 1853. Later in that same year, burdened with debts and in need of another source of income, he began publishing anonymous stories and sketches in both *Harper's New Monthly Magazine* and its younger rival, *Putnam's Monthly Magazine*. From contemporary documents we know that Melville's authorship of certain pieces—especially those carried in *Putnam's Monthly*— was more or less an open secret in literary circles, and that "Bartleby, the Scrivener" and "The Encantadas" in particular provoked much favorable discussion. Between November of 1853 and May of 1856 fourteen of Melville's tales and sketches appeared in the two periodicals along with *Israel Potter*, the longer narrative that George Palmer Putnam brought out in book form in 1855 following its serialization in his magazine. In addition, Melville also submitted "The Two Temples," which Putnam and his editor declined, and composed "The Piazza," written as a new title piece for *The Piazza Tales* (1856), a volume of four hundred and thirty-one pages that reprinted five of Melville's contributions to *Putnam's Monthly* through December of 1855. When Melville proposed this book to the New York firm of Dix & Edwards, which had bought the magazine from Putnam, he was already at work on *The Confidence-Man* (1857) and was no longer writing magazine fiction. But his financial condition, which had steadily worsened since purchase of his Pittsfield farm in 1850, was approaching a crisis in the spring of 1856 when *The Piazza Tales* appeared, and he hoped that its publication would soon bring in some much-needed "returns."[1]

Although contemporary reviewers of *The Piazza Tales* hailed the book as a welcome recovery from the aberrations of Melville's *Pierre*, the volume sold slowly in spite of its generally favorable notices.[2] The years 1856 and 1857 were unpropitious for the book trade. Dix & Edwards dissolved partnership in 1857, apparently without paying Melville any royalties whatsoever for either *The Piazza Tales* or *The Confidence-Man*, and the plates of both volumes were sold for scrap after failing to attract bids at a publishers' auction; in 1857, as Merrell R. Davis and William H. Gilman remark, "no one would risk a dollar on Melville" (*Letters*, p. 188, note 9). Destruction of the plates of course precluded reissue of either volume, and not until the Melville revival of the 1920's was there a complete resetting of *The Piazza Tales*. During the sixty-five years intervening, while Melville's name was virtually forgotten by the general public, a number of his individual stories continued to enjoy a kind of subterranean reputation—something like that of *Moby-Dick*. Two of them, "The Lightning-Rod Man" and "The Bell-Tower," turned up in anthologies, reprinted in each case from the 1856 text of *The Piazza Tales*;[3] others were long remembered from their original appearance in magazines. Henry Mills Alden, the veteran editor of *Harper's* (1869–1919), told Melville's literary executor, Arthur Stedman, that "Cock-A-Doodle-Doo!" (1853) was "about the best short story he ever read,"[4] and in 1880 an anonymous contributor to the *Atlantic Monthly* named "Bartleby, the Scrivener" as one of the articles in *Putnam's* that had excited his "interest, curiosity, and wonder" nearly thirty years before.[5] A dozen years later, when most readers may well have forgotten who Bartleby was, an illustrator for the 1892 deluxe reprint of *Prue and I* by George William Curtis provided a portrait of the character to accompany an allusion by Curtis.[6] And still later, in 1898, Henry James, writing for a London magazine, recalled his "very young pleasure" in "the prose, as mild and easy as an Indian summer in the woods," of Melville, Curtis, and Donald Grant Mitchell as he read their work long before in "the charming Putnam" of "the early fifties."[7]

Perhaps it is too much to suggest, on the basis of such occasional comments, that Melville might have been recognized much earlier as one of the masters of American short fiction had Stedman's 1892 edition of his selected works included a volume of the magazine pieces.[8] But the times were not yet ripe in the 1890's for reassessing any aspect of Melville's literary work, and new printings of the stories were still thirty years in the future. Only after Raymond Weaver had published the first book-length biography—*Herman Melville: Mariner and Mystic*—in 1921 did the stories become readily available to readers and critics. *The Piazza Tales* first reappeared in print in 1922 as a volume in the new collected edition of Melville published by a British firm, Constable and Company, and in that same year Princeton University Press brought together Melville's previously uncollected magazine pieces in *The Apple-Tree Table and Other Sketches by Herman Melville*. In 1924 "The Two Temples," previously unpublished, was first printed from manuscript in *Billy Budd and Other Prose Pieces*, a volume added to the Constable edition with Weaver as editor. The appearance of these volumes and the reprinting of "Benito Cereno," "Bartleby," and "The Encantadas" (along with *Billy Budd* and a provocative introduction by Weaver) in *Shorter Novels of Herman Melville* (New York: Horace Liveright, 1928) not only drew attention to Melville's shorter fiction but also stimulated scholarly and critical interest in this phase of his career. The earliest investigations of Melville's use of source materials in his magazine pieces soon followed: Harold H. Scudder's "Melville's *Benito Cereno* and Captain Delano's Voyages" in 1928 and articles by Leon Howard and Russell Thomas on "The Encantadas" in 1931 and 1932.

The 1940's brought other new developments. The first interpretative essay devoted to a single magazine story or sketch, "Herman Melville's 'Tartarus of Maids'" by E. H. Eby, was published in 1940; small armies of close readers have since followed Eby's lead, explicating other tales and filling professional journals with reports of what they had seen there by way of imagery, symbolism, and allegory ("I, Ishmael, was one of that crew; my shouts had gone up with the rest . . .").[9] Influential new books also began to appear in the 1940's— Egbert Oliver's annotated edition of *The Piazza Tales* (1948), Richard Chase's *Selected Tales and Poems of Herman Melville* (1949), and Jay Leyda's *Complete Short Stories of Herman Melville* (1949)—and by the 1950's "Benito Cereno" and "Bartleby, the Scrivener" had become standard fare in college anthologies. Commentators on the various stories continued to approach them as though they were enigmas to be solved; by pursuing Melville's indirection they sought to find direction out. Leyda was in effect summing up the first decade of interpretation in 1949 when he wrote of the stories as

an artist's resolution of that constant contradiction—between the desperate need to communicate and the fear of revealing too much. In these stories the contradiction is expressed on various levels of tension—the fiercer the pull, the higher the accomplishment. There is also a level, closer to the surface, of *game*, for in "The Tartarus of Maids" Melville gives one the impression of seeing how close he can dance to the edge of nineteenth century sanctities without being caught. (*Complete Stories*, p. xxviii)

Beginning with the decade of the 1940's, there were notable achievements in Melville scholarship that by the 1950's were affecting the tenor of discussion concerning the short fiction. For a long time, as we now recognize, Melville's readers had assumed that much of his writing was transparently autobiographical. His own contemporaries, including the Melville family itself, took such books as *Typee*, *Omoo*, *Redburn*, and *White-Jacket* to be virtual transcripts of personal experience, and some readers then and now saw elements of *Pierre* and the magazine fiction in much the same way. Biographers as late as Arthur Stedman in the 1890's and even Raymond Weaver in the 1920's not only shared this conception but also echoed another idea traceable as far back as the contemporary reviews of *Mardi* and *Moby-Dick*: that indulgence in theological and metaphysical speculation had been Melville's downfall as a popular writer. After World War II, however, the publication of new biographical research steadily undermined the easy assumptions of earlier years about the supposed reflection of Melville's life in his longer works. The old tendency to read the stories biographically had nevertheless persisted, along with a continuing penchant for emphasizing their religious and philosophical dimensions. But criticism of the 1950's and after has grown increasingly more preoccupied with methodology, and for most recent commentators the question of what Melville has to say in the shorter fiction is inseparable from how he says it—from the form and technique of his narrative presentation. Thus the sources of a given story, whether in personal experience or in literary borrowings, may seem less important to the interpreter than its point of view and overall tone; Melville's epistemology may bulk larger than his metaphysics; the issues at stake—in "Benito Cereno," for example, written six years before the Civil War[10]—may be the immediate social and political problems of Melville's day rather than cosmic good and evil, as earlier critics had supposed. Whether these new approaches to the shorter fiction have gone too far, have merely reflected changing fashions in modern criticism, or have at last uncovered the realities of Melville's own outlook in the 1850's remains to be seen. Our cultural historian of the next century may well decide that, in one way or another, they have in fact done all of these things.

i

In 1960 Richard Harter Fogle, who had published essays on "Bartleby," "Benito Cereno," and "The Encantadas" during the 1950's, incorporated his earlier articles in the first book-length treatment of the entire body of Melville's magazine fiction: *Melville's Shorter Tales* (Norman: University of Oklahoma Press). Fogle's readings of the individual stories take account of the best work that had been done over the first four decades of the Melville revival; such a synthesis was still feasible in relatively short compass at the beginning of the 1960's. Ten years ago, in tracing what readers and critics since Melville's day had said about a single story, I referred to Fogle's book as "the most comprehensive of recent discussions" and went on to place Fogle himself "among the least doctrinaire" of those critics who have dealt with the short fiction. In his readings, I continued (and I would still affirm),

> he draws freely upon the insights of earlier commentators. . . . His distinctive approach grows out of his conviction that Melville's writing embraces several levels or layers of significance—among them the biographical—which for him are not mutually exclusive. . . . [His] general conception . . . has all the virtues and possible dangers of an all-inclusive eclecticism, [but] Fogle differs from most of his predecessors and contemporaries alike in a highly important way: because of his governing concern with the aesthetic values of Melville's writing, he repeatedly and rightly insists that to dwell solely on any component part is to risk doing less than justice to the comprehensive artistic whole. On this count, unfortunately, most writers . . . up to the present, whether their preoccupation has been with the life of the author, his metaphysical outlook, or other hidden treasure of their own devising, must plead guilty in some degree.[11]

Both in its own right and as a document of historical record, *Melville's Shorter Tales* stands as a landmark in Melville studies. Writing when he did, Fogle was cautiously determined not to overrate the tales "in proportion as they were underrated in the past"; indeed he pronounced them "very uneven in quality." "Melville," he declared, is "not a craftsman in the ordinary meaning of the term. . . . He is too heavy for the delicate fabric of the kind of tale he is trying to write; what he really has to say is at odds with the limits he has chosen to observe" (p. 12). But this conservative assessment of the stories and the artistry of their author has been vigorously challenged in commentary appearing since Fogle's book—most eloquently, I should say, by Warner Berthoff in *The Example of Melville* (Princeton: Princeton University Press, 1962), a book that has done much to redress earlier neglect of Melville's considerable achievement in prose over the forty years between *Moby-Dick* and *Billy Budd*. As Fogle had surveyed the whole range of the magazine fiction, so Berthoff in turn placed the work of 1853–1856 in the context of Melville's entire development as a writer, dealing briefly but incisively with individual pieces and praising "the high level of craftsmanship apparent through all this magazine work" (p. 59). Berthoff's judgment has been far more influential on subsequent treatment of the stories than the more detailed stylistic and structural analysis provided by another book of the 1960's: *Melvilles Erzählungen*, an untranslated monograph by Klaus Ensslen (Heidelberg: Carl Winter, 1966). Ensslen's work is mentioned in only one of the three books of the 1970's on the short fiction: *The Method of Melville's Short Fiction* (Durham, N.C.: Duke University Press, 1975) by R. Bruce Bickley, Jr., which cites it without comment in a bibliographical footnote (p. x).

"Like Berthoff," Bickley writes in his Preface, "I am convinced that Melville's publications between 1853 and 1856 in fact show more discipline, if not a higher level of craftsmanship, than did the earlier novels" (p. xii). Like Fogle, he surveys all of the stories of these years, and like Ensslen he is particularly concerned with their style and structure. At the same time he is fully aware of other work of the 1960's and early 1970's, observing in his Preface that since the publication of Fogle's book in 1960, "scholarship on Melville's short fiction has proliferated almost too rapidly for acknowledgment and review, much less for proper evaluation. . . . Despite its volume and resourcefulness, however, I am convinced that the short story scholarship remains inadequate; hence this book." Its objectives, he continues, are to look specifically at Melville's experiments with literary techniques, the influences that affected these techniques, and the ways in which Melville's fictional methods "shaped his complex vision artistically" (pp. ix–xi).[12]

When Melville first turned from book-length fiction to shorter tales, Bickley believes, he used models such as Lamb's essays and the stories of Irving and Hawthorne for his own experiments with structure, narration, and characterization. In "Bartleby," for example, "Irving's presence is chiefly felt in the narrative technique . . . and Hawthorne's in the story's metaphysical dimensions" (p. 27). Bickley's discussion of " 'Bartleby' as Paradigm" is as rich as any chapter in the book, providing an effective introduction to the "two basic narrative personae" that he goes on to distinguish in the stories as a whole. A key passage characterizes these two personae as

the genial, sentimental anecdotist who enjoys painting sketches of character or social settings, or writing familiar essays about himself, and . . . the ironic protagonist who, in a sense, becomes the victim of his own story. Works in the first category include "Jimmy Rose" and "I and My Chimney," while

"The Fiddler" and "Cock-A-Doodle-Doo!" feature the second type of narrative pose. "Bartleby" is paradigmatically significant because it illustrates both basic narrative postures: the lawyer is genial and an engaging anecdotist, but he is at the same time an ironic figure of incomplete perceptions. (p. 44)

Bickley's ensuing discussion is divided between examination of Melville's employment of "narrative personae" and "rhetorical irony" and—in the second half of his book—an extended study of the interrelation of "narrative form, epistemology, and vision" in the remaining pieces (p. 44). In essence the book is another commentary on "Melvillean irony and narrative form," to borrow a phrase Bickley himself uses (p. xi, note 3) in acknowledging his indebtedness to Paul Brodtkorb's *Ishmael's White World* (New Haven: Yale University Press, 1965) and John Seelye's *Melville: The Ironic Diagram* (Evanston: Northwestern University Press, 1970). But after all he has to say about "narrative form" in Melville, Bickley seems uneasy about the ultimate implications of "Melvillean irony." His discomfiture becomes especially obvious in the final chapters, those treating "form as vision."

By this stage of his argument, through his discussion of narrative "methodology," Bickley has ostensibly cleared the ground for further definition of Melville's own stance as author and artist in relation to the roles of his various ironic narrators and protagonists. This, after all, is the ultimate engagement implied in Bickley's repeated use of such terms as Melville's "vision" and his reference to the "metaphysical dimensions" of Melville's stories. But the book stops short with discussion of "The Piazza," and a brief "Epilogue" fails, in my judgment, to keep that further engagement. Opening with purely conventional remarks about Melville's achievements in the short fiction, Bickley's "Epilogue" goes on to suggest only that the "vision" shaped by Melville's technical experiments with irony led him inevitably into an aesthetic and philosophical dead end with *The Confidence-Man*, where "indirection and rhetorical irony" are carried "too far" (p. 133). Not until *Billy Budd*, begun some thirty years later, did Melville manage to recover his equilibrium as a story-teller, Bickley believes. He did so by returning to "the methods and themes of earlier days"— which is to say, by abandoning "the ironic confessional mode of his short stories, and the contradictory posing of *The Confidence-Man*" (p. 136). Perhaps so. But surely these controversial assertions seriously undercut Bickley's previous claim that through the methodological experiments of the middle fifties "Melville found new artistic strength" (p. 131). In his closing pages, instead of clinching the case for Melville's "continuing intellectual and artistic growth" that the Preface had envisioned (p. xii), Bickley thus draws back from the deeper abysses of "Melvillean irony," with its implication that "in this world of lies"—Melville's phrase of 1850—the ironic story-teller as well as his ironic protagonist "becomes the victim of his own story."

ii

In the Preface to his *Going Under: Melville's Short Fiction and the American 1850s* (Baton Rouge: Louisiana State University Press, 1977) Marvin Fisher describes the book as "an exercise" in both "cultural history and literary criticism," meeting an unfulfilled need to emphasize the relation between Melville's stories and the culture of the period in which they were written. Comparing Melville himself with such story-tellers as James Joyce and Sherwood Anderson, Fisher values his tales primarily as apocalyptic criticism of "the moral and spiritual paralysis" of their time and place. They

reflect several very grave and distinctively American cultural dilemmas, and in the depths of their disillusionment suggest that mid-nineteenth-century America had betrayed the promises of its inception and fallen victim to its moral faults. They suggest apocalyptically that the social and political ideas of American life and the uniqueness and optimism of the American dream—rather than Melville's talent or intellect—were going under. (p. xi)

A subsequent paragraph explains another implication of the phrase "going under." Melville's social criticism, Fisher believes, was so drastic that to express his views openly would

dismay publishers and offend the majority of potential readers; thus, Melville devised a strategy . . . to publish some unpopular truths through the indirection of symbolism, allusion, and analogy. . . . He chose to *go under* as a literary strategy, to become our first major underground writer at a time when he could not even ascertain that there existed any significant readership capable of understanding or response. (p. xii)

In certain respects Fisher's book antedates Bickley's, though it appeared two years later. Fisher's vision of Melville as an "underground writer," deliberately challenging the social and political evils of his time, is a notion congenial to the American 1960's, when in fact a number of the component chapters were originally written and published. His conception of Melville's "literary strategy" shows minimal indebtedness to recent theorists of "Melvillean irony" such as Brodtkorb and Seelye, whose influence Bickley readily acknowledges, or even to Edgar Dryden, whose analysis of "Hawthorne and His Mosses" is cited in Fisher's opening chapter (p. 2, note 2) along with an essay by Seelye. In this aspect of the book I see a closer kinship between Fisher's approach and that of older critics: for example, Jay Leyda, in his Preface to *Complete Stories*, and Lawrance Thompson and William Charvat, who were writing on Melville in the 1950's. In *Melville's Quarrel with God* (1952) Thompson began with the premise that Melville "took wry and sly pleasure in the irony of disguising his riddle-answers behind the self-protective riddle-masks of his ingenious art; behind various subterfuges of rhetoric and symbol";[13] Charvat, whom Fisher mentions twice in support of his two-fold notion of "going under" (pp. 72, 106), argued that Melville was subversive in treating both his materials and his readers. Thompson did not deal with the shorter fiction, but Charvat held that "under the surface" of the magazine pieces Melville turned their apparently sentimental themes into "devastating commentaries on the idea of progress and the defeat of individualism and the imagination."[14] Fisher's book enlarges upon his own statement of the same basic thesis.

Fisher's vigorous analysis of "Benito Cereno" and its readers then and now is probably the high point of his book. For him it is "a remarkable study in the problems of perception" which has been badly mishandled by critics and classroom teachers (pp. 104–105). More than any other of the stories, it requires "a reader who can abandon the comfort of his social assumptions, relinquish the security of conventional wisdom, liberate himself from the confines of his culture, and gain the perspective of differing points of view" (pp. 106–107). Such readers did not begin to appear "until the 1950s," when with "the acceleration of the civil rights movement, the rise of black consciousness, and the published works of Malcolm X, Frantz Fañon, and Eldridge Cleaver" a few individuals began to recognize "that Babo is an underground hero. . . . Readers in the 1970s are better able to recognize the crippling deficiencies of Delano and Cereno and see Babo as the most fully developed example of manhood in the story—which itself becomes a kind of underground revenge tragedy" (pp. 108–109).

The discussion of "I and My Chimney" in Fisher's final chapter, "A House Divided," is the best single illustration of his critical methodology. "I and My Chimney," he declares, has "important implications which have not been adequately explained and a continuing relevance to the circumstances of American society which warrants further exploration" (p. 199). Fisher rejects "the 'orthodox' interpretation" in terms of Melville's own biography, treats more sympathetically the "revisionist" reading as an explication of Melvillean epistemology, but ultimately concentrates on "the pattern of opposites and divisions" that he himself sees in the story (p. 200): church and state, states' rights and federalism, progressivism and conservatism, youth and age, new and old. "Put most simply, the chimney is the past" (p. 205). The wife, "ludicrously overdrawn," is the "new woman"; the old narrator is a "male chauvinist prig"; the bribable Hiram Scribe "seems a parody of Enlightenment rationalism." The old house of the story, like the American Union as Abraham Lincoln saw it, is "a house divided," and the troubled union of the ill-matched couple is "a fictional means of projecting these larger oppositions" that Fisher has identified (p. 206), divisions which have persisted in American society from Melville's day to our own.

On this note Fisher concludes his book, emphasizing in his final pages

the currency of the conflict that ultimately constitutes Melville's subject—a conflict in the American mind or character capable of crippling or immobilizing society, psychomachia become sociomachia. More profound and less sensational than the myriad schizoid charcteristics of Poe's "House of Usher," Melville's tale of a house divided forecasts the moral paralysis, occasional flare-ups, and ultimate ruin of a domestic cold war—a fertile field for the kind of confidence man who would ask us to trust him to bring us together again. I wonder whether the increasing interest in Melville's short fiction is not due more to the half-realized awareness that his themes strike deep into the collective American psyche (to a level that makes them recurrently contemporary) than to the remarkably innovative technical means he employed. But both theme and technique ultimately served the same purpose: to project the other side of our assumptions and hopes, to deflate our vaunted superiority to Europe, and to assert our partiality and imperfection in what is from the start a fallen world of inevitable duplicity and recurrent deceptions. (pp. 212–213)

This representative passage effectively summarizes the argument of *Going Under*. There will probably never be a stronger presentation of the contemporary relevance, in cultural and social terms, of Melville's shorter fiction. Having said as much, I must nevertheless add my reservations about Fisher's book as about Bickley's: each is but a partial analysis of a subject as formidable as Melville's chimney and as difficult to reduce to any single fomulation.

Another recent publication that points up issues raised by both Fisher and Bickley is *The Feminization of American Culture* by Ann Douglas (New York: Alfred A. Knopf, 1977). The final chapter is entitled "Herman Melville and the Revolt Against the Reader"; a section of the chapter headed "The Magazine Pieces: Going Underground" (pp. 313–320) considers the short stories as Melville's response to readers who would have preferred warmed-over *Typee* to *Mardi, Moby-Dick,* and especially *Pierre.*[15] Like Fisher, Professor Douglas acknowledges the work of William Charvat, whose "Melville" she calls "one of the finest essays to date on Melville and one which has guided my own approach" (p. 386, note 28). She emphasizes "Melville's newly lowered estimation" of his "largely feminine audience" in his writings for the magazines, identifies "the central figure in most of them" as "the 'Ik Marvel' character" made popular by Donald Grant Mitchell but "descended from Irving's Geoffrey Crayon," and argues that through him Melville intended to reflect the taste of both editors and readers of the "feminine fifties." Melville's "distrust" of his narrator figure, she concludes, "never flagged," but he came nevertheless

increasingly to sense and exploit the hostility of this character to the very audience that he had been formed and maimed to serve. In Melville's two latest and in certain ways most interesting magazine stories, "I and My Chimney" and "The Apple-Tree Table," Melville puts himself behind the antagonistic possibilities of his sentimental male narrator, even while he grimly predicts the eventual success of those this personage both flatters and resists. (p. 317)

This is to say that, in the "eventual success" of the narrator's wife and daughters in the two stories, Melville himself was predicting the ultimate triumph of his own "feminine or effeminate" readers and editors, as Douglas calls them (p. 315).

What Charvat and Douglas have had to say about the intended audience and consequent editorial policies of *Harper's* and *Putnam's* lends support to Fisher's supposition that Melville "went underground" in the magazine stories. Douglas resembles Bickley in singling out "the narrator figure" of the tales as central to an understanding of Melville's own relation to the stories which that narrator is given to tell. Unlike Bickley, with his concentration on methodology, she interprets the narrative technique of the short fiction as a response to the cultural context of the 1850's and goes on to establish a positive link between Melville's use of the "mistrusted" narrator figure of the tales with the title character of *The Confidence-Man,* his next book, which Bickley had dismissed as both an aesthetic and a philosophical aberration. "Structure rather than content," she holds, was Melville's "most responsive register and indicator: every change in his sensibility showed up at once as formal instability and transformation" (p. 303). If this observation is valid, as I think it is, then the short fiction needs to be viewed not only against the background of its time and place, as in Fisher's book, but in relation to the whole body of Melville's own writing.

iii

In *Melville's Short Fiction 1853–1856* (Athens: University of Georgia Press, 1977), William B. Dillingham shares one of the basic assumptions that appear in the books by Bickley and Fisher: that Melville practiced "the fine art of concealment." But he takes a noticeably different critical approach and offers far different readings of individual pieces. In observing that earlier critics—Fogle included— underestimated the short fiction, Dillingham concurs with the "overall evaluation" of their quality in Bickley's "refreshing book" while acknowledging that his own interpretations "disagree almost consistently with those in Bickley's study" (p. 6, note 9). Although he too sees Melville as an artistic experimenter, there is no preoccupation in his book with methodology as such: "Structure was not an end in itself" for Melville "so much as it was a means to a still higher aim," Dillingham declares. "His first purpose throughout his short fiction was the delineation of character" (p. 10), and his typical mode of characterization—as both Bickley and Ann Douglas would agree— was to allow a narrator to characterize himself, on both "an overt and a submerged plane." Even the third-person narratives, "The Bell-Tower" and "Benito Cereno," are "impossible to understand . . . without coming to an understanding of the narrative voice" (p. 11). Fisher's name does not appear in Dillingham's Introduction, but their differences on one score are obvious enough.[16] Believing that Melville's ultimate aim was character delineation, Dillingham unequivocally dissents from any assumption that "historical, social, political, economic issues" were "Melville's primary interests. A major premise of this book is that they were not. Wherever they occur they are secondary to the unfolding of character, an unfolding that takes place on the second plane submerged beneath layers of inoffensive wit, congenial reminiscing, and Irvingesque worldly maturity" (p. 11).

It is "Melville's ironic method," Dillingham explains, that determines his own methodology: approaching each story with a "close and persistent scrutiny" that will uncover "submerged characterizations." In some of the first-person narratives "this is the same figure we detected on the surface, but greatly filled out and deepened. In

more cases than not the submerged characterization stands in contrast to the overt one. A stunning, revelatory irony results" (p. 12).
The third-person narratives (treated in two of Dillingham's best chapters) combine

an authorial perspective with what may be called the world's view. The two
have to be carefully identified and separated just as a narrator's words in the
other stories have to be analyzed from the standpoint of both what they say
and what they suggest about the speaker. Melville's own view is submerged
in the image patterns, in allusions, and in dozens of subtle indirections. (pp.
12–13)

It is on the surface level, Dillingham insists, that Melville appealed to
the editors and readers of *Harper's* and *Putnam's* by a wealth of contemporary allusions; here the stories indeed "furnish insights into the
popular culture of mid-nineteenth-century America" (p. 15). He
makes much the same point about Melville's frequent but superficial
use of autobiographical material as a starting-point for several of the
magazine pieces: this practice "does not result in a revelation of what
Melville was like at this period of his life any more than the overt
characterizations of his stories give the best and deepest insights into
his characters" (p. 16). If Melville does reveal himself in the work of
this period, Dillingham observes, it is only in "submerged autobiography," such as the concealed references to his relation with Hawthorne that "flicker in and out of the stories, especially 'The Encantadas' and 'The Piazza'" (p. 17).

Dillingham's fourteen chapters on the stories themselves are longer
and more detailed than either Bickley's or Fisher's and give more attention to previous scholarship. Aware of what Leyda called the "various levels of tension" in individual pieces and dedicated to recovering
what Melville himself "submerged" beneath their deceptive surfaces,
he is never simplistic in his readings nor restricted in his diving to a
search for only one stratum of material, whether biographical, metaphysical, or cultural and political. His breadth of concern resembles
Fogle's, though his aesthetic valuation of the tales is notably higher.
He has obviously profited from the studies of "Melvillean irony and
narrative form" that influenced Bickley, but his consideration of technique remains subordinate to his sensitive response to Melville's use
of language and his consistent emphasis on characterization. Moreover, Dillingham's apprehension of Melville the man keeps in perspective his comments on both the form and the content of the individual stories.

As Dillingham has analyzed the short fiction, it presents two recurrent types of character: those individuals who are dominated by *fear* and those dominated by *anger*. The fearful man, like the lawyer in "Bartleby," takes refuge in a superficial vision of the world and therefore sees too little; his opposite, the angry man, "sees too much, for it is his penetrating vision that creates and feeds his rebellious anger." Melville's Taji, Ahab, and Pierre in the earlier books are men of the latter type, but by the time of the short stories "their flame, if not their heat, has diminished." Here "anger is more likely to be submerged and reflected in actions that either totally puzzle or mislead the ordinary world," as the scrivener's silence, born of "obsessive resentment," baffles his employer. Bannadonna's rage is "channeled into his art"; the narrator of "The Lightning-Rod Man" "seethes beneath his alternating wit and pseudo-piety"; Babo's rage "is directed at far more than his white masters—they simply typify."

The anger of silence, which the world almost always misinterprets, is no less heroic and at the same time no less wrongheaded and destructive than the deafeningly loud roar of Ahab's rebellion. It is simply another form of the same disease, a disease that Melville dreaded perhaps even more than that of fear, for he was born with the germ in his soul. Through anger came the dignity and exhilaration of arrogance, but on the other hand it led to solitude, to a loss of compassionate human feelings, and finally to insanity and self-destruction. Melville admired the defiance that anger creates, but by depicting its negative results in his rebellious characters he kept himself aware that it cannot coexist with love. (p. 369)

Between the extremes of fear and anger is "a kind of emotional middle state," which Dillingham identifies as "fundamentally the one Melville worked out in his own life." The characters in his short fiction achieve such a position through "a willful changing of view" once they have stared overlong at "the white world that underlies life's variety and color." Like Melville himself as Dillingham interprets him, they are *ironists*. An ironist is thus

a person who realizes that sense perception is deceptive but who never loses faith in it completely. . . . An ironist perceives a level beneath the surface, but he does not separate himself from either; he functions in both realms.
The central experience of the ironist in Melville's stories is one first of dangerous encounter and then withdrawal to safety, submersion into himself or into the nature of existence so deeply as to almost drown and emergence back to the surface of ordinary life . . . but, as "The Piazza" makes clear, with a renewed sense of the need to keep his hold on ordinary life while never forgetting what he has seen. (pp. 369–370)

As for the stories themselves, irony "is not only their stylistic method and tone . . . but also a metaphor for their *Weltanschauung*." The short fiction, Dillingham concludes, constitutes "a disguised journal of Melville's plague years and a record of noble survival from the ravages of fear and anger." Not overtly but implicitly, in other words, it is both philosophical and autobiographical.

iv

In Chapter 115 of *Mardi*, Melville's Babbalanja retells a very old story: in his version "nine blind men" confronting "an immense wild banian tree" disagree hopelessly over which of its many trunks is "the original and true one." Melville's critics, I sometimes think, are like the nine blind men. In the case of the short fiction they now appear to be approaching consensus on one point: Melville is an ironist, as the banian tree is a banian tree. But the nature and the objects of his irony seem as various as the predispositions of the critics who acknowledge its existence, and for whom the stories themselves are—to borrow Babbalanja's word—"a polysensuum."

Despite their disagreements over individual readings, most recent critics of the short stories seem to fall into one or two principal camps: those who see Melville employing his irony subversively but aggressively, directing it against the evils of his time and place, and those who see him fighting a kind of rear-guard action against the world outside and the world within, using his irony defensively or even therapeutically. Dillingham, whose interest in Melville's recurrent character-types leads him ultimately into a modernized form of biographical and even philosophical criticism, belongs to the latter group; Fisher, who reads Melville as a social activist speaking to social activists, takes his irony as thrusting aggressively outward. (Bickley— though I may be mistaken—seems to regard irony as an edged tool that may be turned against the writer who commits himself to using it, for whatever purpose.)

I am not "Posterity speaking by proxy," as Melville spoke of Hawthorne in 1850; I lack the perspective of our twenty-first-century historian. Even so, I venture to predict that the field of the short fiction will be divided for some time to come between critics of the school of Fisher and critics of the school of Dillingham, given the diversity of contemporary criticism. On balance, I find Dillingham's approach more responsive to the texture of Melville's writing as I read it than either Fisher's or Bickley's, though I have profited from all three books even while dissenting to some degree from what each of them says about particular stories. No interpreter of Melville, it seems clear, will ever pronounce the last word on any one of his writings, and certainly there will be other essays—probably other books—published on the short fiction between now and the next century. A flurry of articles will undoubtedly appear in the immediate wake of the Northwestern-Newberry volume that includes *The Piazza Tales* and other miscellaneous prose pieces, which is now in press; every major edition of any of Melville's writings, beginning with the Constable edition of the 1920's, has generated renewed interest in some aspect of his work. Not only will the forthcoming volume provide a standard text; it will offer for the short fiction in particular that "'hard-core' scholarship" so essential for really "knowing" Melville, as Robert Milder has recently reminded us;[17] the besetting sin of Melville studies is still the tendency to write interpretation and criticism before the facts are in—or, worse still, to ignore the facts even after they have been established and made readily available.

Although biographical details remain scanty, we now have more documentary evidence about Melville's circumstances in the 1850's, and especially his dealings with his publishers, than was available some years ago: new letters, for example, have turned up; the dating of other letters published by Davis and Gilman has been corrected; more documentary references and reviews have been located. On the basis of these documents, more can now be said about the composition and submission of individual stories, the money Melville received for them, and the response of his reading public than Charvat could say in the 1950's, or that critics following Charvat have said in the 1970's. The audience of *Harper's* and *Putnam's* may not have been as effeminate or obtuse as modern interpreters like to assume without necessarily knowing the magazines themselves as they appeared from issue to issue when Melville himself was reading them. *Putnam's* in particular, for all its timidity over "The Two Temples," was in fact very receptive to Melville's work, under both George Palmer Putnam and his successors Dix & Edwards, and the magazine itself was not only "charming," as Henry James remembered it in after-years, but relatively sophisticated: no less a judge than Thackeray, speaking in 1855, called it "much the best Mag. in the world."[18] The next book on Melville's short fiction, besides taking into account the insights of Bickley, Fisher, and Dillingham, must also weigh these other considerations. We need from its author not only a sensitive reading of the stories themselves but a new consideration of Melville and his audience in the years following *Moby-Dick*, based on first-hand scholarship, and a fuller account of Melville's dealings with editors and publishers during this difficult period of his career, taking into account the documents now available. And whatever his assessment of the short fiction, our author must deal with it in the context not only of the 1850's but of Melville's own writing, exploring that continuity of theme and technique that runs from *Pierre* through the magazine work—not forgetting *Israel Potter*—to *The Confidence-Man* and beyond. Such a book will constitute neither "hard-core" scholarship nor "soft," but the work of a perceptive reader and writer who is equally at home with both.

Melville and Emerson's Rainbow

(1980)

For many years I planned to write an essay on the much-discussed relation between the two major figures that have most engaged my interest as a scholar, Melville and Emerson. In the fall of 1979, while I was on research leave and working on a projected book, *Emerson on the Scholar*, the opportunity came when I was invited to lecture at Oregon State University and subsequently at the University of Victoria, the University of Washington, and Washington State University at Pullman. At that time I prepared a briefer version of "Melville and Emerson's Rainbow" and delivered it as a lecture on the four campuses. The study in its present form, which owes much to the generous assistance of Professors Wallace Williams, Robert Milder, Donald Yannella, William M. Gibson, and Charles N. Watson, Jr., first appeared in *ESQ: A Journal of the American Renaissance*, 26 (2nd Quarter 1980), 53–78; I have restyled some of the citations and made incidental revisions on pp. 254, 256, 264–265, 267–268, 269, and 270.

The two scholars cited in my seventh paragraph have both written me to comment about the essay, and with their permission I quote here from their respective letters. Professor Nina Baym observes that in her "Melville's Quarrel with Fiction" she says "that *Moby-Dick* was (as you quote me) influenced by Emerson's *thought* without specifically assigning sources for that thought. I then use the 'Language' section of *Nature* as a useful place for readers of my essay to consult the aspects of Emerson's thought that I am talking about. One could infer from this use that I think that Melville read *Nature*, but the inference is not necessary, and I did not mean to make that claim. In a general way, the particular Emersonian attitude that I am concerned with is pervasive in his writings, both by direct statement and implication. This attitude has to do with Emerson's sense of what a serious literary person ought and ought not to be doing. He ought to be expressing truth, not devising fables."

Professor Philip Beidler writes with the Baym essay in mind, remarking that he thinks it possible to take his own view "of *Billy Budd* with regard to Emerson and still accept hers of *Moby-Dick*," which "is probably right. This is how my argument might run: like Edgar Dryden, I think that Melville's great theme throughout his career is 'form,' the idea of order itself; this idea of 'form' or 'order,' Melville's philosophical model, so to speak, is also throughout his career basically Emersonian in outline; in *Moby-Dick*, through Ishmael as narrator-artificer, he does seem to respond affirmatively to that 'poetic' of order; from *Pierre* onward, however (as you suggest), his response is negative, and often in explicit ways."

I am grateful for these responses, which deserve quotation here as a matter of record.

Say what they will, he's a great man.

Herman Melville to Evert Duyckinck,
24 February 1849

Nay, I do not oscillate in Emerson's rainbow.

Melville to Duyckinck, 3 March 1849

On 24 February 1849, writing from the home of his father-in-law, Lemuel Shaw, Herman Melville reported to his New York friend Evert Duyckinck how he had been passing his time in Boston, where the Melvilles had gone for the birth of their first child. He had been "exulting" over the plays in a newly purchased seven-volume edition of Shakespeare, "in glorious great type"; he had attended two of Fanny Kemble Butler's Shakespearean readings, of *Macbeth* and *Othello;* he had heard Emerson lecture. Shakespeare, whom he called "the divine William," is "full of sermons-on-the-mount," he told Duyckinck, "and gentle, aye, almost as Jesus. . . . I fancy that this moment Shakspeare in heaven ranks with Gabriel Raphael and Michael. And if another Messiah ever comes twill be in Shakesper's person." Mrs. Butler "makes a glorious Lady Macbeth," he thought, "but her Desdemona seems like a boarding school miss." As for Emerson, who was something of a curiosity to New Yorkers in the 1840's, Melville was favorably impressed: "Say what they will, he's a great man" (*Letters*, pp. 76–78).

Duyckinck's reply has not survived, but its nature can be inferred from Melville's next letter, written on 3 March. As a devout Episcopalian, Duyckinck was obviously shocked by Melville's enthusiastic comparison of Shakespeare with Christ. "To one of your habits of thought," Melville responded, "I confess that in my last, I seemed, but only *seemed* irreverent." What he had said of Mrs. Butler apparently provoked no objections, but his casual reference to Emerson as "great"—"Say what they will"—must also have drawn fire, leading Melville to open his new letter with a fervent denial: "Nay, I do not oscillate in Emerson's rainbow, but prefer rather to hang myself in mine own halter than to swing in any other man's swing" (*Letters*, pp. 78–80).

Why "Emerson's *rainbow*," and why "any other man's *swing*"? Because in all likelihood—though the phrases have never been explained—Duyckinck had clipped and sent to Melville a humorous
squib from the New York *Tribune* of 6 February, illustrated with wood-
cuts, that purported to be a critique of Emerson as a lecturer. "He
takes high flights," the article concludes, "and sustains himself without ruffling a feather. He inverts the rainbow and uses it for a
swing—now sweeping the earth and now clapping his hands among
the stars."[1] Here are the lecturer and his rainbow:

(Courtesy, American Antiquarian Society)

Despite Melville's disavowal to Duyckinck, he too has been charged
repeatedly with swinging "among the stars" in books such as *Mardi*,
then in press, and later in *Moby-Dick* and *Pierre*. None of them was a
favorite with contemporary reviewers, who preferred straightforward "narratives of voyages" like *Typee* and *Omoo*. Some of the critics
of his own day explicitly linked him with Emerson and Transcendentalism. Duyckinck's own *Literary World* found in *Mardi* "poetical,
thoughtful, ingenious moral writing . . . which Emerson would not
disclaim." One English reviewer had already detected what he regarded as Emersonian influence on *Mardi*, and another objected to
Melville's "preaching of certain transcendental nonsense" in its
pages.[2]

Melville himself promised his London publisher that his next book
would contain "no metaphysics, . . . nothing but cakes & ale" (*Letters*,
p. 86), and followed through with *Redburn* (1849) and *White-Jacket*

(1850). But *Moby-Dick* (1851) and *Pierre* (1852) again brought down the wrath of those reviewers who deplored Melville's penchant for what one of them called "philosophy and fantasy." Even the *Literary World* complained of Ishmael's "piratical running down of creeds and opinions," which Duyckinck associated with "the conceited indifferentism of Emerson" and "the run-a-muck style of Carlyle."[3] Several of Melville's relatives in Boston and Albany shared the reviewers' dislike of "philosophy and fantasy," and even in later years, after he had turned to poetry, his cousin Henry Gansevoort grumbled that "he has so much of Emerson & tran[s]cendentalism in his writing that it never will really touch the common heart."[4]

Some twentieth-century critics have continued to associate Melville with Emerson and the Transcendentalists, but in quite a different way. Pointing to satirical passages in *Pierre* and later in *The Confidence-Man* (1857) that openly attack "amiable philosophers of either the 'Compensation,' or 'Optimist' school" (p. 277), they conclude that Melville was entirely hostile to all versions of Transcendental doctrine. But the late Perry Miller, who was sure that at some time or other Melville "must have read much of Emerson," was unwilling to consider his response in either/or terms; if Emerson "had not been there both to stimulate and exasperate Herman Melville," Miller once wrote, "*Moby-Dick* would have emerged as only another sea-story."[5]

After half a century of industrious scholarly work, there is still no consensus among students of Melville today about either the extent or the nature of his engagement with Emerson, or even when it began. Two recent articles illustrate the wide disagreement. In an essay with a provocative title, "Melville's Quarrel with Fiction," Nina Baym, who argues that Melville held "not a Hawthornian, but an Emersonian view of fiction and reading," goes beyond Miller to suggest that his "contact with Emerson's thought was the single most important influence" on what she calls "the shape of *Moby-Dick*."[6] On the other side of the argument is Philip D. Beidler's discussion of *Billy Budd*, Melville's last prose work, as his "Valedictory to Emerson." Beidler joins with those critics who have concluded that Emersonian ideas were wholly foreign to Melville. They point not only to his dismissal of "Compensation" and "Optimism" in *Pierre* but to the unfriendly caricature of Emerson as Mark Winsome, the "mystic" of *The Confidence-Man*—and Winsome's resemblance to Emerson is unmistakable. Beidler posits a "conscious anti-Emersonianism" on Melville's part and argues that in *Billy Budd* he created still another character in Emerson's image as "the Transcendental philosopher-teacher": Captain Vere, whose address to the drumhead court Beidler takes to be "a 'sham' refashioning" of Emerson's first book, *Nature*.[7] Professors Beidler and Baym, for all their obvious differences, agree on one point: Emerson was important for Melville. Yet there is nothing but internal evidence—which can be boggy ground to build on, as Melville himself might say—to suggest that he ever read *Nature*, let alone adapted its ideas in *Moby-Dick* or refuted them in *Billy Budd*.

It is time, I think, to assemble all the evidence concerning Melville's response to Emerson, and to ask again, as Duyckinck did, whether he oscillated in Emerson's rainbow, if only for a time and to some limited degree. And it is in order to point out from the first that the relation between Melville and Emerson was almost entirely one-sided. As far as we know, the two men never met, nor did Emerson hear Melville when he too took to the lecture platform in the late 1850's. There is no mention of Melville either in Emerson's published works or in his journals, letters, and lectures, though he did own a copy of *Typee* in the revised edition published in 1846 by the New York firm of Wiley & Putnam.[8] As for Melville, he assured Duyckinck in 1849 that he knew little of Emerson before hearing him lecture. "I was very agreeably disappointed in Mr Emerson," he declared in his letter of 3 March.

I had heard of him as full of transcendentalisms, myths & oracular gibberish. I had only glanced at a book of his once in Putnam's store—that was all I knew of him, till I heard him lecture.—To my surprise, I found him quite intelligible, tho' to say truth, they told me that that night he was unusually plain.

This letter is the single most important bit of surviving evidence to throw light on Melville's feelings about Emerson; it deserves to be read virtually line by line. Other information outside Melville's various books themselves is sketchy at best. We know from Sophia Hawthorne that during the late summer of 1850, when he was at work on *Moby-Dick*, he spent a morning at the Hawthornes' red cottage in Lenox reading Emerson—which essays from what volume being tantalizingly unspecified. Four books by Emerson have survived from Melville's own library, all from later years: *Poems*, given him in 1859; *Essays* and *Essays: Second Series*, bought in 1862; and *The Conduct of Life*, picked up at second hand in 1870. Whether Melville also owned or borrowed *Nature*, other editions of the *Essays* and *Poems*, or such later works as *Representative Men* (1850) and *English Traits* (1856) is simply not a matter of external record. His marks and notes in the three surviving prose volumes have been known since the 1930's,[9] but, as Miller once remarked, his comments "cast no trustworthy light backward into the time when he wrote his ambiguous report to Duyckinck."[10]

Specifically, these questions have to be addressed: What did Melville really know of Emerson before hearing him lecture? What was Emerson's subject when he lectured in Boston on 5 February 1849? What was the nature of Melville's response to Emerson, both at the time of the lecture and during the writing of *Moby-Dick* in 1850 and 1851? What did Emerson mean to him in later years, from the time of *Pierre* to the time of *Billy Budd*? This essay will address the five questions in turn.

i

Estimating Melville's knowledge of Emerson before 1849 requires answering two subordinate questions. What books by Emerson were available to him by 1848, "in Putnam's store" or elsewhere? Are there authentic signs of Emersonian influence on Melville's early writings? The first answer, which involves matters of fact, is easier to arrive at than the second.

Any New York bookstore, including that of George Palmer Putnam at 155 Broadway, might have carried the Boston editions of three books by Emerson that were still in print in 1848: *Essays* (1841), *Essays: Second Series* (1844), and *Poems* (1846); both series of *Essays* had gone into new editions by 1847. The one title out of print in the United States was *Nature*, the 1836 printing having been exhausted in 1844. Emerson himself did not reprint *Nature* until September of 1849, when it appeared in his *Nature, Addresses, and Lectures*. But there were six unauthorized English printings published between 1841 and 1848,[11] and Putnam, an importer, could have carried one of them. If so, then it was possible for Melville to see any or all of Emerson's first four books "in Putnam's store."

Melville was obviously minimizing his knowledge of Emerson when he wrote Duyckinck; are there further possibilities? Yes, and one of them is that he may have extended his "glance" at Emerson in some New York library. No work of Emerson's is charged to him at the New York Society Library, where he held membership in 1848, or in Duyckinck's own list of "Books Lent," but Duyckinck's collection included Emerson's *Essays* and *Essays: Second Series*, his *Poems*, and one of the pirated English printings of *Nature*. This fourth volume, *Nature, An Essay; and Lecture on the Times* (London: Henry G. Clarke & Co., 1844),[12] had probably been sent over from London when Putnam was the London partner in the firm of Wiley & Putnam, Melville's first American publisher, and Duyckinck was one of its New York editors. Putnam came home from England in 1847 to dissolve the partnership; his new shop, as his son remembered, "depended chiefly on the sale of books and periodicals imported from London" during its first years.[13] This information somewhat increases the possibility, if not the likelihood, that Melville may have seen a copy of *Nature*, either at Putnam's store or in Duyckinck's own library, before 1849.

Melville could also have examined books by Emerson in Boston, but not during the year when he was actively engaged with *Mardi*, 1848; he was in Boston for his marriage to Elizabeth Shaw in August of 1847 and again in the early months of 1849, but during the intervening period he remained in New York. The Shaws, moreover, were not Emersonians. Lemuel Shaw, the distinguished Chief Justice of the Massachusetts Supreme Court, had known the Emerson family for many years, having boarded with Emerson's widowed mother when Emerson himself was a boy driving the family cow to pasture on Boston Common.[14] But Shaw was no Transcendentalist. "Brought up in an atmosphere of strict Calvinistic Congregationalism," as a biographer tells us, he came in time, chiefly through his various associations with Harvard College, to share "what came to be recognized as Orthodox Unitarianism, and refused to follow the new protesting movement of Emerson and Parker. His spirit was satisfied with the advance from doctrinal to ethical religion, but would proceed no further." Although he regularly attended worship in the New-South Meeting House, Unitarian, where he held a pew for many years, he never became a formal communicant.[15]

In 1848 or after, following his daughter's marriage to Melville, Shaw presented her with a six-volume set of the works of William Ellery Channing,[16] whose writings were far closer to his own religious views than Emerson's could have been; Shaw would not have forgotten the controversy in Unitarian circles over Emerson's Divinity School Address of 1838. It seems doubtful, therefore, that Melville would have found anything by Emerson in Shaw's library—or even that Shaw would have taken him to hear Emerson lecture in February of 1849. In the following September, on the eve of departing for Europe, Melville requested Shaw to ask for letters of introduction "from Mr Emerson to Mr Carlyle" and others in London (*Letters*, p. 90), but he did not see Carlyle while he was abroad. There is no evidence that Emerson wrote for Melville to anyone in England or even that Shaw approached him in Melville's behalf; the record as we have it is simply blank.

Is there any sign in *Mardi* itself of Emersonian influence? The late Merrell R. Davis, author of the most detailed study of the book to date, did not investigate the question, saying only that when Melville's Babbalanja defends himself against a charge of inconsistency he is "echoing" Emerson's "Self-Reliance."[17] Maxine Moore, author of the second book-length study of *Mardi*, goes somewhat further, remarking that it "contains passages that seem to be addressed directly to Emerson's 'Nature,'" but she does not pursue the point in any detail. Her principal observation is that Babbalanja "rejects the possibility of a Benevolent Nature, as well as the Romantic tenet that man can draw analogies from Nature."[18] "All vanity, vanity," Babbalanja cries, "to seek in nature for positive warranty to these aspirations of ours. . . . [I]f not against us, nature is not for us" (p. 210).

The most ambitious study of Emersonian elements in *Mardi* is in a chapter of an unpublished 1963 dissertation by Barbara Blansett, "Melville and Emersonian Transcendentalism." *Mardi*, Mrs. Blansett thinks, is evidence of Melville's early attraction to Transcendentalism; she makes a comparative study of passages from the book and from various essays by Emerson.[19] The parallels she cites confirm one's impression that by 1848 Melville had soaked up a good deal of information about transcendental idealism, but they do not necessarily demonstrate that his teacher had been Emerson rather than Plato and Proclus among the ancients[20] or Wordsworth and Coleridge among the moderns. The more "transcendental" passages in *Mardi* I trace to Melville's reading of Plato rather than of Emerson, though I see a resemblance between the self-centered, self-reliant, and generally rebellious questers of Melville's early books and the "I" who speaks out so forcefully in such essays as "Self-Reliance" and "Circles." But the full impact of Emerson's influence, I am convinced, struck Melville only after *Mardi* was behind him.

ii

We do not know who accompanied Melville on the evening of 5 February 1849, when he attended Emerson's lecture in the Freeman Place Chapel in Boston, or who told him that "that night" Emerson "was unusually plain." A likely candidate is his wife's half-brother, Lemuel Shaw, Jr., then a young man in his early twenties who had visited the Melvilles in New York during the previous winter and gone about the city with them; another is Lemuel's younger brother Samuel, then still in his teens, who in later years was to give Melville a copy of Emerson's *Poems*. Until now we have not known the subject of Emerson's lecture. From published scholarship we learn only that it was the fourth of a five-part series on "Mind and Manners in the Nineteenth Century" that had begun on 15 January, when Melville was back in New York.[21] Boston newspapers merely announced the time and place of each lecture in the course without giving individual titles; they respected Emerson's objections to summary reports, which were frequently picked up by exchange and reprinted in other cities he was yet to visit.[22]

Emerson had used the same overall title, "Mind and Manners in the Nineteenth Century," for a somewhat different course of six lectures he had given in London during June of 1848. The first three lectures of both courses, which he grouped under the heading "The Natural History of the Intellect," were essentially the same. In London he filled out the series with three additional lectures, but in Boston and New York in 1849 and 1850 there were only two more, both of them lectures he had first offered in England and Scotland.

Professor Wallace Williams, who is editing Emerson's lecture manuscripts, has identified the fourth and fifth Boston lectures as "Natural Aristocracy" and "The Superlative in Manners and Literature," but he has not been able to establish with certainty the order in which they were presented there. In view of the sequence Emerson followed when lecturing at Concord a month later and again in New York in 1850, he believes that there is "a slightly greater likelihood" that Emerson read "Natural Aristocracy" on 5 February, when Melville was in the audience, and "The Superlative" a week later, but the reverse order would be "almost as likely." He notes also that what remains of the manuscripts indicates that the early versions differ considerably from the synthetic texts assembled for Emerson in his later years by James Elliot Cabot. The manuscript lectures as Emerson last delivered them were collected as "Aristocracy" and "The Superlative" in the posthumous volume *Lectures and Biographical Sketches* in 1883. In particular, Professor Williams describes the early version of "Natural Aristocracy" that Emerson read in Boston, Concord, and New York as "far better" than Cabot's.[25]

My own reading of "Natural Aristocracy" in the text established by Professor Williams persuades me that this is the lecture Melville heard. It opens in the same way as Cabot's later version, explaining that Emerson's concern is with "the permanent traits of the Aristocracy," but there is an increasing divergence in organization in later paragraphs. The representative passages which I quote here are common to both versions: the text is that of Edward Emerson's Centenary Edition, but the arrangement follows the sequence of material in the manuscript text as Professor Williams has established it. As Emerson explains at the outset, he means by the term "aristocrat" not "the accepted and historical peerage," but

a real aristocracy, a chapter of Templars who sit indifferently in all climates and under the shadow of all institutions, but so few, so heedless of badges, so rarely convened, so little in sympathy with the predominant politics of nations, that their names and doings are not recorded in any Book of Peerage, or any Court Journal, or even Daily Newspaper of the world. (*W*, X, 32)

The existence of an upper class is not injurious, as long as it is dependent on merit. (*W*, X, 38)

Aristocracy is the class eminent by personal qualities, and to them belongs without assertion a proper influence. (*W*, X, 38–39)

We are fallen on times so acquiescent and traditionary that we are in danger of forgetting . . . that the basis of all aristocracy must be truth,—the doing what elsewhere is pretended to be done. (*W*, X, 39)

I wish catholic men, who by their science and skill are at home in every latitude and longitude, who carry the world in their thoughts; men . . . who are interested in things in proportion to their truth and magnitude; who know the beauty of animals and the laws of their nature, whom the mystery of botany allures, and the mineral laws; who see general effects and are not too learned to love the Imagination, the power and the spirits of Solitude;—men who see the dance in men's lives as well as in a ball-room, and can feel and convey the sense which is only collectively or totally expressed by a population; men who are charmed by the beautiful Nemesis as well as by the dire Nemesis, and dare trust their inspiration for their welcome; who would find their fellows in persons of real elevation or whatever kind of speculative or practical ability. (*W*, X, 39)

Men "enter the superior class," Emerson continues, in either of two ways. One is through "a commanding talent" demonstrated in practical enterprises (*W*, X, 40); the other is through "Genius," defined as "the power to affect the Imagination, as possessed by the orator, the poet, the novelist or the artist" (*W*, X, 52). Genius, Emerson continues,

has a royal right in all possessions and privileges, being itself representative and accepted by all men as their delegate. It has indeed the best right, because it raises men above themselves, intoxicates them with beauty. (*W*, X, 52)

Elevation of sentiment, refining and inspiring the manners, must really take the place of every distinction whether of material power or of intellectual gifts. The manners of course must have that depth and firmness of tone to attest their centrality in the nature of the man. . . . In the presence of this nobility even genius must stand aside. For the two poles of nature are Beauty and Meanness, and noble sentiment is the highest form of Beauty. (*W*, X, 54–55)

There are certain conditions in the highest degree favorable to the tranquillity of spirit and to that magnanimity we so prize. And mainly the habit of considering large interests, and things in masses, and not too much in detail. (*W*, X, 64)

And finally, in the paragraph that concluded the version of 1849–1850:

I know the feeling of the most ingenious and excellent youth in America; I hear the complaint of the aspirant that we have no prizes offered to the ambition of virtuous young men; that there is no Theban Band; no stern exclusive Legion of Honor, to be entered only by long and real service and patient climbing up all the steps. We have a rich man's aristocracy, plenty of bribes for those who like them; but a grand style of culture, which, without injury, an ardent youth can propose to himself as a Pharos through long dark years, does not exist, and there is no substitute. The youth, having got through the first thickets that oppose his entrance into life, having got into decent society, is left to himself, and falls abroad with too much freedom. But in the hours of insight we rally against this skepticism. We then see that if the ignorant are around us, the great are much more near; that there is an order of men, never quite absent, who enroll no names in their archives but of such as are capable of truth. They are gathered in no one chamber; no chamber would hold them; but, out of the vast duration of man's race, they tower like mountains, and are present to every mind in proportion to its likeness to theirs. The solitariest man who shares their spirit walks environed by them; they talk to him, they comfort him, and happy is he who prefers these associates to profane companions. They also take shape in men, in women. There is no heroic trait, no sentiment or thought that will not sometime embody itself in the form of a friend. That highest good of rational existence is always coming to such as reject mean alliances. (*W*, X, 59–60)

In passages such as these Emerson explicitly formulated ideas that had been seeking expression in Melville's own writing as early as *Typee* and would be emerging even more clearly in *Redburn* and *White-Jacket* and more powerfully in such chapters of *Moby-Dick* as "Knights and Squires." Listening to Emerson in 1849 would have brought Melville ample "confirmation of his own more reserved thoughts"—to borrow another phrase from *Billy Budd*. Perry Miller, pointing to Melville's keen awareness of his own growth and development since his return from the sea—"Three weeks have scarcely passed, at any time between then and now," he once told Hawthorne, "that I have not unfolded within myself" (*Letters*, p. 130)—quotes a pregnant sentence from his letter to Duyckinck about Emerson and Shakespeare: "Any fish can swim near the surface, but it takes a great whale to go down stairs five miles or more." Miller then comments: "Students are free to interpret the letter as they choose; to me it seems the compulsive assertion of a passionate youth who has just heard Emerson tell him more about himself than in any three-week period he had yet discovered."[24] Miller was seldom given to understatement, but in this case his strong words may be very nearly on target.

iii

In examining what Melville wrote on 3 March 1849, about "this Plato who talks thro' his nose," it is well to remember that he was writing nearly a month after hearing Emerson lecture—a fact that Miller overlooked. Moreover, he was answering Evert Duyckinck, a New Yorker with little sympathy for unorthodox religious thought, who had found his previous letter irreverent. Here Melville's praise of Emerson is not only qualified by important reservations; it is sandwiched between comments on charges against both Melville and Emerson that Duyckinck had introduced.

The opening words of the letter—"Nay, I do not oscillate in Emerson's rainbow"—were meant to assure Duyckinck that Melville was in no danger of becoming a Transcendentalist; even so, Melville's next declaration—that he would rather "hang myself in mine own halter than swing in any other man's swing"—sounds like a Melvillean affirmation of Emersonian self-reliance. In concluding the letter Melville returns to Emerson once again after explaining his views on Shakespeare: he agrees with Duyckinck's complaint that Emerson would be out of place "in company of jolly fellows . . . like you & me. Ah, my dear sir," Melville replies, "that's his misfortune, not his fault." Between these nods to Duyckinck comes Melville's independent evaluation, which has more to do with Emerson the man than with the lecture he had heard on 5 February.

On the positive side, Melville places Emerson favorably on the vertical scale that he commonly used in estimating a man's worth: Emerson has both elevation and depth. As for elevation, a term Emerson himself uses repeatedly in "Natural Aristocracy," he is for Melville "an uncommon man. Swear he is a humbug—then is he no common humbug"; again, he is "more than a brilliant fellow." As for depth, he is one of that "whole corps of thought-divers, that have been diving & coming up again with bloodshot eyes since the world began," and Melville, a thought-diver himself, "loves all men who *dive*."[25] Duyckinck had questioned Emerson's originality; Melville, who knew well, after writing three books, that every author borrows from his predecessors, replies, "No man is his own sire." Instinctively—or "instinctuly," as he wrote—we respond to "a something about every man elevated above mediocrity." This undefined "something" Melville sees in "Mr Emerson. And, frankly, for the sake of the argument, let us call him a fool;—then had I rather be a fool than a wise man."

On the negative side, Melville found one "gaping flaw" in Emerson, "notwithstanding his merit": he could confidently tell the Creator Himself how to fashion a better world than the one He had made. (The supercilious smugness that Melville detected in Emerson he would later identify as his "self-conceit.") Moreover, he continues, the man's ideas are destructive rather than constructive; he is one of "the pullers-down" rather than "the builders-up." If this charge seems surprising today, I would suggest that Melville was reacting less to anything he had heard Emerson say than to what conservative New Englanders were saying about him during the 1840's. In Boston there was a lingering distrust of what Transcendentalists themselves called "the newness." "The view taken of Transcendentalism in State Street," Emerson remarked dryly in his journal, "is that it threatens to invalidate contracts" (*JMN*, VIII, 108; cf. *W*, X, 345). In Mount Vernon Street, where the Shaws lived, Lemuel Shaw might well have told Melville that Emerson was still unwelcome at Harvard, where he had outraged orthodox Unitarians with his address to the seniors of the Divinity School more than ten years before. Others who judged Emerson by the company he kept would associate him with miscellaneous reformers—those he himself once described as "picturesque": "Madmen, madwomen, men with beards, Dunkers, Muggletonians, Come-outers, Groaners, Agrarians, Seventh-day Baptists, Quakers, Abolitionists, Calvinists, Unitarians, and Philosophers" (*W*, X, 374). Even Hawthorne in "The Old Manse" could not resist a word about the procession of odd individuals who sought Emerson out at his home in Concord.[26] Melville's own verdict on the Emersonians is harsh: "These men are all cracked right across the brow."

Both the negative and positive impressions of Emerson that Melville recorded in 1849 remained with him for years to come. "These men"—the "cracked" philosophers and reformers with whom Emerson is linked in the letter—turn up three years later in *Pierre* as the ineffectual "Apostles." Their "Grand Master," one Plotinus Plinlimmon, may or may not be modeled after Emerson—critics disagree. But Mark Winsome in *The Confidence-Man* both looks and talks like the lecturer Melville heard some seven years before he wrote the book, and Winsome, coldly and constitutionally temperate, seems equally incapable of swallowing "a draught of ale or a mouthful of cake." Melville's annotations on the essays he read in the 1860's and 1870's record similar reservations about Emerson's seeming coldness and express repeated disagreements—some of them major—with his ideas. Nevertheless, his respect for what he continued to regard as Emerson's "nobility" continued undiminished. "A *noble* expression," he writes in a marginal comment; "he keeps *nobly* on"; "This is *noble* again"; "Still"—in spite of the disagreements—"these essays are *noble*"; the word runs through Melville's marginalia as a virtual refrain. What he set down next to one passage of "The Poet" is in perfect keeping with his response to Emerson's "greatness" in 1849: "All this is nobly written, and proceeds from noble thinking, and a natural sympathy with greatness."[27] His evaluation would apply with equal fitness to "Natural Aristocracy."

iv

"One does not vitally believe in a man," Melville wrote in *Pierre*, "till one's own two eyes have beheld him" (p. 292). And if that man is an author, then one carefully reads his book, perhaps for the first time. So it was, I am persuaded, with Melville and Hawthorne in 1850; so it may have been with Melville and Emerson as well during the previous year.

The most likely place and time for Melville's first careful reading of Emerson would seem to be in Boston in 1849, between his view of Emerson on the lecture platform in February and his return to New York with his wife and new son early in April. His mention of Emerson in the manuscript of "Hawthorne and His Mosses," written in August of 1850, suggests that he knew Emerson's writings by that time, but there is no record of his borrowing any book by Emerson during that year, either from the New York Society Library or from Evert Duyckinck, though late in 1850 Duyckinck loaned him *A Week on the Concord and Merrimack Rivers* by Emerson's protegé, Henry Thoreau.[28] I infer from this information that Melville had probably bought or borrowed one or more of Emerson's books before he left Boston.

If this inference is correct, the essays that Melville read in 1849 could well have been the ones he did *not* mark or annotate in the two volumes of Emerson he acquired in 1862: "History," "Self-Reliance," "Compensation," "Love," "Friendship," "The Over-Soul," "Circles," and "Intellect" in the first series of *Essays*; "Experience" and five other titles in *Essays: Second Series*. Many of these essays, especially those in Emerson's earlier volume, deal with subjects that one would expect Melville to find especially appealing; indeed the 1841 *Essays* is most likely the book he had "glanced at" in 1848 "in Putnam's store" and looked into more closely in 1849 after hearing Emerson lecture. He would surely have responded to Emerson's fascination with energy and movement, process and transformation, expressed in the very imagery of such an essay as "Circles." Similar images, including that of the circle itself, are ubiquitous in Melville's own writing. Melville's protagonists, like the speaker in Emerson's essays, see the world from their own point of view; among them, Captain Ahab is the most literally self-reliant, though scarcely in Emerson's sense of that term. I am one of those readers who regard Ahab's story, with his "lonely death in lonely life," as Melville's implicit criticism of self-reliance as carried to its ultimate secular realization.

In Emerson's "Intellect," one of the 1841 *Essays*, there is a passage that in both imagery and theme resembles the conclusion of Melville's *Mardi*, the "Lee Shore" chapter of *Moby-Dick*, and the distinctive phrasing of Melville's 1849 letter to Duyckinck about "Emerson's rainbow":

God offers to every mind its choice between truth and repose. Take which you please,—you can never have both. Between these, as a pendulum, man *oscillates.* He in whom the love of repose predominates will accept the first creed, the first philosophy, the first political party he meets,—most likely his father's. He gets rest, commodity and reputation; but he shuts the door of truth. He in whom the love of truth predominates will keep himself aloof from all the moorings, and afloat. He will abstain from dogmatism, and recognize all the opposite negations between which, as walls, his being is *swung.* He submits to the inconvenience of suspense and imperfect opinion, but he is a candidate for truth, as the other is not, and respects the highest law of his being. (*W*, II, 341–342; emphasis added)

There is a passage that Melville the truth-seeker would have called "noble" if he read it in Boston in 1849—as I am inclined to believe he did—at the very time when he was denying to Duyckinck that he *"oscillated"* in Emerson's rainbow or *"swung"* in any man's swing but his own. I find that students see a general parallel, just as I do, between Emerson's words in "Intellect" and Chapter 23 of *Moby-Dick*,

"The Lee Shore."[29] What Emerson wrote might well have been applied to Melville himself by either of the Hawthornes, to whom he was soon to open himself as he did to few other men or women in his life; I think of what Hawthorne once wrote of Melville as a man who "can neither believe, nor be comfortable in his unbelief," but is "too honest and courageous not to try to do one or the other" (*Log*, II, 529). To those who know the Emerson of the journals, as Melville of course could not, there is something of the same oscillation between faith and doubt visible in his more private thoughts, and some of the same loneliness too. "Men generally attempt early in life to make their brothers first, afterwards their wives, acquainted with what is going forward in their private theatre," Emerson wrote in 1845, "but they soon desist . . . , and all parties acquiesce at last [each] in a private box with the whole play performed before himself *solus*" (*JMN*, IX, 236).

As Melville's Taji and Ishmael and Ahab become less self-assured and more introverted and self-questioning, they express the loneliness and doubt that both Melville and Emerson knew as the obverse face of American self-reliance. During the 1830's and 1840's, as Perry Miller reminds modern students of our literature, "Emerson and those who were considered his disciples presented themselves to America not as apostles of the serene and inviolable order of nature but as victims of the modern disease of introspection." He then quotes Emerson's own remark that "the young men were born with knives in their brain, a tendency to introversion, self-dissection, anatomizing of motives" (*W*, X, 329).[30] Though Emerson's words were not so intended, of course, I take them as an apposite comment on Melville's strangely "modern" protagonists.

There is some indication of what Emerson meant to Melville by the summer of 1850 in "Hawthorne and His Mosses," the essay he dashed off for Duyckinck's *Literary World* during the eventful August week when he first met Hawthorne and read quickly through his *Mosses from an Old Manse*. In quoting Hawthorne he ignores a specific reference to Emerson and *Nature*. Where Hawthorne writes in "The Old Manse": "It was here that Emerson wrote 'Nature;' for he was then an inhabitant of the Manse, and used to watch the Assyrian dawn and the Paphian sunset and moonrise, from the summit of our eastern hill,"[31] Melville abbreviates: "So all that day, half-buried in the new clover, I watched *this Hawthorne's* 'Assyrian dawn, and Paphian sunset and moonrise, from the summit of our Eastern Hill.'"[32] His curious omission of Hawthorne's reference to Emerson and *Nature* and his apparent assignment of Emerson's phrasing to Hawthorne may mean that he simply did not recognize the fact that Hawthorne was alluding to a passage in "Beauty," Emerson's third chapter.[33] Perhaps Melville had read *Nature* so long before that he had forgotten what Emerson's early style was like, but in my judgment he did not recognize Emerson's words because he had never as yet read *Nature*.

Emerson's name occurs later in the manuscript of "Hawthorne and His Mosses," but not in the essay as it was first printed in Duyckinck's *Literary World* or as it appears in most twentieth-century texts. Before publishing the essay, Duyckinck—with or without Melville's concurrence—deleted Melville's listing of eight leading American authors of the day, in which Hawthorne stands at the very head, Emerson is next, and the others in order are Whittier, Irving, Bryant, Dana, Cooper, and the now nearly forgotten N. P. Willis.[34] It seems unlikely that Melville would have named any author whose work he did not know directly, as he surely knew that of Hawthorne, Irving, Dana, and Cooper and probably that of Whittier, Bryant, and Willis. From these considerations I conclude that by August of 1850 he had indeed been reading Emerson, though probably not *Nature* in either its original edition of 1836 or the revised edition of 1849.

Why Melville should rank Emerson second to Hawthorne in his list of American authors is a question worth discussing. Of course he was writing at a time of high enthusiasm for both Hawthorne and his *Mosses* and without attempting a considered survey of contemporary writers; Longfellow, Lowell, Holmes, and Poe might otherwise have been listed. The reference to Emerson as second only to Hawthorne suggests that both the man and his writings had left a strong impression on Melville since the lecture of 1849. It is Hawthorne, however, that he names in 1850 as "the American, who up to the present day, has evinced, in Literature, the largest brain with the largest heart" (p. 2069). Melville never doubted Emerson's intellectual capacity, but from the time he heard him lecture until the 1860's, as we have seen, he found the man deficient in feeling.

When Melville had written to Duyckinck in 1849 that Emerson's "belly, sir, is in his chest, & his brains descend down into his neck," he was saying that in Emerson's constitutional make-up the heart had somehow become displaced. In "Natural Aristocracy" Emerson himself speaks of "a symmetry between the physical and intellectual powers," adding that when Nature "moulds a large brain" she "joins to it a great trunk to supply it" (*W*, X, 43), but he says nothing in the lecture about the feelings and the emotions. Melville too believed in symmetry, but symmetry of a different kind. "One large brain and one large heart have virtue sufficient to magnetize a whole fleet or an army," he wrote in *White-Jacket*. "True heroism is not in the hand, but in the heart and the head" (p. 112). In Emerson, Melville felt, head overbalanced heart; in Hawthorne, by contrast, intellect and emotion were in balance. With what he called "the shock of recognition," he identified both Emerson and Hawthorne as natural aristocrats. But however elevated and noble Emerson seemed to Melville—"Say what they will, he's a great man"—he never received the kind of praise that Melville lavished on Hawthorne. In Melville's eyes Hawthorne too possessed "a great, deep intellect," but in him its thoughts were "arterialized at his large warm lungs, and expanded in his honest heart."[35]

V

When Melville began *Moby-Dick* early in 1850, he not only knew something of Emerson but was familiar as well with major European authors from Plato to Goethe whose works significantly influenced American Transcendentalism. Emerson once remarked of the Transcendentalists that perhaps they agreed only "in having fallen upon Coleridge and Wordsworth and Goethe, then on Carlyle, with pleasure and sympathy" (*W*, X, 342). By this token Melville too could be charged with Transcendentalist leanings in 1850 and 1851, though in fact he read all of these authors as he read Emerson: with fundamental reservations.

Of the four writers Emerson names, Melville had "fallen upon" Coleridge early in 1848, when he bought a two-volume edition of the *Biographia Literaria*, and he also owned a heavily marked 1839 edition of Wordsworth's poetry.[36] A direct reflection of his recent reading in 1848 and 1849 is his caricature of the "transcendental divine" in *White-Jacket*, a book written at top speed along with the earlier *Redburn* in the summer of 1849 to repair losses in standing and income attending the unpopular *Mardi*. The chaplain's sermons were as "ill calculated to benefit the crew" of his vessel as *Mardi* to please the average reader. Like the author of *Mardi*, the chaplain had tasted of "the mystic fountain of Plato; his head had been turned by the Germans; and . . . White-Jacket himself saw him with Coleridge's Biographia Literaria in his hand" (p. 155). Both the chaplain and Melville must also have been reading Andrews Norton, that distinctly *anti*-transcendental divine who in 1839 had attacked Emerson's Divinity School Address as "the latest form of infidelity"; the chaplain's allusion to an obscure tract by Tertullian and Ishmael's later references in *Moby-Dick* to Gnostic thought apparently come from Melville's own knowledge of Norton's *magnum opus, The Evidences of the Genuineness of the Gospels* (1844), as Professor Thomas Vargish has demonstrated.[37] Perhaps Melville had been reading Norton as well as Emerson while visiting the Shaws during the previous winter.

In the fall of 1849, when Melville was on his way to Europe, he could hold his own in talking "German metaphysics" with a shipboard companion, George Adler, whose philosophy he immediately identified as "Coleridgean."[38] By this time he was interested enough in German writers to buy Goethe's *Auto-Biography* in London and to borrow his *Wilhelm Meister* from Duyckinck after his return to New York;[39] during the summer of 1850, when he was already at work on *Moby-Dick*, he also borrowed three of Carlyle's writings.[40] However much or little of Emerson Melville had read by 1850 and 1851, he obviously knew other Transcendental scripture, and it seems safe to say that his reading of one book in particular—Carlyle's *Sartor Resartus*, with its central idea of "all visible things" as "emblems" of the invisible, and of Nature itself as *"the living visible Garment of God"*[41]—had at least as much to do with the symbolism of *Moby-Dick* as anything in the "Language" chapter of Emerson's *Nature*.

There was a basic reservation in Melville's mind that kept him from giving more than passing allegiance to any form of philosophical idealism, whether he found it in Plato or Proclus or in their modern successors—Carlyle, Goethe, and Emerson. In *Mardi* his Babbalanja had spoken of external nature as something neutral toward mankind rather than benevolent, and in *Moby-Dick* Ishmael makes the dismaying comment that though "in many of its aspects this visible world *seems* formed in love, the invisible spheres *were* formed in fright" (p. 169; emphasis added). Both Ishmael and Ahab, like idealists generally, are of course incurable analogists—so, for that matter, were Hawthorne and the supposedly anti-Transcendental Poe. But Ahab, as Leon Howard has said, is "an imperfect Transcendentalist";[42] "All visible objects," he agrees, "are but as pasteboard masks"—yet "sometimes" he thinks "there's naught beyond" (p. 144).[43] Between such opposite negations, as walls, Melville's own being was also swung.

As Melville worked on *Moby-Dick* at Pittsfield during the fall of 1850 and most of the following year, the Hawthornes were in residence at Lenox, some seven miles away. He had a number of opportunities to discuss Emerson and Transcendentalism with both Hawthorne and his wife; Mrs. Hawthorne had know Emerson before her marriage in 1842 and the Hawthornes' occupancy of the Old Manse in Concord. On at least one occasion Melville and Hawthorne talked of Thoreau (*Log*, I, 407), whom Melville was reading late in 1850, and Emerson may have figured as well when they tackled what Melville called "the Problem of the Universe," discussing "metaphysics" and indulging in "ontological heroics" (*Letters*, pp. 121, 125, 133). Melville's visits to the Hawthornes' cottage sometimes lasted overnight. "He was very careful not to interrupt Mr Hawthorne's mornings," Sophia Hawthorne reported; morning was the time when her husband did his writing. Melville "generally walked off somewhere," she explained. "—& one morning he shut himself into the boudoir & read Mr Emerson's Essays in presence of our beautiful picture."[44]

The ideas of their sometime neighbor in Concord possibly meant more to Sophia Hawthorne than to her husband, who after their marriage, as he wrote in "The Old Manse," came to admire Emerson "as a poet of deep beauty and austere tenderness, but sought nothing from him as a philosopher."[45] Melville valued her judgment and once told her, in response to her praise of of *Moby-Dick*, that with her "spiritualizing nature" she saw "more things than other people" (*Letters*, p. 146). She did not specify which of "Mr Emerson's Essays" occupied Melville during that particular morning at the cottage, which can probably be dated early in September of 1850.[46] Although she could have meant *Essays* or *Essays: Second Series*, she could just as well have been thinking of Emerson's writings in general. By this time the Hawthornes owned presentation copies of every book Emerson had then published, from the first edition of *Nature*, given her when she was Sophia Peabody, to the most recent.[47] While telling Melville of her friendship with the Emersons, she may have shown him any or all of these books. What he read that morning, given his probable familiarity by this time with the Essays of 1841 and 1844, was more likely something later—either *Nature, Addresses, and Lectures*, which had appeared in September of 1849 while he was preparing to sail for Europe, or *Representative Men*, published early in 1850 while he was still abroad.[48]

The case for *Representative Men* as the book Melville read at the Hawthornes' turns on a number of close verbal parallels between Emerson's book and passages both in *Moby-Dick* and in Melville's correspondence of 1850 and 1851. His letters to Hawthorne make occasional references traceable to his recent reading, and where Transcendental writers are involved there are characteristic reservations: Carlyle's *Sartor Resartus*, for example, with its "Everlasting No" and "Everlasting Yea," and "some of Goethe's sayings, so worshipped by his votaries." In each case Melville raises an objection. "All men who say *yes*, lie," he retorted, not only to Carlyle but to the affirmative and optimistic tendencies of the age in general; "the grand truth about Nathaniel Hawthorne" is that *he* "says NO! in thunder" (*Letters*, p. 125). Goethe's pantheistic maxim *"Live in the all"* is simply "nonsense" to "a fellow with a raging toothache," Melville writes—only to add in a postscript that there is "some truth" in "this 'all' feeling," and that "what plays the mischief with the truth is that men will insist upon the universal application of a temporary feeling or opinion" (*Letters*, p. 131). Emerson as an intellectual aristocrat was probably in the back of his mind when he wrote with evident distaste about an idea which "some men have boldly advocated and asserted," that of "an aristocracy of the brain" (*Letters*, pp. 126–127). The one man he names as doing so is not Emerson but Schiller, whose thinking is specifically bracketed with Emerson's in *The Confidence-Man* (p. 215), and in this same letter there is an apparent echo of *Representative Men*.[49]

I now believe that Melville also read *Nature, Addresses, and Lectures*, either at the Hawthornes' or at some later time. Unlike Professor Beidler, I have been unable to satisfy myself that he knew *Nature* itself, however, nor have James Duban, Marvin Fisher, and Beryl Rowland convinced me that Emerson's Divinity School Address, which is printed in this same volume, influenced either *Pierre* or "The Two Temples."[50] Christopher Sten compares Bartleby and the lawyer in Melville's "Bartleby, the Scrivener" with the idealist and the materialist in "The Transcendentalist" and "The Conservative," two of Emerson's lectures that are also in the 1849 volume; he sees the story as "Melville's Dead Letter to Emerson."[51] Although I do not find Sten's general parallels conclusive, I have traced a much-quoted passage in *Moby-Dick* to a strikingly similar passage in "The Transcendentalist,"[52] and I am sure that Melville remembered one of Emerson's most telling images, that of "rare and gifted men" as "superior chronometers," when he composed Plotinus Plinlimmon's "Lecture First," on "Chronometricals and Horologicals," in *Pierre*.[53]

vi

Though a contemporary reviewer dismissed *Pierre* as "one of the most diffuse doses of transcendentalism offered for a long time to the public,"[54] *Pierre* and *The Confidence-Man* now seem of all Melville's books the least hospitable to the Transcendentalist movement and to Emerson. Even so, there are at least three close verbal correspondences between *Pierre* and Emerson's *Essays* of 1841 and 1844.[55] To a dispassionate twentieth-century critic of the book, its introspective hero is like Emerson's "young men . . . with knives in their brain"; he comes to his bad end as "the fool of Truth, the fool of Virtue, the fool of Fate" (p. 358)[56] by pursuing Emersonian goals—or by persuading himself that he is doing so; in this sense *Pierre*, like *Moby-Dick*, may be taken as an implicit criticism of Emerson. When both Pierre and the narrator castigate such philosophers as "Plato, and Spinoza, and Goethe" as "self-imposters," there is no reference to Emerson by name, however; instead, going even farther than Milton in *Paradise Regained*, the narrator finds *all* faith and *all* stoicism and *all* philosophy to be at last ineffectual against "a real impassioned onset of Life. . . . For Faith and philosophy are air, but events are brass. Amidst his gray philosophizings, Life breaks upon a man like a morning" (pp. 208, 289).[57]

The nearest Melville comes to Emerson in *Pierre* may not be in Plotinus Plinlimmon—Emerson too had blue eyes but never wore a beard nor preferred bottles to books—but rather with the "Apostles" his disciples, an urban colony of philosophical idealists settled in what had once been a church, "pursuing some crude, Transcendental Philosophy." Several of them are "well-known Teleological Theorists, and Social Reformers, and political propagandists of all manner of heterodoxical tenets." As Melville had put it in 1849, reflecting conservative Boston's view of the Transcendentalists, "These men are all cracked right across the brow." They are dismissed in *Pierre* as merely "a preposterous rabble of Muggletonian Scots and Yankees, whose vile brogue still the more bestreaks the stripedness of their Greek or German Neoplatonical originals" (pp. 266, 280, 268, 208).

Speaking as one New Yorker to another, Melville told Duyckinck in 1849 that he had heard of Emerson himself as "full of transcendentalisms, myths & oracular gibberish"; he had already satirized philosophical jargon in *Mardi*. In *Pierre* and again in Mark Winsome of *The Confidence-Man* he returns to the attack on the "vile brogue" of the Transcendentalists and their "Greek or German" masters.[58] He must have reread a number of Emerson's essays while he was writing *The Confidence-Man*, since Winsome speaks enough like Emerson, as well as resembling him physically, to make the caricature unmistakable. Melville clearly remembered Emerson's eyes, hair, and angular frame from seeing him in Boston seven years before, and he also recalled his impression of the man's cold intellectuality—so complete a contrast with his own fondness for convivial friendship, or what he called "sociality" and "geniality." Emerson's aloofness from such "jolly fellows" as Duyckinck and Melville himself, Melville had written, was constitutional. In *The Confidence-Man*, Winsome, who seems "more like a metaphysical merman than a feeling man," sits calmly at a table "purely and coldly radiant as a prism," sipping not "genial wine" but his own favorite beverage, chilling ice water. His temperance, we are told, seems a matter of "constitution as much as morality" (pp. 215, 216, 212). Emerson himself, who admitted and deplored his obvious coldness, might have recognized Melville's caricature all too clearly had he read the book: he was born a photometer, he once wrote sadly of himself, and "a photometer," he said, "cannot be a stove" (*Letters*, IV, 33).

Although much has been made of Winsome and his disciple as an attack on Emerson, Thoreau, and the Transcendentalists, it should not be forgotten that a number of other recognizable figures also appear on the deck of the Fidèle or are spoken of there: Judge James Hall and Colonel John Moredock, Poe almost certainly, possibly Fanny Kemble Butler (whom Melville had heard in Boston), and—if Helen Trimpi is right—such prominent Americans as William Cullen Bryant, Theodore Parker, and Horace Greeley as well;[59] each plays a role in the general "masquerade." Neither *The Confidence-Man* nor *Pierre* should be read simply as an anti-Transcendentalist tract, for each is far larger and more complex than that; nor is Melville himself to be neatly categorized as "anti-Emersonian" in his later years on the basis of these books alone.

Overlooked in most discussions of Melville's writing after *The Confidence-Man* is the influence of Emerson's verse, which he studied closely when he himself turned to poetry in the 1850's. His acquaintance with Emerson as a poet could have begun as early as 1846, if he saw the first edition of the *Poems* published in that year, or soon after in 1847, when the ninth issue of Duyckinck's new *Literary World* published its three-page review.[60] No one seems to have noticed that Melville quoted a line from Emerson's "The Problem"—"He builded better than he knew"—in the third paragraph of "The Piazza," written early in 1856 as an introductory sketch for his collected *Piazza Tales* (*The Piazza Tales*, p. 1); the entire poem had appeared in the *Literary World*'s review eight years before.

It was the seventh edition of Emerson's *Poems* that Samuel Shaw, Melville's younger brother-in-law, gave him in 1859; on its table of contents at some later time Melville noted the omission of several of its poems in subsequent editions, thus showing his continuing interest in Emerson's poetic output.[61] There is good reason to believe, moreover, that Emerson's versification and his individual tone as a poet strongly influenced Melville's own often rough poetic lines; he took

very much to heart Emerson's injunction in "Merlin I" to the would-
be poet:

> The kingly bard
> Must smite the chords rudely and hard.
>
> (*W*, IX, 120)

That Melville knew "Merlin" well is evident not only from his scoring
of two passages in his copy of *Poems* but also from an unmistakable if
unintentional verbal appropriation of one of its lines in the opening
stanza of his own "Dupont's Round Fight," a poem of the Civil War
published in his *Battle-Pieces* of 1866.[62]

That poem ends not only with a Northern naval victory but also
with the "victory of LAW"—a rather different theme from either the
"fiery hunt" in *Moby-Dick* or the celebration of spontaneity or instinct
that one finds in such essays of Emerson's as "The Poet," which Melville read during the war years. A change of orientation is visible not
only in Melville's poetry, particularly the verse inspired by his Mediterranean voyage of 1856–1857, but also in his prose; it begins with
the lecture on "Statues in Rome" that he wrote and delivered shortly
after his return from Europe and runs through his last major work
of fiction, *Billy Budd, Sailor*, left in manuscript at his death in 1891.

A comparison of Melville with Emerson will illuminate the point.
Jane Donahue Eberwein, taking her departure from Emerson's chapter on Plato in *Representative Men*, has noted the pronounced differences between Emerson's description of Athens in the Age of Pericles
and Melville's several poems dealing with Attic architecture and landscape. Emerson, she says,

stressed the vitality and spontaneity of the Greeks and pictured them . . .
constructing their perfect works of architecture as readily as nineteenth-
century Americans assembled ships or wove textiles. . . . Emerson saw
energy where Melville saw repose. His stress was on youthfulness while
Melville emphasized the maturity of the culture. And, perhaps most significantly, Emerson was concerned with the vigor and creativity of the artists
even to the implied disparagement of the things made, while Melville
ignored the maker in his admiration for the art itself.[63]

In spite of their marked divergence as Melville grew older, he continually came back to Emerson and his essays. The very chapter of
Representative Men that Mrs. Eberwein cites is undoubtedly the source
of his repeated references to Plato as the fountainhead of modern
knowledge. "Out of Plato," Emerson declared, "come all things that
are still written and debated among men of thought" (*W*, IV, 39).

"What little there was of meaning in the religions of the present day," a young visitor from Williams College quoted Melville as saying in 1859, "had come down from Plato. All our philosophy and all our art and poetry was either derived or imitated from the ancient Greeks" (*Log*, II, 605). Rolfe, the character in Melville's long poem *Clarel* who is most like Melville himself, takes a similar position, asserting that

> even in Physics much late lore
> But drudges after Plato's theme.
> (II.xxi.20–22; p. 208)

In view of the number of parallels between *Representative Men* and various writings of Melville's, ranging from 1850–1851 until the time of *Clarel* (1876), it seems very likely that he owned a copy of the book, which he may have bought for himself after looking into it at the Hawthornes' in the late summer of 1850.[64]

We are aware, of course, that in his forties and fifties Melville bought copies of other works of Emerson: *Essays* and *Essays: Second Series* in 1862 and *The Conduct of Life* in 1870. His purchase of the *Essays* certainly does not foreclose the possibility of an earlier reading or indicate that he had never previously owned copies; he is known to have given away other books he had owned and annotated and then to have bought the same titles again in different editions. Probably the most heavily annotated essay is "The Poet," in *Essays: Second Series*, where his mixed feelings about the man came to their sharpest focus. In the margin of one of its pages he wrote a summation that is as even-handed as it is frank; I would *not* call it "anti-Emersonian":

This is admirable, as many other thoughts of Mr Emerson's are. His gross and astonishing errors & illusions spring from a self-conceit so intensely intellectual and calm that at first one hesitates to call it by its right name. Another species of Mr Emerson's errors, or rather blindness, proceeds from a defect in the region of the heart.[65]

Melville's judgment here, a mixture of severity and admiration, is entirely consistent with what he had written to Duyckinck more than a dozen years before; it reflects his usual uneasiness at any overbalance of intellect at the expense of feeling, as in his letter to Hawthorne dealing with an "aristocracy of the brain" and again in his portrait of Mark Winsome in *The Confidence-Man*.

Obviously Melville's analysis of the source of Emerson's "illusions" and "blindness" had not changed by the 1860's, though he remained interested enough in Emerson's writing to buy *The Conduct of Life* in 1870. And though he repeatedly recognized Emerson's nobility, he felt that his elevation and depth were offset by a correlative lack of warmth and of breadth. This we see clearly in another annotation on a passage of "The Poet" in which Emerson warns all artists, as "expressors of Beauty," against "a life of pleasure and indulgence." To such a restrictive pronouncement Melville could only retort with a volley of negatives: "No, no, no.—Titian, did he deteriorate?—Byron?—Did he.—Mr E. is horribly narrow here. He has his Dardanelles for his every Marmora." And then, striking a characteristic balance after all his objections, he added his customary refrain: "But he keeps nobly on, for all that!"[66]

Throughout Melville's annotations in the two volumes of *Essays* and again in *The Conduct of Life*, bought while he was at work on *Clarel*, he repeatedly faults Emerson for failing to square his idealistic and optimistic vision with the realities of a cruel and evil world. "To one who has weathered Cape Horn as a common sailor," runs a comment on Emerson's "Prudence," "what stuff all this is"![67] A passage in *Clarel* which is probably the latest in time of all Melville's specific comments on the Transcendentalists touches exactly upon the two additional points at which he parted company with Emerson. The speaker is Ungar, the disillusioned Southern veteran of the American Civil War, who, in this instance at least, appears as a surrogate for Melville himself:

> Quite they shun
> A god to name, or cite a man
> Save Greek, heroical, a Don:
> 'Tis Plato's aristocratic tone.
> All recognition they forego
> Of Evil; supercilious skim
> With spurious wing of seraphim
> The last abyss.
> (IV.xx.99–106; p. 478)

If I am right in detecting a faint echo of Emerson's "Uriel" in these lines,[68] then the passage is one more instance of Melville's divided verdict on Emerson, brought in as early as 1849 in his letters to Duyckinck. Though he himself could seldom "oscillate in Emerson's rainbow" nor skim with Uriel "the last abyss," he could still read Emerson—with pleasure but with characteristic reservations—as late as the 1870's. Beyond that time there is no further objective evidence to take us.

This survey of Melville's response to Emerson over the years has necessarily dealt with probabilities rather than with certainties; it is not likely to be the last word about either the affinities or the differences between the two men. Pending the discovery of other evidence, it has reached a number of tentative conclusions which should serve to focus further discussion.

(1) Melville was essentially accurate in telling Evert Duyckinck that he knew little of Emerson before 1849. The book he had "glanced at" in 1848 was most likely Emerson's *Essays* of 1841, which includes "Self-Reliance," but general parallels between Melville's *Mardi* and Emerson's other writings show a common interest in transcendental idealism rather than Emersonian influence on Melville's book.

(2) Melville's sustained interest in Emerson began when he heard Emerson lecture in Boston in February of 1849—probably on "Natural Aristocracy."

(3) Despite the reservations Melville expressed to Duyckinck about Emerson, which reflect contemporary opinion of the Transcendentalists he had heard in both Boston and New York, he became familiar with *Essays* and probably *Essays: Second Series* during 1849 and 1850, though by August of 1850, when he ranked Emerson second only to Hawthorne among American authors, he had probably not read *Nature*.

(4) By the time he wrote *Moby-Dick*, Melville was reading Emerson as he read Coleridge, Wordsworth, Goethe, and especially Carlyle—with evident interest but with major reservations. The Hawthornes, and Mrs. Hawthorne in particular, may have drawn his attention to *Representative Men*, which is echoed in his own writing, and possibly to *Nature, Addresses, and Lectures* as well; if so, it was "The Transcendentalist" rather than *Nature* or the Divinity School Address that most attracted him.

(5) In *Pierre* Melville satirized the Transcendentalists as "the Apostles" even as his narrator and protagonist dismissed as ineffectual *all* faiths and philosophies—notably those of Plato, Spinoza, and Goethe. In *The Confidence-Man*, Mark Winsome is a telling caricature of Emerson, but Emerson is only one of several contemporary figures whose messages or motives are also subjected to scrutiny. In later years Melville honored Emerson's poetry to the point of imitation in his own verse, and during the 1860's and 1870's he was reading or rereading Emerson's prose with his old mixture of admiration for their author's nobility and reservations about Emerson's cold intellectuality, his "self-conceit," his aristocratic tone, and his insufficient apprehension of the fact of evil.

Melville, I conclude, not only read Emerson with understanding over a period of more than twenty years, but knew very well exactly where he agreed and disagreed with Emerson's provocative thinking.

In one sense he did indeed "oscillate" in Emerson's rainbow; the verb captures the mingling of response and rejection with which he read any Transcendental writer. But unlike the Transcendentalists, he never risked playing the mischief with the truth by insisting upon "the universal application of a temporary feeling or opinion." Rainbows, as Ishmael remarks in *Moby-Dick*, "do not visit the clear air; they only irradiate vapor. And so," he continues,

through all the thick mists of the dim doubts in my mind, divine intuitions now and then shoot, enkindling my fog with a heavenly ray. And for this I thank God; for all have doubts; many deny; but doubts or denials, few along with them, have intuitions. Doubts of all things earthly, and intuitions of some things heavenly; this combination makes neither believer nor infidel, but makes a man who regards them both with equal eye. (p. 314)

Ishmael's "dim doubts" are but a prelude to the epistemological darkness visible of Melville's later works, where the "divine intuitions" that Emerson celebrates are seen—if they appear at all—only as momentary and delusive. But for all Melville's reservations about Emerson, he continued to respect the man's "noble" writing, which, like his own, proceeded "from noble thinking, and a natural sympathy with greatness."

Melville

and the Platonic Tradition

[1980]

This essay was written especially for the present volume. I regard it as a sequel to "Melville and Emerson's Rainbow," not merely because it was drafted a year later but also because I had to clear the ground for it by considering Melville's response to Emerson in particular before taking up his relation to the Platonic tradition in general. Some Melville scholarship has erred, I believe, either in underestimating or in overestimating his reaction to philosophical idealism, which has usually been discussed only in terms of his comments on Emerson and the New England Transcendentalists. But to several students of Melville I have remarked, "Where you see Emerson, I see Plato."

My justification for such a statement grows out of my study of all three authors, which began in the 1930's and has continued with my later teaching and research. I first discussed Melville's debt to Plato in three chapters of my doctoral dissertation, "Herman Melville's Reading in Ancient Philosophy," completed in 1942, but what I said there never completely satisfied me. After World War II, as I was teaching Plato and Emerson as well as Melville and editing both Melville and Emerson, I found myself comparing and contrasting the Emersonian and Melvillean responses to Plato and Platonism. But not until 1980, after assessing Melville's knowledge of Emerson, did I at last feel ready to address in print the larger issues that are dealt with here. To be writing on this subject is thus to be fulfilling an old ambition, and to publish my findings is to discharge a professional obligation incurred many years ago when I first juxtaposed Melville with the Platonic tradition.

What is demonstrated here is that Melville's first-hand acquaintance with the Platonic dialogues antedated his knowledge of Emerson, beginning early in 1848 and constituting a major influence on both *Mardi* and *Moby-Dick*. With *Pierre* came an evident revulsion against *all* faith and philosophy, but in later years Melville continued to read Plato as he read other philosophical idealists in the Platonic tradition: with mingled satisfaction and reservations.

One read his superscription clear—
A genial heart, a brain austere—
And further, deemed that such a man
Though given to study, as might seem,
Was no scholastic partisan
Or euphonist of Academe,
But supplemented Plato's theme
With dædal life in boats and tents
A messmate of the elements. . . .

"Rolfe," in Clarel, I.xxxi.13–21

O f the various philosophers whose thought was familiar to Melville, either directly from their works or through intermediate sources, Plato is clearly the preeminent influence on his thinking and writing. That "Plato is philosophy, and philosophy, Plato," as Emerson had said, is a statement Melville must have endorsed wholeheartedly when he came upon it in *Representative Men*.[1] Both writers regarded Plato as the fountainhead of modern knowledge; Melville took his very name as a generic term for philosophers, applying it to thinkers as diverse as Benjamin Franklin, that "homely sage, and household Plato," as he is called in Chapter 7 of *Israel Potter* (1855), and Emerson himself, "this Plato who talks thro' his nose" (*Letters*, p. 79). Since Melville admitted knowing little of Emerson at first hand until after he had finished *Mardi* (1849), "the more 'transcendental' passages" in that book must have derived from non-Emersonian sources already familiar to him. This was my contention in "Melville and Emerson's Rainbow," where I endorsed the essential accuracy of his own statement to Evert Duyckinck about his knowledge of Emerson and argued that his first intensive reading of Emerson's *Essays* probably took place in February, March, or early April of 1849. While at work on *Mardi* in the previous year he was already "soak[ing] up a good deal of information about transcendental idealism," however—not from Emerson, but from other writers, including the founder of the idealistic tradition in philosophy, Plato himself.[2]

Although Melville's allusions to Plato, Plato's Socrates, and various Platonic dialogues far outnumber his references to other philosophers, published scholarship has taken relatively little notice of his significant debt to Plato since K. H. Sundermann in 1937 pointed out a number of passages in *Mardi* and its successors that unmistakably reflect Platonic thought.[3] The dialogues deserve further attention as a significant influence on the content and perhaps even the shifting form of *Mardi*, for in its later chapters and again in such later works as *The Confidence-Man* (1857) and *Clarel* (1876) Melville was following a principle that Montaigne attributes to Plato: in Montaigne's words, Plato was a writer who "seems to have affected this method of philosophising in dialogues, . . . that he might with greater decency from several mouths deliver the diversity and variety of his own fancies."[4] So in the latter two-thirds of *Mardi* Melville speaks through the "several mouths" of old Mohi the chronicler, young Yoomy the poet, and—most talkative of all—the bedeviled Babbalanja the philosopher, whose attendant demon Azzageddi marks him as an aberrant Mardian Socrates. There is Platonism in *Mardi*, clearly enough, though it is found strangely mixed with the humor and satire of a Rabelais and the indiscriminate learning of a Robert Burton.

It should be observed that neither Plato nor Platonism had any special prominence in Melville's life or work earlier than *Mardi*. Although the title character of *Pierre* (1852) is said to recall "the simple page, which in his father's edition prefixed the vast speculations of Plato" (p. 249), no volume of the dialogues is known to have survived from the libraries of Melville's own father or his other relatives among either the Melvilles or the Gansevoorts. Melville's absorption during his later years in ancient philosophy and literature as well as in Greek and Roman biography and history may be traceable to an abiding interest first developed at the Albany Academy and the Albany Classical School in the early 1830's. He possibly learned something of the old philosophers in 1830–1831 while enrolled in the Fourth Department at the Academy, where the standard preparatory course included "Universal, Grecian, Roman and English History" and "Classical Biography," or in 1836–1837, when his study of "the Latin Language" may have involved some "recitations" in Greek as well.[5] Even so, there is no mention of philosophy and philosophers in any of his extant writings earlier than a passing reference in Chapter 26 of *Typee* (1846) to "a Platonic affection" (p. 189). But by the time of *Mardi* he owned at least one work of ancient philosophy, *Seneca's Morals by Way of Abstract*, which Babbalanja quotes approvingly in Chapter 124,[6] and in Chapter 119, entitled "Dreams," the narrator-protagonist who is called Taji declares that both "divine Plato" and Proclus (the esoteric fifth-century commentator on Platonic thought) are among the "many worthies" who "converse" within himself (p. 367)— most of them writers whose names form a kind of bead-roll of Melville's own recent reading.

Included in that reading were the celebrated versions of Plato and his Neoplatonic successors by Thomas Taylor "the Platonist" (1758–1835), the mathematician-philosopher and translator whose work so strongly influenced the English Romantic poets. Taylor's translations had also attracted Emerson, who told Wordsworth in 1848—the very year in which Melville was completing *Mardi*—that they were to be found "in every American library."[7] Although some of Taylor's publications were rarer than Emerson realized, the five-volume Taylor-Sydenham version of Plato was indeed available to Melville on the shelves of the New York Society Library, where he became a shareholder in January of 1848. Since he is not recorded as withdrawing any volume of this translation,[8] he presumably used it either in the Library's own rooms or in some other unidentified collection that must also have included Taylor's translation of *The Six Books of Proclus . . . on the Theology of Plato*, a two-volume set published in only five hundred copies that belonged neither to the Library nor to Melville's friend Duyckinck, from whom he was then borrowing other "old Books" (*Log*, I, 273). He took nothing more substantial from Proclus than some abstruse Neoplatonic terminology that became the butt of his satires on philosophical "gibberish" in both *Mardi* and *The Confidence-Man*, as I have shown elsewhere.[9] But from Plato himself, in addition to the pattern of philosophical dialogue that informs so much of *Mardi*, Melville drew seminal themes and images that first emerged there and reappeared in key passages of his later writings.

i. Platonic Elements in *Mardi*

Four general themes that can properly be called "Platonic" are identifiable in Melville's *Mardi*. The first two of these concern literary composition rather than formal philosophy. (1) The relation between a writer and his cultural heritage, a concern of both Babbalanja the philosopher and the narrator who is called Taji, is explored in terms of the Platonic concept of knowledge as reminiscence or recollection, set forth in Plato's *Phaedo* and *Republic*. Melville also entertains the related ideas of the soul's preexistence and transmigration. Thus Babbalanja reduplicates his favorite author Bardianna, whom he is constantly quoting, and "many, many souls" are in Taji, whose memory is "a life beyond birth" (pp. 367–368). (2) Both Babbalanja and his friend Yoomy the poet exemplify the themes of poetic inspiration and divine frenzy or madness, set forth in Plato's *Phaedrus;* so too does their predecessor Lombardo, who wrote his epic "Kozstanza" much as Melville himself composed *Mardi*: "When Lombardo set about his work," says Babbalanja, "he knew not what it would become. He did not build himself in with plans; he wrote right on; and so doing, got deeper and deeper into himself" (p. 595). (3) What Melville later called "Plato's aristocratic tone" (*Clarel*, IV.xx.102) is echoed in King Media, whose thinking about both metaphysics and politics and his reservations about poetry somewhat resemble the hierarchical character of Platonic thought in the *Republic*. (4) Melville's knowledge of psychology, cosmology, and what are called "old ontologies" (p. 591) is apparent in a number of scattered passages that seem to reflect his reading in the myths and figures of the *Republic*, *Phaedrus*, and *Timaeus*, and possibly of various Neoplatonic writings as well.

(1) *The writer and his heritage*. Among the "old Books" that Melville borrowed from Duyckinck early in 1848 were three volumes of the works of Sir Thomas Browne, the seventeenth-century English essayist echoed in *Mardi* "to the length of ventriloquism."[10] Babbalanja's first set speech in Chapter 78—nine chapters after his first appearance in the book—is a meditation on human mortality in the vein of Browne's *Urn-Burial*. Babbalanja and his companions discuss death and the possibility of an afterlife more often than the characters of any of Melville's other works, though without the intensity of feeling and imaginative richness with which the same topics are treated three years later in *Moby-Dick* or still later in *Clarel*. Melville's speculative interest in these subjects in 1848 may well have been awakened by his reading of Browne's somber pages. As a writer in the Platonic tradition, moreover, Browne was another author like "Plato and Proclus among the ancients or Wordsworth and Coleridge among the moderns" who represented philosophical idealism to Melville before his encounter with Emerson in 1849.[11] Since there are passages in *Mardi* that show the combined influence of Browne and Plato, I infer that he was becoming acquainted with both authors at about the same time: late February or early March of 1848.

Two related ideas that Melville encountered in Plato and Browne and promptly introduced into *Mardi* through Babbalanja and Taji are the Pythagorean concept of metempsychosis, or transmigration of souls, and Plato's own theory of knowledge as reminiscence, or recollection of ideas latent in the mind since a prior state of existence; the latter notion is doubly familiar to modern readers, as it may have been to Melville, through Wordsworth's affirmation in the "Immortality" ode that our birth in this life is "but a sleep and a forgetting." A passage of dialogue from Chapter 126 of *Mardi* will illustrate Melville's mingling of Platonic influence with that of Browne and possibly that of Wordsworth; it also shows that his fundamental concern involves no serious doctrinal commitment but rather a way of acknowledging his own imaginative response to the mind of the past as he had encountered it in his omnivorous private reading.

In this amusing chapter, where Babbalanja "quotes from the old Authors right and left" and levies in particular on Bardianna, his special favorite, King Media finally calls a halt. "A truce to your everlasting pratings of old Bardianna," he cries; "why not speak your own thoughts, Babbalanja?" The garrulous philosopher's reply can be taken as a kind of justification for Melville's own practice; it was his wide reading and attendant habit of literary allusion that was making *Mardi* so different a book from his earlier "narratives of voyages," as he called its two predecessors.

> "May you not possibly mistake, my lord? for I do not so much quote Bardianna, as Bardianna quoted me, though he flourished before me; and no vanity, but honesty to say so. The catalogue of true thoughts is but small; they are ubiquitous; no man's property; and unspoken, or bruited, are the same. When we hear them, why seem they so natural, receiving our spontaneous approval? why do we think we have heard them before? Because they but reiterate ourselves; *they were in us, before we were born.* The truest poets are but *mouth-pieces;* and some men are duplicates of each other: *I see myself in Bardianna."* (p. 397; emphasis added)

The immediate source of this apologia appears to be an observation in Browne's *Religio Medici:*

> For, as though there were a metempsychosis, and the soul of one man passed into another, opinions do find, after certain revolutions, men and minds like those that first begat them. *To see ourselves again, we need not look for Plato's year:* every man is not only himself; there have been many Diogeneses, and as many Timons, though but few of that name; men are lived over again; the world is now as it was in ages past; there was none then, but there hath been some one since, that parallels him, and is, as it were, *his revived self.*[12]

And though Babbalanja's speech here, like others in *Mardi,* shows his conviction that through him his forebears are speaking, it also specifically echoes Plato's doctrine of innate ideas. As Socrates argues in the *Phaedo,*

> it is necessary we should have received the science of all these *before we were born.* . . . And if, since we receive these sciences, we did not forget each of them, we should always be born knowing, through the whole course of our life. (IV, 286)

The basic concepts in the quoted passages are obviously similar: Browne is discussing the persistence of character-types, if not a literal transmigration of souls; Plato's Socrates is affirming the soul's preexistence before its birth in the present life; Melville's Babbalanja is acknowledging both the ubiquity of "true thoughts" and a kind of fellowship of "the truest poets" extending across the ages, making possible that "shock of recognition" Melville himself was to write of in "Hawthorne and His Mosses" (1850). There are other links between Browne and Plato in Melville's later writings; here, Browne's reference to "Plato's year"—the notion that the heavenly bodies complete a cycle by returning to their original positions relative to one another—is worth noting, since studies of the process of verbal recollection show the vital part played by linking words and names in establishing a whole chain of association.

Both Babbalanja and Taji return to the themes of reincarnation and reminiscence in other chapters of *Mardi*, though with adaptations of their own. "In some universe-old truths, all mankind are disbelievers," Taji declares in Chapter 97. "Do you believe that you lived three thousand years ago? . . . No. But for me," he goes on to say, "I was at the subsiding of the Deluge"—and at well over a dozen historical events down the ages that he proceeds to enumerate (p. 297). "I am full with a thousand souls," he exclaims in Chapter 119, "Dreams," sometimes "speaking one at a time, then all with one voice" (p. 367). Babbalanja takes up the theme in Chapter 123, speculating that "the thoughts of men are each a soul" (p. 385); in Chapter 180 he carries this idea well beyond anything Melville had found in Plato or Browne: "We are full of ghosts and spirits; we are as grave-yards full of buried dead, that start to life before us. And all our dead sires, verily are in us; *that* is their immortality. . . . Every thought's a soul of some past poet, hero, sage. We are fuller than a city" (pp. 593–594).[13]

(2) *Poetic inspiration.* The concept of the soul's existence both before its mortal birth and after death occurs repeatedly in Plato. Another dialogue evidently known to Melville at the time he was writing *Mardi* was the *Phaedrus*, where Socrates holds that the soul fettered to body lacks the perfect spiritual vision she possessed before birth. This teaching is embodied in the mythical representation of the preexistent soul as "winged" (III, 322). Upon descending into body, the soul loses her wings—that is, her spiritual vision; but the true philosopher, being spiritually pure, may recover them under the quickening power of Love. Thus a partial restoration of spiritual vision is granted him even before his death.

In *Mardi*, the notion of the soul's preexistence reappears in Chapter 188 when Babbalanja is transported in a vision to the realm of preexistent souls and given instruction there through a sixth sense "concerning things unsearchable" to ordinary mortals. He later tells his earthly companions that his sixth sense "sleeps again, with all the wisdom that it gained" from this experience (p. 635), but he does recall seeing "spirits in their essences . . . vital with intelligence, which seeks embodiment."

"This it is, that unbeknown to Mardians, causes them to strangely start in solitudes of night, and in the fixed flood of their enchanted noons. From hence, are formed your mortal souls; and all those sad and shadowy dreams, and boundless thoughts man hath, are *vague remembrances* of the time when the soul's sad germ wide wandered through these realms." (p. 636; emphasis added)

In a similar vein Socrates declares in the *Phaedrus*, with reference to familiar Platonic doctrine, that "this is *a recollection* of what our soul formerly saw with divinity, when in a perfect condition of being" (III, 326; emphasis added).

Babbalanja's vision of the spiritual realm and the recurrent emphasis in *Mardi* on the power of Love may have been suggested as much by Dante as by Plato, since Melville was also reading the *Divine Comedy* in 1848.[14] But Love in the *Phaedrus* takes the distinctive form of a divine madness, which alike inspires the lover, the prophet, the poet, and the philosopher. As a lover of things heavenly, the philosopher sums up in himself all these manifestations of inspiration. He recalls true spiritual beauty in beholding even imperfect earthly loveliness, or in figurative language, he "may recover his wings." He then struggles "to fly away," but being unable to do so, "*like a bird looking on high* and despising inferior concerns, he is accused as one *insanely affected*" (III, 327; emphasis added). So Melville's Babbalanja, inspired to the madness of inspiration by the promptings of his demon Azzageddi, is deemed mad by matter-of-fact Mardians. He and the other seekers after Yillah—interpreted either as true spiritual beauty or as its earthly approximation—are likened to "birds, with pinions clipped" (p. 435), and when Taji meets the sensual Hautia and touches her hand, down drops "a dead bird from the clouds" (p. 650). In the *Phaedrus* the winged soul seeks to return to the eternal realm from which she came; in *Mardi*, Melville gives these words to Taji in Chapter 75: "Thus deeper and deeper into Time's endless tunnel, does *the winged soul*, like a night-hawk, wend her wild way; and finds *eternities before and behind; and her last limit is her everlasting beginning*" (p. 230; emphasis added).

Mardi is abundant in bird-imagery, much of it applied to poets.[15] Each Mardian poet, moreover, is in full agreement with Socrates in the *Phaedrus* that poetry is produced solely by inspiration. "My lord, I seldom think," says Yoomy; "I but give ear to the voices in my calm" (p. 486). The poet Lombardo, according to Babbalanja, was "a mere amanuensis writing by dictation" (p. 596), and Taji himself declares in "Dreams" that a "mad brood of eagles" is devouring him:

fain would I unsay this audacity; but an iron-mailed hand clenches mine in a vice, and prints down every letter in my spite. Fain would I hurl off this Dionysius that rides me; my thoughts crush me down till I groan; in far fields I hear the song of the reaper, while I slave and faint in this cell. The fever runs through me like lava; my hot brain burns like a coal; and like many a monarch, I am less to be envied, than the veriest hind in the land. (p. 368)

When Babbalanja seeks to explain Lombardo's inspiration he refers once again to the Platonic doctrine of innate ideas: "My lord, all men are inspired; fools are inspired; your highness is inspired; for *the essence of all ideas is infused.* Of ourselves, and in ourselves, we originate nothing" (p. 595; emphasis added). Thus Yoomy, Lombardo, Babbalanja, and Taji himself are not only familiar with Platonic doctrine but have experienced that "possession and madness descending from the Muses," as Socrates has it in the *Phaedrus*, "which receiving a soul tender and solitary," rouses and inspires it to literary composition (III, 319).

Both Melville and the Socrates of the *Phaedrus*, it is clear, have similar conceptions of inspiration: both emphasize the purity of the poet and go on to stress his resemblance to the philosopher and the isolation of each of them from the multitude; both employ the imagery of wings and flying in treating these subjects. Plato's Socrates in the *Phaedrus*, crediting inspiration to the power of Love, quotes the following Homeric verse:

> By men Love's *flying* called; but, forced to fly,
> He's named *the winged*, by the powers on high.
> (III, 332)

In *Mardi*, Chapter 137, Yoomy takes a comparable view of his art in a speech to King Media, and Babbalanja concurs:

"My lord, my lord!" cried Yoomy. "The air that breathes my music from me is a mountain air! *Purer than others am I;* for though not a woman, I feel in me a woman's soul."

"Ah, have done, silly Yoomy," said Media. Thou art becoming *flighty*, even as Babbalanja, when Azzageddi is uppermost."

"Thus ever: ever thus!" sighed Yoomy. "*They comprehend us not.*"

"Nor me," said Babbalanja. "Yoomy: *poets both*, we differ but in seeming;

thy airiest conceits are as the shadows of my deepest ponderings; though Yoomy *soars*, and Babbalanja dives, both meet at last. Not a song you sing, but I have thought its thought. . . . Poets are we, Yoomy." (p. 438; emphasis added)

And as Babbalanja says elsewhere to his own detractors, "I am wrong in seeking to invest sublunary sounds with celestial sense. Much that is in me is incommunicable by this ether we breathe. But I blame ye not" (pp. 352–353).

Babbalanja's words in *Mardi* anticipate Ishmael's in Chapter 93 of *Moby-Dick*, "The Castaway," which accounts for the madness of "the little negro Pippin" after he is all but lost in "the awful lonesomeness" of the open ocean.

The sea had jeeringly kept his finite body up, but drowned the infinite of his soul. Not drowned entirely, though. Rather carried down alive to wondrous depths. . . . He saw God's foot upon the treadle of the loom, and spoke it; and therefore his shipmates called him mad. So man's insanity is heaven's sense; and wandering from all mortal reason, man comes at last to that celestial thought, which, to reason, is absurd and frantic; and weal or woe, feels then uncompromised, indifferent as his God. (p. 347)

Melville's study of madness in *Moby-Dick* reflects his reading of *King Lear*, where Shakespeare's Lear and his Fool prefigure Ahab and Pip. But back of Melville's Ahab and Pip are his own previous studies of the inspired characters in *Mardi*, and Ishmael's notion that "man's insanity is heaven's sense" seems traceable in part to Babbalanja and ultimately to Plato's Socrates in the *Phaedrus*. "In all of us lodges the same fuel to light the same fire," Melville himself told Duyckinck in 1849. "And he who has never felt, momentarily, what madness is has but a mouthful of brains" (*Letters*, p. 83).

(3) *The Platonic hierarchy.* Plato's Socrates in the *Phaedrus*, like Melville's Babbalanja in *Mardi*, is sympathetic to poets, but Plato's Socrates in the *Republic* is distrustful of their art, which he regards as potentially subversive of good government in both the state and the individual. "There is an antient variance," he declares in Book X, "between philosophy and poetry" (I, 459). Along with all imitative art, poetry stands "third distant from real being," he charges (I, 451), and the imitator himself has "neither knowledge, nor right opinion about what he imitates" (I, 454). Moreover, his art appeals to the baser part of the soul, the passions, and thus "nourishes and waters those things which ought to be parched, and constitutes as our governor, those which ought to be governed, in order to our becoming better and happier, instead of being worse and more miserable" (I, 459).

Seen in relation to the entire scheme of the *Republic*, these three charges are related to the Platonic hierarchy of ideas, which Socrates develops in Books VI and VII through his celebrated allegory of the cave and figure of the divided line, and to his theory of justice in both the state and the individual, which holds that the rational element in both should control the lesser faculties and those who are dominated by them. As knowledge of reality is superior to mere belief or opinion, so the wisest men and women will be trained through a rigorous system of education, culminating in the study of dialectic, not only to know reality but to become Guardians of the state—and so to stand at the top of a political hierarchy compatible with the Platonic hierarchy of ideas. Socrates puts the case this way in Book V:

Unless either philosophers . . . govern in cities, or those who at present are called kings and governors philosophize genuinely and sufficiently, and these two, the political power and philosophy, unite in one; and till the bulk of those who at present pursue each of these separately are of necessity excluded, there shall be no end . . . to the miseries of cities, nor . . . to those of the human race; nor till then shall ever this republic . . . spring up to a possibility, and behold the light of the sun. (I, 312–313)

In Chapter 179 of *Mardi* the questers visit an island ruled by "the care-free bachelor Abrazza," who cleaves ever to its sunny side and banishes "all things uncongenial" from his company. With obvious irony, Babbalanja calls him a "king-philosopher" (p. 589), using a Platonic term that could be more fittingly applied to royal Media. King Media's charge that poets are guilty of "stirring up all Mardi" with their lays (p. 437) may be a humorous echo of Socrates' strictures in the *Republic;* in his political thinking, which possibly reflects Melville's own views in 1848, he also sounds something like a Greek aristocrat. The mysterious scroll delivered to the Vivenzans in Chapter 161, which Media may have written,[16] offers a critique of contemporary American society that is not unlike the picture of democracy and the democratic man drawn in Book VIII of the *Republic*. One passage even makes an informed reference to Greek city-states. Addressing the self-governing Vivenzans as "sovereign-kings," the writer declares that they

"are not meditative philosophers like the people of a small republic of old [Athens]; nor enduring stoics, like their neighbors [the Spartans]. Pent up, like them, may it please you, your thirteen original tribes had proved more turbulent, than so many mutinous legions. Free horses need wide prairies; and fortunate for you, sovereign-kings! that you have room enough, wherein to be free." (p. 526)

Plato's account of his ideal commonwealth calls for government of the state by its best and wisest—its aristocrats; such a government is presented as superior to all other forms of political organization, democracy of course included. In *Mardi*, King Media, a ruling monarch, is likewise distrustful of government by the many. As for Melville himself, despite the "ruthless democracy on all sides" he professed to Hawthorne (*Letters*, p. 127), there is an aristocratic strain throughout his writing, and to describe his political outlook, as Lewis Mumford long ago remarked, "some such compound word as aristodemocracy" seems necessary.[17] Though he objected in later years to the "aristocratic tone" he detected in both Plato and Emerson, he responded favorably to Emerson's lecture of 1849 on "Natural Aristocracy"—an aristocracy of merit.[18]

In *Mardi* the Vivenzans are told that "though all men approached sages in intelligence, some would yet be more wise than others; and so, the old degrees be preserved" (p. 527). The Serenians of Chapter 187 have no kings, but even they realize that "equality is not for all. . . . Such differences must be" (p. 627). That Melville himself held similar views seems evident in *Redburn* (1849), where the title character also discusses social stratification. "There are classes of men in the world, who bear the same relation to society at large, that the wheels do to a coach: and are just as indispensable," he declares in Chapter 29. But "no contrivance, no sagacity, can lift *them* out of the mire; for upon something the coach must be bottomed; on something the insiders must roll" (p. 139). Though such observations reflect Melville's own experience afloat and ashore, they have their parallel in the *Republic*, which may have contributed to his conservative political and social thinking during 1848, that year of revolution abroad, when he was reading Plato and completing *Mardi*. That his acceptance of the principle of degree did not extend to approval of slavery, however, is apparent from Chapter 162, where a visit to "the extreme South of Vivenza" by Taji and his party draws condemnation of the practice even from King Media.

Media appears a more sympathetic character in such a setting than in an earlier episode related in Chapter 60, where he scornfully rejects a petition from his own Mardian subjects to substitute trial by jury for the monarch's arbitrary legal decisions. "Away!" he cries.

"As unerring justice dwells in a unity, and as one judge will at last judge the world beyond all appeal; so—though often here below justice be hard to attain—does man come nearest the mark, when he imitates that model divine. Hence, one judge is better than twelve.

"And as Justice, in ideal, is ever painted high lifted above the crowd; so, from the exaltation of his rank, an honest king is the best of those unical judges, which individually are better than twelve. And therefore am I, King Media, the best judge in this land." (p. 185)

Behind the self-serving logic of Media's speech lies a conception not unlike Plato's of a two-world system, comprising a world of actuality where justice is indeed "hard to attain" and a transcendent world where "Justice, in ideal," is "high lifted above the crowd." The *Republic* itself opens as an inquiry into the nature of justice and goes on to envision it as written large in an ideal commonwealth. According to the Platonic theory of ideas, all entities having an earthly or material embodiment are patterned after transcendent spiritual forms which are eternal and unchangeable. No actual state can realize the ideal form, nor can any physical entity. All visible objects, which Ahab in *Moby-Dick* calls "pasteboard masks" (p. 144), are for Plato but the shadows of reality, and the material world perceived by the senses is therefore a realm of shadowy illusion. True reality exists only in the world of ideas, to be seen only by the spiritual eye when illuminated by the sun of reason, and in Books VI and VII of *Republic* Socrates identifies perception of shadows as the lowest form of sense perception (I, 352, 358).

Such teaching is the essence of idealistic philosophy, and Melville clearly echoes it in *Mardi*. Socrates objects to imitative art as thrice removed from ideal forms: just as the artist's conception imperfectly realizes the ideal, so the work of art in turn imperfectly realizes what the artist had in mind. The Mardian poet Lombardo, whose experience as a creative writer parallels Melville's own, is enough of a Platonist to confess that what he has written seems to him "but a poor scrawled copy of something within, which, do what he would, he could not completely transfer" (p. 601). And to Melville's Babbalanja, "The shadows of things are greater than themselves; and the more exaggerated the shadow, the more unlike to the substance" (p. 362). Through Babbalanja, here and elsewhere in *Mardi*, Melville repeatedly employs the language of philosophical idealism as he had found it in Plato, but without endorsing Platonic doctrine itself. Even Babbalanja is as much a skeptic with regard to the world of mind as he is concerning the material world: "things visible are but conceits of the eye," he declares; "things imaginative, conceits of the fancy. If duped by one, we are equally duped by the other" (pp. 283–284). On this subject Media has the last word. "The free, airy robe of your philosophy is but a dream, which seems true while it lasts," he tells Babbalanja in Chapter 120; "but waking again into the orthodox world, straightway you resume the old habit. And though in your dreams you may hie to the uttermost Orient, yet all the while you abide where you are. Babbalanja, you mortals dwell in Mardi, and it is impossible to get elsewhere" (p. 370).

(4) *Psychology, cosmology, ontology*. The philosophical dialogue in *Mardi*, which becomes increasingly prominent in the later chapters as Babbalanja is given more and more to say, is not the only part of the book with Platonic overtones; the allegorical quest for the maiden Yillah also involves elements of Platonism. Yillah, says Taji in Chapter 51, is the tangible "substance" of a "spiritual image" previously revealed to him in dreams; he describes her as "the earthly substance of that sweet vision, that haunted my earliest thoughts" (p. 158). But in some mysterious way Yillah is related to the temptress Hautia, who perennially seeks to ensnare Taji once Yillah is lost to him. Sundermann has pointed out a broad resemblance between the triangle of Taji, Yillah, and Hautia in *Mardi* and one of the best known passages of the *Phaedrus*, Plato's figurative analysis of the human soul into three component parts: a charioteer driving a "winged chariot" drawn by a pair of horses (III, 322–324).[19] One of the horses, restrained and obedient, desires to draw him only toward the pleasures of virtue and philosophy; the other, representing the appetites, is passionate and impulsive, eager to carry the charioteer toward sensual indulgence. The two women in *Mardi* offer comparable alternatives to Taji; the same dualism of spirit and flesh appears again in *Pierre*, with Lucy and Isabel replacing Yillah and Hautia while Pierre himself succeeds Taji as the "charioteer."[20]

Both books seem to reflect Plato's tripartite psychology, which is also developed in Book IV of the *Republic*. There Socrates holds that proper government of the soul requires control by its "rational part," with "the irascible part" as its auxiliary, the two of them working in harmony to manage "the concupiscible part, which in every one is the greater part of the soul, and in its nature most insatiably desirous of being gratified" (I, 284). The result will be analogous to good government in the state: a form of justice and internal harmony, the three components being attuned "in the most natural manner, as three musical strings, base, tenor, and treble, or whatever others may chance to intervene" (I, 285).[21] In *Mardi* Melville makes incidental use of the image: Yoomy, for example, is "miraculously gifted with three voices; and, upon occasions, . . . was a concert of sweet sounds in himself" (pp. 559–560), and Babbalanja responds to a "divine harmony" within that is "overheard by the rapt spirit alone" (p. 562).[22] "Not in a spirit of foolish speculation altogether, in no merely transcendental mood, did the glorious Greek of old fancy the human soul to be essentially a harmony," Melville was soon to write in *Redburn* (p. 249); in *Redburn*, with Carlo's hand-organ, and especially in *Pierre*, with Isabel's guitar, there is further treatment of the musical figure.

In contrast to the inner harmony prized alike by Socrates and Babbalanja is the conflict within the Mardian philosopher objectified in the outbursts of his "demon," Azzageddi. To the extent that Azzageddi represents the visitations of divine madness that Plato treats in the *Phaedrus* he may be regarded as deriving from Melville's reading, but he is clearly unlike the tutelary dæmon of Socrates as characterized by Plato in the *Apology*. Socrates appears in that dialogue as a man "not conscious to myself that I am wise," as he tells his judges, but rather as "a certain fly," sent by Divinity to excite, persuade, and reprove his sluggish fellow citizens (IV, 203, 214). "Ah! my lord," says Melville's Babbalanja in his own apology to King Media, "think not that in aught I've said . . . I would assert any wisdom of my own. I but fight against the armed and crested Lies of Mardi" (p. 430).[23] Babbalanja is no system-builder; on the contrary, he is "forever pruning" himself "down to the standard of what is unchangeably true" (p. 390). In the *Timaeus* Socrates asserts that "no one is voluntarily bad" (II, 563); in *Mardi* Babbalanja quotes "the sage lawgiver Yamjamma," who "roundly asserts, that all men who knowingly do evil are bedeviled" (p. 317). This is in Chapter 104, where Babbalanja ascribes to his beloved Bardianna the notion that "All men are possessed by devils" (p. 317); here Babbalanja's psychology is beginning to diverge from Plato's.

In this same chapter, where Babbalanja's own devil emerges, we see clearly how he differs from the Socratic dæmon. Azzageddi prompts Babbalanja to the frequent outbursts that his fellow Mardians take as evidence of madness; the tutelary spirit of Socrates acts only as a restraining influence, as he makes clear in the *Apology*. Again in the *Phaedrus* Socrates speaks of the "dæmoniacal and usual signal" which is sometimes sent to him, explaining that "whenever this takes place," it "always prohibits me from accomplishing what I was about to do" (III, 311). Melville's exploration of the possessed Babbalanja, who is more like the inspired lover-poet-philosopher of the *Phaedrus* than the restrained Socrates, probably drew less on his reading than on his own experience as he, like Lombardo, "got deeper and deeper into himself" in writing *Mardi*. In the words of Lewis Mumford, the release of an Azzageddi through the utterances of Babbalanja was "the first sign of Melville's maturity."[24]

Babbalanja's perplexed conception of mankind as either inspired or bedeviled raises fundamental questions for the reader, as it did for Melville himself, about human nature and man's place in the governance of the universe. As we have seen, Babbalanja's vision of Paradise in Chapter 188 somewhat offsets his view of mortal limitation, preparing him for a religious conversion. Plato too, it should be noted, provides glimpses of the afterlife, both in the *Phaedrus* and in the *Republic*. In Book X of the *Republic* Socrates relates the celebrated myth of Er ("Erus" in the Taylor-Sydenham translation), a Pamphylian slain in battle, who visits the world beyond the grave and returns to tell of what he saw there. He had witnessed the arrival from earth of the souls of the dead, some of whom were condemned to be cast into Tartarus while others were permitted to ascend into the upper world; after a period of several days, he declares, the latter group were brought before the Three Fates to receive lots and samples of the lives which they would assume in their next earthly incarnation. "Souls of a day!" they are hailed.

> *The beginning of another period of men of mortal race.* The dæmon shall not receive you as his lot, but you shall choose the dæmon: He who draws the first, let him first make choice of a life, to which he must of necessity adhere: . . . the cause is in him who makes the choice, and God is blameless. (I, 474; emphasis added)

In Chapter 175 of *Mardi*, "A Book from the 'Ponderings of old Bardianna,'" where the prose cadences resemble those of *Urn Burial* or *Religio Medici*, Melville seems to have remembered this assertion of human freedom and example of Platonic theodicy.[25] Either his recollection was imperfect or else a copyist or printer omitted a key phrase, however: "Fellow men!" cries Babbalanja, quoting Bardianna, "our mortal lives have an end; but that end is no goal: no place of repose. Whatever it may be, it will prove but as *the beginning of another race*" (p. 575; emphasis added). Or as Bardianna has it in his "roundabout chapter on Cycles and Epicycles," it is "a perpetual cycling with us, without progression" (p. 460). Babbalanja, like Melville himself, is fond of drawing analogies from the cycles of nature; his observation in Chapter 123 that "death is but a mode of life" (p. 385) may reflect the argument of Socrates in the *Phaedo* that death and life produce one another just as other contraries produce their opposites (IV, 277 ff.). But Babbalanja's skepticism is recurrent. "Our souls belong to our bodies, not our bodies to our souls," he declares later. "Simpletons show us, that a body can get along almost without a soul; but of a soul getting along without a body, we have no tangible and indisputable proof" (p. 505). Melville ultimately allows Babbalanja a haven on the Mardian island of Serenia as a professed follower of Alma (Christ), but closes his book with the willful Taji still in pursuit of Yillah "over an endless sea" (p. 654).

Further cosmological and ontological implications of *Mardi* also deserve comment in the light of both Platonic and Neoplatonic thought. Sundermann has suggested that certain passages in the book show the influence of Plato's *Timaeus*, which deals with the creation of the world.[26] To Socrates in the *Timaeus*, the world is "an animal, endued with intellect, and generated through the providence of Divinity . . . , containing within itself all such animals as are allied to its nature" (II, 479). So Babbalanja declares in Chapter 143 that "Mardi is alive to its axis."

"Daily the slow, majestic throbbings of its heart are perceptible on the surface in the tides of the lagoon. Its rivers are its veins; when agonized, earthquakes are its throes; it shouts in the thunder, and weeps in the shower; and as the body of a bison is covered with hair, so Mardi is covered with grasses and vegetation, among which, we parasitical things do but crawl, vexing and tormenting the patient creature to which we cling." (p. 458)

In the *Timaeus* Socrates maintains that what he calls "the plastic artificer" (II, 549) molded the world out of the preexistent matter of chaos; in Chapter 75 of *Mardi* Taji remarks that "the controversialists have debated, whether indeed the All-Plastic Power itself can do more than mold" (p. 229). "Time may have been," he goes on to say, "when the whole material universe lived its Dark Ages; yea, when the Ineffable Silence, proceeding from its unimaginable remoteness, espied it as an isle in the sea" (p. 230).[27]

In Neoplatonic thought, with which Melville also had some acquaintance, Plato's soul of the world becomes the World Soul, the third member of an ontological triad linking the transcendental and terrestrial realms; certain passages of *Mardi* seem to derive either from Plato or from some version of Neoplatonism. Chapter 170, for example, shows Babbalanja erupting in a torrent of Neoplatonic terminology: "the Adyta, the Monads, and the Hyparxes; the Dianoias, the Unical Hypostases, the Gnostic powers of the Psychical Essence, and *the Supermundane and Pleromatic Triads;* to say nothing of the Abstract Noumenons." In the same passage, when Yoomy interrupts his singing "in the middle" of a song about Yillah, Babbalanja objects: "Mysticism!" he cries.

"What, minstrel; must nothing ultimate come of all that melody? no final and inexhaustible meaning? nothing that strikes down into the soul's depths; till, intent upon itself, it pierces in upon its own essence, and is resolved into *its pervading original;* becoming a thing constituent of *the all embracing deific;* whereby we mortals become part and parcel of the gods; our souls to them as thoughts; and we privy to all things occult, ineffable, and sublime? Then, Yoomy, is thy song nothing worth." (p. 561; emphasis added)

Here Babbalanja's language seems to be a parody of terminology Melville had found in *The Six Books of Proclus . . . on the Theology of Plato,* but other related passages may derive either from Proclus again, from Plato himself, perhaps from Thomas Taylor's translation of *Select Works of Plotinus,* which was available to Melville in the New York Society Library,[28] or even from Plutarch's *Morals,* from which he drew material at the time of *Moby-Dick.* The successors of Plato, seeking to avoid the dualism of matter and spirit inherent in the old accounts of creation, had recourse to the monistic doctrine of emanation: all things both spiritual and material emanate from a single source, the ineffable One, which for Plotinus is the fountain of all being. "In all the universe is but one original," Taji affirms in Chapter 75; "and the very suns must to their source for their fire" (p. 229); in Chapter 184 Babbalanja declares that with Oro, the Mardian God, "the sun is co-eternal; and the same life that moves that moose, animates the sun and Oro. All are parts of One" (p. 615). As for mankind, we mortals "are but a step in a scale, that reaches further above us than below" (p. 575).[29] But though Melville was evidently attracted by philosophical monism and even by pantheism while he was writing *Mardi,* he was unable to reconcile such concepts with the fact of evil. In Babbalanja's words,

"Oro [God] is *in* all things, and himself *is* all things—the time-old creed. But since evil abounds, and Oro is all things, then he can not be perfectly good; wherefore, Oro's omnipresence and moral perfection seem incompatible." (p. 427)

It is the fact of evil that above all else prevented Melville's adherence to philosophical idealism in any form. "Though all evils may be assuaged; all evils cannot be done away," reads the anonymous scroll in Chapter 161. "For evil is the chronic malady of the universe; and checked in one place, breaks forth in another" (p. 529). Or as Melville was to write many years later, in *Clarel,*

> Evil and good they braided play
> Into one chord.
> (IV.iv.28–29)

By the time Melville finished *Mardi* he had obviously managed through his reading to become well versed in the major topics of philosophy. Certainly he knew the meaning of philosophical idealism; as early as Chapter 11 he jokingly calls an idealist "an aerial architect; a constructor of flying buttresses" (p. 36), and in Chapter 20 he alludes with tongue in cheek to "my Right Reverend friend, Bishop Berkeley—truly, one of your lords spiritual—who, metaphysically speaking, holding all objects to be mere optical delusions, was, notwithstanding, extremely matter-of-fact in all matters touching matter itself" (p. 63). As for Plato, this survey of Platonic elements in *Mardi* reveals him not as a confirmed Platonist by any means, but rather as a receptive and retentive reader of at least two of the dialogues and probably others as well, though the influence of the *Republic* and *Phaedrus* is especially evident. Sometimes, as we have seen, he took Platonism as lightly as he apparently took Berkeleian idealism. More seriously, he responded to those Platonic themes that spoke to his own experience as a writer, such as poetic inspiration and knowledge as recollection, though he adapted them in ways Plato might not have recognized. Melville's concurrent reading in other authors such as Sir Thomas Browne, himself something of a Platonist, helped to fix certain themes in his mind and suggest how they might be assimilated into his own way of writing.

In a letter to Duyckinck written in December of 1849, after the generally unfavorable reception of *Mardi* by readers and critics, Melville made a comment on the book that implies a fundamental reservation about both Platonic inspiration and the teachings of other idealists among his own contemporaries: "I am but a poor mortal, & I admit that I learn by experience & not by divine intuitions. Had I not written & published 'Mardi,' in all likelihood, I would not be as wise as I am now, or may be" (*Letters*, p. 96). One aspect of *Mardi* that troubled him was the sheer weight of Platonic influence on the book as he came to feel it in later years. If Book XVIII of *Pierre*, "Pierre, as a Juvenile Author, Reconsidered," is based on Melville's own experience as a writer, then Pierre's earliest publication, "*The Tropical Summer: A Sonnet*" (p. 263), corresponds to *Typee* and *Omoo;* and when in Book XXI "Pierre Immaturely Attempts a Mature Work" the obvious analogue is *Mardi*. What Melville has to say about Pierre's bookishness is a judgment on the role of Plato in his own development that—ironically—is actually couched in Platonic terms. Pierre, says Melville's narrator, "did not see" while he was writing—or at least could not yet put the idea into words—that "the heavy unmalleable element of mere book-knowledge would not congenially weld with the wide fluidness and ethereal airiness of spontaneous creative thought" (p. 283). Specifically, he failed to see

that though Plato was indeed a transcendently great man in himself, yet Plato must not be transcendently great to him (Pierre), so long as he (Pierre himself) would also do something transcendently great. He did not see that there is no such thing as a standard for the creative spirit; that no one great book must ever be separately regarded, and permitted to domineer with its own uniqueness upon the creative mind. . . . He did not see . . . that all the great books in the world are but the mutilated shadowings-forth of invisible and eternally unembodied images in the soul; so that they are but the mirrors, distortedly reflecting to us our own things; and never mind what the mirror may be, if we would see the object, we must look at the object itself, and not at its reflection. (pp. 283–284)

A reader of the present day, who may well be surprised by the sheer number of Platonic echoes identifiable in *Mardi*, must surely regard the passage in *Pierre* as a remarkable piece of self-criticism. The *Republic* and *Phaedrus* had indeed served Melville as "mirrors"; if they distorted whatever images in his own mind they reflected, they at least revealed to him what lay there waiting for original expression. After *Mardi*, as Melville came to realize, he must look even more deeply into himself—not through Plato or any other author, but directly—if he would "do something transcendently great."

ii. From *Mardi* to *Moby-Dick*

During the opening months of 1849, when Melville was shuttling between New York and Boston while awaiting the birth of his first child and the publication of *Mardi*, he found time to do some significant reading. In Boston he bought a new edition of Shakespeare and an old set of Bayle's *Dictionary;* in New York during March he ordered the thirty-seven volumes of Harper's Classical Library from his publisher and then or later he probably bought William Gowans' new edition of Plato's *Phædon*.[30] His letters to Duyckinck written at Boston refer to his purchase of the Shakespeare and Bayle and also mention the *Phædon;* his familiarity with all of these works is evident in *Redburn* and *White-Jacket*, the two books he drove himself to write during the spring and summer of 1849 once it had become clear that *Mardi* was unsuccessful with both the critics and the public.

The familiar name of Sir Thomas Browne also turns up in Melville's correspondence of this period in association with both Plato and Emerson. After Melville had heard Emerson lecture in February of 1849 and praised him to Duyckinck as "a great man," Duyckinck must have replied with an unfavorable comparison of the essayist with Browne; Melville's response, in a letter of 3 March, reads like a passage from *Mardi:*

Lay it down that had not Sir Thomas Browne lived, Emerson would not have mystified—I will answer, that had not Old Zack's father begot him, Old Zack [General Zachary Taylor] would never have been the hero of Palo Alto. The truth is that we are all sons, grandsons, or nephews or great-nephews of those who go before us. No one is his own sire. (*Letters*, p. 78)

As we know, Melville had already linked Browne with Plato in composing *Mardi*, and in another letter to Duyckinck he did so again. "I bought a set of Bayle's Dictionary the other day," he wrote on 5 April, "& on my return to New York intend to lay the great old folios side by side & go to sleep on them . . . with the Phaedon in one hand & Tom Brown[e] in the other" (*Letters*, pp. 83–84). There are allusions to Plato in both *Redburn* and *White-Jacket*, and "the Phædon"—spelled as in the title of Gowans' new edition—is specifically named in *White-Jacket* and again in *Moby-Dick*.

Since Melville kept his promise of "no metaphysics" in *Redburn* (*Letters*, p. 86), there is little from Plato in that short book about a sailor's first voyage. In Chapter 49, describing young Carlo and his hand-organ, is an allusion to Book IV of the *Republic* already noted: the idea of that "glorious Greek of old" that the human soul is "essentially a harmony" (p. 249).[31] Chapter 58 is concerned with death at sea, a topic that leads Redburn to remark that "in every being's ideas of death, and his behavior when it suddenly menaces him, lies the best index to his life and his faith."

Though the Christian era had not then begun, Socrates died the death of the Christian; and though Hume was not a Christian in theory, yet he, too, died the death of the Christian,—humble, composed, without bravado; and though the most skeptical of philosophical skeptics, yet full of that firm, creedless faith, that embraces the spheres. Seneca died dictating to posterity; Petronius lightly discoursing of essences and love-songs; and Addison, calling upon Christendom to behold how calmly a Christian could die; but not even the last of these three, perhaps, died the best death of the Christian. (p. 291)

In this passage, which in subject matter and tone anticipates Ishmael's meditations on death in *Moby-Dick*, is the first mention of the name of Socrates in Melville's published works or surviving letters. The allusion in such a context suggests that he was thinking of "the

Phaedon"; in his next book, dealing with life aboard a man-of-war, his White-Jacket characterizes the old sailor Ushant, who "was wont to talk philosophy," as "a sort of sea-Socrates" (p. 353) and describes the ship's chaplain as a "transcendental divine" who "learnedly" alludes to "the Phædon of Plato" (p. 155) and to both Plato and Socrates (p. 157). White-Jacket himself seems to know the *Republic*, like Redburn; he echoes the same passage in Book X on fate and free choice that Melville had drawn upon in Chapter 175 of *Mardi* for Bardianna's "Ponderings."[32]

From these several allusions to Platonic themes and to Socrates, in Melville's correspondence and in both *Redburn* and *White-Jacket*, I conclude that Plato was still fresh in his mind during the spring and summer of 1849, either because he remembered his reading of the year before while he was at work on *Mardi* or because he was then rereading at least one or two of the dialogues. In view of his consistent spelling "Phaedon" and his further allusions to that dialogue in *Moby-Dick*, I am reasonably sure that he was using Gowans' new edition, and from this point on I shall therefore follow the same spelling and cite Gowans' 1849 text.[33] As for the other dialogues, it seems likely that by the time of Melville's removal from New York to Pittsfield in the late summer of 1850 he had begun to acquire his own copies of *The Works of Plato* in the new Bohn edition, translated in six volumes by Henry Cary, Henry Davis, and George Burges, which in *Billy Budd, Sailor*, he was to call "the authentic translation" (p. 75).[34] The first three volumes, published in 1848, 1849, and 1850, would have been available to him by the time he finished *Moby-Dick* in 1851;[35] in a letter to Hawthorne written in response to Hawthorne's praise of that book he made an unmistakable allusion to the *Symposium*, or *Banquet*, which is included in the third volume. There Alcibiades gives his celebrated account of Socrates' outer ugliness and inward beauty (III, 561–564); in a similar vein Melville's letter declares that Hawthorne

did not care a penny for the book. But, now and then as you read, you understood the pervading thought that impelled the book—and that you praised. . . . You were archangel enough to despise the imperfect body, and embrace the soul. Once you hugged the ugly Socrates because you saw the flame in the mouth, and heard the rushing of the demon,—the familiar,— and recognized the sound; for you have heard it in your own solitudes. (*Letters*, p. 142)

Given such clear evidence that Melville was reading Plato in Pittsfield, I shall therefore cite the text of the Bohn edition from this point

on in quoting from Plato's works other than the *Phædon*.[36] In turning
to Platonism in *Moby-Dick* I shall first consider Ishmael, who went to
sea "with the Phædon . . . in his head" (p. 139); then Ahab, whom
Melville repeatedly associated with the thought and imagery of the
Republic; and finally the implications of Platonic thought for the book
as a whole—as Melville conceived it and as it appears to the modern
reader.

(1) *Ishmael.* In "The Mast-Head," Chapter 35 of *Moby-Dick*, the narrator Ishmael addresses a half-humorous warning to Nantucket ship-
owners against

enlisting in your vigilant fisheries any lad with lean brow and hollow eye;
given to unseasonable meditativeness; and who offers to ship with the
Phædon instead of Bowditch in his head. Beware of such an one, I say; your
whales must be seen before they can be killed; and this sunken-eyed young
Platonist will tow you ten wakes round the world, and never make you
one pint of sperm the richer. (p. 139)

Is Ishmael then a Platonist? By his own confession, he too "kept but
sorry guard" while on duty at the mast-head. "With the problem of
the universe revolving in me, how could I—being left completely to
myself at such a thought-engendering altitude,—how could I but
lightly hold my obligations to observe all whale-ships' standing orders, 'Keep your weather eye open, and sing out every time.'"

Yes, Ishmael himself is one of those "absent-minded young philosophers," the very "Platonists" he warns against, at least at the beginning of his voyage. Therefore he too runs the risk of losing his identity by taking "the mystic ocean at his feet for the visible image of that
deep, blue, bottomless soul, pervading mankind and nature," as he
puts it in this same chapter,[37] and of having his spirit ebb away "to
whence it came" and so forgetting the material world altogether. "But
while this sleep, this dream is on ye," he cautions himself and other
philosophical idealists,

move your foot or hand an inch; slip your hold at all; and your identity
comes back in horror. Over Descartian vortices you hover. And perhaps, at
mid-day, in the fairest weather, with one half-throttled shriek you drop
through that transparent air into the summer sea, no more to rise for ever.
Heed it well, ye Pantheists! (p. 140)

As we soon learn from the opening chapters, Ishmael may also be
taken as a successor to Taji and his questing companions in *Mardi*.
There is no Yillah in his thoughts, however. For him, "meditation
and water are wedded for ever" (p. 13), and the sea itself is his special
image for what he calls "the ungraspable phantom of life" (p. 14).

Moreover, he seems preoccupied with death and dying. Going to sea, he tells us, is his "substitute for pistol and ball. With a philosophical flourish Cato throws himself upon his sword; I quietly take to the ship" (p. 12). As a professed reader of the *Phædon* he should of course know that "a man enlightened by philosophy ought to die with courage," as Socrates reminds his friends in that dialogue, which Cato was reading before his suicide. "True philosophers make it the whole business of their lives to learn to die" (*Phædon*, p. 57). Ishmael goes farther, however, in actively courting death by going to sea, and now, being moved to undertake his first whaling voyage by "the overwhelming idea of the great whale himself" (p. 16), he has come to behold still more images in his "inmost soul"—"endless processions of the whale, and, midmost of them all, one grand hooded phantom, like a snow hill in the air" (p. 16), that anticipates what he is yet to learn about the death-dealing White Whale, Moby Dick himself.

Even before Ishmael embarks from Nantucket, while he is visiting Father Mapple's chapel for seamen in New Bedford, he reads in its memorial tablets "the fate of the whalemen who had gone before me. Yes, Ishmael, the same fate may be thine," he reflects, for "there is death in this business of whaling—a speechlessly quick chaotic bundling of a man into Eternity" (p. 41). It is just at this point, as he is thinking of death and Eternity, that Ishmael's Platonism first begins to emerge. "But what then?" he asks, rhetorically, going on to answer his own question in unmistakably Platonic language.

Methinks we have hugely mistaken this matter of Life and Death. Methinks that what they call my shadow here on earth is my true substance. Methinks that in looking at things spiritual, we are too much like oysters observing the sun through the water, and thinking that thick water the thinnest of air. Methinks my body is but the lees of my better being. In fact take my body who will, take it I say, it is not me. And therefore three cheers for Nantucket; and come a stove boat and stove body when they will, for stave my soul, Jove himself cannot. (p. 41)

A little-noticed article of 1933 by H. N. Couch, commenting on Ishmael's striking figure of "oysters observing the sun through the water," cites a parallel to this passage in the *Phædon*.[38] There Socrates tells of two earths: the one where mortals dwell and "another pure earth above the pure heaven where the stars are, which is commonly called æther. The earth we inhabit is properly nothing else but the sediment of the other." We mortals

fancy we inhabit the upper part of the pure earth . . . , as if one dwelling in the depths of the sea, should fancy his habitation to be above the waters;

and when he *sees the sun and stars through the waters*, should fancy the sea to be the heavens. . . . This is just our condition, we are mewed up within some hole of the earth, and fancy we live at the top of all, we take the air for the true heavens, in which the stars run their rounds. And the cause of our mistake, is our heaviness and weakness, that keep us from surmounting this thick and muddy air. (*Phædon*, pp. 160–161)

The Platonism in Ishmael's words, which like those of Socrates in the *Phædon* concern the limitations of mortal men's spiritual vision, Couch regarded as "too patent to be the chance creation of a similar figure by an independent mind." He suggested an unconscious reproduction of the image on Melville's part, believing that Melville would not have brought *oysters* into the context "if his memory had served him better." Actually his memory had ranged elsewhere in Plato, a fact which escaped the notice of Couch in his citation of only the single parallel with the *Phædon*.

In the *Phaedrus* as well as in the *Phædon* Socrates discusses the impediment to the soul of its mortal frame—"this which we now carry about with us and call the body, fettered to it like an *oyster* to its shell" (Bohn, I, 326; emphasis added).[39] Here is the probable source of Ishmael's phraseology. The notion that "my body is but the lees of my better being" is strongly reminiscent of Socrates' theme in the two dialogues, culminating in the *Phædon* with his reply to Crito's inquiry regarding an appropriate burial: "But how will you be buried?" "Just as you please," answers Socrates, "if you can but catch me, and if I do not give you the slip." For, as he goes on to explain, Crito "confounds me with my corps[e]; and in that view asks how I must be buried. . . . [W]hen he sees my body burnt or interred" he should "not despair, as if I suffered great misery, and say at my funeral, that Socrates is laid out, Socrates is carried out, Socrates is interred. . . . You should . . . say, that my body is to be interred. That you may inter as you please" (*Phædon*, pp. 172–173). In exactly this same vein is Ishmael's remark in *Moby-Dick*: "take my body who will, take it I say, it is not me."[40]

Going back to the passage first quoted from the *Phædon*, we find there that Socrates, after first observing that "our heaviness and weakness . . . keep us from surmounting this thick and muddy air," continues as follows:

If any could mount up with wings to the upper surface, he would no sooner put his head out of this gross air, than he would behold what is transacted in those blessed mansions; *just as the fishes skipping above the surface of the water, see what is done in the air in which we breathe*, and if he were a man fit for long contemplation, *he would find it to be the true heaven* and the true light; in a word, to be the true earth. (*Phædon*, p. 161; emphasis added)

With a characteristic touch, Melville also adapted the suggestion of this remark to the motif of *Moby-Dick*. "With a frigate's anchors for my bridle-bits and fasces of harpoons for spurs," Ishmael exclaims in a later chapter, 57, "would I could mount that whale and *leap the topmost skies, to see* whether *the fabled heavens* with all their countless tents really lie encamped *beyond my mortal sight!*" (p. 233; emphasis added). Here man's mortal vision and the question of life after death are Ishmael's subjects, as they were for Socrates in the *Phædon*, but the skeptic in him—and in Melville himself—cannot speak of an afterlife with the sure conviction of the Greek philosopher; for him the heavens are *fabled* heavens still.

In reviewing the passages from both Melville and Plato we see that in a single paragraph of *Moby-Dick* Melville's Ishmael is sufficiently a Platonist to be able to draw readily on two separate passages of the *Phædon* and one of the *Phaedrus*, combining three related images, and to introduce a further recollection of the longest of the passages nearly two hundred pages later in his narrative. In each passage Socrates is discussing either the impediment to the soul of the mortal body, the prospect of an afterlife, or both; what is taken over into *Moby-Dick* centers on a single vivid picture that was easily adaptable to its new context. Thus Socrates' lifeless body is not Socrates, and Ishmael's body is not Ishmael. Again, a fish's clouded vision and an oyster fettered to its shell combine into "oysters observing the sun through the water," and a fish emerging from the sea to behold the earth becomes a man riding a leaping whale to behold the heavens, as Socrates said a man might do could he "mount with wings to the upper surface."

That two of these instances concern the sea is understandable enough, for one need not read far in Melville to become aware of the quick play of his mind about anything touching either the sea or ships. In another borrowing from the *Phædon* he manages to make a maritime application of that "speculative indifference as to death" that Ishmael characterizes as "Platonian" (p. 284).[41] "All men, except the philosophers, are only brave and valiant through fear," Socrates remarks (*Phædon*, p. 67), and in *Moby-Dick* the conventionally minded Starbuck bears out his observation: as first mate of the Pequod he will have no man in his boat "who is not afraid of a whale" (p. 103). But Ishmael takes Socrates' point: "if you be a philosopher," he affirms, "though seated in the whale-boat, you would not at heart feel one whit more of terror, than though seated before your evening fire with a poker, and not a harpoon, by your side" (p. 241).

Later in the narrative, however, Ishmael appears to lose his allegiance to Socrates and the *Phædon*. Although he speaks at one point of his "doubts of all things earthly, and intuitions of some things heavenly" (p. 314), his faith in the beneficence of the spiritual realm is anything but Platonic once the voyage is under way and Ahab secures a pledge from the crew to join him in hunting the White Whale to his death. In the *Phædon* Socrates had affirmed that the soul is "an invisible being, that goes to a place like itself, marvellous, pure, and invisible, . . . and returns to a God full of goodness and wisdom" (*Phædon*, pp. 96–97). "Though in many of its aspects this visible world seems formed in love," Ishmael declares, he goes on to state without qualification that "the invisible spheres were formed in fright" (p. 169). This flat rejection of idealistic doctrine comes in Chapter 42, "The Whiteness of the Whale," which follows the crew's oath of allegiance to Ahab: now, he says, "Ahab's quenchless feud seemed mine" (p. 155). Whiteness for Ishmael is "at once the most meaning symbol of spiritual things" and yet "the intensifying agent in things the most appalling to mankind"; for him and for his readers it raises unanswerable questions:

Is it that by its indefiniteness it shadows forth the heartless voids and immensities of the universe, and thus stabs us from behind with the thought of annihilation, when beholding the white depths of the milky way? Or is it, that as in essence whiteness is not so much a color as the visible absence of color, and at the same time the concrete of all colors; is it for these reasons that there is such a dumb blankness, full of meaning, in a wide landscape of snows—a colorless, all-color of atheism from which we shrink? (p. 169)

Once Ishmael commits himself to Ahab's quest he ceases to be the dreamy "young Platonist" of "The Mast-Head." Thoughts of atheism and annihilation, of which "the Albino whale" is the fitting symbol (p. 170), have replaced the *Phædon* in his head, and he makes few additional references to Plato or Platonism in the remaining chapters. One of them is in Chapter 78, where Queequeg rescues Tashtego from perishing within "the secret inner chamber and sanctum sanctorum" of a sperm whale's head. Ishmael can recall "only one sweeter end":

—the delicious death of an Ohio honey-hunter, who seeking honey in the crotch of a hollow tree, found such exceeding store of it, that leaning too far over, it sucked him in, so that he died embalmed. How many, think ye, have likewise fallen into Plato's honey head, and sweetly perished there? (p. 209)[42]

(2) *Ahab.* If one thinks of Ishmael as playing a role in *Moby-Dick* like Taji's as the narrator of *Mardi*, then Ahab stands in relation to Ishmael as Babbalanja stood with respect to Taji. Like Babbalanja, Ahab is driven by a demon, "the gliding great demon of the seas of life" (p. 162)—"that demon phantom that, some time or other, swims before *all* human hearts" (p. 204; emphasis added). The words are Ishmael's, but the possession, or obsession, is Ahab's.

All that most maddens and torments; all that stirs up the lees of things; all truth with malice in it; all that cracks the sinews and cakes the brain; all the subtle demonisms of life and thought; all evil, to crazy Ahab, were visibly personified, and made practically assailable in Moby Dick. He piled upon the whale's white hump the sum of all the general rage and hate felt by his whole race from Adam down; and then, as if his chest had been a mortar, he burst his hot heart's shell upon it. (p. 160)

Like Taji, Babbalanja, and Ishmael himself, moreover, Ahab is in part a philosophical idealist, a Platonist, even something of a transcendentalist, and his own words have what Ishmael in another context calls "a transcendental and Platonic application" (p. 372). Witness what he tells Starbuck, his first mate, in Chapter 36:

"All visible objects, man, are but as pasteboard masks. But in each event—in the living act, the undoubted deed—there, some unknown but still reasoning thing puts forth the mouldings of its features from behind the unreasoning mask. If a man will strike, strike through the mask! How can the prisoner reach outside except by thrusting through the wall? To me, the white whale is that wall, shoved near to me. Sometimes I think there's naught beyond. But 'tis enough. He tasks me; he heaps me; I see in him outrageous strength, with an inscrutable malice sinewing it. That inscrutable thing is chiefly what I hate; and be the white whale agent, or be the white whale principal, I will wreak that hate upon him." (p. 144)

Citing this speech by Ahab to Starbuck and the crew, Michael E. Levin, in the fullest and most challenging comment to date on the Platonic strain in *Moby-Dick*,[43] has recently called attention to "some overall similarities between Ahab and Plato's paradigm philosopher, Socrates." Both, as he notes, are old, "perhaps in conformity with Plato's belief that only a man of advanced age is prepared to grasp the Forms"—those supreme principles that stand at the very head of the Platonic hierarchy of ideas developed in Books VI and VII of the *Republic.* ("Ahab has not studied mathematics or harmony," which

Plato's Socrates prescribes there as essential preparation for philosophical dialectic, "but he has in his way studied astronomy," as Levin remarks.) Both Ahab and Socrates

are men of extraordinary physical endurance: Socrates standing at Potidaea, Ahab standing "for hours and hours . . . gazing dead to windward" in a gale so violent that the crew have lashed themselves to the rail. Both have fathered children when old. In sum, for both Ahab and Socrates physical and spiritual fortitude are of a piece. Finally, Ahab compares himself to a prisoner of this world in his first exchange with Starbuck: "How can the prisoner reach outside except by thrusting through the wall? To me, the white whale is that wall." (p. 65)

Ahab's comparison of himself to a prisoner has at least two Platonic analogues. One is Socrates' image in the *Phædon* of the soul imprisoned in the body—"glued" inside of it, in Ishmael's phrase (p. 137). The other, which is more applicable to Ahab's immediate point, is the allegory of the cave in Book VII of the *Republic*, which illustrates the plight of men who are prisoners of the limited world of sense experience: chained within the cave, they can see only shadows cast upon a wall by physical objects moved between that wall and the flickering light of a fire. But the philosopher, as Socrates explains, is like a prisoner removed from the cave and taught to behold not only real objects but ultimately the sun itself. In Levin's words, he "ascends from the dark realm of illusion into the light of knowledge, there to discover the source of being and goodness" (p. 61). The sequel requires him to reenter the cave in order to govern those incapable of making the ascent—men who may well misunderstand his motives and resist his good offices. In *Moby-Dick*, Levin argues, Ahab's spiritual progress exactly reverses Plato's upward movement from darkness to light: "Ahab descends from the illusion of light into the profundity of darkness, there to discover the evil reality beneath the 'masks' of everyday life. Like the Socratic philosopher, Ahab returns to the realm of illusion, where he is thought mad by those who have never left—but he brings them darkness instead of enlightenment" (p. 61). In short, his story is the myth of the cave *inverted*.

In support of his reading of *Moby-Dick* Levin cites a series of passages that illustrate a consistent pattern of imagery involving light and darkness. "Truth and profundity," he finds, "are always identified with darkness; light, and the sun, with shallowness and illusion" (pp. 67–68). Moreover, he suggests that Ahab's apparent madness, the result of his encounter with dark reality, is "underscored" by Melville through what happens to Pip—"a miniature Ahab," as Levin calls him.

Pip, like Ahab, has been transformed by a glimpse into the dark essence of things: "carried down alive to wondrous depths . . . among the joyous, heartless, ever-juvenile eternities, Pip . . . saw God's foot upon the treadle of the loom, and spoke it; and therefore his shipmates called him mad." Thus, "from that hour the little negro went about the deck an idiot; such, at least, they said he was." Here we have . . . the suggestion that Pip (and Ahab) are not mad at all—it is the blind crew that misperceive the return of the man transformed by knowledge. (pp. 66–67)

Finally Levin, like Ahab and Ishmael before him, must confront Moby Dick himself, whom he comes close to identifying with the Platonic Forms even though he is properly cautious about Melville's own intentions. The White Whale, as he notes, seems preternatural—especially in the "unearthly conceit" of whalemen that he is "not only ubiquitous, but immortal (for immortality is but ubiquity in time)." Here Levin is quoting Ishmael in Chapter 41 (p. 158); one thinks too of Babbalanja's remark in *Mardi* that "true thoughts . . . are ubiquitous; . . . they were in us, before we were born" (p. 397; see p. 283 above). "Ubiquity," according to Levin, is "the very mark" of the Platonic Forms, the attribute that

gives them their distinctive ontological and explanatory role and . . . makes them single abstract rather than scattered concrete objects. Melville could not have intended anything so flatly literal as making the whale out to be a Form; but its ubiquity does suggest that the whale, like the Forms, inhabits some ulterior reality from which it sends out manifold projections, none of which are more than partially adequate. (p. 67)

He adds that Melville may be emphasizing that latter point through Ishmael's insistence that "there is no *earthly* way of finding out precisely what the whale really looks like" (p. 228; emphasis added).

That Levin is correct in recognizing what he calls "Melville's high regard for the *Republic* and especially the *Phaedo*" (p. 62) is amply borne out by what has been reviewed here—from *Mardi*, *Redburn*, and *White-Jacket* as well as from *Moby-Dick*. He is well aware that there is more to Ahab and to the book as a whole than inverted Platonism; as he admits himself, his reading "risks imposing an allegorical pattern so mechanically that it rubs the texture of narrative suggestion threadbare and compresses character down to a single dimension" (p. 61). This is finely said at the very outset. Moreover, in concluding his presentation he is willing to grant that neither Melville nor any other author consciously *intended* "the meaning we attribute to him," though he has proposed the reading he offers because "I have found it impossible to understand *Moby-Dick* without attending to the dark inverted Platonism that moved Melville himself." Melville's "particular use of light imagery," he maintains, was "cued" by "its appropriateness to the pessimistic dualism jockeying with much else for position in his mind" (p. 71).

To understand that "pessimistic dualism," I would add, we must remember also that for Ahab—and for Melville—there were many things in heaven and earth undreamt of in Plato's philosophy. Not Platonism but Zoroastrianism, Gnosticism, and perhaps even Hinduism "cued" the most powerful imagery of light and dark in the entire book: that in Ahab's defiant address to the "white flame" of the corpusants in Chapter 119, "The Candles."

> "Oh! thou clear spirit of clear fire, whom on these seas I as Persian once did worship . . . ; I now know that thy right worship is defiance. To neither love nor reverence wilt thou be kind. . . . Come in thy lowest form of love, and I will kneel and kiss thee; but at thy highest, come as mere supernal power; and though thou launchest navies of full-freighted worlds, there's that in here that still remains indifferent. . . . Light though thou be, thou leapest out of darkness; but I am darkness leaping out of light, leaping out of thee! . . . But thou art but my fiery father; my sweet mother, I know not. . . . Thou knowest not how came ye, hence callest thyself unbegotten; certainly knowest not thy beginning, hence callest thyself unbegun. I know that of me, which thou knowest not of thyself, oh, thou omnipotent! There is some unsuffusing thing beyond thee, thou clear spirit, to whom all thy eternity is but time, all thy creativeness mechanical. . . . I leap with thee; I burn with thee; would fain be welded with thee; defyingly I worship thee!" (pp. 416–417)

Back of this impassioned defiance lay Melville's reading in a wide variety of primary and secondary works ranging far beyond Greek philosophy; one of the most influential, Pierre Bayle's *Historical and Critical Dictionary*, he had bought in 1849 at the same time that he was reading Plato, Browne, and Emerson.[44] This very eclecticism is in keeping with Melville's injunction in *Pierre* against letting any "one great book . . . domineer with its own uniqueness upon the creative mind"; instead, "all existing great works must be federated in the fancy" as "simply an exhilarative and provocative" to the aspiring writer. "Even when thus combined," moreover, they will constitute "but one small mite, compared to the latent infiniteness and inexhaustibility" in the author himself (p. 284).

(3) *"Like a magician's glass."* Both Ahab and Ishmael, though steeped in Platonism as they so obviously were, would subscribe only in part to what Levin identifies as three of its principal tenets (pp. 62–63). First, to borrow Levin's convenient phrasing, Plato's "sharp distinction between a realm of appearance and a realm of reality" means

that "genuine knowledge (of reality) requires active transcendence of appearance." But here one remembers Ishmael's insistence throughout the book that no man has ever really known "the living whale," that formidable being which,

> in his full majesty and significance, is only to be seen at sea in unfathomable waters; and afloat the vast bulk of him is out of sight, like a launched line-of-battle ship. . . . And the only mode in which you can derive even a tolerable idea of his living contour, is by going a whaling yourself; but by so doing, you run no small risk of being eternally stove and sunk by him. Wherefore, . . . you had best not be too fastidious in your curiosity touching this Leviathan. (pp. 227–228)

Again in a later chapter Ishmael restates his basic position that whatever knowledge of the whale a man can grasp is not transcendental or absolute but relative and existential: "Only in the heart of quickest perils; only when within the eddyings of his angry flukes; only on the profound unbounded sea, can the fully invested whale be truly and livingly found out" (p. 378).

Ahab is more of an absolutist, though even he cannot be sure whether the whale is but a whale or the intermediate "agent" of some higher and necessarily malevolent power (p. 144). "Sometimes" he thinks "there's naught beyond" the realm of appearance that he variously calls the "unreasoning mask" or imprisoning "wall" of visible objects: as he puts it in Chapter 125, "The dead, blind wall butts all inquiring heads at last" (p. 427). (One recalls Media's reminder to Babbalanja in *Mardi:* "you mortals dwell in Mardi, and it is impossible to get elsewhere.") Still, Ahab continues to adhere to what Levin distinguishes as Platonism's second tenet: "reality is mind-like." Here Ahab is the consistent idealist: "Oh! how immaterial are all materials!" he cries in Chapter 127. "What things real are there, but imponderable thoughts?" (pp. 432–433). "All the things that most exasperate and outrage mortal man," he complains, are intangible— "bodiless" (p. 461). But Ishmael, whenever he forgets "our horrible oath" to hunt Moby Dick, draws apart from Ahab as well as from his own earlier Platonism, and in Chapter 94, speaking in the narrative present, he makes this distinctly non-Platonic affirmation:

> For now, . . . by many prolonged, repeated experiences, I have perceived that in all cases man must eventually lower, or at least shift, his conceit of attainable felicity; *not placing it anywhere in the intellect or the fancy;* but in the wife, the heart, the bed, the table, the saddle, the fire-side, the country. (p. 349; emphasis added)

Ishmael's "shift" from the realm of intellect to the realm of tangible entities is a repudiation of the Platonic scale of values and the idealistic assumption that "goodness comes from the source of being"— Levin's third tenet of Platonism. What feelings he has about "the source of being" are apparent in "The Whiteness of the Whale." As for Ahab, it is *evil*, not goodness, that he attributes to ultimate reality; his quarrel with the cosmos itself carries him even beyond Platonism in "The Candles" and eventually to his death in "The Chase." The alternatives, it would seem, are to come to terms with the realm of appearance, as Ishmael recommends, or to transcend it—and transcendence is *not* to be attained in this life. "We can never arrive at the wisdom we court till after death," even Socrates admits in the *Phædon* (p. 63); "Our souls are like those orphans whose unwedded mothers die in bearing them," says Ahab: "the secret of our paternity lies in their grave, and we must there to learn it" (p. 406).[45]

In *Moby-Dick* Melville has dramatized this dilemma that confronts all mortals by creating both Ishmael and Ahab and sending them to sea, there to front Moby Dick. Each is meditative, philosophical, even idealistic, but each in his own way is both more and less than a Platonist. Certain aspects of Ahab's idealism, for instance, seem less like that of the Platonic dialogues than what Melville himself had encountered in the thought of his nineteenth-century contemporaries. "O Nature, and O soul of man!" Ahab exclaims at one point, "how far beyond all utterance are your linked analogies! not the smallest atom stirs or lives in matter, but has its cunning duplicate in mind" (p. 264); this is essentially the conception of symbolic correspondence between matter and spirit to be found in Carlyle and Emerson. Again, both Ahab and Ishmael as nineteenth-century characters are intensely subjective almost to solipsism, as the Greeks were not. In "The Doubloon," Chapter 99, Ishmael reports how seven men of the Pequod, ranging from Ahab to Pip, in turn see themselves projected in the gold coin Ahab has nailed to the mainmast. "Some certain significance lurks in all things," Ishmael himself muses, "else all things are little worth, and the round world itself but an empty cipher" (p. 358). His implication is that "significance" may well lie in the eye of the beholder; Ahab is even more explicit. "This round gold," he soliloquizes aloud,

"is but the image of the rounder globe, which, like a magician's glass, to each and every man in turn but mirrors back his own mysterious self. Great pains, small gains for those who ask the world to solve them; it cannot solve itself. Methinks now this coined sun wears a ruddy face; but see! aye, he enters the sign of storms, the equinox! and but six months before he wheeled out of a former equinox at Aries! From storm to storm! So be it, then. Born in throes, 'tis fit that man should live in pains and die in pangs! So be it, then! Here's a stout stuff for woe to work on. So be it, then." (pp. 359–360)

What Ishmael and Ahab say in this chapter is written large throughout *Moby-Dick* in terms of its dominant symbol, the sea. To go to sea, as Ishmael tells us from the beginning, is to search for truth; he makes the point most plainly in Chapter 23, "The Lee Shore"—a chapter echoing Emerson[46]—when he sets forth "that mortally intolerable" principle that

all deep, earnest thinking is but the intrepid effort of the soul to keep the open independence of her sea; while the wildest winds of heaven and earth conspire to cast her on the treacherous, slavish shore[.]

But as in landlessness alone resides the highest truth, shoreless, indefinite as God—so, better is it to perish in that howling infinite, than be ingloriously dashed upon the lee, even if that were safety! (p. 97)[47]

Moving along what I like to think of as the "horizontal" axis of *Moby-Dick*, Ishmael's narrative carries forward the continuous quest that Melville had begun in *Typee*, a quest that in *Mardi* was extended into what Taji calls "the world of mind" (p. 557). By the time of *Moby-Dick*, however, this horizontal movement was displaying a tendency to circle back on itself. The helmsman Bulkington, the "tall, new-landed mariner" memorialized in "The Lee Shore," is a man "who in midwinter just landed from a four years' dangerous voyage," had "unrestingly push[ed] off again for still another tempestuous term. The land seemed scorching to his feet" (p. 97). He may well be the very steersman whom Ahab is addressing in Chapter 52—"Up helm! Keep her off round the world!"—when Ishmael comments:

Round the world! There is much in that sound to inspire proud feelings; but whereto does all that circumnavigation conduct? Only through numberless perils to the very point whence we started, where those that we left behind secure, were all the time before us.

Were this world an endless plain, and by sailing eastward we could for ever reach new distances, and discover sights more sweet and strange than any Cyclades or Islands of King Solomon, then there were promise in the voyage. But in pursuit of those far mysteries we dream of, or in tormented chase of that demon phantom that, some time or other, swims before all human hearts; while chasing such over this round globe, they either lead us on in barren mazes or midway leave us whelmed. (p. 204)

Here Ishmael is voicing an idea recurrent in Melville's later thought: that whether for the individual or for the race, progress is a delusion. He returns to the theme in Chapter 98, which includes a reference to metempsychosis far different from anything in *Mardi:*

hardly have we mortals by long toilings extracted from this world's vast bulk its small but valuable sperm; and then, with weary patience, cleansed ourselves from its defilements, and learned to live here in clean tabernacles of the soul; hardly is this done, when—*There she blows!*—the ghost is spouted up, and away we sail to fight some other world, and go through young life's old routine again.

Oh! the metempsychosis! Oh! Pythagoras, that in bright Greece, two thousand years ago, did die, so good, so wise, so mild; I sailed with thee along the Peruvian coast last voyage—and, foolish as I am, taught thee, a green simple boy, how to splice a rope! (p. 358)[48]

To the degree that the voyage of the Pequod is the figurative representation of a philosophical quest, the death of Ahab and survival of Ishmael—whether by fate, necessity, or chance, which for Ishmael has "the last featuring blow at events" (p. 185)—may seem to have alternative implications, though I would not reduce *Moby-Dick* to the level of a cautionary tale. Instead, I prefer to return the discussion to the issue of idealistic subjectivism by way of what I call the "vertical" axis of *Moby-Dick*, which begins with the "water-gazers" of Chapter 1.

Why is almost every robust healthy boy with a robust healthy soul in him, at some time or other crazy to go to sea? Why upon your first voyage as a passenger, did you yourself feel such a mystical vibration, when first told that you and your ship were now out of sight of land? Why did the old Persians hold the sea holy? Why did the Greeks give it a separate deity, and make him the own brother of Jove? Surely all this is not without meaning. And still deeper the meaning of that story of Narcissus, who because he could not grasp the tormenting, mild image he saw in the fountain, plunged into it and was drowned. But that same image, we ourselves see in all rivers and oceans. It is the image of the ungraspable phantom of life, and this is the key to it all. (pp. 13–14)

"The story of Narcissus," with all its implications for other "plunges" in *Moby-Dick*—young Platonists teetering above the water at the mast-head, Tashtego actually falling into the whale's head, Pip "carried down alive to wondrous depths," the Pequod ultimately stove and sunk by Moby Dick, with Ishmael himself "escaped alone to tell thee" (p. 470)—has earlier analogues in Melville's writing. Yoomy in *Mardi* "soars" while Babbalanja "dives"; Melville himself told Duyckinck in 1849, with Emerson in mind, "I love all men who *dive*," going on to praise "the whole corps of thought-divers, that have been diving & coming up again with bloodshot eyes since the world began" (*Let-*

ters, p. 79). When he wrote *White-Jacket* later in that same year he ordained a sea-change for his title character through a fall from a yard-arm of the Neversink (Chapter 92). In *Moby-Dick* there are innumerable references to all that lies below the surface of the ocean, which to the idealistic pantheist of Chapter 35 symbolizes "that deep, blue, bottomless soul, pervading mankind and nature";

and every strange, half-seen, gliding, beautiful thing that eludes him; every dimly-discovered, uprising fin of some undiscernible form, seems to him the embodiment of those elusive thoughts that only people the soul by continually flitting through it. (p. 140)

Is the ocean a Neoplatonic soul of the world, or only the projecting mind of the beholder? Ishmael cannot finally say, though the question has obviously occurred to him and to Melville. Beneath the track of the Pequod "rush herds of walruses and whales" (p. 63); in that "everlasting terra incognita" (p. 235) swims what both Ishmael and Fleece call accursed, the shark (pp. 235, 252);[49] and there too glides Moby Dick.

What thoughts the White Whale "embodies" for Ahab we know, and we know too, through physical analogies reported by Ishmael, how much Ahab has come to resemble outwardly the projected image of his inner torment, for both are old and wrinkled, humped and scarred. But for Ishmael, by contrast, what he associates with whales in general and Moby Dick in particular is not fixed and set. Instead, his conceptions continually shift as he moves from rumors and superstitions about the whale through actual experience as a whaleman to his first glimpse of Moby Dick himself. During much of the narrative he of course shares Ahab's hatred for the White Whale, though in such later chapters as 94, "A Squeeze of the Hand," he has already moved somewhat apart from Ahab and from Ahab's unchanging obsession. In Chapter 96, "The Try-Works," he partly casts off Ahab's spell, his power of blackness; there is perhaps even a faint recollection of the allegory of the cave as Ishmael cries:

Look not too long in the face of the fire, O man! Never dream with thy hand on the helm! Turn not thy back to the compass; accept the first hint of the hitching tiller; *believe not the artificial fire*, when its redness makes all things look ghastly. Tomorrow, *in the natural sun*, the skies will be bright; those who glared like devils in the forking flames, the morn will show in far other, at least gentler, relief; *the glorious, golden, glad sun, the only true lamp— all others but liars!*

Nevertheless the sun hides not Virginia's Dismal Swamp, nor Rome's cursed Campagna, nor wide Sahara, nor all the millions of miles of deserts and of griefs beneath the moon. *The sun hides not the ocean, which is the dark side of this earth, and which is two thirds of this earth.* So, therefore, that mortal man who hath more of joy than sorrow in him, that mortal man cannot be true—not true, or undeveloped. With books the same. (pp. 354–355; emphasis added)

Ishmael concludes this deliberate weighing of light against dark with a characteristic injunction that in its imagery of diving and soaring recalls both *Mardi* and Plato's *Phaedrus:*

Give not thyself up, then, to fire, lest it *invert thee, deaden thee, as for the time it did me.* There is a wisdom that is woe; but there is a woe that is *madness.* And there is a Catskill eagle in some souls that can alike *dive down* into the blackest gorges, and *soar out* of them again and become invisible in the sunny spaces. And even if he for ever flies within the gorge, that gorge is in the mountains; so that even in his lowest swoop the mountain eagle is still higher than other birds upon the plain, even though they soar. (p. 355; emphasis added)

The same effort to weigh and balance and a recurrence of the idea of subjective projection are both apparent when we examine Ishmael's glimpses of whales in the later chapters of his narrative. In Chapter 86, describing the "peaking of the whale's flukes," he is moved to remark that "in gazing at such scenes, it is all in what mood you are in; if in the Dantean, the devils will occur to you; if in that of Isaiah, the archangels" (p. 317). A chapter later, in "The Grand Armada," his mood is less Dantean than Platonic once again. Through water "to a considerable depth exceedingly transparent" he is looking down at "the nursing mothers of the whales":

as human infants while suckling will calmly and fixedly gaze away from the breast, as if leading two different lives at the same time; and while yet drawing mortal nourishment, be still *spiritually feasting upon some unearthly reminiscence;*—even so did the young of these whales seem looking up towards us, but not at us. (p. 325; emphasis added)

But it is another sight altogether in Chapter 133 when Moby Dick himself at last appears:

A gentle joyousness—a mighty mildness of repose in swiftness, invested the gliding whale. Not the white bull Jupiter swimming away with ravished Europa clinging to his graceful horns; his lovely, leering eyes sideways intent upon the maid; with smooth bewitching fleetness, rippling straight for the nuptial bower in Crete; not Jove, not that great majesty Supreme! did surpass the glorified White Whale as he so divinely swam.

On each soft side . . . the whale shed off enticings. No wonder there has been some among the hunters who namelessly transported and allured by all that serenity, had ventured to assail it; but had fatally found that quietude but the vesture of tornadoes. Yet calm, enticing calm, oh, whale! thou glidest on, to all who for the first time eye thee, no matter how many in that same way thou may'st have bejuggled and destroyed before.

And thus, through the serene tranquillities of the tropical sea, . . . Moby Dick moved on, still withholding from sight the full terrors of his sub-merged trunk, entirely hiding the wrenched hideousness of his jaw. But soon the fore part of him slowly rose from the water; for an instant his whole marbleized body formed a high arch, like Virginia's Natural Bridge, and warningly waving his bannered flukes in the air, the grand god revealed himself, sounded, and went out of sight. (pp. 447–448)

What Ishmael is setting before us here is no Platonic Form. In this climactic passage Moby Dick is a tangible and believable whale whose emergence before our eyes has been prepared for in some way, di-rectly or obliquely, by every chapter of Ishmael's long narrative. The majesty of the White Whale as he finally appears to us is first of all the majesty of physical nature itself, with all the ambiguous mingling of beauty and terror that pertains to the natural world. At the same time, our realization that he has risen from the depths of the sea, out of what seems to some the very soul of that world, may suggest still further implications—if one attends to the specific imagery of the passage and relates it to the book's metaphysical and theological di-mensions. Here as elsewhere Moby Dick carries attributes not of the Forms but of divinity, itself both beautiful and terrible; yet Ishmael has already provided the basis for alternative readings, either natu-ralistic or subjective, of what the White Whale is and does. Ahab's obviously subjective vision of his antagonist and all the variations on the Narcissus myth we have noted throughout Ishmael's narrative suggest that the whale and the water in which he swims are like the doubloon and the round globe itself: mirrors of each man's "own mysterious self." Whether qualities and values are "actually inherent" in any natural object, whales included, or whether they are merely "laid on from without"—to borrow phrases from "The Whiteness of the Whale" (p. 170)—is an epistemological issue that Ishmael never finally decides. Taken subjectively, metaphysically, or even on the purely physical level, the White Whale remains ambiguous for him to the final chapter, where Ahab meets his death, the Pequod sinks, and the sea, like a shroud, rolls on "as it rolled five thousand years ago" (p. 469).

Between the writing of *Mardi* and the writing of *Moby-Dick*, during the years when he also turned out *Redburn* and *White-Jacket*, Melville developed from an author who entertained philosophical ideas into a full-fledged philosophical novelist. In *Mardi* the characters talk philosophy; in *Moby-Dick*, for good or for ill, both Ahab and Ishmael put their philosophy to the test of experience in the course of Ahab's doomed quest for Moby Dick. In *Mardi* Taji is narrator, protagonist, and quester all in one and Babbalanja is the inveterate philosopher; in *Moby-Dick* the narrator's role falls to Ishmael but both he and Ahab have their own stories in which each is at once protagonist, quester, and philosopher as well. If the book is "the tragedy of Captain Ahab," John Halverson has remarked, "it is also the novel of Ishmael." [50]

"A philosophical novelist like Melville," says Michael Levin in his analysis of *Moby-Dick* as inverted Platonism,

supplies something generally lacking in the formal development of a philosophical system: what it is like to experience the world as the system represents it. The system-builder's job is to refine his system, give reasons for accepting it, and perhaps draw from it some practical consequences. A novelist like Melville is trying to articulate the world as seen through the lens of the system. He need not even subscribe to the system to appreciate its interest as an aesthetic object—perhaps not Ahab but the sceptical Ishmael speaks for Melville. (pp. 61–62)

"What it is like to experience the world" as a philosophical idealist is a state of mind and feeling that Melville first communicated with genuine success in *Moby-Dick* with Ishmael and Ahab, though he had dramatized elements of idealistic thought in a line of characters extending from Taji and Babbalanja through the vignette of the unnamed "transcendental" chaplain of *White-Jacket*. Levin recognizes a difference between Ahab, with his philosophy of ultimate blackness, and "the sceptical Ishmael," but he does not analyze the movement of Ishmael's narrative and therefore takes no account of Ishmael's inclination toward Platonism in the opening chapters, his loss of idealistic faith once his allegiance is transferred from Socrates to Ahab, or his ultimate awareness of what Emerson meant when he wrote in "Experience" that "Life is a train of moods like a string of beads":

as we pass through them they prove to be many-colored lenses which paint the world their own hue, and each shows only what lies in its focus. . . . We animate what we can, and we see only what we animate. Nature and books belong to the eyes that see them. It depends on the mood of the man whether he shall see the sunset or the fine poem. There are always sunsets, and there is always genius; but only a few hours so serene that we can relish nature or criticism. [51]

"Oh! time was," Ahab soliloquizes, "when as the sunrise nobly spurred me, so the sunset soothed. No more. This lovely light, it lights not me; all loveliness is anguish to me, since I can ne'er enjoy" (p. 147). "It is all in what mood you are in" when you behold the whale, Ishmael tells us, as though his subjectivism were Emerson's; it is not a doctrine he had learned from the *Phædon*.

Does Ahab speak for Melville in such passages, or does Ishmael? The reader need not choose; the advantage of "this method of philosophising in dialogues," as Melville had read in Montaigne, is the opportunity to deliver "from several mouths . . . the diversity and variety" of an author's "own fancies." Ahab's philosophy, like his purpose in pursuing Moby Dick, is fixed—"laid with iron rails," as he says, "whereon my soul is grooved to run" (p. 147); Ishmael's is far more flexible. "So far gone" is Ahab "in the dark side of earth," as he himself realizes, "that its other side, the theoretic bright one, seems but uncertain twilight to me" (p. 433). Ishmael will grant that "the dark side of this earth" (which he identifies with the ocean) is "two thirds of this earth," but there is another side as well, where the natural sun outshines the artificial fire of the Pequod's try-works. "Give not thyself up, then, to fire," he tells us, "lest it invert thee, deaden thee; as for the time it did me"; though there is "a wisdom that is woe," there is also "a woe that is madness."

From Ahab's mouth, as from Babbalanja's in *Mardi* when Azzageddi is in the ascendant, come Melville's own darker, deeper fancies; "for any good man, in his own proper character, to utter, or even hint of them," in the words of "Hawthorne and His Mosses" (1850), "were all but madness."[52] At one remove from Ahab (and from Moby Dick) stands Ishmael, for Melville and for us. He too knows what madness is, having more than "a mouthful of brains," in Melville's phrase. He is both poet and philosopher—Yoomy as well as Babbalanja—and can soar as well as dive; it is he who survives the wreck to report the Pequod's voyage.

iii. From *Moby-Dick* to *Pierre*, and Beyond

In Chapter 73 of *Moby-Dick* Ishmael tells us that the crew of the Pequod, with "a Sperm Whale's prodigious head" already hanging at her side, is directed by Ahab to capture a Right Whale as well. "I wonder what the old man wants with this lump of foul lard," Stubb remarks to Flask after the second whale is taken. "Wants with it?" Flask replies,

"did you never hear that the ship which but once has a Sperm Whale's head hoisted on her starboard side, and at the same time a Right Whale's on the larboard; did you never hear, Stubb, that that ship can never afterwards capsize?"
    "Why not?"
    "I don't know, but I heard that gamboge ghost of a Fedallah saying so, and he seems to know all about ships' charms." (p. 275)

Flask goes on to remark of Fedallah that he doesn't "half like that chap," and Stubb agrees: "I take that Fedallah to be the devil in disguise. . . . He's the devil, I say." But Ishmael himself, whatever he may think of Fedallah as man or devil, has little use for his "ships' charms." As Flask had predicted, Ahab orders "this right whale's head hoisted up opposite that parmacetti's," and Ishmael describes the result:

As before, the Pequod steeply leaned over towards the sperm whale's head, now, by the counterpoise of both heads, she regained her even keel; though sorely strained, you may well believe. So, when on one side you hoist in Locke's head, you go over that way; but now, on the other side, hoist in Kant's and you come back again; but in very poor plight. Thus, some minds for ever keep trimming boat. Oh, ye foolish! throw all these thunderheads overboard, and then you will float light and right. (p. 277)

Ishmael's words in this much-quoted passage clearly reflect Melville's knowledge of philosophy: "Only a man at home with his metaphysics," as Michael Levin remarks in his essay on *Moby-Dick*, "could so deftly balance an empiricist against a rationalist" (p. 64). But the passage also demonstrates Melville's awareness of the controversy current in his day between adherents of John Locke's empirical philosophy, which had long been taught in American colleges, and the so-called Transcendentalists of New England, who had begun their celebrated revolt against the Lockeian position during the 1830's. By the time this chapter of *Moby-Dick* was written, Melville, as we now know, had read Emerson's published lecture "The Transcendentalist" (1849),[53] which points out that the term "Transcendental" had been applied to contemporary philosophical idealism—"the Idealism of the present day"—from its use by Immanuel Kant. As Melville was writing here about "Locke's head" and "Kant's" he was surely thinking of this very passage, in which Emerson goes on to explain that Kant

replied to the skeptical philosophy of Locke, which insisted that there was nothing in the intellect which was not previously in the experience of the

senses, by showing that there was a very important class of ideas or imperative forms, which did not come by experience, but through which experience was acquired; that these were intuitions of the mind itself; and he
denominated them *Transcendental* forms. The extraordinary profoundness
and precision of that man's thinking have given vogue to his nomenclature,
in Europe and America, to that extent that whatever belongs to the class
of intuitive thought is popularly called at the present day *Transcendental*.[54]

What Ishmael is given to say in *Moby-Dick* about "these thunderheads" has less to do with Locke and Kant in particular than with the
general schools of philosophy they represent, the empiricists and the
idealists. A corresponding division within Melville's own mind between the claims of experience and reflection, skepticism and intuition, doubt and faith is apparent in Ishmael, whose words in Chapter
73 were prompted not only by Melville's current reading in Emerson
but by his ambivalent response to philosophy itself. Even in *Mardi*,
where his fascination with philosophical topics is first manifest, there
were other voices than the philosopher's to speak for Melville, and
more recently in *White-Jacket*, after calling philosophy "the best wisdom that has ever in any way been revealed to our man-of-war
world," he had gone on to characterize it as "but a slough and a mire,
with a few tufts of good footing here and there" (p. 186). In *Pierre* his
reservations were to grow into virtual repudiation as Plato and his
successors in the idealistic tradition became objects of bitter attack for
both the narrator and the title character. Pierre as we first meet him
is a young idealist, in every sense of the word, but as his story unfolds
"his Faith-born, enthusiastic, high-wrought, stoic, and philosophic
defenses" ultimately crumble. "For there is no faith, and no stoicism,
and no philosophy," the narrator tells us in Book XXI,

that a mortal man can possibly evoke, which will stand the final test of a real
impassioned onset of Life and Passion upon him. Then all the fair philosophic or Faith-phantoms that he raised from the mist, slide away and dis-
appear as ghosts at cock-crow. For Faith and philosophy are air, but events
are brass. Amidst his gray philosophizings, Life breaks upon a man like a
morning. (p. 288)

(1) *Pierre*. As we know from Melville's reference to "the ugly Socrates" in a letter to Hawthorne, Plato's *Symposium* was fresh in his
mind in November of 1851, when *Moby-Dick* was newly published and
he had already begun work on his next book. It is not surprising to
find further echoes of the *Symposium* in its opening pages—especially
those of Book II which deal with the romance of young Pierre and
Lucy Tartan. Lucy's mother had long planned a match between them,

we are told, but "the thing demanded no manœuvering at all. The two Platonic particles, after roaming in quest of each other, from the time of Saturn and Ops till now; they came together before Mrs. Tartan's own eyes; and what more could Mrs. Tartan do toward making them forever one and indivisible?" (p. 27). The allusion is of course to the celebrated myth related by Aristophanes in Plato's dialogue: "Each of us," says Aristophanes, "is but the counterpart of a human creature, as having been cut . . . from one into two. Hence each one is in search of his counterpart" (Bohn, III, 512). The several speeches celebrating Love in the *Symposium* may also have suggested some of the extravagant language Melville's narrator uses in the fourth chapter of Book II, again in praise of Love. In succeeding chapters, however, we learn that Pierre is haunted by a vision of a mysterious face— not Lucy's—and therefore fears that "the invisible agencies are plotting treasons against our loves" (p. 37).

The face Pierre has seen is that of Isabel Banford, and her growing influence upon him threatens his betrothal to Lucy Tartan.

> Pierre now seemed distinctly to feel two antagonistic agencies within him; one of which was just struggling into his consciousness, and each of which was striving for the mastery; and between whose respective final ascendencies, he thought he could perceive, though but shadowly, that he himself was to be the only umpire. (p. 63)

That Pierre's situation as it develops is like that of Taji in *Mardi*, torn between Yillah and Hautia, is an idea that has already occurred to the commentators; that he also resembles Plato's charioteer in the *Phaedrus*, striving to control his opposing steeds, is also suggested by still other phrasing like that just quoted. "He seemed placed between them, to choose one or the other," the narrator flatly declares in Book VII (p. 129).

Though he strives "diligently" to "drive the phantom from him" (p. 53), the persistent vision of Isabel's face evokes strange fancies in Pierre. "For me," he cries in an apostrophe to the face, "thou hast uncovered one infinite, dumb, beseeching countenance of mystery, underlying all the surfaces of visible time and space" (p. 52). From this point on he must deal with the old Platonic dualism of appearance and reality, like Ishmael and Ahab in *Moby-Dick*, as he becomes increasingly aware of the disparity between the visible surface of things and the mysterious realm beneath or beyond it. He complains of Fate in language like Ahab's: "Thou Black Knight, that with visor down, thus confrontest me, and mockest at me; Lo! *I strike through thy helm,* and will see thy face, be it Gorgon! . . . From all idols, I tear all veils; henceforth I will see the hidden things; and live right out in my own hidden life!" (pp. 65–66; empasis added). What he comes to see—or to think he sees—is that Isabel is in all likelihood his father's illegitimate daughter. On his initiation into this "saddened truth" (if truth it be) the narrator comments that such a revelation

is not so much accomplished by any covertly inductive reasoning process . . . as it is the magical effect of the admission into man's inmost spirit of a before unexperienced and wholly inexplicable element, which like electricity suddenly received into any sultry atmosphere of the dark, in all directions splits itself into nimble lances of purifying light; which at one and the same instant discharge all the air of sluggishness and inform it with an illuminating property; so that objects which before, in the uncertainty of the dark, assumed shadowy and romantic outlines, now are lighted up in their substantial realities; so that in these flashing revelations of grief's wonderful fire, we see all things as they are; and though, when the electric element is gone, the shadows once more descend, and the false outlines of objects again return; yet not with their former power to deceive; for now, even in the presence of the falsest aspects, we still retain the impressions of their immovable true ones, though, indeed, once more concealed. (p. 88)

Had Melville not known Plato's allegory of the cave in the *Republic* he could never have written this remarkable sentence, which uses typical Platonic imagery—light and dark, shadow and substance—to convey a most unplatonic thought. It is not Plato's dialectic, the light of "reasoning," that reveals to us "things as they are"; it is "grief's wonderful fire."

Although *Pierre*, like *Mardi* and *Moby-Dick*, has metaphysical and theological dimensions, the reader is thus made aware from the outset that it is deeply concerned with epistemological questions—*what can we know?* and *how can we know?* The very subtitle, "*The Ambiguities*," emphasizes the epistemological issues, which in turn have ethical implications for the idealistic Pierre. His intuitive assumption that Isabel is indeed his half-sister prompts his ill-advised decision to become her champion, to give up both his fiancée and his mother for her sake, and to protect his dead father's name by representing Isabel to the world as Mrs. Pierre Glendinning. At first he is blind to the fact that sheer physical attraction has drawn the two of them together; he was not "consciously" aware of any such thing (p. 142), and Isabel herself insists that there is "no sex" in their supposedly "immaculate" relationship (p. 149). Ultimately "a terrible self-revelation" comes to Pierre, however (p. 192), as he realizes what has been his strongest motivation all along. If what passes for intuitive certainty is traceable no farther than to the workings of human psychology and biology,

Melville is saying, then its epistemological claims may be grossly inflated.

As Melville was well aware, the philosophical idealists of his own day set great store on intuitive truth. His exposure of what is really motivating Pierre is an implicit critique of a basic assumption of the New England Transcendentalists.[55] "Whatever belongs to the class of intuitive thought," he had read in Emerson, "is popularly called at the present day *Transcendental*." In the second half of *Pierre*, as the young protagonist takes Isabel to live in the midst of a Transcendentalist colony in an unnamed city, the critique develops into an explicit attack on philosophical idealism in general. This new turn in the story begins in the opening paragraph of Book XIV with the narrator's unqualified declaration that "Silence is the only Voice of our God" (p. 204); it continues with his further statement a few pages later that unless "the enthusiast youth . . . can find the talismanic secret, to reconcile this world with his own soul, then there is no peace for him, no slightest truce for him in this life" (p. 208). What follows is directed against idealist philosophers both ancient and modern:

Now without doubt this Talismanic Secret has never yet been found; and in the nature of human things it seems as though it never can be. Certain philosophers have time and again pretended to have found it; but if they do not in the end discover their own delusion, other people soon discover it for themselves, and so those philosophers and their vain philosophy are let glide away into practical oblivion. Plato, and Spinoza, and Goethe, and many more belong to this guild of self-impostors, with a preposterous rabble of Muggletonian Scots and Yankees, whose vile brogue still the more bestreaks the stripedness of their Greek or German Neoplatonical originals. That profound Silence, that only Voice of our God, which I before spoke of; from that divine thing without a name, those impostor philosophers pretend somehow to have got an answer; which is absurd, as though they should say they have got water out of stone; for how can a man get a Voice out of Silence? (p. 208)

What Melville gives his narrator to say in Book XIV is reduplicated in Book XXII when Pierre, "immaturely" attempting to write "a mature work" (p. 282), ascribes these words to *his* "apparent author-hero, Vivia":

"Away, ye chattering apes of a sophomorean Spinoza and Plato, who once didst all but delude me that the night was day, and pain only a tickle. Explain this darkness, exorcise this devil, ye can not. Tell me not, thou inconceivable coxcomb of a Goethe, that the universe can not spare thee and thy immortality, so long as—like a hired waiter—thou makest thyself 'generally useful.' Already the universe gets on without thee, and could still spare a million more of the same identical kidney. Corporations have no souls, and thy Pantheism, what was that? Thou wert but the pretentious, heartless part of a man." (p. 302)

In this extract, we are told, Pierre "seems to have directly plagiarized from his own experience"; more specifically, he is echoing the narrator's earlier attack on these same writers—Plato, Spinoza, and Goethe—so that the words he ascribes to "Vivia" stand at three removes from what was previously set down in Book XIV. As Melville perhaps intended to suggest, the situation illustrates Plato's charge in the *Republic* that artists render but a copy of a copy; the passage may also constitute deliberate self-parody. Certainly young Pierre exaggerates some of Melville's own literary mannerisms; here he is clearly violating Mrs. Glendinning's injunction in Book I never to *rave* or *rant.* "Your father never did either," she had told him; "nor is it written of Socrates; and both were very wise men. Your father was profoundly in love . . . but I never heard him rant about it. He was always exceedingly gentlemanly: and gentlemen never rant. Milk-sops and Muggletonians rant, but gentlemen never" (p. 19). *Pierre* is scarcely a light-hearted book, but in writing it Melville did not wholly deny expression to what he once called his "infirmity of jocularity" (*Letters,* p. 193).[56]

What Pierre and the narrator unite in saying against Plato, Spinoza, and Goethe (but not Socrates) does not differ substantially from other objections to philosophical idealism raised in Melville's earlier writings. The first charge is made on epistemological grounds: idealists deceive themselves and others by pretending to have got "a Voice out of Silence." The second involves the problem of evil: they make darkness seem light and "pain but a tickle." The third, which applies particularly to Goethe rather than Plato, is an objection to pantheism that is coupled with Melville's familiar hostility to aristocratic intellectuality: "Thou wert but the *pretentious, heartless* part of a man." The narrator also extends Melville's old comments about philosophical "gibberish" to contemporary followers of Carlyle and Emerson, calling them "Muggletonian Scots and Yankees" whose "vile brogue" is even more deplorable than that of Proclus or Kant—"their Greek or German Neoplatonical originals." All of this is epitomized in Book XX with the narrator's devastating sketch of Pierre's not-very-bright boyhood friend Charlie Millthorpe, a young man "possessing a certain constitutional, sophomorean presumption and egotism" (p. 276) who at twenty-two is now "following the law for a corporeal living" while "pursuing some crude, transcendental Philosophy." He is one of the Apostles, with their "peculiar secret, theologico-politico-social schemes" (p. 280), for he too naturally inclines toward those "amiable philosophers of either the 'Compensation,' or 'Optimist' school," who minimize the fact of human misery (p. 277). For Charlie, as yet unmarried, "the great men are all bachelors, you know. Their family is the universe . . . and Plato their uncle"; but Pierre, having the responsibility of a wife, should go into politics, he says, and "Stump the State on the Kantian Philosophy!" (p. 281).

With his portrait of Millthorpe the narrator shifts the reader's attention from Plato to the contemporary Transcendentalists; the movement from ancient to modern continues in Books XIV and XXI with his presentation of *Plotinus* Plinlimmon, "the Grand Master of a certain mystic Society among the Apostles" (p. 290). Something "latently visible" in Plinlimmon the narrator finds repellent, calling it "neither Malice nor ill-will" but rather "Non-Benevolence" (p. 290). When Pierre himself beholds Plinlimmon's face he is affected almost as strongly as in earlier chapters by his first glimpse of Isabel.

Only through two panes of glass—his own and the stranger's—had Pierre hitherto beheld that remarkable face of repose,—repose neither divine nor human, nor any thing made up of either or both—but a repose separate and apart—a repose of a face by itself. One adequate look at that face conveyed to most philosophical observers a notion of something not before included in their scheme of the Universe. (p. 291)

"Repose," it might be noted, was a special word for Melville, one that both Ahab and Ishmael apply to whales in *Moby-Dick* (pp. 237, 447) and that in his own person he would later associate with Plato in a poem on Greek landscape (*Poems*, p. 246). As for Piere, we are told that Plinlimmon's face, though itself passive and inscrutable, "at last wore a sort of malicious leer to him. But the Kantists might say, that this was a *subjective* sort of leer in Pierre" (p. 293). From this sentence I infer that knowledge of Kant as well as of Emerson may have contributed to the subjectivism seen earlier in the differing responses to the doubloon and the whale by the various characters of *Moby-Dick*.

What Plinlimmon advocates, if we may judge from the torn fragment of his lecture on "Chronometricals and Horologicals" quoted in Book XIV, is a form of ethical relativism that dilutes both Platonic and Christian teaching by advocating "a virtuous expediency" as "the highest desirable or attainable earthly excellence for the mass of men, and . . . the only earthly excellence that their Creator intended for them" (p. 214). Though man's own "earthly wisdom" may be "heavenly folly," Plinlimmon argues, God's "heavenly wisdom," conversely, is "an earthly folly to man" (p. 212). For mere mortals it would be "positively wrong in a world like this" to aim at "the highest abstract heavenly righteousness" (p. 213); indeed, such an attempt may actually lead to "strange, *unique* follies and sins" (p. 213), as it in fact does in Pierre's misguided efforts in behalf of the ambiguous Isabel. Plinlimmon's objection to Christianity, that "after 1800 years' inculcation from tens of thousands of pulpits, it has proved entirely impracticable" (p. 215), is akin to the narrator's even more sweeping declaration that "no faith, and no stoicism, and no philosophy" can finally avail a man in the event of "a real impassioned onset of Life and Passion." Along with Plato and Spinoza and Goethe, in other words, the narrator is literally rejecting *all* faith and philosophy, Christian or pagan.

Is he then speaking for Melville himself? To this question, the Kantists might say, a critic will return a *subjective* sort of answer. My own response, based on what documentation has come down to us, is not a flat yes or no; I think first of Hawthorne's much-quoted words of 1856 that his friend "can neither believe, nor be comfortable in his unbelief," and "will never rest until he gets hold of a definite belief" (*Log*, II, 529). Confining the question specifically to philosophy and to Plato, I find it evident from the writing of his later years that Melville continued to read ancient philosophy as he continued to read Emerson's essays: with mingled satisfaction and reservations. In *Pierre* itself, as we have seen, he employed Platonic images to illustrate unplatonic or even anti-Platonic insights—as when the narrator contrasts "two books," one which the world sees in its printed form and the other written only in its author's soul (p. 304), or when Pierre perverts Plato's shadow imagery to declare to Isabel that "a nothing is the substance, it casts one shadow one way, and another the other way; and these two shadows cast from one nothing; these, seems to me, are Virtue and Vice" (p. 274).[57] And the narrator, we remember, acknowledges that "though Plato was indeed a transcendently great man in himself, yet Plato must not be transcendently great" to an author—Pierre or Melville himself—who "would also do something transcendently great."

Although there are Platonic elements in *Pierre*, they are not as significant in the overall effect of the book as the pervasive Platonism of either *Mardi* or *Moby-Dick*. *Pierre* is the work in which Melville takes the measure of metaphysical and ethical idealism, Plato's included, and finds them both wanting. Continuing the movement from metaphysics to epistemology that is evident in *Moby-Dick*, he went on in *Pierre* to explore those psychological processes below the level of conscious thought that ultimately find expression in literary creation as well as in overt action. His method is more rhetorical than philosophical, making use of images and symbols rather than abstract concepts: faces and portraits, spiral stairs and pyramids, the well of childhood and the flowing river of consciousness. What resulted is by no means his best book, but with respect to its remarkable images of mental processes *Pierre* is his most experimental and certainly one of his most original works. "All the great books in the world," his narrator remarks after warning authors against excessive Platonic influence, are but "mirrors, distortedly reflecting to us our own things"; if we would see the object within, "we must look at the object itself," not at its reflected rendering in Plato or any other writer (pp. 283–284). In some of the most striking pages of *Pierre*—and the least Platonic—Melville was following his own Platonic injunction.

(2) *The later 1850's.* There is but one reference to Plato in Melville's magazine writing of 1853–1856 that followed *Pierre*, though he mentioned Socrates in two published pieces.[58] His most significant uses of Platonic themes during these years occur in "The Piazza," composed early in 1856 as a title piece for *The Piazza Tales* (1856), and in Chapter 22 of *The Confidence-Man*, finished in that same year—a chapter that ironically professes to emulate "the polite spirit" of Cicero's Tusculan Disputations (p. 129). In "The Piazza," as Rosemary Kenny has written, the mountain girl Marianna is drawn by Melville as

a parody of the literary artist who strives to see beyond appearances and express his insights through his art. Specifically, Marianna is a parody of both the Hawthornean and the Platonic artist. She exists between two worlds but participates "in neither." And like the artist in Plato's *Republic*, she exists at a third remove from reality. She sees neither the objects which cast the shadows, nor even the shadows themselves.[59]

In *The Confidence-Man*, which I think of as another philosophical dialogue like *Mardi*, Melville attempts "to define every important ethical problem known to man"; the book "tries to dramatize man's epistemological problems; it tries to provide a voice for each way of looking at these problems." I quote H. Bruce Franklin, who takes note of the caricature of Emerson as Mark Winsome in Chapter 36 and who sees in Chapter 22 "an incarnation of Plato's Socrates"—the man from the Philosophical Intelligence Office (p. 129)—arguing with "an incarnation of Diogenes," the Missourian Pitch, "about innate knowledge and innate virtue." Franklin makes an excellent case for interpreting "this modern philosophical dialogue" as "a carefully constructed parody of Plato's *Meno*."[60]

Among Plato's objects in the *Meno*, according to George Burges, the Bohn translator of the dialogue, was "to inquire into the nature of Virtue in the abstract" and "to ascertain whether it can or cannot be taught"; Burges's Introduction is relevant both to *The Confidence-Man* and to Melville's own interpretation of the character of Socrates.

> On the first of these points Plato, as usual, arrives at no conclusion. For Socrates, who is merely Plato's mouth-piece, and not, as many imagine, the exponent of his own opinions, never pretended to know any thing in the abstract. He was therefore content to show, that for the development of Virtue a correct moral conduct, founded on prudence, temperance, and justice, is all that is requisite.
> With regard to the question, whether Virtue can or cannot be taught, we are told that, as Virtue is not a science, it cannot, like a science, be made the subject of teaching; and that the virtuous person is such, rather by an act of the deity than by any efforts made by man. (Bohn, III, 1)

In *The Confidence-Man* the Missourian, who has no confidence in boys, is finally persuaded to hire "a very promising little fellow" after the man from the Intelligence Office convinces him, through specious analogies, that a boy can indeed become virtuous. "The petty vices of boys," he argues, "are like the innocent kicks of colts, as yet imperfectly broken. Some boys know not virtue only for the same reason they know not French; it was never taught them" (p. 144). The parody in Chapter 22, Mark Winsome's Emerson-like allusion to Proclus "on the theology of Plato" in Chapter 36 (p. 217), and an earlier reference in Chapter 7 to "that notion of Socrates, that the soul is a harmony" (p. 42) are the only specific signs of possible Platonic influence on *The Confidence-Man* that I have detected. In Melville's later writings there is a differentiation between Socrates the man and Socrates as "Plato's mouth-piece" that may reflect the remarks of Burges on the *Meno* that I have quoted above.

Melville spent the winter of 1856–1857 on a visit to the Mediterranean, financed by his father-in-law, that provided material for a number of his later writings. The immediate product was a lecture, "Statues in Rome," that he gave during the winter of 1857–1858, based in part on his manuscript journal of the trip that also provided material for *Clarel*; between 1857 and 1860 he wrote a number of poems for a projected volume of verse that was never placed with a publisher. A section of *Timoleon* (1891) headed "Fruit of Travel Long Ago" probably includes some of these pieces, two of which, on "The Attic Landscape" (*Poems*, pp. 245–246), give some sense of the "pure outline," "linear charm," and "repose" that he had found so attractive in both Greek architecture and Greek literature:

A circumambient spell it is,
   Pellucid on these scenes that waits,
   Repose that does of Plato tell—[61]
   Charm that his style authenticates.

"Statues in Rome" includes descriptions of portrait busts of both Plato and Socrates that Melville had seen in Italy early in 1857. Most of what he wrote about the statues must have been from memory, since the only relevant entry in his journal is a brief reference to a single bust of Plato.[62]

According to newspaper accounts of the lecture, Melville's comments on Plato in "Statues in Rome" ran something to this effect:

> The first view of Plato surprises one, being that of a Greek Grammont or Chesterfield. Engaged in the deep researches of philosophy as he was, we certainly should expect no fastidiousness in his appearance, neither a carefully adjusted toga or pomatumed hair. Yet such is the fact, for the long flowing locks of that aristocratic transcendentalist were as carefully parted as a modern belle's and his beard would have graced a Venetian exquisite. If this bust were true, he might have composed his works as if meditating on the destinies of the world under the hand of a hairdresser or a modern *valet-de-chambre*, as Louis XIV mused over documents while he smelled his Cologne bottle.[63]

Although these were not Melville's exact words, the paragraph has an air of authenticity, since it repeats phrasing that he himself applied to Plato in *Moby-Dick*, where Ishmael had linked "transcendental" and "Platonic" (p. 372), and later in *Clarel*, where Ungar mentions "Plato's aristocratic tone" (IV.xx.102).

"The bust of Socrates," it was reported, struck Melville as "a kind of anomaly," for in it

> we see a countenance more like that of a bacchanal or the debauchee of a carnival than of a sober and decorous philosopher. At a first glance it reminds one much of the broad and rubicund phiz of an Irish comedian. It possesses in many respects the characteristics peculiar to the modern Hibernian. But a closer observer would see the simple-hearted, yet cool, sarcastic, ironical cast indicative of his true character.[64]

Here again the newspaper phrasing is in general harmony with words of Melville's own in other contexts. Concerning the philosopher's physical appearance, he had not only mentioned "the ugly Socrates" to Hawthorne in 1851, as noted above, he had also described a London waiter in "The Paradise of Bachelors" (1855) as having "a head like Socrates";[65] as for simple-heartedness, Ishmael in *Moby-Dick* had characterized the "calm self-collectedness of simplicity" in savages like Queequeg as "Socratic wisdom" (p. 52). Melville's remarks on the "cool, sarcastic, ironical cast" of the portrait bust anticipate his own ironic comments on Socrates made in the 1860's and 1870's that will be touched upon in subsequent discussion.

Both "Statues in Rome" and Melville's lecture of the next season, "The South Seas," are testaments to his rejection of nineteenth-century faith in human progress. When two young Hawaiian-Americans from Williams College visited him at Pittsfield in 1859, hoping to hear him talk about his adventures in the Pacific, "he preferred to pour forth his philosophy and his theories of life," as one of them wrote. "The shade of Aristotle arose like a cold mist between myself and Fayaway." The other student found him

disgusted with the civilized world and with our Christendom in general and in particular. The ancient dignity of Homeric times afforded the only state of humanity, individual or social, to which he could turn with any complacency. What little there was of meaning in the religions of the present day had come down from Plato. All our philosophy and all our art and poetry was either derived or imitated from the ancient Greeks. (*Log*, II, 605)

What Melville said to the young collegians in praise of Plato echoed Emerson's laudatory comments in *Representative Men*, as I have shown in "Melville and Emerson's Rainbow."[66] But though, following Emerson's lead, he continued to acknowledge the indebtedness of modern thought to Plato and the Greeks in many areas, including even modern physics, he expressed reservations in later years about Plato's political thought, which did not square with his own view of human nature and human rationality. It was probably about the time of his conversation with the two students that he made the one direct written comment that has survived on the ideal commonwealth drawn in the *Republic*. The following quatrain appears on a manuscript leaf that may have been part of the never-published volume of poetry he completed by 1860:

A Reasonable Constitution

What though Reason forged your scheme?
'Twas Reason dreamed the Utopia's dream:
'Tis dream to think that Reason can
Govern the reasoning creature, man.

Appended to the verse is a note in prose: "Observable in Sir Thomas More's 'Utopia' are First its almost entire reasonableness. Second its almost entire impracticability[.] The remark applies more or less to the Utopia's prototype 'Plato's Republic'" (*Log*, II, 617). Both the verse and the prose comment are reminiscent of Melville's old preference for heart over head and his consequent reservations about any purely intellectual aristocracy.

(3) *The "silent years."* During the long period that Willard Thorp once called Melville's "silent years," after he had given over both fiction and lecturing and taken an obscure position as Inspector of Customs in New York, he in fact published four little-noticed volumes of poetry: *Battle-Pieces and Aspects of the War* (1866), *Clarel* (1876), and two privately printed collections, *John Marr and Other Sailors* (1888) and *Timoleon and Other Ventures in Minor Verse* (1891). Plato and Socrates do not figure prominently in any of these works, but incidental comments there and in other writings of the late years serve to round out Melville's final judgments of both philosophers. *Clarel* in particular has a number of references to Plato and Platonism, most of them made by Rolfe. A partial self-portrait of Melville, Rolfe is described as one who "supplemented Plato's theme"—philosophy—with "dædal life in boats and tents / A messmate of the elements" (I.xxxi.19–21). It is Rolfe, fittingly enough, who echoes Melville himself in his three references to Plato in Book II: first in speaking of modern Greece— "Where is Pericles? / Plato is where? Simonides?" (viii.32–33); then in remarking that even nineteenth-century physics "drudges after" Plato (xxi.20–21); and again in recalling

> those Hebrews, which of old
> Sharing some doubts we moderns rue,
> Would fain Eclectic comfort fold
> By grafting slips from Plato's palm
> On Moses' melancholy yew.
>
> (xxii.79–83)

Here Rolfe has in mind the Neoplatonists of Alexandria who sought to combine Hellenic and Hebraic traditions, as Melville himself had long ago noted (*Log*, I, 370).[67]

In Melville's other compositions of the 1870's and after there are several allusions to Plato's *Symposium*, or *Banquet*, that may have been prompted by a rereading of the dialogue in Shelley's translation.[68] One of them occurs in "After the Pleasure Party," where the feminine protagonist recalls the myth related in the dialogue by Aristophanes concerning the two sexes—"the two Platonic particles" of *Pierre* (p. 27).[69] Two other references appear in the series of lighter pieces in both prose and verse that I have called the "Burgundy Club Sketches," undertaken during and after the writing of *Clarel*.[70] A prose sketch of the Marquis de Grandvin mentions "a richer than

Plato's 'Banquet'";[71] a verse symposium of master artists "at Delmon-ico's" presents them as conversing

> On themes that under orchards old
> The chapleted Greek would frank unfold,
> And Socrates, a spirit divine,
> Not alien held to cheerful wine,
> That reassurer of the soul.
>
> (*Poems*, p. 334)

Here Melville presumably had in mind the remark of Alcibiades in Plato's dialogue that though Socrates was "generally unwilling to drink, yet when forced to do so, he beat all the rest; and what is the most wonderful of all, no one ever saw Socrates intoxicated" (Bohn, III, 570).

From these and other instances emerges a rough outline of the character of Socrates as Melville came to envision it in his later years—the Socrates of history, in effect, as distinguished from the "mouth-piece" for Plato that the Bohn translator saw in the dia-logues. To fill in that outline, one needs to remember the always fa-vorable references to Socrates in earlier works: *Redburn* ("the glorious Greek of old"), *White-Jacket* ("a sort of sea-Socrates"), and *Moby-Dick* ("simplicity" is "Socratic wisdom"). Socrates is absent from the "guild of self-impostors" scorned in *Pierre*, a group in which Plato himself is conspicuous. In "Cock-A-Doodle-Doo!" (1853) the narrator-protago-nist mentions the "bird rightly offered up by the invincible Socrates, in testimony of his final victory over life"; here Melville himself was obviously thinking of the *Phædon*[72]—and perhaps of his own remark in *Redburn* that in a man's behavior in facing death "lies the best index to his life and his faith." In later years he also recalled the Socrates of Plato's *Apology* as he confronted his accusers and judges. "'You are undermining the laws, and are dangerous to the young,' said the judges to Socrates. They said the truth," Melville wrote ironically, "& *from this point of view*"—emphasis added—"were just in condem[n]ing him." As "a self-constituted agent for the conservation of youthful persuasions[?]," Melville added, "——I suppress the inference." He set down these words in 1862 or after;[73] during the 1870's he made another ironical reference to the timeless wisdom of a Socrates that expresses his own jaundiced view of modern "progress," already voiced in the earlier lectures and again in *Clarel*: "What could a sage of the nineteenth century teach Socrates? Why, nothing more than something about Cyrus Feilds [Field] and the ocean telegraph, and the Sewing Machine."[74]

With Schopenhauer, whom he was reading during the last months
of his life, Melville probably shared "Plato's dictum, that the multitude can't be philosophers,"[75] but for all his own belief in degree—
manifest in *Mardi* and *Redburn*—even philosopher-kings stood below
the summit of his private scale of spiritual values. Ishmael had remarked in *Moby-Dick* that "to the purely spiritual, the intellectual but
stand in a sort of corporeal relation" (p. 183); the narrator of *Clarel*
similarly distinguishes an almoner at the monastery of St. Saba as
belonging to

> Another order, and more rare—
> As high above the Plato mind
> As this above the Mammon kind.
> (*Clarel*, III.xxx.49–51)

When Clarel in the same poem recognizes his fellow pilgrims Rolfe
and Vine as "exceptional natures" (I.xxxi.45) I assume that Melville
himself is distinguishing them from "the multitude" on the one hand
and from both an intellectual and a "purely spiritual" aristocracy on
the other. They are akin to the small group of what are again called
"exceptional" men who appear in later works—notably the unfinished novella *Billy Budd, Sailor*, where both Billy Budd and Captain
Vere are characterized as "two of great Nature's nobler order" who
share "the rarer qualities" of human nature (p. 115).[76]

The title character of "Timoleon" (1891), a poem based on Plutarch's *Lives* (*Poems*, pp. 209–215), is another man of the same noble
stamp. The poem is set in classical Greece:

> The time was Plato's. Wandering lights
> Confirmed the atheist's standing star;
> As now, no sanction Virtue knew
> For deeds that on prescriptive morals jar.

Timoleon is a Corinthian patriot who exhibits "a virtue beyond man's
standard rate." Like Melville's Pierre, he heeds a voice "whose man-
date calls, / Or seems to call, peremptory from the skies"; at its behest
he frees Corinth from tyranny by slaying its despotic ruler, his own
evil brother. Then, coming to doubt his own motives—again like
Pierre—he contemplates suicide and ultimately quarrels with the
gods themselves "as compromised in wrong," though he also borrows
a Platonic image to raise Melville's old question:

> Are earnest natures staggering here
> But fatherless shadows from no substance cast?
> Yea, *are* ye, gods?

The contrast between the virtuous Timoleon and his vicious brother Timophanes is not unlike the pairing of opposites in *Billy Budd, Sailor*, where the narrator sets Billy Budd's simple goodness over against what he calls John Claggart's "depravity according to nature" (p. 75). He makes reference to a list of definitions attributed to Plato appearing in the final volume of the Bohn edition (VI, 143), adding that the concept of "Natural Depravity" supposedly held by Plato is intended to apply only to individuals rather than to all of mankind.[77] Such persons as Claggart are uncommon, he observes. They "have no vulgar alloy of the brute in them, but invariably are dominated by intellectuality" (p. 75), and what especially marks "so exceptional a nature" is this:

Though the man's even temper and discreet bearing would seem to intimate a mind peculiarly subject to the law of reason, not the less in heart he would seem to riot in complete exemption from that law, having apparently little to do with reason further than to employ it as an ambidexter implement for effecting the irrational. (p. 76)

These words in *Billy Budd* provide a striking coda to the earlier quatrain headed "A Reasonable Constitution," where Melville had called it a "dream" to think with Sir Thomas More or Plato that "Reason can / Govern the reasoning creature, man." The pallid Claggart, whose evil nature is "born with him and innate," is as much a madman as Ahab, though for a different cause; his "lunacy" is "not continuous, but occasional," we are told, and in "method" and "outward proceeding" it is "always perfectly rational" (p. 76). In both intellect and education he is superior to rosy-cheeked Billy, for the handsome young sailor is "one to whom not yet has been proffered the questionable apple of knowledge" (p. 52). An illiterate, Billy is still a "child-man" in whom "intelligence, such as it was, had advanced while yet his simple-mindedness remained for the most part unaffected" (p. 86).

According to Sundermann and others, Captain Vere stands in relation to Billy and Claggart as Plato's charioteer in the *Phaedrus* is related to his two winged horses—like Taji with Yillah and Hautia in *Mardi* and Pierre with Lucy and Isabel in *Pierre*.[78] There are difficulties with this analogy, however, since the duality of the two horses in the *Phaedrus* involves reason versus sensual appetite while the dichotomy of Billy and Claggart repeats Melville's old pattern of heart versus head. Even so, Vere must decide between them when Claggart falsely accuses Billy of fomenting mutiny; and when Billy, his speech impaired by a stammer, responds with a fatal blow to Claggart's forehead, "so shapely and intellectual-looking a feature" (p. 99), Vere becomes another judge like Media in *Mardi* who faces the disparity between "Justice, in ideal," and justice in the world of actuality. Billy's trial before Vere's drumhead court takes place in a man-of-war world where justice is not absolute but relative; the Articles of War, in the language of *Pierre*, are drawn up according to merely horological rather than chronometrical principles. Prompted by Vere, an "exceptional" man who comprehends the natures of both Billy and Claggart and is fully aware of all that is at stake in the young sailor's case, the court condemns Billy to death by hanging, and Billy, unprotesting, goes to his death with a blessing for Vere on his lips.

The disparity between Billy Budd's "essential innocence" (p. 121) and his physical responsibility for the death of his superior, John Claggart, is plain enough to Vere, who is equally conscious of his own position as commander of a naval vessel at sea in time of war with a crew whose loyalty might well have been compromised by the Great Mutiny of recent date. Vere's decision and Melville's presumed view of it have provoked a seemingly endless debate among readers and critics of *Billy Budd*. According to the late Yvor Winters, Vere can see "only one solution" to the problem posed by Billy's deed, "the solution of Socrates"—namely, "to act according to established principle, which supports public order, and, for the margin of difference between established order and the facts of the particular situation, to accept it as private tragedy."[79] Whether or not Melville himself had Socrates in mind we have no basis for saying, but when Vere moves the court to follow the military code to the letter and condemn Billy he does in fact influence its members as strongly as Socrates had influenced the judges at his own trial. From *one* point of view, as Melville had said of the Greek court, they *were* "just" in condemning him. On the spiritual level Billy is not touched, and as serenely as Socrates he goes to his death. Between his fate and his innocence is the margin of private tragedy, perhaps felt most keenly by Captain Vere despite his "philosophic austerity" (p. 129). Like Socrates in the *Phædon*, Billy is better prepared to die than those about him, and as he awaits execution, "a serene happy light born of *some wandering reminiscence or dream* would diffuse itself over his face, and then wane away only anew to return" (pp. 119–120; emphasis added). The Platonic language here, which recalls comparable passages of *Mardi* and *Moby-Dick*, helps to emphasize Billy's purity and innocence without obliging the narrator or author to hold out any assurance of an afterlife.

A strikingly different reading of *Billy Budd* with reference to Socrates is that of Thomas J. Scorza, who sees Claggart rather than Billy or Vere as the Socratic figure in the story—a narrative through which, for Scorza, Melville "reveals himself as an enemy of Socrates and Socratism." When Billy's blow strikes Claggart "full upon the forehead," Scorza writes, one witnesses the destruction of Claggart, "who is as pale as the Socrates of Aristophanes' *Clouds*, and who, like the Socrates of the *Symposium*, 'never allows wine to get within [his] guard,' and who, like the Socrates of the *Meno*, has a numbing effect on speech like a 'torpedo fish.'"[80] In this interpretation, moreover, Socrates becomes the representative of philosophy in that "antient variance between philosophy and poetry" that Plato alludes to in Book X of the *Republic;* according to Scorza, Melville belongs "wtih Aristophanes on the side of the poets." Poets and philosophers, he argues, are rival claimants to knowledge and wisdom and therefore to the role of teacher. The poet's knowledge is

not the product of reason but of a far more comprehensive process whereby [he] claims to have been inspired by the cosmic dimensions of life. . . . [W]hile the poet sees the philosopher's exclusive celebration of the power of reason as the quintessential human claim of superiority to nature and its truths, he sees his own openness to the fullness of nature as a celebration of nature itself. (p. 178)

I disagree completely with Scorza's remarks on Claggart as a Socratic figure, which run counter to the many tokens of Melville's unflagging esteem for the man as a true spiritual hero. As for the type figure of the philosopher, with his "exclusive celebration of the power of reason," as Scorza puts it, it was Plato rather than Socrates who repeatedly came to Melville's mind as standing both for philosophy and for human rationality itself. As we have seen, he distinguished "the invincible Socrates" of the *Phædon* and *Apology*, with his imperturbable courage, from the Socrates of those other dialogues where he is but a "mouth" for Plato to speak through. Moreover, that Platonic Socrates who praises love and the madness of inspiration in the *Symposium* and *Phaedrus* must have seemed to Melville a more congenial figure than the surrogate for Plato the rationalist who in the *Republic* would banish poets from his ideal commonwealth. Melville himself knew well enough how to create fictional characters to voice "his own fancies," and as early as *Mardi* he was speaking not only as philosopher but also as poet through Babbalanja and Yoomy—"poets both" who "differ but in seeming": "though Yoomy soars, and Babbalanja dives, both meet at last"—and in Ishmael they become in effect one voice.

What I do value in Scorza's approach to Melville is his recognition of that general distrust both of pure rationality and of what he calls "modernity," an attitude that informs not only *Billy Budd, Sailor,* but also Melville's writing in general from at least the time of *Pierre;* the Mediterranean trip of 1856–1857, which took him to Egypt and Palestine, Greece and Rome, only reinforced his long-standing regard for the achievements of the ancient world, as we know from his journal and from "Statues in Rome." As a poet, he took a stand both in his verse and in *Billy Budd* against what Scorza calls "the major representatives of modernity," from "the enlightened philosophy of his day" to "Burkean" conservatism on the right and Romanticism's celebration of "its natural man" on the left (pp. 178–179). This generalization I can accept, though I disagree with Scorza's farther statement that Melville's "attack on modern science and philosophy does not lead [him] back to ancient science and philosophy but . . . rather to an attack on philosophy as such" (p. 176); convincing evidence to the contrary is assembled here from Melville's own writings.

An idealist who mistrusted idealism, Melville persistently loved philosophy even while criticizing philosophers and philosophical systems; moreover, the course of his love never did run smooth—witness *Mardi, Moby-Dick,* and especially *Pierre* from his work of the 1840's and 1850's. As for Platonism, despite his reservations about Plato's aristocratic intellectuality, it is evident that he went back once again to the dialogues, along with other works of philosophy, during his later years, when he is known to have been reading Aristotle, Diogenes Laertius, and perhaps other ancient writers as well[81]—just as he returned to Emerson's essays after attacking Transcendentalists both ancient and modern in *Pierre* and *The Confidence-Man. When* a writer flourished made little difference to Melville, as he had long been saying; in the words of *Mardi,* "The catalogue of true thoughts is but small; they are ubiquitous; no man's property; and unspoken, or bruited, are the same." A characteristic injunction positing this very point appears in "Lone Founts," a poem included in the *Timoleon* volume of 1891 (*Poems,* p. 229) that helps to explain his lasting interest in Plato, in Socrates, and even in the Platonic tradition itself:

> Stand where Posterity shall stand;
> Stand where the Ancients stood before,
> And, dipping in lone founts thy hand,
> Drink of the never-varying lore:
> Wise once, and wise thence evermore.

PART IV
PURSUING MELVILLE

And thus, pursuers and pursued
flew on, over an endless sea.

Mardi, Chapter 195

A Letter to Henry A. Murray

D ear Harry,

Forty years ago, when Eleanor Metcalf sent me to talk to you
and Charles Olson about my piece on "I and My Chimney," you told
me that those who study Melville do so out of some personal need. I
agreed then and I agree now, though I have to wonder in a few cases
just how seriously they study and what motivating force generates
their need. In a recent letter—the one dated the 29th of May, 1980—
you made another comment that has been agitating my conscience
ever since, as no doubt it was intended to do. Among the Mel*villains*,
as I like to call them, you were distinguishing, if not actually naming,
"the fact-interpreters" and "the fact-reporters," going on to charge
that "All you diligent disciples of Prof. Williams have chosen to remain with the fact-collectors, as if literary criticism should be made
into a kind of quasi-science." Then you wrote another sentence to
take the sting off that one, adding: "But then I think of your enlightened 'I and My Chimney' which refutes my conception of a lot of sub-
sub-librarians who are academically conditioned against the use of
disciplined imagination & intuition."

You're right, of course, in saying that we "sub-subs" interested in
HM have worked diligently to get the facts straight. It hasn't been
just Stanley Williams' students, either, though he certainly fired up a
whole generation of Yale Ph.D.'s: Foster, Bezanson, Hillway, Hayford,
Pommer, Baird, Davis, Gilman, Feidelson, Haave, Wright, Fiess,
Creeger, and Finkelstein, to name only those Melvillains who worked
with him as I did. There were others writing on Melville—Anderson,
Thorp, Vincent, Leyda, and Howard, for example—whose books of
the thirties, forties, and fifties were intended first of all to get the

facts properly *logged*. More often than not we've all walked respectfully and admiringly in your own footsteps, knowing you had been there as a researcher before we were. But how many of us have filled your shoes?—or, to switch the metaphor, have worn all the additional hats you've sported so bravely, as in that sparkling "Bartleby and I," where you appear variously as not only psychologist and biographer but as "first critic," "second critic," and commentator and then as surrogate for the attorney, the scrivener, and even Melville himself!

In short, *you've* produced a good deal more concerning HM than just the facts. But have *we*? Did we *all* choose "to remain with the fact-collectors"? Or, to put your question even more broadly, has my generation mostly abjured genuine criticism in favor of a kind of literary scholarship that lacks "disciplined imagination & intuition"?

You've asked damnable and damning questions of anyone professing concern with literature, especially if American literature is what he professes for a living. By and large, we "disciples of Prof. Williams" weren't embryo novelists and dramatists and poets to begin with, and what we wanted to do primarily and professionally was to study books and authors and to work with other students, not to write fiction or poetry ourselves. That's a strike against us, of course, with anyone who assumes automatically and immediately that those who can, do, and those who can't, teach. But as Emerson said in "The American Scholar," there's creative reading as well as creative writing, and colleges "can only highly serve us when they aim not to drill, but to create." (I have sat in your classroom, you'll remember, and it wasn't "drill" that you were aiming at.) Who can honestly claim to be either a student or a teacher of literature, let alone a *professor*, without the gift of "imagination & intuition"? Ishmael said it finely in Chapter 42 of *Moby-Dick:* "in a matter like this, subtlety appeals to subtlety, and without imagination no man can follow another into these halls."

Melville, as we both have reason to know, read a good deal of Matthew Arnold, including Arnold's essay "The Function of Criticism at the Present Time," an essay which defends imaginative criticism as essential to creativity in much the same way that I am moved to defend imaginative scholarship as essential to criticism. "For the creation of a master-work of literature," Arnold held in 1864, "two powers must concur, the power of the man and the power of the moment." Power is essential to both, as he recognized. But "the man is not enough without the moment." His point is applicable to the issue between us. In terms of American literary scholarship, which as a discipline isn't much older than the Melville revival itself, we can see now, from the perspective of the 1980's, that much of what

Weaver and Mumford and their contemporaries wrote about Melville in the 1920's and 1930's was imaginative enough, even brilliantly so, but unhappily it too often lacked the mundane scholarly underpinnings that literary study has to have in order to stand as permanently reliable. Even as in science, it isn't facts *or* imagination, but imagination playing upon fact.

What Stanley Williams inspired many of us to do (I use the word "inspired" quite deliberately) was to put down good foundations for the future, beginning in his seminars in the later 1930's and 1940's and working in areas where our own experience and inclinations might intersect with the current need for reliable information accurately presented and soundly interpreted. As I see it now, he was saying to us as would-be scholar-teachers dealing with American literature what Thoreau had said to his neighbors and friends a hundred years earlier in *Walden:* "If you have built castles in the air, your work need not be lost; that is where they should be. Now put the foundations under them."

This is the spirit in which we "disciples" began our careers. Our writing on Melville, mine certainly included, involved a good deal of what Williams called "spade-work." He meant basic research, digging out the substratum of biographical fact, establishing the canon and the texts. This is a labor that literary scholars have a professional obligation to do, as he repeatedly told his graduate seminars, but he never said or implied that literary study should stop with research—quite the contrary. Research is the essential preliminary to larger and more recognizably imaginative projects, and literary history and biography, literary criticism, and the classroom teaching of literature can be no sounder than the scholarship on which they are based.

"You were born for research," Williams once said to me when we were talking about my work of the 1940's on Melville's library. But I hope that I was born for something else as well, and I think that he thought I was. What Emerson called "the true scholar" is no pedant but a creator, one who teaches with the authority that comes with first-hand knowledge. What Stanley Williams and *his* generation of scholar-teachers did for American literary scholarship was first to create and establish it as a discipline, then to train and inspire their own successors as its practitioners and teachers. *My* generation has tried, though not always with success, to maintain and extend what they passed along to us, with the thought that American literary study—if the humanities survive at all—is still to come fully into its own in the years ahead. There's a gamble involved here, and perhaps some errors of choice or emphasis as well, though only time will finally tell.

As you and I know, much of the so-called "hard" scholarship of the past forty years on Melville has been biographical and textual, as I'm sure it had to be. Anyone who still thinks that everything we need to know about HM was chronicled by Davis or Gilman or Leyda by the early 1950's hasn't yet read what's been turned up as recently as the late 1970's—by Patricia Barber, for instance, or by Walter Kring and Jonathan Carey, or by Fred and Joyce Kennedy. After all, Jay himself wrote in 1951 that *The Melville Log* might well have been called *The Endless Study*. Reliable texts are another matter. Some major American authors and books had gone out of print altogether when I was a graduate student, and many others were to be had only in corrupt texts that couldn't be trusted. What kind of criticism could we hope to write as long as the texts we needed to work with were unreliable if we could find them at all? You yourself responded in the 1940's just as I did, by turning editor. Your *Pierre* in the Hendricks House edition was brilliant. But that edition as a whole was never completed, and the Northwestern-Newberry Melville now in progress—I wish it well—stands at six volumes in print (1968–1971), with nine still to go as of 1980.

We needed good editions of American authors in 1940, and we still do. Producing them isn't easy and it certainly isn't cheap; I know from my own experience in editing both Melville and Emerson how great the cost in Time, Strength, Cash, and Patience, not to chronicle personal frustrations and disappointments. But I'm also aware of how very much I've learned about the ways of creativity through the close absorption in the text and its biographical milieu that good editing requires, especially where manuscripts must be ordered and interpreted, and I'm sure that other editors have commonly profited as I did. Good editing isn't synonymous with mere pedantry; as both editor and critic of *Pierre* you can't very well deny that it demands the "disciplined imagination & intuition" you call for. But wasn't it a waste of time and talent, or at least a sacrifice, to set virtually a whole generation of American literary scholars to work on largely editorial tasks instead of producing genuine criticism? Yes—if all we've done since the 1940's is to bury our authors and not to praise them. The editorial job needed doing, nevertheless; it's at last well on the way to completion despite faltering and delay; the next generation of scholar-teacher-critics should profit accordingly. My question, like the related ones you raised in your letter, can't really be answered until it's known whether the ground we've plowed has become a cemetery or a seedbed.

With students of my own I've tried to share the lessons I learned from the precepts and examples of my predecessors, and I've tried also to add flavor extracted from the fruits of my own experience as scholar-teacher. To teach, after all, is to try out ideas and intuitions on human pulses, not just on the typewriter. Sharing with others the sheer fun of learning should be a real joy for both students and teachers, and both should know the excitement of discovery. They need to know also that there's hard work involved, and disappointments major and minor, while the pursuit is on. You and I while pursuing Melville, or being pursued by him, have learned how to decipher HM's tracks as he prowled through bookstores and swam through libraries and created his own world of mind. That pursuit has been your avocation, not your profession; as for me, my object, if not to be a critic in your sense of the word or a creator in Olson's, has been to combine the avocation with the calling—"yield who will to their separation," as Frost once put it.

For me, pursuing Melville all these years has meant trying to understand a mystery that allures, to explain a need to myself, and to share with others not only what I have learned but my sense of the mystery and the need and the perennial attraction of the chase. The scholar in search of answers is a hunter; if not an Ahab or a Leatherstocking he's at least a problem-solver like Poe's detective, satisfying his private rage for order. In reporting his findings he ought to be opening an intercourse with the world as Hawthorne did, or writing the world a letter like Emily Dickinson, though his medium will be essays rather than stories or poems; he should communicate not only his solutions but a feeling of what their pursuit is worth in itself. The good researcher isn't always the good teacher or writer—that I must dutifully and honestly say. Still, the very best scholar-teachers I've known among my own mentors and colleagues and students have all been alive *in* the classroom because they were already alive outside and beyond it, as humane men and women and as dedicated professionals. You, sir, have been just such a man; so too was Stanley Williams.

Sincerely,

Merton Sealts

P.S. I hope that the papers I've collected in this volume reflect something of what I learned from Stanley Williams as a scholar-teacher. If they have caught his spirit, they ought to illustrate sound basic scholarship as it passes over into biography and criticism, at the point where spade-work and foundation-building have culminated in some new genuinely critical understanding of Herman Melville and the writings that have engaged so many of us so enthusiastically and so long. For me, I want to add, every research project I've tackled has meant not only hard scholarly work but the thrill of discovery and the satisfaction of bringing some kind of order out of Chaos and old Night, always with the feeling of surprise at learning what I never could have anticipated, either at the outset or during the intermediate stages of our endless pursuit.

APPENDIX
NOTES
INDEX

Appendix:

Additions and Changes in the "Check-List of Books Owned and Borrowed" (1966)

Following the publication in book form of *Melville's Reading: A Check-List of Books Owned and Borrowed* (University of Wisconsin Press, 1966), revised and expanded after its original appearance in the *Harvard Library Bulletin* (1948–1950, 1952), enough additions and changes accumulated to warrant two supplementary notes, which were published in the *Bulletin*, 19 (July 1971), 280–284, and 27 (July 1979), 330–335. With the kind permission of the *Bulletin's* editor, Edwin E. Williams, these and subsequent additions and changes in the "Check-List of Books Owned and Borrowed" are consolidated here. The listings which follow employ the same system of numbering and other conventions such as abbreviations and symbols that were used in these earlier compilations.

Five references should be deleted from the list of abbreviations and symbols given on pp. 32–34 of the 1966 volume: "Long," "Mott," "Murray," "Sealts," and "Seelye"; the following additions and changes should be made to the remaining items:

BCHS	Berkshire County Historical Society, Pittsfield, Massachusetts
BUL	Brown University Library
CUL	Columbia University Library
Current	The Current Co., Bristol, Rhode Island
Dietrich	The Dietrich Brothers Americana Corporation, Wilmington, Delaware
Levenson	*For* Minneapolis, Minnesota *read* Charlottesville, Virginia
Marshall	The collection of Mrs. Roderick Marshall, Oxford, England
NL	The Newberry Library, Chicago

Sackman   *For* East Rockaway, New York *read* South Deerfield, Massa-
              chusetts
Simmons   Larry Simmons, 12342 Broadstreet, Detroit, Michigan
              48204
Woodstock   Library of the Woodstock Theological Center, George-
              town University, Washington, D.C.

Within the "Check-List of Books Owned and Borrowed," pp. 35–106 of the
1966 volume, the following additions and changes should be made on the
pages and in the numbered entries indicated:

Page *Number*
35   4   [Adams, William Henry Davenport. The Buried Cities of Cam-
                pania . . .]
                For . . . Herculaneum, Their . . . *read* . . . Herculaneum,
                Their History, Their . . .
36   11   [Alger, William Rounseville. The Solitudes of Nature and of
                Man . . .]
                For 3rd ed. *read* 2nd ed.
36   12a   American Unitarian Association. Hymn and Tune Book for
                the Church and the Home. Revised Edition. Boston: American
                Unitarian Association, 1877.
                    Stamped 'Melville' on front cover; title page lacking. (BCHS)
36   14.1   Arichandra, the Martyr of Truth: a Tamil Drama Translated
                into English by Mutu Coomàra Swàmy. London, Smith, Elder,
                1863.#
                    'To Rear Admiral, Sir Rodney Mundy, K.C.B. from the au-
                thor, with his compliments.'; 'H. Melville, Nov. 17, '71 N.Y.'
                Annotated by the late Roderick Marshall. (Marshall)
37   21   [Arnold, Matthew. Poems . . .]
                For Murray *read* BeA.
37   21a   ['Atlas of the Heavens.']: *delete; see No. 101a.*
37   21d   Baldwin, Simeon Eben. A Brief Memorial of Philip Marett.
                Read by Simeon E. Baldwin before the New Haven Colony
                Historical Society, September 22d, 1890. New Haven, Tuttle,
                Morehouse & Taylor, Printers, 1890.
                    Unlocated. Philip Marett (1792–1869) was the father of El-
                len Marett Gifford (18?–1889), a cousin of Elizabeth Shaw
                Melville and benefactor of her family. In a letter of 3 March
                1891 (Baldwin Family Papers, Yale University Library;
                quoted by authorization of the Library) Mrs Melville thanked
                Baldwin 'for the very interesting "Memorial" which you
                were kind enough to send me. . . . Both my husband and I
                have read with great interest this appreciative and friendly
                "Memorial" and he begs to add to mine his thanks and re-
                gards.'

39   51   *Revise to read:* Bayle, Pierre. An Historical and Critical Dictio-
             nary . . . (Tr. Jacob Tonson.) London, Harper, [etc.], 1710. 4 v.
             Add: That Melville owned and used the Tonson translation
             is demonstrated by James Duban, 'The Translation of Pierre
             Bayle's *An Historical and Critical Dictionary* Owned by Mel-
             ville,' *PBSA*, 71 (1977), 347–351.
41   62a   Bible. O. T. Psalms. English. 1796. The Psalms of David, with
             Hymns and Spiritual Songs, Having the proper Metre pre-
             fixed to each. Also, The Cathechism, Compendium, Confes-
             sion of Faith and Liturgy, of the Reformed Church in the
             Netherlands. For the Use of the Reformed Dutch Church in
             North-America. Albany, Charles R. and George Webster,
             1796.
             Stamped 'Maria Gansevoort' on front cover. (NL)
41   *In the cross-reference to* Blake, William *delete* '533' *and add* 520.
42   73a   Book [unidentified].
             'Herman Melville from his Aunt, Priscille [Priscilla] Melville,
             Boston, March, 1846.' The inscription, described as 'Signa-
             ture and two lines, apparently cut from a book, 1½ X 7½
             inches,' is quoted in Kenneth W. Rendell, Inc., Catalogue
             44; *Autograph Letters, Manuscripts & Documents* (62 Bristol
             Road, Somerville, Mass., January 1970), Lot 121.
42   75a   Book [unidentified].
             For No. 21a *read* No. 101a.
43   86.1 Braun, Emil. Handbook of the Ruins and Museums of Rome.
             A Guide for Travellers, Artists and Lovers of Antiquity. Bruns-
             wick, Frederick Vieweg; Rome, J. Spithöver, 1856.
             Probably acquired by Melville in Italy in 1857. Mrs Melville
             cited 'Brauns Handbook' along with No. 375 in her un-
             paged *Pocket Diary, 1866*, which is in BeA.
43   87a   Broughton, Thomas Duer. Selections from the Popular Poetry
             of the Hindoos. Arranged and Translated by Thomas Duer
             Broughton. London, Martin, 1814.
             'H Melville'. Marked. (CUL)
44   94a   Bunyan, John. Divine Emblems, or, Temporal Things Spiritu-
             alised, &c. With Preface by Alexander Smith . . . London,
             Bickers & Son, [186–].
             'H. Melville 1871 N.Y.' (NL)
45   101a Burritt, Elijah Hinsdale. Atlas, Designed to Illustrate the Ge-
             ography of the Heavens . . .
             Edition unidentified. According to Mrs Metcalf, in the Mel-
             ville household in New York there was a large atlas in paper
             covers, creased in the middle and kept with Chambers's *Cy-
             clopaedia* (No. 128 or No. 128b), containing colored plates of
             the constellations in soft colors; she did not recall the exact

title. The Perkins Observatory, Delaware, Ohio, has an edition of Burritt's *Atlas* (New York, F. J. Huntington, c. 1835) that fits Mrs Metcalf's description (letter from John M. J. Gretchko, 24 June 1978). See No. 75a.

45   107   [Byron, George Gordon Noël Byron, 6th Baron. The Complete Works . . .]

For Mott . . . 107 *read* NL.

47   121   [Carlyle, Thomas, tr. German Romance . . .]

Add: v. 1: Carlyle's Preface, Musæus ('Dumb Love,' 'Libussa,' 'Melechsala'), Fouqué ('Aslauga's Knight'), Tieck ('The Fair-Haired Eckbert,' 'The Trusty Eckart,' 'The Runenberg,' 'The Elves,' 'The Goblet'); v. 2: Hoffman ('The Golden Pot'), Richter ('Army-Chaplain Schmelzle's Journey to Flätz,' 'Life of Quintus Fixlein').

48   128b   Chambers's Encyclopaedia: A Dictionary of Useful Knowledge for the People. London, W. & R. Chambers, 1868. 10 v.

Possibly owned by Melville or his family; see No. 21a. Mrs Melville, among undated memoranda written over the years in an unpaged *Pocket Diary, 1866* (BeA), wrote: 'It is erroneously stated in Chambers' Encyclopedia that "in 1860 Herman M. left his farm and made a voyage round the world in a whaling vessel"'; *Chambers's* article on Melville (VI, 397), after giving the erroneous date of 1860 for the publication of *Israel Potter*, continues: 'when he left his farm in Massachusetts and embarked in a whaling vessel on a voyage round the world.' One American edition of *Chambers's* (Philadelphia, Lippincott, 1875 and 1891) mentions no such voyage; another (New York, Collier, 1886) reads: 'In 1860, he embarked in a whaling-vessel for a new tour round the world' (V, 321).

53   158.1   Cooper, James Fenimore. The Last of the Mohicans; a Narrative of 1757. By the Author of 'The Pioneers.' Philadelphia, H. C. Carey & I. Lea, 1826. 2 v.

V. 1: 'Augusta Melville'. Marked; clipping dated (1874) on flyleaf of v. 1. (NL)

55   178a   [De Grey, Thomas. The Complete Horse-Man . . . #]

Delete (Sold . . . unknown) *and add* (Dietrich).

58   197a   [Eagle Hill; or, Selections in Prose and Verse . . .]

For Sealts *read* BeA.

59   *Following No. 209, add this cross-reference*: Evening Hymn, The: see Burns, James Drummond, comp. (No. 99a)

60   218   [FitzGerald, Edward. Polonius . . .]

For Opposite the title-page . . . *read* On the title-page . . .

62   228   [Goethe . . . The Auto-Biography . . .]

For Murray *read* BeA.

62 231 [Goldsmith, Oliver. The Deserted Village . . .]
For Binnian *read* BCHS.
62 232 [Goldsmith, Oliver. The Vicar of Wakefield . . .]
For Sealts *read* BeA.
62 232a Goody Two Shoes. The History of Goody Two-Shoes. Embellished with Plates. To which is Added, The Fisherman's Son. New York, N. B. Holmes, 1826.
Laid in is note inscribed by the late Mrs Walter B. Binnian: 'This is very valuable for some Herman Melville collection'. Possibly a gift to Melville himself (b. 1819) as a child, or to one of his children. His first child, Malcolm, was born in February of 1849; there is an allusion to 'Goody Two Shoes' in Melville's 'Hawthorne and His Mosses,' published in August of 1850. (BCHS)
63 234b Grimm, Jakob Ludwig Karl. German Popular Stories, with Illustrations after the Original Designs of George Cruikshank. Edited by Edgar Taylor, with Introduction by John Ruskin. London, Hotten, 1868.
[In Melville's hand:] 'Miss Fanny Melville. Xmas. 1874. N.Y.' (BUL)
64 244 [Hawthorne, Julian. Nathaniel Hawthorne and His Wife . . .]
To imprint add 3rd ed.
64 245 [Hawthorne, Nathaniel. The Blithedale Romance . . .]
After st—' *add* ; 'Mrs Herman Melville' and a date(?) '—' erased from title-page.
69 283 [Hope, Thomas.] *For* The Costumes of the Ancients . . . *read* The Costume of the Ancients . . .
69 284 [Horne, Richard Henry. Exposition of the False Medium and Barriers excluding Men of Genius from the Public . . .]
Delete E. C. Stedman's . . . to Mrs Melville *and add* Present location unknown. Given to E. C. Stedman by Mrs Melville. According to a typed copy (CUL) of her letter of 4 Feb 1892 to Stedman (the original is said to be inserted in the volume), Melville had 'much prized the book (accidentally picked up at a book-stall)'. Mrs Melville's letter asked whether her late husband's 'surmise was correct in that the pencillings on the title page were by the author's own hand—and possibly the markings through the book—none of which were Mr. Melville's with a few exceptions in heavier lines.' Stedman's reply *continuing as before*
70 292a [Irving, Washington. Works . . .]
Add: NL has an identical copy of v. I only, inscribed 'Mrs Allan Melville from A. P. Lathers'.
77 346 [Maistre, Xavier, Comte de. A Journey round My Room . . .]
For Long *read* Simmons.

77   348   Marlowe, Christopher. *For* 'Plays'. *and* Edition unidentified.
            read The Dramatic Works . . . with Prefatory Remarks, Notes,
            Critical and Explanatory. By W. Oxberry. London, W. Simpkin,
            R. Marshall, C. Chapple, [1820?].
            'H. Melville London, December 1849.' *Continue as before,*
            adding Contains eight plays separately paged: *The Jew of*
            Malta (1818), *Edward the Second* (1818), *Dr. Faustus* (1818),
            Lust's Dominion (1818), *The Massacre of Paris* (1818), *Tambur-*
            laine, I and II (1820), *Dido Queen of Carthage* (n.d.). Anno-
            tated. (HCL)

78   356   [The Men of the Time . . .]
            For Sealts *read* HCL.

78   356a [Menken, Adah Isaacs. Infelicia . . .]
            Insert from p. 79 the item erroneously numbered 358a.

80   366   *Revise to read*: Montaigne, Michel Eyquem de. The Complete
            Works . . . Comprising; The Essays (Translated by [Charles]
            Cotton); The Letters; The Journey into Germany and Italy;
            Now First Translated; A Life, by the Editor . . . William Hazlitt
            [(1811–1893)]. London, John Templeman, 1842, *or* the 'Sec-
            ond Edition' [i.e., second impression], London, C. Temple-
            man, 1845.
            Delete Title and edition unidentified. *and at end of entry add*:
            Aretta J. Stevens, 'The Edition of Montaigne Read by Mel-
            ville,' *PBSA*, 62 (1968), 130–134, concludes that Melville
            bought either the 1842 or more likely the 1845 impression
            of Hazlitt's edition.

84   393   [Omar Khayyám. Rubáiyát of Omar Khayyám . . .]
            Delete Edition . . . text. *and substitute* On 15 Feb 1886, accord-
            ing to Mrs Melville, James Billson sent Melville a '"semi-
            manuscript" copy . . . translated by Fitzgerald'; this Melville
            acknowledged in his letter of 2 Apr 1886 to Billson as a
            'semi-manuscript "Omar"— . . . in that unique form' (cf. p.
            25 above). Billson himself, in a letter of 21 Aug 1935 to Prof
            Willard Thorp (NL), explained that his friend the poet
            James Thomson 'had Omar Khayyam in M.S. form in his
            own hand writing. At that time, there were no correct copies
            available here & I copied from his M.S. & lent it to the Book
            editor at the Secular Hall [at Leicester, England] who made
            a large number of copies which he sold at a trifling cost. It
            was one of these I sent to Melville.'

86   404b The Poetry of Love, from the Most Celebrated Authors, with
            Several Original Pieces. Selected by the Editor of "Poetry of
            the Affections." Philadelphia, Thomas Wardle, 1844. #
            'Fanny from Herman N.Y. June 1868'. (Current)

90   435a [Salt, Henry Stephens.] The Life of James Thomson ("B.V.")

with a Selection from His Letters and a Study of His Writings
. . . London, Reeves and Turner, 1889.

Arthur Stedman, in a letter to Salt of 4 May 1892 (NL),
stated that 'Mrs. Melville has given me the copy of the life of
James Thomson which her husband purchased before you
sent him one. He paid $3.75 for it at a time when he was a
very poor man.' Present location unknown.

90   436.1   Samuels, Samuel. From the Forecastle to the Cabin. New York,
Harper, 1887.

'For M^r. Herman Melville from his friends H & B [Harper
& Brothers?]. May 27, 1887.' (Sackman)

91   445   [Schopenhauer, Arthur. Religion: A Dialogue . . .]
Add to imprint: 2nd ed.

95   478   [Smith, Joseph Edward Adams. Taghconic . . .]
Add: Another copy, paperbound, is in NL, inscribed 'Augusta Melville, with the Love of Her Brother, John C. Hoadley, Pittsfield, April 23^d 1855–'.

98   496   [Taylor, John (1694–1761). The Scripture Doctrine of Original Sin . . .]
Following 1701 *in imprint, insert* [*sic*; i.e., 1740 or later ed.—
possibly 1741] *and add to the comment* T. Walter Herbert, 'Calvinism and Cosmic Evil in *Moby-Dick*,' *PMLA*, 84 (October
1969), 1613, n. 4, finds it 'almost certain' that Melville's copy
'contained the supplement to the first edition' of 1740 and
must therefore have been one of five later editions: 1741,
1746, 1750, 1767, or 1845. In a letter of 13 Nov 1967, noting that the edition of 1741 is described in the British Mu-
seum *Catalogue* as incorrectly dated '1761', he conjectured
that the compiler of the Goldsmith catalogue may have
made the further error of copying '1701' for '1761'.

102   532   *Revise to read*: United States Exploring Expedition, 1838–1842.
United States Exploring Expedition. During the Years 1838,
1839, 1840, 1841, 1842. Under the Command of Charles
Wilkes, U.S.N. . . . In Five Volumes, and an Atlas. Philadelphia, Lea & Blanchard, 1845. 6 v.

17 Apr 1847: '1 Wilkes U.S. Exploring Expedition 6 Vol^s
Sheep [$]21.00' (HCL-WP, 1 Jul 1847). Presumably the is-
sues numbered 2B or 3 plus the *Atlas*, 17B, in Daniel C.
Haskell, *The United States Exploring Expedition, 1838–1842,
and Its Publications, 1844–1874* (The New York Public Library, 1942), pp. 37–41, 46–47.[1]

---

[1]Haskell's 2B and 17B were 'unofficial' issues of a thousand copies each; the 'official'
issues printed for the use of Congress were of only a hundred copies (nos. 1, 17).
Commenting on differences between the respective issues, Haskell, pp. 21–22, notes

103 543a Walpole, Horace. Anecdotes of Painting in England. Reprint of the Edition of 1786. London, Alexander Murray, 1871.
'H. Melville Jan. 5, '72 N.Y.' Card enclosed: 'Miss Eleanor Melville Thomas 63 Montrose Avenue South Orange [N.J.]' inscribed 'I am sending one of Grandfather Melville's books, with warm Christmas greetings. The markings are his. E. M. T.' The recipient was Rev Samuel Hines Bishop: see p. 121 below, n. 5. (NL)

103 544 [Walpole, Horace . . . The Castle of Otranto . . .]
Delete No. 544 . . . n. 5.

104 [Wellington, Arthur Wellesley . . . The Words of Wellington . . .]
Correct 544 *to* 554.

106 563a Wordsworth, William. The Complete Poetical Works . . . Together With a Description of the Country of the Lakes in the North of England . . . Edited by Henry Reed. Philadelphia, James Kay, Jun. and Brother; Boston, James Munroe and Company; Pittsburgh, C. H. Kay & Co., 1839. Rebound.
Melville's signature on title page lost by trimming during rebinding. 'Pacific Ocean, Sep. 14th 1860 / 5°60″ N.L. / Gulf of Mexico ⟨Oct⟩ Nov 6th 1860 / Steamer "North Star"'. Annotated. (Woodstock)

106 187a [*In 'Addendum'*: Doddridge, Philip . . . Life of . . . James Gardiner . . .]
For [17–] *in imprint read* [after 1763]; *for* Seelye *read* NL.

These additions and changes will of course affect the listings in the "Analytical Index to the Check-List," pp. 109–115. On p. 121, note 5, "possibly No. 544" should now read "No. 543a." Note 88, p. 132, concerning books that Melville took with him on his voyage around Cape Horn in 1860, should also be revised to read "At least nine . . . 278, 439, and 563a."

---

that those classed as 'official' carry no publisher's imprint, that their original binding was dark green morocco while the unofficial issues 'were usually bound in black cloth,' and that 'the official issue does not assign a number to the atlas to Wilkes' *Narrative* while the unofficial does, calling it vol. 6.' A contemporary publication, Roorbach's *Bibliotheca Americana*, lists at $25 a 6-volume edition published by Lea & Blanchard.

Notes

The following short titles designate works frequently cited in these notes:

Billy Budd, Sailor (Chicago, 1962).   *Billy Budd, Sailor (An Inside Narrative)*.
By Herman Melville. Reading Text and Genetic Text, Edited from the
Manuscript with Introduction and Notes by Harrison Hayford and
Merton M. Sealts, Jr. Chicago: The University of Chicago Press, 1962.
Complete Stories.   *The Complete Stories of Herman Melville.* Edited, with an
introduction and notes, by Jay Leyda. New York: Random House,
1949.
Hendricks House Edition.   *Complete Works of Herman Melville.* Howard P.
Vincent, General Editor. Chicago and New York: Hendricks House,
1947–.
Published to date: *Collected Poems*, edited by Howard P. Vincent
(1947); *Piazza Tales*, edited by Egbert Oliver (1948); *Pierre, or, The
Ambiguities*, edited by Henry A. Murray (1949); *Moby-Dick, or, The
Whale*, edited by Luther S. Mansfield and Howard P. Vincent (1952);
The Confidence-Man: His Masquerade, edited by Elizabeth S. Foster
(1954); *Clarel: A Poem and Pilgrimage in the Holy Land*, edited by Wal-
ter E. Bezanson (1960); *Omoo: A Narrative of Adventures in the South
Seas*, edited by Harrison Hayford and Walter Blair (1969).
Letters.   *The Letters of Herman Melville.* Edited by Merrell R. Davis and Wil-
liam H. Gilman. New Haven: Yale University Press, 1960.
Log.   Jay Leyda, *The Melville Log: A Documentary Life of Herman Melville
1819–1891.* 2 vols. New York: Harcourt, Brace and Company, 1951;
reprinted, with a new supplementary chapter, New York: Gordian
Press, 1969.
Melville's Reading.   Merton M. Sealts, Jr., *Melville's Reading: A Check-List of
Books Owned and Borrowed.* Madison, Milwaukee, and London: The
University of Wisconsin Press, 1966.
Moby-Dick (New York, 1967).   Herman Melville, *Moby-Dick.* An Authorita-
tive Text, Reviews and Letters by Melville, Analogues and Sources,

Criticism. Edited by Harrison Hayford and Hershel Parker. New
York: W. W. Norton & Company Inc., 1967.
Northwestern-Newberry Edition.   *The Writings of Herman Melville.* Edited
by Harrison Hayford, Hershel Parker, and G. Thomas Tanselle.
Evanston and Chicago: Northwestern University Press and The New-
berry Library, 1968–.
Published to date: *Typee* (1968), *Omoo* (1969), *Redburn* (1969), *Mardi*
(1970), *Pierre* (1971).
Standard Edition.   *The Works of Herman Melville.* 16 vols. London: Con-
stable and Company, 1922–1924.

The World of Mind: Melville's Theory of Knowledge

1 In a marginal comment at this point Professor Williams wrote "interesting" and added "worth a special paper?" Out of our joint observations
grew the idea of a dissertation on Melville's reading in philosophy, which
in turn led to my further study of his reading in general.
2 Professor Williams circled the phrase "human nature" and in the margin
wrote "True?"
3 Professor Williams circled the word "plumbing" and in a subsequent conference chided me for using it. I let the phrase "profound plumbing"
stand here unchanged as a lamentable example for scholarly authors to
ponder.
4 Lewis Mumford, *Herman Melville* (New York: Harcourt, Brace & Company, 1929), p. 104.
5 Once again Professor Williams circled this word!

Herman Melville's "I and My Chimney"

Citations of Melville's works are to the Standard Edition.

1 In the Introduction to his edition of Melville's *Journal up the Straits, October
11, 1856–May 5, 1857* (New York: The Colophon, 1935), p. xii.
To Herman Melville's granddaughter, Mrs. Eleanor Melville Metcalf,
and to the Committee on Higher Degrees in the History of American
Civilization, Harvard University, I am indebted for permission to quote
from manuscript material as indicated below. This material, hitherto unpublished [as of 1941], is now in the Melville Collection of the Harvard
University Library. Mr. William Braswell of Purdue University has also
allowed me to quote from his unpublished dissertation, "Herman Melville
and Christianity." For these and other favors connected with the preparation of this article, I am grateful.

2 [Published anonymously in *Putnam's Monthly Magazine*, 7 (March 1856), 269–283; from a reference in George W. Curtis's editorial correspondence with Joshua A. Dix it is now known that the manuscript was in the editors' hands prior to 7 September 1855. Jay Leyda, *The Melville Log*, II, 504, suggests that Melville may have submitted it as early as mid-July of that year.—MMS, 1966.]

3 Raymond Weaver, *Herman Melville: Mariner and Mystic* (New York: George H. Doran Company, 1921), p. 308.

4 "I and My Chimney," in *Billy Budd and Other Prose Pieces* (vol. XIII in the Standard Edition).

5 Weaver, *Herman Melville*, pp. 308 ff.

6 John Freeman, *Herman Melville* (London: Macmillan & Co., 1926), p. 52.

7 Lewis Mumford, *Herman Melville* (New York: Harcourt, Brace & Company, 1929), p. 236.

8 Ibid., p. 238.

9 E. H. Eby, "Herman Melville's 'Tartarus of Maids,'" *Modern Language Quarterly*, 1 (March 1940), 95–100. Eby holds that here "Melville's main intention is to represent through the medium of the story the biological burdens imposed on women because they bear the children. This is conveyed by symbolism remarkably consistent and detailed" (p. 97).

10 Weaver prints this notation with the text of the story in the Standard Edition, p. 287. He is inaccurate in his accompanying statement that it is taken from the *manuscript* of the story, which has apparently not survived. Mrs. Melville made her notation on a printed copy of the story which, with clippings of other periodical pieces by her husband, she collected in a binder. [This volume, formerly in the possession of her granddaughter, the late Mrs. Henry K. Metcalf, is now in the Harvard College Library. What Mrs. Melville termed the "purely mythical" proposal to remove the chimney may have been suggested by alterations made at the nearby Broadhall in 1851 after Melville's friends the J. R. Morewoods bought the property from the family of his late uncle Thomas. As Mrs. Morewood explained in a letter of 7 November 1851 to George L. Duyckinck (Duyckinck Collection, New York Public Library), "a chimney had to come down" in order to allow enlargement of the dining room. J. E. A. Smith, *The History of Pittsfield, 1800–1876* (Springfield, Mass., 1876), p. 7, referring to the alterations at that time, mentions "removal of the broad chimney and the old-fashioned balustrade which surrounded the roof."—MMS, 1966.]

11 Apis was "supposed to be the image of the soul of Osiris. . . . He was also regarded as the reincarnation (or the son) of Ptah—except by Greek writers" (*Encyclopaedia Britannica*, 14th ed., II, 99).

12 Note the significance of other references to the pyramids: in a letter to Hawthorne written in 1851 as printed by Julian Hawthorne, *Nathaniel Hawthorne and His Wife*, 2 vols. (Boston, 1885), I, 405 ff.; a passage in "Bartleby the Scrivener," *Piazza Tales*, p. 64; the profound effect on Mel-

ville of the pyramids themselves, described in his *Journal up the Straits*, pp. 56–59.

13 For still another physiological connotation, cf. pp. 286 ff.: the "mysterious closet." This passage should be read in the light of Eby's article, cited above, and with reference to the chronology of Melville's family life in 1855. Those familiar with E. L. Grant Watson's article, "Melville's *Pierre*," *New England Quarterly*, 3 (April 1930), 195–234, should also compare the description of Pierre's chambers (*Pierre*, pp. 413 ff.), noting reference to "the dining room" there as in the present story (p. 292).

14 Compare the dedication of *Israel Potter* (dated 17 June 1854) to the Bunker Hill Monument.

15 The ensuing dispute over the ash-hole is a strange passage, dealing with the wife, the cat, and St. Dunstan's devil. Compare Isabel's mention of the cat in *Pierre*, "softly scratching for some hidden thing among the litter of the abandoned fire-places" (p. 163).

16 From an unpublished letter dated Albany, 15 January 1832, now in the Melville Collection of the Harvard University Library, printed with permission of Mrs. Eleanor Melville Metcalf and authorities of Harvard University. Peter Gansevoort had touched upon the matter five days earlier in a letter to Thomas Melvill, Jr., now in the Gansevoort-Lansing Collection of the New York Public Library: see Willard Thorp, *Herman Melville: Representative Selections* (New York: American Book Company, 1938), p. xii and note. [Relevant extracts from both letters were printed in 1951 by Jay Leyda (*Log*, I, 51).—MMS, 1981.]

17 Note the similarity in terms employed by Lewis Mumford, *Herman Melville*, pp. 220 ff.; E. L. Grant Watson, "Melville's *Pierre*," p. 201; George C. Homans, "The Dark Angel: The Tragedy of Herman Melville," *New England Quarterly*, 5 (October 1932), 723; William Braswell, "The Satirical Temper of Melville's *Pierre*," *American Literature*, 7 (January 1936), 431, note; Willard Thorp, *Herman Melville: Representative Selections*, p. lxxx.

18 Weaver prints a lengthy quotation from Mrs. Melville's pocket diary in his Introduction to Melville's *Journal up the Straits*, pp. xv ff. [In *The Early Lives of Melville* (1974), pp. 167–177, I have printed Mrs. Melville's surviving memoranda in their entirety.—MMS, 1981.]

19 William Braswell, "Herman Melville and Christianity" (Diss. University of Chicago 1934), p. 166 and note, quoted with permission of the author. [See William Braswell, *Melville's Religious Thought* (Durham, North Carolina: Duke University Press, 1943), p. 106.—MMS, 1966.] See also Weaver's discussion in his Introduction to Melville's *Journal up the Straits*, pp. xii–xxiv.

20 Concerning *Mardi* Mrs. Melville had written her stepmother: "I suppose by this time you are deep in the 'fogs' of 'Mardi'—if the mist ever does clear away, I should like to know what it reveals to *you* . . . "(from an unpublished letter dated New York, 30 April 1849, now in the Melville Collection of the Harvard University Library, printed with permission of Mrs.

Eleanor Melville Metcalf and authorities of Harvard University). Melville himself told Mrs. Hawthorne that she was "the only *woman*" who liked *Moby-Dick*, but that with her "spiritualizing nature" she could "see more things than other people" (from a letter dated New York, 8 January 1852, printed in part in "An Unpublished Letter from Herman Melville to Mrs. Hawthorne in Explanation of 'Moby-Dick.'" *American Art Association–Anderson Galleries Catalogue of Sale*, No. 3911, p. 9 [New York, 1931]). [In the Berkshire Athenaeum, as a bequest of the late Miss Agnes Morewood, granddaughter of Melville's brother Allan, is a copy of *Putnam's* for March 1856, inscribed "Allan Melville. Arrowhead— / Pittsfield / Mass. / (I and my chimney)"; there are question marks in the margins of the sketch on pages 269, 272, 277 (two), 280, and 283 and a check mark in the margin of page 280.—MMS, 1966.]

21 Compare "I and My Chimney," pp. 309 ff.
22 Introduction to *Journal up the Straits*, p. xvi. Note the reference to sciatica in "I and My Chimney," pp. 287 ff.; this may be of some value in confirming the suggested date of the story.
23 See a letter of Evert A. Duyckinck to his wife dated Pittsfield, 6 August 1850, printed by Luther S. Mansfield, "Glimpses of Herman Melville's Life in Pittsfield, 1850–1851," *American Literature*, 9 (March 1937), 29–31; M. B. Field, *Memories of Many Men and of Some Women* (New York, 1874), p. 202.
24 Robert S. Forsythe, reviewing Weaver's edition of *Journal up the Straits*, *American Literature*, 8 (March 1936), 85.

Melville and the Philosophers

Citations of Melville's works are to the Standard Edition.

1 See my "Melville's 'Neoplatonical Originals'" (1952), drawn from Chapter 5 of the dissertation, pp. 126–135.
2 "I and My Chimney," in *Billy Budd and Other Prose Pieces* (vol. XIII in the Standard Edition), p. 309. In 1942, when few of us recognized the aesthetic distance Melville maintained between himself and his narrators, I wrote "he" rather than "his narrator" as my sentence now properly reads.
3 The same thought is presented figuratively in *Moby-Dick*, I, 300, where Ishmael remarks that circumnavigating the globe conducts us only "to the very point whence we started."
4 "I and My Chimney," p. 289; *Billy Budd*, also in *Billy Budd and Other Prose Pieces*, p. 29.
5 In his copy of Matthew Arnold's *Essays in Criticism* (Boston, 1865), purchased in 1869, Melville marked a quotation from Joubert on "the failure of every system of metaphysics," underlining as follows: "Not one of them has succeeded; for the simple reason, that in every one *ciphers* have been

constantly used instead of *values*, artificial ideas instead of native ideas, jargon instead of idiom" (p. 215). In the preface by the translator, T. B. Saunders, of Schopenhauer's *Religion: A Dialogue* (London, 1890), Melville marked the statement that Schopenhauer's scheme of things "shares the common fate of all metaphysical systems in being unverifiable, and to that extent unprofitable" (p. viii).

6 Stanley Geist, *Herman Melville: The Tragic Vision and the Heroic Ideal* (Cambridge: Harvard University Press, 1939), p. 42.

7 Compare his contrast of the modern era with "old Greek times, before man's brain went into doting bondage, and bleached and beaten in Baconian fulling-mills, his four limbs lost their barbaric tan and beauty" (*Pierre*, p. 276).

8 "Hawthorne and His Mosses," in *Billy Budd and Other Prose Pieces*, p. 129.

9 See *Pierre*, Book XXII, Chapter iv, on Pierre at work on a book: "Is it creation, or destruction?" (p. 424).

The Records of Melville's Reading

1 I have revised the foregoing paragraph with respect both to current holdings of Melville's books and to the numbers of titles that have now been tabulated and located. The figures do not include those titles advertised by the Bodley Book Shop of New York City during the 1960's and 1970's; see my comment in *Melville's Reading* (1966), p. 123, note 15. What is described as "Melville's pencilled autograph" on the title page of one of the volumes in question is reproduced in *Emerson Society Quarterly*, No. 63 (Spring 1971), p. 49.

2 David K. Titus, "Herman Melville at the Albany Academy," *Melville Society Extracts*, No. 42 (May 1980), p. 1; see also pp. 4–10. Titus and John P. Runden (note 3 below) have recently extended and in some respects corrected the late William H. Gilman's pioneering study of Melville's formal education in his *Melville's Early Life and "Redburn"* (New York: New York University Press, 1951). Titus, an alumnus of the Academy and a professional librarian, presented his initial findings in "'Herman Melville, formerly a well-known author . . . ,'" *Albany Academy Alumni Quarterly*, 20 (May 1979), 10–11—an article brought to my attention by another alumnus, Professor Ricardo Quintana.

3 John P. Runden, "Columbia Grammar School: An Overlooked Year in the Lives of Gansevoort and Herman Melville," *Melville Society Extracts*, No. 46 (May 1981), pp. 1–3. Runden cites both a contemporary "Register of the Pupils of the Grammar School of Columbia College" and also McDonald Sullivan and Ross Dixon, *The Columbia Grammar School—1764–1964—A Historical Log* (1965), a publication previously overlooked by Melville scholars.

4 Titus, "Herman Melville at the Albany Academy," p. 6.

5 For examples, see three of the editorial notes that I contributed to the Hayford-Sealts edition of *Billy Budd, Sailor* (Chicago, 1962), pp. 139 ("*sinister dexterity*"), 143 ("*prior to Cain's city and citified man*"), and 165 ("*the reactionary bite of that serpent*," with particular attention to the derivation of "remorse"). In conversation with me, Gilman once objected to these comments on the ground that Melville knew no Latin.

6 Wilson L. Heflin, "New Light on Herman Melville's Cruise in the *Charles and Henry*," *Historic Nantucket*, 22 (October 1974), 6–27; the passage quoted here (p. 11) is followed by the list of titles as Professor Heflin has identified them (pp. 11–15). The entire article has been reprinted as a pamphlet by The Melville Society.

7 This information concerning the frigate United States, generously sent to me by Professor Heflin with letters of 9 December 1974 and 2 September 1978, is summarized with his kind permission. These two paragraphs on the ships Charles and Henry and United States first appeared in "A Second Supplementary Note to *Melville's Reading* (1966)," *Harvard Library Bulletin*, 27 (July 1979), 330–331.

8 It has recently been learned that among New York book stores Melville was seen from time to time in that of Albert L. Luyster at 138 Fulton Street between 1870 and 1875; see Frederick J. Kennedy, "Dr. Samuel Jones and Herman Melville," *Extracts / An Occasional Newsletter* (The Melville Society), No. 32 (November 1977), pp. 3–7. Kennedy quotes a letter of 7 January 1900 from Dr. Jones to Professor Archibald MacMechan recalling Melville as he had seen him at Luyster's store: "he was the quietest, meekest, modestest, retiringest man you can imagine. He moved from shelf to shelf so quietly—I never saw him speak to anyone—and his air was that of shrinking timidity: by no stretch of the imagination would one have thought him an author of any repute" (pp. 4–5).

9 See "The Library Call-Slips" in *Melville's Reading* (1966), pp. 117–120.

Toward the Whole Evidence on Melville as a Lecturer

1 *The Heart of Emerson's Journals*, ed. Bliss Perry (Boston and New York: Houghton Mifflin Company, 1909), p. 296.

2 "Melville and His Public: 1858," *American Notes and Queries*, 2 (August 1942), 70.

3 *The American Lyceum* (New York: Oxford University Press, 1956), p. 132.

4 *The Heart of Thoreau's Journals*, ed. Odell Shepard (Boston: Houghton Mifflin Company, 1927), pp. 311–312. Compare Vern Wagner's survey of "The Lecture Lyceum and the Problem of Controversy," *Journal of the History of Ideas*, 15 (January 1954), 119–135: however valuable the lyceum was in other ways, according to Wagner, it "was not the arena for serious and vital controversy" except during the single decade of the 1860's (p. 135).

5 Bode, *The American Lyceum*, pp. 218, 237.
6 "Melville and His Public: 1858," p. 67.
7 *Philological Quarterly*, 20 (January 1941), 57.

The Ghost of Major Melvill

Citations of Melville's "Jimmy Rose" are to its first printing in *Harper's New Monthly Magazine*, 11 (November 1855), 803–807; citations of other works are to *Complete Stories;* to the Hendricks House Edition; and to *Melville's Billy Budd*, ed. F. Barron Freeman (Cambridge: Harvard University Press, 1948).

1 The sketch, "John Marr," is reprinted in *Collected Poems*, pp. 159–164.
2 William H. Gilman, *Melville's Early Life and "Redburn"* (New York: New York University Press, 1951), p. 65. "Thomas Melvill, Jr., and most of his descendants continued to spell their name ... without the 'e,'" even though Herman Melville's mother and her children adopted the form "Melville" after the deaths of the senior Allan Melvill and Thomas Melvill, Sr., in 1832: see Melville's *Pierre*, Hendricks House Edition, note 1.10, pp. 429–430; Gilman, p. 309, note 74.
3 *The History of Pittsfield, (Berkshire County,) Massachusetts, from the Year 1800 to the Year 1876*, compiled and written under the general direction of a committee, by J. E. A. Smith (Springfield, Mass., 1876). A condensation of the opening paragraphs and extracts from the body of the memoir are printed on pp. 399–400 of the *History;* the complete text exists in an unpublished fair copy in an unknown hand consisting of ten pages of manuscript and a covering sheet inscribed "Sketch / of Major / Thos. Melvill Jr. / Copy" (now in the Gansevoort-Lansing Collection of the New York Public Library [Manuscripts and Archives Division]). Although Smith's own biographical sketch of Herman Melville (Pittsfield, 1897) states that the memoir was written "subsequent to 1871" (p. 19), there is an internal reference in the manuscript copy to the Melvill property at Pittsfield as "now 1870" belonging to John R. Morewood. The wording of the extracts in the printed text agrees substantially with that of the manuscript copy, which has been drawn upon in the quotations which follow for passages omitted in the published version.
4 In France Major Melvill had married Françoise Raymonde Marie des Douleurs Lamé Fleury, born in Cadiz in 1781, who bore him six children. The memoir does not mention the loss of two of them, Napoleon and Peter Francis, at the time of her own death in 1814.
5 Melville's memory for dates, as notoriously inaccurate as his spelling, led to several errors and omissions in the memoir. The manuscript copy incorrectly dates his Illinois visit (unmentioned in the published text) as taking place in 1841; contrast his "Trophies of Peace: Illinois in 1840" in *Collected Poems*, p. 266. The years of Major Melvill's birth and death are

left open in the manuscript copy; that of his death is incorrectly supplied as 1846 in the *History*. These and similar oversights (see note 7 below) suggest that Melville meant John Marr to have emigrated to the prairies in the same year as Major Melvill, 1837: in the later sketch he actually wrote "about the year 1838."

6 "I first saw him . . . in 1831, I think," Melville wrote in the memoir (the passage is omitted from the published text), "at evening, after a summer day's travel by stage from Albany." The occasion is noted in Allan Melvill's diary for 11 August 1831 (*Log*, I, 48). But in the memoir Melville "evidently forgot his first visit to Pittsfield in 1823," according to William H. Gilman, "when he probably saw his uncle" (*Melville's Early Life*, p. 308, note 57).

7 In 1834; both the manuscript copy and the published text of the memoir read "1836," though Gilman has demonstrated that Melville was otherwise occupied in that year (*Melville's Early Life*, p. 312, note 95). Gilman and Leyda (*Log*, I, 42, 63) agree in assigning his stay at Pittsfield to the summer and autumn of 1834.

8 Letter to Evert Duyckinck, Pittsfield, 16 August 1850, printed in *Herman Melville: Representative Selections*, ed. Willard Thorp (New York: American Book Company, 1938), pp. 379–381. The desk reappears in both "The Apple-Tree Table" (1856) and the second chapter of *The Confidence-Man* (1857).

9 Quoted from the manuscript copy; lacking in the published text.

10 Quoted from the manuscript copy; lacking in the published text.

11 Leyda, *Complete Stories*, p. 468, compares the location with that of "the second house in New York City occupied by the Melville family after Herman's birth," at 55 Courtland Street, where they lived until he was five years old.

12 The magazine text at this point (p. 805) reads "Persian roses," which in view of the context may have been written "Parisian roses" in Melville's manuscript. Persian roses, however, reappear in late works where rose-symbolism recurs: e.g., the prose sketch "Under the Rose" and the poem "The Rose Farmer."

13 In the manuscript copy of the memoir is a reference to Major Melvill's father (original of Holmes's "The Last Leaf") as a member "of the Boston Tea Party and an officer of the Revolution, with whose cocked hat and small-clothes, worn to the end of his life, passed away probably the last vestige in New England of the old costume."

14 Gilman, *Melville's Early Life*, pp. 65–67 and notes, pp. 312–313, discussing Major Melvill's financial difficulties, points out that he even served "several terms in jail for debt." In the memoir Melville himself speaks of his uncle's "enterprising and sanguine temper—too much so indeed," and cautions lest it "be inferred herefrom that the amiable side of my uncle's character partook of indolence. On the contrary he was of a very industrious and methodical turn of mind. Mighty folios of accounts, dating back to the days when he was commissary, with laborious diaries of the

farm, remain monuments to his diligence." (This passage was omitted from the published text.) Major Melvill's monetary troubles, which also involved his father and necessitated the intervention of Daniel Webster, are the subject of many of the family papers now in the Melville Collection of the Harvard College Library and the Shaw Collection of the Massachusetts Historical Society.

15 Portions of the prose sketches are somewhat inaccurately printed in *Billy Budd and Other Prose Pieces* (vol. XIII in the Standard Edition) from manuscripts now in the Harvard College Library. The references to this material which follow are based on a study of the manuscripts themselves in preparation for a new edition [Hendricks House] of Melville's late prose writings.

16 In "Jack Gentian's Decoration" the badge is compared favorably to that of the Knights of the Golden Fleece; the association recalls Melville's earlier description of the "Parisian-looking birds" in the chamber of the peacocks as "all rubies, diamonds, and Orders of the Golden Fleece."

17 R. R. Palmer, "Herman Melville et la Révolution Française," *Annales Historiques de la Révolution Française*, 26 (July–September 1954), 254–256.

18 This passage, omitted from the *History*, is quoted from the manuscript copy. It should perhaps be noted that Jimmy Rose in his late years "kept himself informed of European affairs and the last literature, foreign and domestic. And of this, when encouragement was given, he would largely talk. But encouragement was not always given" (p. 806).

19 *Herman Melville* (New York: Harcourt, Brace & Company, 1929), p. 259.

20 Leyda, *Complete Stories*, p. 467, has also nominated Major Melvill as a "likely" original of the elderly uncle in Melville's short story "The Happy Failure" (1854), where the failure of an invention "made a good old man" of the uncle and "a wise young one" of the narrator.

Melville's Burgundy Club Sketches

Citations of Melville's works are to the Hendricks House Edition; to the Standard Edition; and to *Melville's Billy Budd*, ed. F. Barron Freeman (Cambridge: Harvard University Press, 1948).

1 In *Poems* (vol. XVI in the Standard Edition), pp. 356–403, and later by Howard P. Vincent in *Collected Poems* (Hendricks House Edition), pp. 311–368.

2 Quoted from the manuscript—now forming, with the other Burgundy Club materials, part of the Melville Collection in the Harvard College Library. Raymond Weaver, in *Poems*, pp. 352–353, prints the entire prefatory note; Vincent, in *Collected Poems*, p. 484, combines it with other manuscripts as though all were part of a single "prose chapter."

3 In *Billy Budd and Other Prose Pieces* (vol. XIII in the Standard Edition), pp. 346–381, and *Poems*, p. 355 ("To M. de Grandvin," used by Weaver to introduce "At the Hostelry").

4 *Collected Poems*, p. 360.

5 Reproduced in facsimile by Jay Leyda, *Log*, II, 741. Vincent, in *Collected Poems*, pp. 483–484, quotes from the revised version of this title page that is discussed below; Weaver, in *Poems*, p. 351, prints the title page in its final form.

6 See notes to *Collected Poems*, pp. 476, 483.

7 Presumably by August, when Peter Gansevoort, his uncle, offered to subsidize its publication. Melville may have been finishing the manuscript when his wife, in a letter of 9 March 1875 to her step-mother (quoted in *Log*, II, 740–741), described him as "very busy . . . writing poetry"; if *Clarel* was already complete by March, however, the "poetry" may have been part of the projected "Parthenope."

8 Separately printed in *Billy Budd and Other Prose Pieces*, p. 381, as "Fragment."

9 *Melville's Billy Budd* (1948).

10 It may be significant that Melville's method of preparing the surviving manuscripts of this period is in accordance with the instructions to contributors published in the revived *Putnam's Magazine*, n.s. 2 (1868), viii: "to write on SMALL NOTE PAPER, (not on foolscap,)" so as to permit mailing "in a flat package rather than a roll." The issue for January 1868 quoted letters of acceptance from various "eminent writers" invited to contribute, Melville among them (*Log*, II, 694).

11 See Leon Howard, *Herman Melville: A Biography* (Berkeley and Los Angeles: University of California Press, 1951), pp. 321, 324.

12 *Herman Melville* (New York: Harcourt, Brace and Company, 1929), p. 337.

13 *Collected Poems*, p. 394.

14 "Inscription Epistolary" to *John Marr and Other Sailors* (1888); in *Collected Poems*, p. 468.

15 *Herman Melville*, p. 348.

16 *Herman Melville: A Critical Study* (New York: The Macmillan Company, 1949), p. 159.

17 John Thomas Gulick, visiting Melville at Pittsfield in 1859, had described Melville's own countenance as "slightly flushed with whiskey drinking" (*Log*, II, 605).

18 Toward which Melville had been unsympathetic at the time, on the evidence of his "Authentic Anecdotes of 'Old Zack,'" a series of humorous articles published in *Yankee Doodle* in 1847, and the later *Mardi* (1849).

19 *The History of Pittsfield, (Berkshire County,) Massachusetts, from the Year 1800 to the Year 1876*, ed. J. E. A. Smith (Springfield, Mass., 1876), pp. 399–400.

20 See Merton M. Sealts, Jr., "The Ghost of Major Melvill" (1957), reprinted above.

21 A reproduction of the portrait appears in Raymond Weaver, *Herman Melville: Mariner and Mystic* (New York: George H. Doran Company, 1921), facing p. 40.

22 *Herman Melville*, pp. 38–39.

23 *Pierre* (Hendricks House Edition), p. 437, note 11.19.

24 Freeman, *Melville's Billy Budd*, p. 243, notes 95, 96.

A Correspondence With Charles Olson

1 On 17 May 1947, Olson remarked that Roosevelt "comprehended ⌐the mass⌐ by way of body and intimacy with intimates, alone." Here and throughout, insertions are indicated by paired arrows (⌐ . . . ⌐); deletions are indicated by angle brackets (< . . . >).

2 Richard Chase had then published "An Approach to Melville," *Partisan Review*, 14 (May–June 1947), 285–294; "Dissent on *Billy Budd*," *ibid.*, 15 (November 1948), 1212–1218; and *Herman Melville: A Critical Study* (New York: The Macmillan Company, 1949).

3 Robert J. Bertholf, "Charles Olson and the Melville Society," *Extracts / An occasional newsletter* (The Melville Society), No. 10 (January 1972), p. 3. "Lear and Moby-Dick" was published in *Twice a Year*, 1 (Fall–Winter 1938), 165–189; see also note 15 below, on Matthiessen and Olson.

4 "David Young, David Old," *Western Review*, 14 (Fall 1949), 63–66.

5 "Letter for Melville" is included in *The Distances: Poems by Charles Olson* (New York: Grove Press, and London: Evergreen Books, 1960), pp. 46–54. For the identifications, see Bertholf, "Charles Olson and the Melville Society" (note 3 above).

6 Olson was thinking in particular of Wilson L. Heflin, "Melville's Third Whaler," *Modern Language Notes*, 64 (April 1949), 241–245; William H. Gilman, "Melville's Liverpool Trip," *ibid.*, 61 (December 1946), 543–547; Harrison Hayford, "Two New Letters of Herman Melville," *ELH, A Journal of English Literary History*, 11 (March 1944), 76–83; and Leon Howard, "Melville and Spenser—A Note on Criticism," *Modern Language Notes*, 46 (May 1931), 291–292. Olson's memory failed him with respect to Howard's article, which he recalled as "Scudder's job years ago on M's use of Spenser in the Encantadas"; H. H. Scudder wrote "Melville's *Benito Cereno* and Captain Delano's Voyages," *PMLA*, 43 (June 1928), 502–532.

7 *Modern Language Notes*, 67 (February 1952), 80–86.

8 See *Mardi*, Ch. 119: "divine Plato, and Proclus, and Verulam are of my counsel. . . ."

9 See *Moby-Dick*, Ch. 78: "How many, think ye, have likewise fallen into

Plato's honey head and sweetly perished there?"; *Pierre*, Book XIV, Ch. iii: "Bacon's brains were mere watch-maker's brains; but Christ was a chronometer. . . ."

10 Olson was thinking of Arvin's *Herman Melville* (New York: William Sloane Associates, 1950).

11 Olson applied the concept of "negative capability" to Melville in a later article, "Equal, That Is, to the Real Itself," *Chicago Review*, 12 (Summer 1958), 98–104. See also William V. Spanos, "Charles Olson and Negative Capability: A Phenomenological Interpretation," *Contemporary Literature*, 21 (Winter 1980), 38–80.

12 Professor George Butterick informed me in a letter of 17 February 1972 that two of Olson's poems in the *Maximus IV, V, VI* volume were written just before and just after the date of this letter, 18 February 1962. One is "from the 16th, the other dated the 22nd—both dry and factual, fixing the dates for the settlement of Dogtown before he writes the magnificent Gravelly Hill poem in March." As Professor Butterick remarked, "that season was a critical point in the poet's life—no money, bills due, the offer from Buffalo still to come."

13 Here, as on other occasions, Olson was thinking of E. H. Eby, "Herman Melville's 'Tartarus of Maids,'" *Modern Language Quarterly*, 1 (March 1940), 95–100.

14 Olson had treated Stern's book harshly in "Equal, That Is, to the Real Itself" in 1958 (note 11, above); ostensibly a review, the article is in fact a discussion of Melville's apprehension of reality.

15 In his "Lear and Moby-Dick" (1938), pp. 172–173, Olson had noted and transcribed "what seem to be rough jottings for *Moby-Dick*" in the last volume of Melville's set of Shakespeare, containing *King Lear, Hamlet,* and *Othello:*

> Ego non bapitzo te in nominee Patris et
> Filii et Spiritus Sancti—sed in nomine
> Diaboli.—Madness is undefinable—
> It & right reason extremes of one,
> —not the (black art) Goetic but Theurgic magic—
> seeks converse with the Intelligence, Power, the
> Angel

F. O. Matthiessen, *American Renaissance: Art and Expression in the Age of Emerson and Whitman* (New York: Oxford University Press, 1941), p. 457, note 6, quotes the same passage, reading the sixth word as "nomine"; Olson follows Matthiessen's reading in *Call Me Ishmael* (New York: Reynal & Hitchcock, 1947), p. 52, except that he does not capitalize "Madness" in the third line. In none of the three versions does either Olson or Matthiessen read "woe" for "one" at the end of the fourth line, and I am therefore unable to account for Olson's question in his letter.

Melville's "Geniality"

Citations of Melville's works are to *White-Jacket* (New York: United States Book Company, 1892); to *Moby-Dick, Pierre, The Confidence-Man, Clarel,* and *Collected Poems* in the Hendricks House Edition; to *Complete Stories;* and to *Billy Budd, Sailor* (Chicago, 1962).

1 The phrase is Newton Arvin's, applied to Melville in his Introduction to *Hawthorne's Short Stories* (New York: Alfred A. Knopf, 1946), p. xv.

2 R. E. Watters, "Melville's 'Sociality,'" *American Literature*, 17 (March 1945), 33–49; "Melville's 'Isolatoes,'" *PMLA*, 60 (December 1945), 1138–1148.

3 Edward H. Rosenberry, *Melville and the Comic Spirit* (Cambridge: Harvard University Press, 1955), p. 3.

4 As reprinted in *Collected Poems*, p. 161.

5 In this book alone are more than seventy occurrences of "genial" and its cognates, concentrated in thirteen of the forty-six chapters: 9–11, 13, 23–24, 27–31, 34, 36. For still other instances, see the related fragment "The River" and Melville's draft of projected chapter titles, both printed in the Hendricks House Edition of *The Confidence-Man*, pp. 380, 381.

6 *Melville and the Comic Spirit*, p. 53. I am particularly indebted to Mr. Rosenberry's treatment of the "gastronomic" comedy in *Mardi* and its predecessors, which goes far beyond the necessarily limited discussion here.

7 *White-Jacket*, Chs. 4, 91.

8 In "Benito Cereno" (1855) Captain Delano, "like most men of a good, blithe heart, . . . took to negroes, not philanthropically, but genially, just as other men to Newfoundland dogs" (*Complete Stories*, p. 307). In *The Confidence-Man*, Chapter 11, the bogus stock salesman holds Negroes to be "by nature a singularly cheerful race" who "even from religion" dismiss "all gloom" (p. 64).

9 *Moby-Dick*, Chs. 10, 30, 37, 93, 49.

10 *Pierre*, Bk. XX, Ch. 1.

11 Jimmy's misfortunes are somewhat like those of Charlemont in Chapter 34 of *The Confidence-Man*, except that the latter is ultimately restored to "genial friendships" (p. 209).

12 *The Critic*, as quoted by Elizabeth Foster in her invaluable Introduction to the Hendricks House edition, p. xxxv.

13 There is possibly a coda to this encounter. The stock salesman, taking a hint from the merchant's reference in Chapter 11 to "a shrunken old miser . . . stretched out, an invalid, on a bare plank in the emigrants' quarters" (p. 63), later visits this man, succors him with a glass of water, and before leaving his side extracts from him "ten hoarded eagles" for an unspecified investment (Ch. 15). The miser's flesh is described as "dry as combustibles" (p. 82); when he reappears, tottering, in Chapter 20, he is seen as "dried-up . . . , with the stature of a boy of twelve" (p. 114). Except for the implication that the miser has not previously left the emigrants'

cabin, one might infer from this studied phrasing that he is to be identified with the "little, dried-up man" seated in the cabin (p. 58) who had resisted the salesman's proffered wine and other blandishments. It is possible that at one point Melville intended some connection between the two figures.

14 Entitled "A Philanthropist Undertakes to Convert a Misanthrope, but Does Not Get Beyond Confuting Him." An earlier version of this title had called overt attention to their emblematic pipe and rifle: "The Philanthropist & Misanthrope. *The Rifle* & Pipe [*The Pipe* & Rifle?]." See p. 381.

15 The name he gives in Chapter 29, where the cosmopolitan identifies himself as Francis Goodman; both names are palpably false. Miss Foster terms Noble's middle name, "Arnold," a "visible tag of treachery" (p. lxxiii); "Charlie Noble," as Melville surely knew, is a sailor's term for the smoke-pipe of a ship's galley: see Leland P. Lovette, *Naval Customs, Traditions, and Usage* (Annapolis, Maryland, 1939), p. 222.

16 Compare what Melville had said of Jack Chase in Chapter 4 of *White-Jacket:* "No one could be better company . . . ; no man told such stories, sang such songs" (p. 16).

17 Melville's scornful rejection of the notion of "progress" runs through his correspondence of the mid-fifties and his subsequent lectures on "Statues in Rome" and "The South Seas." The latter embraces his familiar animadversions against his old target the missionaries; compare the satirical thrust at missionary "progress" in Chapter 7 of *The Confidence-Man*, where the man in the gray coat proposes to "quicken" Christian missions with the modern "Wall street spirit" and so convert the Chinese "*en masse* within six months" (pp. 45–46)! Elsewhere, the repeated linking of geniality with tippling, particularly in the cosmopolitan's story of the deacon's wife and her "jug of Santa Cruz" (p. 152), may involve hits at religious enthusiasts.

18 Like the "honest scholar" and "writer whom few know" of *Billy Budd, Sailor*, pp. 74, 114; other examples in Melville are cited in editorial discussion (note, p. 161). John C. Cawelti, "Some Notes on the Structure of *The Confidence-Man*," *American Literature*, 29 (November 1957), 278–288, also finds in the "parable of the wine-drinker" a clue to Melville's own position, with its characteristic recognition that "there are at least two opposing sides to everything" (p. 287). I am indebted here to this provocative discussion. But I do not concur in Mr. Cawelti's specific identification of the wine-drinker with the "genial misanthrope" of Chapter 30, since like Miss Foster I believe that Melville intended the phrase "genial misanthrope" to apply particularly to the cosmopolitan just as "surly philanthropist" in the same context clearly applies to his opposite number the Missourian.

19 Sealts, *Melville as Lecturer* (Cambridge: Harvard University Press, 1957), p. 182.

20 "Genial" in the sense of pleasant, warm, gay is applied variously to the

Greek climate and people (III.vi.87–88 and 111; compare "The Parthenon" in *Collected Poems*, p. 247), to Rolfe's heart (I.xxxi.14), to the spirits and heart of the liberal churchman Derwent (II.xxix.43, III.xvi.189–190), to the gestures of the wine-loving Arnaut (III.xi.150–151), and to the faith that Rolfe would instill in Clarel (IV.xxiii.76–77). Conversely, it is said that the apostate Margoth fixes "no genial glance" (II.xxix.103); and that events "overrode the genial part" of Ungar (IV.v.138–140), making him misanthropic. Modern religion, for Rolfe, has lost its "deity / So genial" (II.xxi.65–66); to Ungar, modern democracy lacks "free / And genial catholicity" (IV.xix.151–152).

21 See "Melville's Burgundy Club Sketches" (1958), reprinted above, which explores the relation of these pieces to the aspects of Melville under discussion here.

22 In, respectively, a manuscript fragment on Shakespeare among the Melville papers in the Harvard College Library and a letter of 1886 printed in *Letters*, p. 283.

23 Elsewhere, Melville characterizes the manner of the surgeon as "less genial than polite" (p. 124).

24 *Collected Poems*, p. 94. Melville applied his line to Shakespeare; of himself he once said that though "neither pessimist nor optomist [*sic*]," he "relished" pessimism in the poetry of Thomson "if for nothing else than as a counterpoise to the exhorbitant hopefulness, juvenile and shallow," of the time (*Letters*, p. 277).

Melville's Chimney, Reexamined

The books, articles, and reviews referred to in Parts ii, iii, and iv of this essay are listed here in the order in which they are mentioned.

1940–1955: William Braswell, *Melville's Religious Thought: An Essay in Interpretation* (Durham, N.C.: Duke University Press, 1943); William Ellery Sedgwick, *Herman Melville: The Tragedy of Mind* (Cambridge: Harvard University Press, 1945); Willard Thorp, review of Braswell, *American Literature*, 16 (November 1944), 240–243; Jay Leyda, ed., *The Complete Stories of Herman Melville* (New York: Random House, 1949); Richard Chase, *Herman Melville: A Critical Study* (New York: The Macmillan Company, 1949); Richard Chase, ed., *Selected Tales and Poems by Herman Melville* (New York: Rinehart & Co., 1950); Newton Arvin, "Melville and the Gothic Novel," *New England Quarterly*, 22 (March 1949), 33–48; Newton Arvin, *Herman Melville* (New York: William Sloan Associates, 1950); Geoffrey Stone, *Melville* (New York: Sheed and Ward, 1949); Jay Leyda, *The Melville Log: A Documentary Life of Herman Melville 1819–1891*, 2 vols. (New York: Harcourt, Brace and Company, 1951): Leon Howard, *Herman Melville: A Biography* (Berkeley and Los Angeles: University of California Press, 1951); Leon Howard, *Herman Melville*, University of Minnesota Pamphlets on American Writers, No. 13 (Minneapolis: University of Minnesota Press, 1961); Leon Howard, "Herman Melville," in *Eight American Writers: An Anthology of American Literature*, ed. Norman Foerster and Robert P. Falk (New York: W. W. Norton & Company, 1963); Leon Howard, "The Mystery of Melville's Short Stories," *Americana-Austriaca: Festschrift des Amerika-Instituts der Universität Innsbruck*, ed. Klaus Lanzinger (Wien IX-Stuttgart: Wilhelm Braumüller, 1966); Edward H. Rosenberry, *Melville and the Comic Spirit* (Cambridge: Harvard University Press, 1955).

1955–1965: Merlin Bowen, *The Long Encounter: Self and Experience in the Writings of Herman Melville* (Chicago: University of Chicago Press, 1960); Harry Levin, *The Power of Blackness: Hawthorne, Poe, Melville* (New York: Alfred A. Knopf, 1958); Leslie Fiedler, *Love and Death in the American Novel* (New York: Criterion Books, 1960); William G. Crowley, "Melville's Chimney," *Emerson Society Quarterly*, No. 14 (I Quarter 1959), pp. 2–6; E. Hale Chatfield, "Levels of Meaning in Melville's 'I and My Chimney,'" *American Imago*, 19 (Spring 1962), 163–169; Darwin T. Turner, "Smoke from Melville's Chimney," *CLA Journal*, 7 (December 1963), 107–113; Dorothee Metlitsky Finkelstein, *Melville's Orienda* (New Haven: Yale University Press, 1961); Stuart C. Woodruff, "Melville and His Chimney," *PMLA*, 65 (June 1960), 283–292; William J. Sowder, "Melville's 'I and My Chimney': A Southern Exposure," *Mississippi Quarterly*, 16 (Summer 1963), 128–145; William Bysshe Stein, "Melville's Chimney Chivy," *Emerson Society Quarterly*, No. 35 (II Quarter 1964), Pt. 3, pp. 63–65; Richard Harter Fogle, *Melville's Shorter Tales* (Norman: University of Oklahoma Press, 1960); Judith Slater, "The Domestic Adventurer in Melville's Tales," *American Literature*, 37 (November 1965), 267–279.

After 1965: Warner Berthoff, *The Example of Melville* (Princeton: Princeton University Press, 1962); A. W. Plumstead, "Bartleby: Melville's Venture into a New Genre," and Henry A. Murray, "Bartleby and I," in *Melville Annual 1965 / A Symposium: Bartleby the Scrivener*, ed. Howard P. Vincent (Kent, Ohio: Kent State University Press, 1966).

Alien to His Contemporaries: Melville's Last Years

1 Stephen Birmingham, *Life at the Dakota* (New York: Random House, 1980), p. 45, recording information from the Schirmers' granddaughter, Mrs. W. Rodman Fay of New York. Mrs. Fay also told Professor Donald Yannella in October of 1980 that the dinner "—which had taken place when she was about five—was common knowledge in the family and that no written record had survived if there ever had been one—no thank you note from Elizabeth or Herman, or any other documents. She had noth-

ing more to report than the information Mr. Birmingham had offered in *Life at the Dakota*." See Kathleen and Donald Yannella, "Dinner at the Dakota," *Melville Society Extracts*, No. 44 (November 1980), pp. 10–11; the Yannellas also report Birmingham's statement that he had not embroidered at all on the information given him by Mrs. Fay; in their words, "the only interpolation he had offered was the comment about Melville being 'charming but a little sad.'"

2 For (1) reproductions of Mrs. Ferris's essay and Mrs. Melville's letter, (2) a transcription of the letter, and (3) two associated articles that I have drawn upon here—Dorothy V. B. D. R. McNeilly, "The Melvilles and Mrs. Ferris," and an essay of my own, "Mary L. D. Ferris and the Melvilles"— see *Extracts: An Occasional Newsletter* (The Melville Society), No. 28 (November 1976), pp. 1–11.

3 Greenslet's vivid recollections of Melville deserve fuller notice, as several readers remarked to me at the time *The Early Lives* was published. In *Extracts*, No. 28 (November 1976), pp. 12–13, I provided a more generous quotation from Greenslet's letter of 22 November 1946 to Willard Thorp (Melville Collection, The Newberry Library; used with permission of the Library and the Ferris Greenslet Trust). Greenslet wrote that in the summer of 1886 or 1887, when a boy of about eleven or twelve, he had listened to "a singularly vital and impressive" man of about seventy who was spinning yarns in a barbershop in Glens Falls, New York. (It should be noted that Melville's cousin Stanwix Gansevoort, 1822–1901, was then a resident of Glens Falls.) The barber's customer announced that he had driven by buggy "some eight or nine miles" from Gansevoort, New York, "in a flat hour."

Clad in a blue double-breasted suit of a seagoing flavor, he was seventy-ish, with a lot of hair and a beard well grizzled, a vigorous body, "plump sphericity," a well tanned countenance, a bright and roving eye, all making up a singularly vital and impressive personality. I remember no one that I have met in the fifty odd years since more vividly.

The barber, "having apparently ministered to his patient before," then said to him, in Greenslet's account,

"Tell us some more about those adventures you had in the South Seas when you were a boy." Whereupon he began a flow of joyous narrative, which I did not identify with TYPEE until nearly half a century later.

The thing went on better and better until after my own job was finished, and I continued to listen spellbound. The climax came when the barber inquired:

"Weren't there any girls down there?"

"My God!" said the whiskerando, "I'll say there were! I went back to the island a couple of years after I left there on board a man-of-war and the first thing I saw when I went ashore was my own little son about a year and a half old running around naked in the sun on the beach."

"How did you know it was your son?" asked the barber.

"He had to be," said the story teller. "He carried his bowsprit to starboard!"

These, I assure you, were his *ipsissima verba*. On the surface of him at least there was every indication of a central *joie de vivre*, which is not without interest considering that just at that time he must have been writing, or at any rate thinking about, BILLY BUDD.

Henry A. Murray has told me that Greenslet, in giving him an independent account of this same well remembered incident, again emphasized that he had no idea until long afterward that the barber's loquacious customer was Herman Melville.

The Chronology of Melville's Short Fiction, 1853–1856

1 *Harper's New Monthly Magazine*, 8 (January 1854), 145.

2 Davis and Gilman tentatively date the letter "13 August [1854?]" (*Letters*, p. 171). In attempting to identify the "three articles" they cite three pieces which subsequently appeared in *Harper's:* "The Paradise of Bachelors and the Tartarus of Maids" (April 1855), "Jimmy Rose" (November 1855), and "The 'Gees" (March 1856). But the two-part article had already been paid for, as noted above, by 25 May 1854, and "Jimmy Rose" and "The 'Gees" appear to be the "brace of fowl—wild fowl" that Melville sent to Harper & Brothers "by Express" on 18 September [1854?] (*Letters*, p. 172). Thus the letter of 13 August clearly fits the circumstances of Melville's magazine writing of 1853 rather than his situation in the following year. He had evidently agreed by the early summer of 1853 to contribute to *Harper's:* according to his wife's stepmother, Hope Savage Shaw, writing confidentially on 27 July to Samuel H. Savage, "the Harpers have persuaded Herman to write for him [*i.e.*, them]; and he is admirably paid." (Mrs. Shaw's letter is quoted in Frederick J. Kennedy and Joyce Deveau Kennedy, "Additions to *The Melville Log*," *Extracts / An Occasional Newsletter* [The Melville Society], No. 31 [September 1977], p. 8.) Moreover, as Davis and Gilman acknowledge in their textual notes, p. 354, Melville's letter of 18 September (No. 115, now in the Pierpont Morgan Library) "is written on different paper [white] from that of the other letters to the Harpers" that they assign to 1854, all of which are on blue paper.

3 This letter (now in the Pierpont Morgan Library) is quoted in part by Davis and Gilman, *Letters*, p. 172, note 3; their conjectural date, "Sept 20 [1854?]," is obviously in error, since in March of 1854 George Palmer Putnam sold his magazine to Dix & Edwards and Briggs lost his editorship at that time.

4 Melville to Lemuel Shaw, 22 May 1856; see Patricia Barber, "Two New Melville Letters," *American Literature*, 49 (November 1977), 420.

5 *Letters*, p. 169, note 8.

6 Melville had probably composed Sketch Eighth, the longest of the ten sketches of "The Encantadas," before 24 November 1853, when he re-

ported to Harper & Brothers that his proposed book was "pretty well on towards completion." In "The Sources and Genesis of Melville's 'Norfolk Isle and the Chola Widow,'" *American Literature*, 50 (November 1978), 398–417, Robert Sattelmeyer and James Barbour have shown that his tale of Hunilla is based in part on one or more newspaper accounts of an Indian woman recently rescued from a Pacific island eighteen years after her abandonment there (p. 399). A front-page story of this "female Robinson Crusoe" appeared in the Albany *Evening Journal* for 3 November 1853; the Springfield, Massachusetts, *Republican* printed "a more complete but otherwise identical piece" on 22 November (p. 400).

7 *Journal of a Visit to London and the Continent by Herman Melville 1849–1850*, ed. Eleanor Melville Metcalf (Cambridge: Harvard University Press, 1948), p. 75 (entry for 18 December 1849).

8 See Catalogue 68 (1970), Paul C. Richards Autographs, Brookline, Massachusetts, Lot 1, for a full transcription of the letter and an accompanying facsimile reproduction. The letter itself is now in the Barrett Collection of The University of Virginia Library.

9 See the publisher's notes at the end of the first bound volume (I, January–June 1853, unpaged) and the beginning of the second (II, July–December 1853, [iii]).

10 Frank Luther Mott, *A History of American Magazines*, 5 vols. (New York: D. Appleton and Co., 1930; Cambridge: Harvard University Press and The Belknap Press of Harvard University Press, 1938–1957), II, 20, 116.

11 In 1943 William Charvat estimated that Melville received "a little over $725" in all for his magazine work of this period, or "an average of about $240 a year." See Charvat, "Melville's Income," *American Literature*, 15 (November 1943), 255; reprinted in *The Profession of Authorship in America, 1800–1870: The Papers of William Charvat*, ed. Matthew J. Bruccoli (Columbus: Ohio State University Press, 1968), p. 194.

12 See note 2 above.

13 See Carolyn L. Karcher, "Melville's 'The 'Gees': A Forgotten Satire on Scientific Racism," *American Quarterly*, 27 (October 1975), 421–442, "slightly expanded" in her *Shadow over the Promised Land: Slavery, Race, and Violence in Melville's America* (Baton Rouge and London: Louisiana State University Press, 1980), pp. 160–185.

14. Elizabeth Shaw Melville, "Herman Melville," in Merton M. Sealts, Jr., *The Early Lives of Melville: Nineteenth-Century Biographical Sketches and Their Authors* (Madison and London: University of Wisconsin Press, 1974), p. 169.

15 Elizabeth Foster, Introduction to *The Confidence-Man* (Hendricks House Edition), p. xxiii, notes that "Chapter 13, about one-fourth of the way through the book," was evidently written before 8 October 1855, and that Chapter 24 apparently alludes to a costume picnic given at Pittsfield early in September.

16 "Don't have the Harpers," Melville was to tell his brother Allan four years later, on 22 May 1860, when he wrote a memorandum "concerning the publication of my verses" (*Letters*, p. 198).

The Reception of Melville's Short Fiction

1 Melville to Lemuel Shaw, 22 May 1856, as printed in Patricia Barber, "Two New Melville Letters," *Ameican Literature*, 49 (November 1977), 421.

2 Hugh W. Hetherington, *Melville's Reviewers British and American, 1846–1891* (Chapel Hill: University of North Carolina Press, 1961), pp. 248–255, surveys the book's contemporary reception. Steve Mailloux and Hershel Parker, "Checklist of Melville Reviews" (The Melville Society, 1975), pp. 65–68, covers both earlier notices of the tales as they appeared in magazines and subsequent reviews of *The Piazza Tales*. See also Merton M. Sealts, Jr., "The Publication of Melville's *Piazza Tales*," *Modern Language Notes*, 59 (January 1944), 56–59, and G. Thomas Tanselle, "The Sales of Melville's Books," *Harvard Library Bulletin*, 17 (April 1969), 195–215.

3 See Richard Colles Johnson, "Melville in Anthologies," *American Book Collector*, 21 (Summer 1971), 7–8.

4 Arthur Stedman, "Melville of Marquesas," *Review of Reviews* (New York), 4 (November 1891), 428–430, as reprinted in Merton M. Sealts, Jr., *The Early Lives of Melville: Nineteenth-Century Biographical Sketches and Their Authors* (Madison and London: University of Wisconsin Press, 1974), p. 112.

5 *Atlantic Monthly*, 45 (June 1880), 858, as quoted in George Monteiro, " 'Bartleby the Scrivener' and Melville's Contemporary Reputation," *Studies in Bibliography*, 24 (1971), 196.

6 Curtis's reference to "Bartleby" had originally appeared in his "Sea from Shore," published in *Putnam's Monthly* for July 1854, after that magazine had carried Melville's story; the sketch was subsequently included in Curtis's collection *Prue and I* (1856 and nine later editions). Barton Levi St. Armand, "Curtis's 'Bartleby': An Unrecorded Melville Reference," *Publications of the Bibliographical Society of America*, 71 (1977), 220, remarks that Curtis's allusion and the illustration of 1892 (by Albert Edward Sterner) "must have puzzled many contemporary readers, who were [by 1892] as unfamiliar with the tale as they were with its once-popular author."

7 The quoted phrases are from James's "American Letters," *Literature* (London), 2 (11 June 1898), 676–677, as quoted in George Monteiro, "More on Herman Melville in the 1890's," *Extracts / An Occasional Newsletter* (The Melville Society), No. 30 (May 1977), p. 14.

8 In *The Early Lives of Melville*, p. 74, I have conjectured that Stedman might have preferred a new edition of *The Piazza Tales*—possibly enlarged to include other magazine pieces uncollected by Melville himself—to *Israel Potter*, which had been mentioned as a possible addition to the four volumes issued in 1892 by the United States Book Company: *Typee*, *Omoo*, *White-Jacket*, and *Moby-Dick*. The publisher's bankruptcy precluded the appearance of a fifth volume.

9 The steady proliferation of discussion since the 1940's is reflected in the chapters on Melville in successive editions of *Eight American Authors:* in the 1956 edition Stanley Williams was able to cover in two paragraphs the pioneering work on the short stories published up to that time; in the

revised edition of 1971 Nathalia Wright's tightly packed review of subsequent scholarship runs to nearly five full pages. In 1967, when Howard Vincent edited a symposium on "Bartleby, the Scrivener" for the Melville Society, a survey compiled for the volume by Donald Fiene listed 117 items bearing on that story alone which had appeared since 1856. That the accelerated interest of the 1960's in the short fiction has continued into the 1970's is evident from such annual surveys as the *MLA International Bibliography* and *American Literary Scholarship*.

10 As early as 1950, Joseph Schiffman was arguing, in "Critical Problems in Melville's 'Benito Cereno,'" *Modern Language Quarterly*, 11 (September 1950), 317–324, that "Melville betray[s] his sympathies" in the story: by depicting in Don Alexandro Aranda and Captain Amasa Delano "the short-sightedness of those who thought slavery was acceptable to other people, Melville was condemning slavery" (pp. 321–322).

11 "Melville's Chimney, Reexamined" (1969), reprinted above.

12 Professor Bickley's book is the outgrowth of his earlier doctoral dissertation, "Literary Influences and Techniques in Melville's Short Fiction: 1853–1856" (Duke University, 1969); see *Dissertation Abstracts International* (1970), 4935A.

13 *Melville's Quarrel with God* (Princeton: Princeton University Press, 1952), p. 3.

14 *The Profession of Authorship in America: The Papers of William Charvat*, ed. Matthew J. Bruccoli (Columbus: Ohio State University Press, 1968), p. 258. Two essays by Charvat are the most systematic studies to date of Melville's relation to the reading public of his day: "Melville," left in manuscript at Charvat's death and first published in this volume (pp. 204–261), and "Melville and the Common Reader," read before the English Institute in 1957, first published in the following year, and reprinted here (pp. 262–282).

15 An earlier version of her discussion of the magazine pieces was read before the Melville Society in December of 1973 and abstracted under the title of "Herman Melville and the Feminine Fifties" in *Extracts*, No. 17 (February 1974), p. 2. As early as 1971 Fisher was already referring to Melville as perhaps "the first major American writer to have written for an underground audience"; see his "Melville's 'Tartarus': The Deflowering of New England," *American Quarterly*, 23 (Spring 1971), 80, and its adaptation in *Going Under*, p. 72.

16 Fisher's name appears frequently in Dillingham's footnotes, which offer a running commentary on the body of interpretation that has grown up about the various stories; Dillingham has read and sometimes taken specific issue with the earlier articles that Fisher brought together in *Going Under*, but Bickley's book "appeared too late" for him to consider it in detail (p. 6, note 9). Dillingham's survey of previous criticism and scholarship, more comprehensive than the compilations of Bickley and Fisher, is one of the strengths of his book.

17 Robert Milder, "'Knowing' Melville," *ESQ: A Journal of the American Renaissance*, 24 (2nd Quarter 1978), 96–117; see note 37, p. 116.
18 Curtis to Joshua Dix, 7 September 1855, as quoted in Laura Wood Roper, "'Mr. Law' and *Putnam's Monthly:* A Note on a Phase in the Career of Frederick Law Olmsted," *American Literature*, 26 (March 1954), 92.

Melville and Emerson's Rainbow

Citations of Melville's works are to the five published volumes of the Northwestern-Newberry Edition; to *Moby-Dick* (New York, 1967); to *The Piazza Tales, The Confidence-Man, Clarel,* and *Collected Poems* in the Hendricks House Edition; and to *Billy Budd, Sailor* (Chicago, 1962). Citations of Emerson's writings are to *The Complete Works of Ralph Waldo Emerson,* ed. Edward Waldo Emerson, 12 vols. (Boston and New York: Houghton Mifflin Co., 1903–1904), abbreviated as "*W*"; to *The Journals and Miscellaneous Notebooks of Ralph Waldo Emerson,* ed. William H. Gilman et al. (Cambridge: The Belknap Press of Harvard University Press, 1960–), abbreviated as "*JMN*"; and to *The Letters of Ralph Waldo Emerson,* ed. Ralph L. Rusk, 6 vols. (New York: Columbia University Press, 1939), abbreviated "*L*."

1 "An Illustrated Criticism," carried under "City Items" in the New York *Tribune*, Tuesday, 6 February 1849, p. 2, col. 5 (see *ESQ*, 26 [1980], 54–55). The Boston *Daily Evening Transcript* for Thursday, 8 February 1849, p. 2, col. 2, reproduced the entire item, including the illustrations, with a prefatory explanation: "The Boston Post contained the other day a very fanciful critique upon Mr Ralph Waldo Emerson as a lecturer; and the New York Tribune of Monday [*sic*] happily hits off the article in a parody, followed by some clever wood cut illustrations. . . . We copy the article and the accompanying engravings, as there has been considerable inquiry for the latter among the curious." I am indebted to Nolan Smith for calling my attention to the article in the *Transcript*, which in turn led me to that in the *Tribune*.
2 See Brian Higgins, *Herman Melville: An Annotated Bibliography*, vol. I: 1846–1930 (Boston: G. K. Hall & Co., 1979), pp. 47 (B34), 41 (B3), 51 (B58).
3 See Hershel Parker and Harrison Hayford, eds., *Moby-Dick as Doubloon: Essays and Extracts (1851–1970)* (New York: W. W. Norton & Company, 1970), p. 51. "We do not like to see . . . the most sacred associations of life violated and defaced," the pious Duyckinck went on to say.
4 On Fitz-James O'Brien's terms "philosophy and fantasy" as "code words, among nineteenth-century critics and the Melville family alike, for all the otherwise undefined tendencies in *Mardi* and its successors that made them different from *Typee* and *Omoo*," see Merton M. Sealts, Jr., *The Early*

Lives of Melville: Nineteenth-Century Biographical Sketches and Their Authors (Madison and London: University of Wisconsin Press, 1974), pp. 75–77.

5 Perry Miller, "Melville and Transcendentalism," in *Moby-Dick Centennial Essays*, ed. Tyrus Hillway and Luther S. Mansfield (Dallas: Southern Methodist University Press, 1953), p. 146, and Introduction to *The Golden Age of American Literature* (New York: George Braziller, 1959), p. 12.

6 Nina Baym, "Melville's Quarrel with Fiction," *PMLA*, 94 (October 1979), 915.

7 Philip D. Beidler, "*Billy Budd:* Melville's Valedictory to Emerson," *ESQ: A Journal of the American Renaissance*, 24 (4th Quarter 1978), 227, note 12; 222.

8 Walter Harding, *Emerson's Library* (Charlottesville: The University Press of Virginia, 1967), p. 189.

9 William Braswell, "Melville as a Critic of Emerson," *American Literature*, 9 (November 1937), 317–334, gives a full report of Melville's numerous markings and annotations.

10 "Melville and Transcendentalism," p. 146.

11 See *Emerson's "Nature": Origin, Growth, Meaning*, ed. Merton M. Sealts, Jr., and Alfred R. Ferguson, 2nd ed., enlarged (Carbondale and Edwardsville: Southern Illinois University Press, 1979), p. 66 and note.

12 All four titles appear in the inventory of Duyckinck's library made after his death by the Lenox Library and now available at The New York Public Library; see *Lenox Library Short-Title Lists*, VIII, 20, and XII, 33. Duyckinck while an editor with Wiley & Putnam had written Emerson in 1845 seeking contributions to the firm's Library of Choice Reading and Library of American Books; in 1846 Emerson asked him to consider publishing the manuscript of Thoreau's *A Week on the Concord and Merrimack Rivers*, which the firm declined. By 1851–1852, if not earlier, Emerson was reading Duyckinck's *Literary World;* see *L*, III, 296–297, 301–302, 307–308, 384; IV, 267–268, 289.

13 George Haven Putnam, *George Palmer Putnam: A Memoir* (New York and London: G. P. Putnam's Sons, 1912), p. 125. Putnam imported at least one English book for Melville, in 1850; see Merton M. Sealts, Jr., *Melville's Reading: A Check-List of Books Owned and Borrowed* (Madison, Milwaukee, and London: University of Wisconsin Press, 1966), pp. 39–40: No. 52. In 1853–1855 Putnam and Melville corresponded concerning Melville's contributions to *Putnam's Monthly Magazine*, which began publication in 1853.

14 F. B. Sanborn and William T. Harris, *A. Bronson Alcott: His Life and Philosophy*, 2 vols. (1893; reprinted, New York: Biblo and Tannen, 1965), I, 300, note; Ralph L. Rusk, *The Life of Ralph Waldo Emerson* (New York: Charles Scribner's Sons, 1949), p. 54.

15 Frederick Hathaway Chase, *Lemuel Shaw* (Boston and New York: Houghton Mifflin Co., 1918), pp. 313–316. It was probably Shaw's second wife, Hope Savage Shaw, stepmother of Elizabeth Shaw Melville, who placed Lemuel Shaw, Jr., in Bronson Alcott's ill-fated Temple School during the

mid-1830's. Sanborn and Harris, who mention young Shaw as one of Alcott's students, remark also (in the note cited above) that Mrs. Shaw was a friend and distant kinswoman of Mrs. Alcott.

16 *Melville's Reading*, pp. 48–49: No. 120.

17 Merrell R. Davis, *Melville's "Mardi": A Chartless Voyage* (New Haven: Yale University Press, 1952), p. 179. Elsewhere Davis notes that Babbalanja's argument against an innate moral sense takes issue with a position held by Emerson and others (p. 181, note 4), and that Emerson's poem "The Sphynx" affords an appropriate commentary on the meaning of *Mardi* (p. 199).

18 Maxine Moore, *That Lonely Game: Melville, "Mardi," and the Almanac* (Columbia: University of Missouri Press, 1975), p. 174 and note. She also observes another minor parallel: in Chapter 67, island chiefs at the court of King Peepi retire from the king's presence "with their heads between their thighs. . . . All objects look well through an arch" (pp. 202–203); in *Nature*, Chapter 6, Emerson tells his reader to shift perspective "by looking at the landscape through your legs" (*W*, I, 51).

19 Barbara Ruth Nieweg Blansett, "Melville and Emersonian Transcendentalism," Diss. University of Texas 1963, Chapter 3, pp. 39–66. Mrs. Blansett nowhere claims that Melville "drew his ideas *direct* from Emerson at the time he wrote *Mardi*," recognizing that "there is not sufficient evidence available as to his reading in this period to warrant such a conclusion. He had, however, been reading many of the same works that had been read earlier by Emerson, and whether he arrived at his like conclusions independently, or whether he paraphrased them from Emerson is not really of vital concern" in her study (p. 40).

20 Melville does not name Emerson in *Mardi* but in Chapter 119, "Dreams," Taji declares that "Plato, and Proclus, and Verulam [Francis Bacon] are of my counsel" (p. 367); on Melville's use of Proclus in both *Mardi* and *The Confidence-Man*, see Merton M. Sealts, Jr., "Melville's 'Neoplatonical Originals,'" *Modern Language Notes*, 67 (February 1952), 80–86. "With Babbalanja's 'all-embracing deific; whereby we mortals become part and parcel of the gods' [*Mardi*, p. 561], may be compared the famous passage in Part I of Emerson's *Nature*: 'The currents of the Universal Being circulate through me; I am part or parcel of God' [*W*, I, 10]" (p. 82, note 5).

21 He had returned to finish reading the last proofs of *Mardi*, which was then in press, but was in Boston again on 30 January. On the evening of 12 February, when Emerson concluded his course, Melville attended one of Fanny Kemble Butler's readings.

22 Emerson had found such summaries especially annoying while he was lecturing in England and Scotland; in 1851 he complained to Duyckinck that reports of his recent lectures in Boston were copied by New York papers before he could repeat them there (*L*, IV, 267–268). Since there were no summaries of the "Mind and Manners" series of 1849 in the Boston papers, it is possible that a request not to summarize accompanied the

complimentary tickets of admission he provided for five of them. See *JMN*, XI, 68.

23 Professor Williams in letters of 27 October and 9 November 1979 generously summarized his research on the sequence of lectures in the "Mind and Manners" series and commented on the two manuscripts. The six lectures of the course as given in London were reported at some length in *Douglas Jerrold's Newspaper*, which identified the last three as "Politics and Socialism," "Poetry and Eloquence" (a version of which Emerson had read in Boston in 1847, when the Boston *Journal* printed a long summary), and "Natural Aristocracy." In October of 1848 Emerson listed seven possible lectures for an American course to include the group of three that he called "Natural History of the Intellect" plus "The Superlative," "Reading," "Natural Aristocracy," and "Spirit of the Age" (*JMN*, XI, 18). "Reading" and "Spirit of the Age" include material that Emerson read at other times in Boston; both "Natural Aristocracy" and "The Superlative"—the latter read as an extra lecture following Emerson's Portman Square series in London—qualify as "London Lectures," the term he applied in a letter of 3 February 1849 to the Boston version of the "Mind and Manners" course (*L*, IV, 132). For the two essays essentially as Cabot prepared them, see *W*, X, 29–66 ("Aristocracy," with further changes), and 161–179 ("The Superlative").

24 "Melville and Transcendentalism," pp. 142–143.

25 This sentence has been variously interpreted. Heyward Ehrlich, "A Note on Melville's 'Men who *Dive*,'" *Bulletin of the New York Public Library*, 69 (December 1965), 661–664, quotes a letter from Evert Duyckinck to his brother George, 4 March 1839, explaining that "Duycking" in the family coat of arms "means *diving*—that is to say seeking the hidden pearls of truth." Ehrlich, assuming that Melville is punning on the name "Duyckinck," argues that Duyckinck rather than Emerson is the man who dives. I agree that Melville, with his own knowledge of things Dutch from his Gansevoort family background, is punning on the name, as he would do again in *Pierre*. But I do not see that in the letter he is commenting solely on *either* Emerson or Duyckinck, since he refers to "*all* men who *dive*." "I'm not talking of Mr Emerson now," he continues in the letter, "but of the *whole corps* of thought-divers"—not excluding Herman Melville himself.

26 "The Old Manse," in *Mosses from an Old Manse* (Columbus: Ohio State University Press, 1974), pp. 31–32: "Never was a poor little country village infested with such a variety of queer, strangely dressed, oddly behaved mortals" who "were simply bores of a very intense water."

27 For the quoted phrases, see Braswell, "Melville as a Critic of Emerson," pp. 320, 322, 325, 321, 320–321 (emphasis added).

28 *Melville's Reading*, p. 101: No. 524.

29 See S. A. Cowan, "In Praise of Self-Reliance: The Role of Bulkington in *Moby-Dick*," *American Literature*, 38 (January 1967), 547–556. Cowan's ar-

ticle is directed at critics who see Melville's response to Emerson and Transcendentalism as preponderantly negative.

30 "Melville and Transcendentalism," p. 132.

31 *Mosses from an Old Manse*, 2 vols. in one (New York: Wiley & Putnam, 1846), I, 3; this is the edition owned and marked by Melville. See *Melville's Reading*, p. 65: No. 248.

32 "Hawthorne and His Mosses," in *The Norton Anthology of American Literature*, ed. Ronald Gottesman et al., 2 vols. (New York and London: W. W. Norton & Company, 1979), I, 2058 (emphasis added). Pending publication of vol. IX of the Northwestern-Newberry Edition of Melville, the Norton text of "Hawthorne and His Mosses," prepared by Hershel Parker, is the best version available.

33 *Nature* (Boston: James Munroe and Company, 1836), pp. 21–22: "Give me health and a day, and I will make the pomp of emperors ridiculous. The dawn is my Assyria; the sun-set and moon-rise my Paphos, and unimaginable realms of faerie; broad noon shall be my England of the senses and the understanding; the night shall be my Germany of mystic philosophy and dreams."

34 "Hawthorne and His Mosses," in *The Norton Anthology*, I, 2063. The passage, which occurs on Leaf 15 of the manuscript (now in the Duyckinck Collection, Manuscripts and Archives Division, The New York Public Library), is heavily revised; the eight names are lined out in favor of substitute phrasing inscribed in Evert Duyckinck's hand: "but even were there no strong literary individualities among us, as there are some dozen at least." Melville's cancelled wording will be restored in the Northwestern-Newberry text as well as in the Norton.

35 For the quoted phrases from "Hawthorne and His Mosses," see pp. 2065, 2059, 2062.

36 On Melville's purchase of *Biographia Literaria*, see *Melville's Reading*, p. 52: No. 154. He also knew something of both Coleridge's poetry and Wordsworth's: see his reference to "The Ancient Mariner" in a note to Chapter 42 of *Moby-Dick*, "The Whiteness of the Whale" (p. 165), and to Wordsworth in Chapter 11 of *White-Jacket* (p. 40); Thomas F. Heffernan, "Melville and Wordsworth," *American Literature*, 49 (November 1977), 338–351.

37 On Melville's possible use of Norton, see Thomas Vargish, "Gnostic *Mythos* in *Moby-Dick*," *PMLA*, 81 (June 1966), 272–277. He also read about the Gnostics in Pierre Bayle's *Historical and Critical Dictionary*, which he bought in Boston in March or April of 1849; see *Melville's Reading*, p. 39: No. 51, and "Melville and the Platonic Tradition," pp. 298, 308 below.

38 *Journal of a Visit to London and the Continent by Herman Melville 1849–1850*, ed. Eleanor Melville Metcalf (Cambridge: Harvard University Press, 1948), p. 5.

39 *Melville's Reading*, p. 62: No. 228. Melville's interest in Goethe was perhaps stimulated by his conversations on shipboard with Adler, who sent him a

382 Notes to pp. 268-269

translation of *Iphigenia in Tauris* early in 1851 (No. 229). If Melville read "Goethe; or, The Writer" in *Representative Men* at some time in 1850, as there is reason to believe he did, it is possible that reading Emerson's discussion of *Wilhelm Meister* (*W*, IV, 227–280) led him to borrow Goethe's novel (No. 230) from Duyckinck in the late summer of that year.

40 *Melville's Reading*, pp. 47–48: Nos. 121–123. Melville first borrowed *Sartor Resartus* and *On Heroes, Hero-Worship, and the Heroic in History*, probably in June or July, and then Carlyle's translations of *German Romance*, probably in August or September.

41 For the quoted phrases, see Thomas Carlyle, *Sartor Resartus*, ed. William Savage Johnson (Boston: Houghton Mifflin Company, 1924), pp. 51 and 39. Julie Ann Braun has studied "Melville's Use of Carlyle's *Sartor Resartus*: 1846–1857" (Diss. University of California at Los Angeles 1967). Morse Peckham, arguing that in *Moby-Dick* "the various styles are derived from various stages of Romanticism, just as the ideas are," discusses relations between the book and Emersonian Transcendentalism, the poetry of Wordsworth, and particularly "The Rime of the Ancient Mariner" and *Sartor Resartus;* see his "Hawthorne and Melville as European Authors," in *Melville and Hawthorne in the Berkshires: A Symposium*, ed. Howard P. Vincent (Kent, Ohio: Kent State University Press, 1968), pp. 58–60.

42 Introduction to *Moby-Dick or, The Whale* (New York: The Modern Library, 1950), p. xiii.

43 On the contrast between Ahab's view of nature and Emerson's, see E. J. Rose, "Melville, Emerson, and the Sphynx," *New England Quarterly*, 36 (June 1963), 249–258.

44 Eleanor Melville Metcalf, *Herman Melville: Cycle and Epicycle* (Cambridge: Harvard University Press, 1953), p. 91; *Log*, II, 925. The "boudoir," according to Rose Hawthorne Lathrop, *Memories of Hawthorne* (Boston and New York: Houghton, Mifflin and Co., 1897), p. 185, was a small sitting room on the first floor of the cottage overlooking lake, meadow, and mountains and furnished with pictures and bookshelves; the "beautiful picture" was an engraving of Raphael's *Transfiguration* that Emerson and Elizabeth Hoar had given Mrs. Hawthorne before her marriage. At Lenox, the engraving first hung "over the ottoman" in the drawing room, as Mrs. Hawthorne told her mother in a letter of 23 June 1850; see Julian Hawthorne, *Nathaniel Hawthorne and His Wife*, 2 vols. (Boston: James R. Osgood and Company, 1884), I, 368. When Melville and Evert Duyckinck visited the Hawthornes on 8 August 1850, it had evidently been moved to the "boudoir"; see Duyckinck's letter to his wife, 9 August 1850, in Luther Stearns Mansfield, "Glimpses of Herman Melville's Life in Pittsfield, 1850–1851: Some Unpublished Letters of Evert A. Duyckinck," *American Literature*, 9 (March 1937), 34.

45 "The Old Manse," in *Mosses from an Old Manse* (Columbus: Ohio State University Press, 1974), p. 31.

46 Leyda, *Log*, II, 924–925, dates the visit as "September 5–6."

47 Emerson sent presentation copies of *Nature* and the 1841 *Essays* to Sophia

Peabody (*JMN*, V, 263; VII, 546). To Hawthorne he sent *Essays: Second Series, Poems, Nature, Addresses, and Lectures*, and *Representative Men* (*JMN*, IX, 129, 456; XI, 156, 189).

48 Melville probably read what the *Literary World* said about the two books during his absence. In reviewing *Nature, Addresses, and Lectures* (V, No. 144 [3 November 1849], 374–376) Duyckinck contrasted Emersonian self-reliance with Christian self-renunciation, mentioning in conclusion his "horror" at Emerson's "irreverent blasphemy, his cool, patronizing way of speaking" of Christ. The review of *Representative Men* (VI, No. 158 [9 February 1850], 123–124), which consists largely of extracts from the book, calls it "Mr. Emerson's best work," but objects that Emersonian self-reliance, "this stoicism of the nineteenth century," leads ultimately to "moral indifference." In his later review of *Moby-Dick*, it will be recalled, Duyckinck deplored traces in Ishmael of "the conceited indifferentism of Emerson."

49 Here Melville writes of the "fastidious" feeling which an aristocrat may develop, "similar to that which, in an English Howard, conveys *a torpedo-fish thrill* at the slightest contact with a social plebeian" (*Letters*, p. 126; emphasis added); there are comparable passages in Melville's *Clarel*, I.xxiii.78–80, and *Billy Budd, Sailor*, p. 98. Emerson declares in his chapter on "Napoleon" that Napoleon's "absorbing egotism was deadly to all other men. It resembled the torpedo, which inflicts a succession of shocks on any one who takes hold of it . . . until he paralyzes and kills his victim" (*W*, IV, 257–258). Emerson probably derived the figure in turn from the *Meno* of Plato, a work that Melville knew also (see "Melville and the Platonic Tradition," pp. 326–327 and 335 below). In Plato's dialogue Meno compares Socrates with "that broad sea-fish, called the torpedo; for that too produces a numbness in the person whoever approaches and touches it." See the Bohn edition of *The Works of Plato*, 6 vols., first published in 1848–1854, III, 18; this is the edition Melville alludes to in *Billy Budd, Sailor*, p. 75.

At least one passage of *Moby-Dick* obviously echoes *Representative Men*. In Chapter 80, "The Nut," Melville refers to the "German conceit, that the vertebræ are absolutely undeveloped skulls" (p. 294); Goethe, according to Emerson, "assumed that one vertebra of the spine might be considered as the unit of the skeleton: the head was only the uttermost vertebræ transformed" (*W*, IV, 275). Further parallels between *Representative Men* and Melville's later writings are discussed below, and other apparent echoes of Emerson essays are also noted in "Melville and the Platonic Tradition," pp. 316–317 and 317–319 below and note 57, p. 393.

50 James Duban, "The Spenserian Maze of Melville's *Pierre*," *ESQ*, 23 (4th Quarter 1977), 217–225—especially pp. 221–222; Marvin Fisher, "Focus on Melville's 'The Two Temples': The Denigration of the American Dream," in *American Dreams, American Nightmares*, ed. David Madden (Carbondale and Edwardsville: Southern Illinois University Press, 1970), pp. 76–86, and *Going Under: Melville's Short Fiction and the American 1850s* (Ba-

ton Rouge and London: Louisiana State University Press, 1977), pp. 51–61; Beryl Rowland, "Melville Answers the Theologians: The Ladder of Charity in 'The Two Temples,'" *Mosaic*, 7 (Summer 1974), 1–13, especially pp. 7–10.

51 Christopher Sten, "Bartleby the Transcendentalist: Melville's Dead Letter to Emerson," *Modern Language Quarterly*, 35 (March 1974), 30–44.

52 With "The Transcendentalist," *W*, I, 339–340, on Locke and Kant, compare *Moby-Dick*, Chapter 73, where the Pequod is laboring under the double burden of a sperm whale's head ("Locke's," says Ishmael) and a right whale's ("Kant's") hanging from her sides. See "Melville and the Platonic Tradition," pp. 317–319 below.

53 "The Transcendentalist," *W*, I, 358; *Pierre*, pp. 210–215. "Bacon's brains were mere watch-maker's brains," according to Plinlimmon; "but Christ was a chronometer" (p. 211). In "The Transcendentalist," Emerson cites Timoleon as one of several examples of individuals who refuse "all measure of right and wrong except the determinations of the private spirit" (*W*, I, 336–337). William H. Shurr, "Melville and Emerson," *Extracts: An Occasional Newsletter* (The Melville Society), No. 11 (May 1972), p. 2, compares Melville's late poem "Timoleon," observing that though Plutarch and other sources "enriched the development of Melville's thought in this poem, . . . Emerson's essay clearly provides the suggestion."

54 The London *Athenæum*; see *Log*, I, 464. The *Athenæum* regarded *Pierre* as second-hand Germanism, with nothing American or original in its pages; see Higgins, *Herman Melville: An Annotated Bibliography*, I, 126 (B77).

55 In letters of 15 and 30 January 1980, Professor Robert Milder of Washington University, who read this essay in typescript, generously called these parallels to my attention; I note them here with his concurrence. (1) The narrator's figure of "new truth" overturning man "as the Tartars did China; for there is no China Wall that man can build in his soul, which shall permanently stay the irruptions of those barbarous hordes which Truth ever nourishes" (p. 167), may well echo Emerson's reference in "Spiritual Laws" to "a Chinese wall which any nimble Tartar can leap over" (*W*, II, 137). (2) Pierre's angling in "the well of his childhood, to find what fish might be there" (p. 284), resembles Emerson's statement in "Intellect" that in later years we "still run back to the despised recollections of childhood, and always we are fishing up some wonderful article out of that pond" (*W*, II, 334). (3) The image of the human heart as "a spiral stair in a shaft, without any end" (pp. 288–289), may derive from Emerson's remark at the beginning of "Experience" that we "find ourselves on a stair" with "stairs below us" and others "above us . . . which go upward and out of sight" (*W*, III, 45). Still other parallels between *Pierre* and Emerson's "Fate" are difficult to account for, as Professor Milder observes, since Melville is not known to have heard "Fate" as a lecture in 1851 or 1852, when Emerson first gave it, and Emerson did not publish it

as an essay until 1860, in *The Conduct of Life*. Perhaps both authors were drawing upon a common source.

56 In the 1870's, when Melville was reading Emerson's essay "Illusions" in his copy of *The Conduct of Life*, he "heavily marked an old Persian proverb which Emerson praised: 'Fooled thou must be, though wisest of the wise: / Then be the fool of virtue, not of vice.'" See Braswell, "Melville as a Critic of Emerson," p. 326.

57 Compare p. 302, where Pierre's "apparent author-hero, Vivia" echoes the narrator in a soliloquy, addressing "ye chattering apes of a sophomorean Spinoza and Plato" and "thou inconceivable coxcomb of a Goethe. . . . [T]hy Pantheism, what was that?" As Melville associates "pantheism" with Goethe and Spinoza in particular, so he links transcendental idealism with Plato and Kant, its philosophical fathers.

58 Melville's satire began in *Mardi;* Babbalanja the philosopher charges Yoomy the poet with "Mysticism"—only to burst out himself in the very kind of professional jargon that Mohi the historian had already dismissed as "gibberish" (pp. 561, 340). Melville found his esoteric terminology in the Greek Neoplatonic philosopher Proclus and his *Six Books . . . on the Theology of Plato*, written in the fourth century, translated into English by Thomas Taylor, and published in London in 1816; though Melville would not have known it, Emerson owned Taylor's translations of both Plato and Proclus (Harding, *Emerson's Library*, pp. 215–216, 220). In *The Confidence-Man*, Mark Winsome quotes "a sentence of Greek" allegedly from the *Theology* (p. 217).

59 See Egbert S. Oliver, "Melville's Picture of Emerson and Thoreau in *The Confidence-Man*," *College English*, 8 (November 1946), 61–72; Elizabeth S. Foster, Introduction to *The Confidence-Man*, pp. lxxiii–lxxxii; Hershel Parker, "Melville's Satire of Emerson and Thoreau: An Evaluation of the Evidence," *American Transcendental Quarterly*, Nos. 7 (Summer 1970), 61–67, and 9 (Winter 1971), 70; Robert Sattelmeyer and James Barbour, "A Possible Source and Model for 'The Story of China Aster' in Melville's *The Confidence-Man*," *American Literature*, 48 (January 1977), 577–583; Egbert S. Oliver, "Melville's Goneril and Fanny Kemble," *College English*, 18 (December 1945), 489–500; Harrison Hayford, "Poe in *The Confidence-Man*," *Nineteenth-Century Fiction*, 14 (December 1959), 207–218; Helen P. Trimpi, "Three of Melville's Confidence Men: William Cullen Bryant, Theodore Parker, and Horace Greeley," *TSLL: Texas Studies in Language and Literature*, 21 (Fall 1979), 368–395.

60 *Literary World*, 1 (3 April 1847), 197–199; the review had noted "the comparatively cold reception of Mr. Emerson among his countrymen" (p. 197). Its author was not Duyckinck but his friend Cornelius Mathews, as Duyckinck told his brother George in a letter of 28 April 1847; I am indebted for this information to Professor Donald Yannella, who is editing the Duyckinck papers, writing on 28 January 1980. On 8 April Ma-

thews himself had also written Emerson about *Poems* and his review; see Ralph L. Rusk, *The Life of Ralph Waldo Emerson*, pp. 323, 535.

61 *Melville's Reading*, p. 59: No. 206.

62 Lucy Marie Freibert, "Meditative Voice in the Poetry of Herman Melville," Diss. University of Wisconsin–Madison 1970, pp. 77–79, demonstrates the parallel between line 127 of "Merlin II," "*In perfect time and measure* they", and the opening line of "Dupont's Round Fight": "*In time and perfect measure* move"; see *W*, IX, 124 (emphasis added), and *Collected Poems*, p. 15 (emphasis added). She also notes a general similarity between Melville's "Art" and the motto for Emerson's "Spiritual Laws," with the words "flame" and "freeze" occurring both in line 5 of "Art" (*Collected Poems*, p. 231) and in line 10 of the motto (*W*, II, 129; IX, 275); see "Meditative Voice," pp. 42–43 and note 1, pp. 350–351.

63 Jane Donahue, "Melville's Classicism: Law and Order in His Poetry," *Papers on Language and Literature*, 5 (Winter 1969), 66.

64 Philip Beidler, "*Billy Budd*," p. 227, note 17, remarks on "some intriguing textual parallels" between *Billy Budd* and *Representative Men*—especially Emerson's chapter on Montaigne.

65 Braswell, "Melville as a Critic of Emerson," pp. 330–331; the context in "The Poet," *W*, III, 22, deals with language as "fossil poetry."

66 "Melville as a Critic of Emerson," p. 322; for the context in "The Poet," see *W*, III, 28.

67 "Melville as a Critic of Emerson," p. 329; the context in "Prudence," *W*, II, 237, concerns drovers and sailors.

68 Emerson's Uriel troubled both "war-gods" and "*seraphs*" by expressing his heretical ideas, among them the pronouncements that "*Evil* will bless" and that good may be "of *evil* born"; "now and then, truth-speaking things / Shamed the angels' veiling *wings*" (*W*, IX, 13–15; emphasis added).

Melville and the Platonic Tradition

Citations of Melville's works are to the six published volumes of the Northwestern-Newberry Edition; to *Moby-Dick* (New York, 1967); to *The Confidence-Man, Collected Poems*, and *Clarel* in the Hendricks House Edition; to *Complete Stories*; to *Billy Budd and Other Prose Pieces* in the Standard Edition; and to *Billy Budd, Sailor* (Chicago, 1962).

1 See "Melville and Emerson's Rainbow," pp. 269, 273 above.

2 Ibid., p. 257.

3 K. H. Sundermann, *Herman Melvilles Gedankengut: Eine kritische Untersuchung seiner weltanschaulichen Grundideen* (Berlin: Arthur Collignon, 1937), *passim*.

4 "Apology for Raimond de Sebonde," *Essays*, Book II, Chapter xii, quoted from William Hazlitt's version of the translation by Charles Cotton, 4 vols.

(London: Reeves & Turner, 1902), II, 358. The volume of Montaigne that Melville bought in July of 1848 was probably the second impression (1845) of Hazlitt's edition, first published in London in 1842 (*Melville's Reading*, p. 80: No. 366; p. 352 above).

5 See David K. Titus, "Herman Melville at the Albany Academy," *Melville Society Extracts*, No. 42 (May 1980), pp. 6 and 8; p. 38 above.

6 *Melville's Reading*, pp. 92–93: No. 458; William Braswell, "Melville's Use of Seneca," *American Literature*, 12 (March 1940), 98–104.'

7 *The Complete Works of Ralph Waldo Emerson*, ed. Edward Waldo Emerson, 12 vols. (Boston and New York: Houghton Mifflin Co., 1903–1904), V, 295.

8 The *Alphabetical and Analytical Catalogue of the New York Society Library* (New York, 1850), p. 351, lists *The Works of Plato*, translated by Floyer Sydenham and Thomas Taylor, 5 vols. (London: T. Taylor, 1804). All references to Plato's dialogues as discussed in relation to Melville's *Mardi* will be to the Taylor-Sydenham edition, cited parenthetically within the text. Of the four titles charged to Melville at the Library, only one could be considered a work of a philosophical nature: David Hartley's *Observations on Man, His Frame, His Duty, and His Expectations* (London, 1801), borrowed between 17 January and 22 February 1848 (*Melville's Reading*, p. 64: No. 243).

9 In "Melville's 'Neoplatonical Originals,'" *Modern Language Notes*, 67 (February 1952), 80–86, I demonstrated Melville's use of *The Six Books . . .* , 2 vols. (London: A. J. Valpy, 1816), in both *Mardi* and *The Confidence-Man*. When I published this note I supposed that Melville had been led to both Plato and Proclus through his reading of Emerson, but it is now apparent that he knew both authors a year before his first significant encounter with Emerson and his writings; see "A Correspondence with Charles Olson," pp. 121–122, and 127 above, for comments on this point.

10 The phrase is from F. O. Matthiessen, *American Renaissance: Art and Expression in the Age of Emerson and Whitman* (New York: Oxford University Press, 1941), p. 123; it is quoted in "The Records of Melville's Reading," p. 47 above, where Melville's response to Browne is discussed. The first allusion to Browne in *Mardi* occurs in Chapter 13: "while exploding 'Vulgar Errors,'" he "heartily hugged all the mysteries in the Pentateuch" (p. 39); Chapter 32, "Xiphius Platypterus" (pp. 103–105), echoes Browne's prose cadences, as do later passages in both *Mardi* and *Moby-Dick*.

11 See "Melville and Emerson's Rainbow," p. 257 above.

12 *Sir Thomas Browne's Works . . .* , ed. Simon Wilkin, 4 vols. (London: Pickering, 1835–1836), II, 10–11 (emphasis added). Melville borrowed three of the four volumes of this edition from Duyckinck between mid-February and 18 March of 1848 (*Melville's Reading*, p. 44: No. 89).

13 "In nations," according to the anonymous scroll read to the people of Vivenza in Chapter 161, "there is a transmigration of souls" (p. 527). Here Melville is probably echoing not Plato or Browne, but Robert Burton, *The Anatomy of Melancholy* (New York: John Wiley, 1847), which he acquired

on 8 February 1848 (*Melville's Reading*, p. 45: No. 102): "once in 600 years," according to Burton (p. 134), providence orders "a transmigration of nations, to amend and purify their blood."

14 *Melville's Reading*, p. 55: No. 174.

15 James Albert Key has written "An Introduction to Melville's Bird Imagery" (Diss. Tulane University 1966); see *Dissertation Abstracts*, 27, 1369A.

16 Melville obscures authorship of the scroll by noting the absence of both Media and Babbalanja immediately before the scroll is discovered (p. 524), by making each of them charge the other with its composition (p. 530), and by having Media say that to the Vivenzans "a tyrant would prove a blessing." "My lord, that last sentiment decides the authorship of the scroll," says Babbalanja (p. 541). To the angry Vivenzans, it came from some benighted "tory, and monarchist" (p. 530).

17 Lewis Mumford, *Herman Melville* (New York: Harcourt, Brace & Company, 1929), p. 296.

18 See "Melville and Emerson's Rainbow" above, p. 259. "The tension in Melville's social thought" between democratic leanings and an aristocratic sense of personal superiority to the mass of mankind has recently been examined by Larry J. Reynolds in a study of *White-Jacket*, one of the books Melville wrote in 1849 after he had heard Emerson lecture: "Antidemocratic Emphasis in *White-Jacket*," *American Literature*, 48 (March 1976), 13–28. In presenting the man-of-war's crew, as Reynolds notes (p. 18), White-Jacket "establishes a convenient hierarchy with his own group literally and figuratively at the top."

19 Sundermann, *Melvilles Gedankengut*, p. 203, note 18.

20 According to Sundermann, the pattern is repeated not only in *Pierre* but also in *Moby-Dick*, with Ahab, Starbuck, and Fedallah, and *Billy Budd*, where Budd and Claggart seemingly externalize contending forces within the third principal character, Captain Vere. John A. Heitner's dissertation finds still other characters grouped in threes throughout the Melville canon: see "Melville's Tragic Triad: A Study of His Tragic Visions," *Dissertation Abstracts*, 29 (1968), 229A–230A.

21 The doctrine of the soul as a harmony is treated also in Plato's *Phaedo*, where it is introduced into the discussion of immortality by Simmias but is rejected by Socrates on two grounds: it contradicts the theory of knowledge as recollection and it makes the soul dependent upon the mortal body as music is dependent upon the strings of a harp (IV, 299–310). Melville's allusions to the doctrine show that he had the *Republic* rather than the *Phaedo* in mind when he recalled it.

22 The account of Babbalanja's vision in Chapter 188 includes references to a melody in his "inmost soul," described as an "inward harmony," and to a celestial harmony of gladness seemingly mixed with sadness (pp. 632–633).

23 Babbalanja, says Yoomy, "only seem[s] wise, because of the contrasting follies of others," not of any great wisdom in himself (p. 281).

24 Mumford, *Herman Melville*, p. 104. Concerning Babbalanja's demon, see

also note 29 below. It is possible that Melville was influenced not only by Plato but by Charles Anthon's edition of *Xenophon's Memorabilia of Socrates* (New York, 1848); he probably saw a review of it in the New York *Literary World* for 14 October 1848, which commented on "the mysterious demon of Socrates" and Anthon's theory that Socrates was "laboring under the influence of a mental hallucination on this subject. It is somewhat unpleasant to associate the idea of monomania with the man . . . judged wisest of men," the reviewer remarked; "but . . . the honest and sublime morality of Socrates will always command the respect of mankind" (III, 726).

25 Sundermann, *Melvilles Gedankengut*, p. 95 and note 8, p. 208, also compares the passage on Fate in Chapter 75 of Melville's *White-Jacket* (1850):

> But all events are mixed in a fusion indistinguishable. What we call Fate is even, heartless, and impartial; not a fiend to kindle bigot flames, nor a philanthropist to espouse the cause of Greece. We may fret, fume, and fight; but the thing called Fate everlastingly sustains an armed neutrality.
>
> Yet though all this be so, nevertheless, in our own hearts, we mold the whole world's hereafters; and in our own hearts we fashion our own gods. *Each mortal casts his vote for whom he will to rule the worlds;* I have a voice that helps to shape eternity; and my volitions stir the orbits of the furthest suns. In two senses, we are precisely what we worship. Ourselves are Fate. (pp. 320–321; emphasis added)

He also goes on to suggest that Melville took the term "Parcae," which he uses in Chapter 19 of *Israel Potter*, from the myth of Er; see p. 96 and note 15, p. 209.

26 Sundermann, *Melvilles Gedankengut*, p. 94 and note 62, p. 208.

27 What might appear to be an indication of Melville's direct familiarity with Platonic or Neoplatonic cosmology is Babbalanja's remark later in this same paragraph that *"were all space a vacuum, yet would it be a fullness; for to Himself His own universe is He"* (p. 230; emphasis added); instead it probably echoes *Paradise Lost*, VII, 168–169 (emphasis added):

> Boundless the Deep, because I am who fill
> Infinitude, *nor vacuous the space.*

I cite this example to show the difficulties of untangling Melville's indebtedness when he knew several authors writing on a common theme.

28 The 1850 *Catalogue*, pp. 351–352, lists Taylor's *Select Works of Plotinus, The Great Restorer of the Philosophy of Plato: and Extracts from the Treatise of Synesius on Providence. . . . With an Introduction Containing the Substance of Porphyry's Life of Plotinus* (London: The Author, 1817). Babbalanja's fable of the philosopher Grando, who had "a sovereign contempt for his carcass" (p. 505), may have come from Porphyry's statement as paraphrased by Taylor, p. xi, that Plotinus was "ashamed that his soul was in body." His "vehement love for intellectual pursuits, and contempt for body, made him disdain to sit for his picture" (Taylor's italics omitted). "*Plotinus* Plinlimmon" is a character in *Pierre*, where the narrator scorns attempts to fit man's "dog of a body" for heaven (p. 299) and the protagonist pointedly refuses to sit for *his* picture (p. 254). When Plotinus was speaking, according to Porphyry, "a certain attenuated and dewy moisture appeared on

his face" (*Select Works*, p. xlvii); Ishmael in *Moby-Dick* is "convinced that from the heads of all ponderous profound beings, such as Plato, Pyrrho, the Devil, Jupiter, Dante, and so on, there always goes up a certain semi-visible steam, while in the process of thinking deep thoughts" (p. 313). All of these parallels may suggest that Melville read Taylor's Introduction, but I have found nothing in *Select Works* or two other translations of Plotinus by Taylor, *On Suicide* (London, 1834) and *Five Books of Plotinus* (London, 1794), to show that he drew on Plotinian thought to any significant extent.

29 The concept of a scale of being is of course a familiar one in many writers ancient and modern—Milton, for example. Sir Thomas Browne wrote in *Religio Medici* that the greatest interval on the scale is that between men and angels (*Works*, II, 47–48). Taylor's annotations to his several translations of Plato and the Neoplatonists set forth a whole system of gods, demi-gods, and daemons that may have influenced *Mardi*. Taji appears to the Mardians as a demi-god (p. 166); most of the Mardian kings claim homage as demi-gods, as Media does (p. 175); both Babbalanja's tutelary spirit Azzageddi and those "invisible spirits, ycleped the Plujii," of Chapter 86 (p. 262) may be Melvillean versions of Greek daemons.

30 On the Shakespeare, the Bayle, and Harper's Classical Library, see *Melville's Reading*, p. 93: No. 460; p. 39: No. 51, and p. 349 above; pp. 51–52: No. 147. As for the *Phædon*, Gowans was a New York bookseller where in 1847 Melville had bought a volume that was once his father's (*Melville's Reading*, p. 45: No. 103; p. 37 above); in the *Literary World* for 17 March 1849 appeared an advertisement for Gowans' *Phædon: or, a Dialogue on the Immortality of the Soul. By Plato. Translated from the Original Greek by Madam Dacier. With Notes and Emendations. To Which is Prefixed the Life of the Author, by Fenelon* (New York: William Gowans, 1849). Melville was in New York between 2 and 15 March 1849, according to a letter written by Hope Savage Shaw quoted in Joyce Deveau Kennedy and Frederick J. Kennedy, "Elizabeth Shaw Melville and Samuel Hay Savage," *Melville Society Extracts*, No. 39 (September 1979), p. 4; he first mentioned "the Phaedon" in a letter of 5 April (*Letters*, pp. 83–84).

Another "*Phædon*" translated from the German of Moses Mendelssohn (London, 1789) would have been available to Melville at the New York Society Library, according to its 1850 *Catalogue*, p. 294, but Gowans' more recent publication seems the likelier text. Duyckinck, it might be noted, owned a copy of an earlier English version of the Dacier rendering (New York, 1833), but there is no record of Melville's borrowing it.

31 See pp. 291–292 above and p. 388, note 21.

32 See p. 293 above and p. 389, note 25, which quotes the passage from *White-Jacket*, Chapter 75.

33 Parenthetically within the text as "*Phædon*."

34 London: Henry G. Bohn, 1848–1854. In *Billy Budd, Sailor*, Melville quotes a definition of "natural depravity" from what he calls a "list of

definitions" that is to be found in the Bohn edition (VI, 143) but is lacking in later nineteenth-century translations by Whewell and Jowett. See p. 333 below and note 77, p. 395.

35 On 27 January 1849 the New York bookseller John Wiley advertised the first volume in the *Literary World;* this volume includes the *Apology, Crito, Phaedo, Gorgias, Protagoras, Phaedrus, Theaetetus, Euthyphron,* and *Lysis.* The second volume (1849) includes the *Republic, Timaeus,* and *Critias;* the third (1850), the *Meno, Euthydemus, Sophist, Statesman, Cratylus, Parmenides,* and *Banquet.*

36 Parenthetically within the text as "Bohn."

37 Elsewhere he writes of the sea as "the great mundane soul" (p. 201).

38 H. N. Couch, *"Moby Dick* and the *Phaedo," Classical Journal,* 28 (February 1933), 367–368.

39 A note in the Hendricks House edition of *Moby-Dick,* p. 614, correctly identifies Melville's source for the image of "oysters," citing the Jowett translation of the *Phaedrus.* Overlooking Couch's article, the note also proposes Plato's allegory of the cave in Book VII of the *Republic* as Melville's further source in the passage.

40 In "The Mast-Head," Ishmael refers to the soul as "glued inside of its fleshly tabernacle," the body (p. 137); his image may have come from Cary's translation of a passage in the *Phaedon* where Socrates speaks of the soul as "bound and glued to the body" (Bohn, I, 86). (The Gowans *Phædon,* p. 102, uses the phrase "tied and chained" at this same point.)

41 To Ishmael, the sperm whale appears elsewhere as a "Platonian leviathan" (p. 228); Melville probably knew from *Anthon's Classical Dictionary* that the name Plato (Πλατών, from πλατύς, "broad") was given the Greek philosopher "from either the breadth of his shoulders or of his forehead." In the present passage Ishmael sees the sperm whale as "a Platonian, who might have taken up Spinoza in his latter years"; the right whale, with his "enormous practical resolution in facing death," he sees as "a Stoic" (p. 284). Ishmael's tone here may be light, but the distinction between Platonists and Stoics was a real one for Melville himself. In *Mardi,* it will be recalled, Babbalanja quotes the Stoic Seneca, the "antique pagan" of Chapter 124, as well as Bardianna (p. 280 above), and either he or Media differentiates Athenians from Spartans as "meditative philosophers" rather than "enduring stoics" (p. 526; see p. 288 above).

42 It has not been observed that Melville's phrase "Plato's honey head" recalls an old tradition—one that he may have come across in William Browne's *Britannia's Pastorals,* which he borrowed from Evert Duyckinck in 1850 (*Melville's Reading,* p. 44; No. 91). In Book I, Song 2, lines 439–440, Browne writes:

> And as when Plato did i' th' cradle thrive,
> Bees to his lips brought honey from their hive. . . .

The head as a "hive" is an image Melville later applied both to Benjamin

Franklin in Chapter 7 of *Israel Potter* and to Babo in "Benito Cereno" (1855). Franklin, called a "household Plato" (as noted above), has a "hive of a head," and Babo's severed head is a "hive of subtlety"; see *Complete Stories*, p. 353.

43 Michael E. Levin, "Ahab as Socratic Philosopher: The Myth of the Cave Inverted," *ATQ: The American Transcendental Quarterly*, No. 41 (Winter 1979), pp. 61–73; further reference to this article will be made parenthetically within the text. Levin is a member of the Department of Philosophy, The City College of The City University of New York.

44 *Melville's Reading*, p. 39: No. 51, and p. 349 above; see "Melville and Emerson's Rainbow," p. 263 above. Melville's knowledge of Gnosticism seems to have come both from Bayle and from Andrews Norton; see Millicent Bell, "Pierre Bayle and *Moby-Dick*," *PMLA*, 66 (September 1951), 626–648; and for specific comment on the passage just quoted, Thomas Vargish, "Gnostic *Mythos* in *Moby-Dick*," *PMLA*, 81 (June 1966), 272–277. On Melville and Zoroaster, see Dorothee Metlitsky Finkelstein, *Melville's Orienda* (New Haven and London: Yale University Press, 1961), pp. 152–164; on Ahab's notion of worship by defiance, see H. B. Kulkarni, *Moby-Dick: A Hindu Avatar. A Study of Hindu Myth and Thought in "Moby-Dick"* (Logan, Utah: Utah State University Press, 1970), pp. 36–38. As Levin himself remarks (p. 66), Melville's out-of-the-way learning at the time of *Moby-Dick* led him to note in a new copy of the Bible that certain books of the Apocrypha combined Platonism and Judaism; see also *Melville's Reading*, pp. 40–41: No. 62; and *Log*, I, 370.

45 Although quotation marks are absent from the received text at this point, the passage quoted follows a paragraph on Ahab and precedes companion meditations attributed to Starbuck and Stubb. I take the words to be Ahab's.

46 See "Melville and Emerson's Rainbow," p. 264 above.

47 The antithesis of sea and land is recurrent in *Moby-Dick*. In Chapter 58, for example, Ishmael draws "a strange analogy": "as this appalling ocean surrounds the verdant land, so in the soul of man there lies one insular Tahiti, full of peace and joy, but encompassed by all the horrors of the half known life. . . . Push not off from that isle, thou canst never return!" (p. 236).

48 Here as in *Mardi* Melville was probably drawing on Sir Thomas Browne, who wrote in *Religio Medici:* "I cannot believe the wisdom of Pythagoras did ever positively, and in a literal sense, affirm his metempsychosis" (*Works*, II, 55). In *Moby-Dick*, compare Chapter 114: "There is no steady unretracing progress in this life; we do not advance. . . . [O]nce gone through, we trace the round again" (p. 406, in a paragraph I attribute to Ahab; see note 45 above). In "I and My Chimney" (1856) the narrator likens his home to "a philosophical system": "Going through the house, you seem to be forever going somewhere, and getting nowhere. . . . [I]f you arrive at all, it is just where you started"; see *Complete Stories*, p. 389.

49 "Queequeg no care what god made him shark; wedder Fejee god or Nantucket god; but de god wat made shark must be one dam Ingin" (p. 257).

50 John Halverson, "The Shadow in *Moby-Dick*," *American Quarterly*, 15 (Fall 1963), 444. Halverson's entire essay (pp. 436–446) investigates the abundant shadow imagery of the book in terms of psychological archetypes; he remarks incidentally that "Jung did not discover the shadow side of man. Among countless earlier instances, let Plato's black horse of the *Phaedrus* parable suffice as an example" (p. 436). Melville's imagery is closest to Plato's when Ishmael is dealing with Fedallah in Chapter 130. The crew of the Pequod seem uncertain "whether indeed he were a mortal substance, or else a tremulous shadow cast upon the deck by some unseen being's body" (p. 438). Ahab and Fedallah gaze upon one another "as if in the Parsee Ahab saw his forethrown shadow, in Ahab the Parsee his abandoned substance." Sometimes he appears as Ahab's slave, Ishmael declares; "again both seemed *yoked together*, and an unseen tyrant driving them" (p. 439; emphasis added).

51 Emerson, *Works*, III, 50.

52 Melville had in mind Shakespeare as speaking his own thoughts through the "mouths" of his "dark characters" in the tragedies; see "Hawthorne and His Mosses" in *The Norton Anthology of American Literature*, ed. Ronald Gottesman et al., 2 vols. (New York and London: W. W. Norton & Company, 1979), I, 2061.

53 See "Melville and Emerson's Rainbow," p. 270 above.

54 Emerson, *Works*, I, 339–340.

55 This aspect of *Pierre* will be examined in more detail in a chapter of Professor James Duban's forthcoming book on Melville. Reading his chapter in draft has shown me that Melville was more familiar with finer points of Unitarian theology than I had supposed when I wrote "Melville and Emerson's Rainbow," and I am grateful for the opportunity to learn from his thorough research and careful analysis.

56 Raymond J. Nelson, "The Art of Herman Melville: The Author of *Pierre*," *Yale Review*, 59 (Winter 1970), 197–214, holds that the tone of *Pierre* is "much more comic than has been generally recognized" (p. 200) and argues that the book Pierre is writing about "Vivia" is actually *Pierre* itself—a wholly reflexive narrative. The points considered in this paragraph have some bearing on Nelson's unorthodox thesis, which deserves more scrutiny than it has yet received.

57 Here Melville may well be echoing not Plato but Emerson's discussion of subjectivism in "Experience": "Perhaps these subject-lenses have a creative power," Emerson writes; "perhaps there are no objects. . . . Nature and literature are subjective phenomena; every evil and every good thing is *a shadow which we cast*" (*Works*, III, 76; emphasis added).

58 In *Israel Potter*, Chapter 7, as noted above, Benjamin Franklin is called a "household Plato"; the story was first serialized in *Putnam's Monthly Magazine* in 1854–1855. Socrates is mentioned in both "Cock-A-Doodle-Doo!"

(1853) and "The Paradise of Bachelors and the Tartarus of Maids" (1855); see *Complete Stories*, pp. 128 and 191 (the name is repeated on pp. 193 and 194).

59 Rosemary Austin Kenny, "Melville's Short Fiction: A Methodology of Unknowing," Diss. University of Wisconsin 1980, p. 320.

60 H. Bruce Franklin, *The Wake of the Gods: Melville's Mythology* (Stanford: Stanford University Press, 1963), p. 154 and note 1, p. 216. Franklin credits his wife with first pointing out Melville's parody and shrewdly cites Emerson's essay on Plato in *Representative Men* as influencing Melville's "picture of Socrates" in the man from the Intelligence Office. "There is much else in Emerson's essay," he adds, "which casts light on the character of the PIO man, the Cosmopolitan, and the ethical and metaphysical issues in *The Confidence-Man*" (p. 216). On Plato's image in the *Meno* of the torpedo fish (Bohn, III, 18), which struck both Emerson and Melville, see "Melville and Emerson's Rainbow," note 49, p. 383 above.

61 "Emerson saw energy" in the Greeks "where Melville saw repose," as Jane Donahue Eberwein points out; see "Melville and Emerson's Rainbow," p. 273 above.

62 "Plato (hair & beard & imperial)"; see Melville's *Journal of a Visit to Europe and the Levant October 11, 1856–May 6, 1857*, ed. Howard C. Horsford (Princeton: Princeton University Press, 1955), p. 183.

63 Merton M. Sealts, Jr., *Melville as Lecturer* (Cambridge: Harvard University Press, 1957), pp. 133–134; here and below I have emended the reconstructed text published in 1957 to take account of additional newspaper reports, as in the revised text I prepared in 1975 for volume IX of the Northwestern-Newberry Edition of Melville's writings.

64 *Melville as Lecturer*, p. 132—again with subsequent emendations incorporated in the present extract.

65 *Complete Stories*, p. 191.

66 See pp. 273–274 above.

67 See note 44 above.

68 In 1873 Melville acquired a copy of *Essays, Letters from Abroad, Translations and Fragments*, edited by Mrs. Shelley, 2 vols. (London: Moxon, 1852), which includes Shelley's version (I, 61–135); see *Melville's Reading*, p. 94: No. 468.

69 The relevant passage (*Poems*, p. 219) reads as follows:

> For, Nature, in no shallow surge,
> Against thee either sex may urge,
> Why hast thou made us but in halves—
> Co-relatives? This makes us slaves.
> If those co-relatives never meet
> Self-hood itself seems incomplete.

70 See "Melville's Burgundy Club Sketches," reprinted above.

71 Printed in *Billy Budd and Other Prose Pieces* (vol. XIV of the Standard Edition), p. 351.

72 *Complete Stories*, p. 128; in the *Phædon* the last words of Socrates, addressed to Crito, are: "We owe a cock to Æsculapius, discharge this vow for me, and do not forget it" (p. 178).

73 Quoted in part from Melville's annotation in his copy of Madame de Staël's *Germany*, 2 vols. (New York: Derby and Jackson, 1859), I, 26; the date of 4 March 1862 appears in his hand in this volume (*Melville's Reading*, p. 96: No. 487).

74 Quoted in part from Melville's annotation in his copy of Matthew Arnold's *New Poems* (Boston: Ticknor and Fields, 1867), p. 28; Melville bought the book on 13 February 1871 (*Melville's Reading*, p. 37: No. 20). Field's Atlantic cable was in operation in 1868.

75 Marked in Melville's copy of Arthur Schopenhauer's *Religion: A Dialogue, and Other Essays*, translated by T. B. Saunders (London: Sonnenschein, 1890), p. 19; see *Melville's Reading*, p. 91: No. 445.

76 See *Billy Budd, Sailor*, p. 75, where the narrator discusses "that finer spiritual insight indispensable to the understanding of the essential in certain exceptional characters, whether evil ones or good"; p. 96, where he notes "something exceptional in the moral quality of Captain Vere"; and p. 174, where the editors comment on the latter observation.

77 Although the attribution to Plato may be open to question, there is a similar idea advanced in the *Republic*, Book X, where Socrates describes "natural depravity" as that depravity which "is revealed within the soul of the tyrant." I quote Thomas J. Scorza, *In The Time Before Steamships:* Billy Budd, *the Limits of Politics, and Modernity* (De Kalb: Northern Illinois University Press, 1979), p. 81, who also remarks that "Socrates' description places the tyrannical man's depravity at the opposite pole of rationality and the 'divine part' of our natures: Socrates' tyrant is the opposite of the philosopher. Nevertheless, in *Billy Budd*, the embodiment of 'natural depravity'"—Claggart—"is said to be 'dominated by intellectuality,'" which Scorza identifies as "the ultimate depravity within man" for Melville. In my judgment this is an overstatement of Melville's evident distrust of the purely intellectual element in human nature.

78 See note 20 above.

79 Yvor Winters, "Herman Melville, and the Problems of Moral Navigation," in *Maule's Curse* (Norfolk, Connecticut: New Directions, 1938), pp. 86–87; reprinted in his *In Defense of Reason* (New York: The Swallow Press & William Morrow and Company, 1947), pp. 230–231.

80 *In the Time Before Steamships* (note 77 above), p. 177; on the torpedo fish, mentioned in note 60 above, see "Melville and Emerson's Rainbow," note 49, p. 383 above. When Scorza cites Melville's remark on Socrates' trial that I quoted above, he takes no account of its obvious irony. He found the passage in *The Socratic Enigma*, ed. Herbert Spiegelberg (Indianapolis: Library of Liberal Arts, 1964), p. 135; I had called the passage to Professor Spiegelberg's attention in earlier years when he and I were colleagues at Lawrence College.

81 See *Melville's Reading*, pp. 36–37 and 56: Nos. 14a, 14b, and 183a, all rebound in uniform bindings at some time after 1889–1890, when the two volumes of No. 14a were published in London. Other more esoteric books may have been among the "many 'theological' works" from Melville's library that were scrapped by A. F. Farnell; see "The Records of Melville's Reading," p. 35 above.

Index

DESIGNED BY DESIGN FOR PUBLISHING, BOB NANCE
COMPOSED BY GRAPHIC COMPOSITION, INC., ATHENS, GEORGIA
MANUFACTURED BY THOMSON-SHORE, INC., DEXTER, MICHIGAN
TEXT AND DISPLAY LINES ARE SET IN BASKERVILLE

Library of Congress Cataloging in Publication Data

Sealts, Merton, M.
Pursuing Melville, 1940–1980.
Includes index.
1. Melville, Herman, 1819–1891—Miscellanea.
2. Sealts, Merton M.   3. Olson, Charles,
1910–1970—Correspondence.   I. Title.
PS2386.S43   813'.3   81–70014
ISBN 0–299–08870–7   AACR2